"Addictive reading for anyone interested in greed, outrageous behavior, epic bad planning and character, lousy luck, and worst of all, comically bad manners. Wilkie knows precisely where the skeletons, the cash boxes, and the daggers are buried along the Mississippi backroads. And he knows, ruefully—which is why this book demands a wide audience—that the South, no matter its looney sense of exceptionalism, is pretty much just like the rest of the planet."　—Richard Ford

"In telling a great legal story about a great legal storyteller, Wilkie has produced a page-turning masterpiece that explores power, greed, hubris, and the human condition. *The Fall of the House of Zeus* is a Greek tragedy set in the modern South. Lawyers, clients, and anyone interested in seeing how the sausages of justice get made will love this book."　—Alan Dershowitz, author of *The Trials of Zion*

"*The Fall of the House of Zeus* is a riveting American saga of ambition, cunning, greed, corruption, high life, and low life in the land of Faulkner and Grisham. These are good ol' boys gone bad with flair, private jets, and lots of cash to carry. Curtis Wilkie, a child of the South and a reporter's reporter, is the perfect match for this wild ride."
—Tom Brokaw

"Fascinating, breath-holding action . . . The undisputed accuracy of recorded dialogue will fan embers that will keep this story alive for decades—not only in Mississippi . . . but anywhere obscene wealth, arrogance, and narrow-mindedness grant us human beings a look into the darkest rooms of our hearts."　—Clyde Edgerton, *Garden & Gun*

"The legendary yet factual Curtis Wilkie has been the right man in the right place at an uncanny number of extraordinary times."
—Roy Blount Jr.

"A fascinating and eye-opening modern-day account of politics, greed, hate, and their power over men."　—*Memphis Lawyer*

ALSO BY CURTIS WILKIE

Dixie: A Personal Odyssey Through Events That
Shaped the Modern South

Arkansas Mischief: The Birth of a National Scandal
(with Jim McDougal)

CURTIS WILKIE

THE FALL OF

Broadway Paperbacks / New York

THE HOUSE OF ZEUS

The Rise and Ruin

of America's

Most Powerful

Trial Lawyer

Library of Congress Cataloging-in-Publication Data
Wilkie, Curtis.
    The fall of the house of Zeus / Curtis Wilkie.
1. Scruggs, Dickie. 2. Lawyers—Mississippi—Biography. 3. Judicial corruption—
Mississippi—History I. Scruggs, Dickie. II. Title.
    KF373.S342W55 2010
    340.092—dc22
    [B]
                                                                2010004503

ISBN 978-0-307-46071-4
eISBN 978-0-307-46072-1

Printed in the United States of America

BOOK DESIGN BY ELINA D. NUDELMAN
COVER DESIGN BY DAVID TRAN
COVER PHOTOGRAPHS BY CONNIE COLEMAN, © STONE COLLECTION/GETTY IMAGES

See page 395 for photograph insert credits.

10 9 8 7 6 5 4 3 2 1

First Paperback Edition

For Nancy

Principal Characters

The Defendants

Dick Scruggs, wealthy trial lawyer and engineer of groundbreaking tobacco lititgation

Zach Scruggs, his son and law partner

Sid Backstrom, junior partner in the Scruggs Law Firm

Tim Balducci, ambitious lawyer who envisioned a superfirm

Steve Patterson, former state auditor, Democratic chairman, and Balducci's partner

Joey Langston, prominent lawyer specializing in criminal defense and plaintiff lawsuits

Bobby DeLaughter, state judge and former prosecutor who helped convict assassin Byron De La Beckwith

Their Antagonists

Johnny Jones, Jackson lawyer who sued Scruggs Katrina Group

Grady Tollison, Oxford attorney who represented Jones

Alwyn Luckey, former Scruggs partner in Asbestos Group

Roberts Wilson, former member of Asbestos Group

Charlie Merkel, Clarksdale attorney who represented both Luckey and Wilson in lawsuits against Scruggs

George Dale, state insurance commissioner driven from office by Scruggs

Henry Lackey, state judge who reported improper approach by Balducci

The Prosecutors

Jim Greenlee, U.S. attorney in Oxford

John Hailman, prosecutor who initiated the investigation before retiring

Tom Dawson, chief deputy in U.S. Attorney's Office

Bob Norman, who took charge of the Scruggs case after Dawson's retirement

The Defense Lawyers

John Keker, San Francisco attorney representing Dick Scruggs

Mike Moore, former Mississippi attorney general and close friend of Scruggs who represented Zach Scruggs

Frank Trapp, Jackson attorney representing Sid Backstrom

Rhea Tannehill, Oxford friend and attorney for Backstrom

Tony Farese, attorney who first represented Zach Scruggs, and then, Langston

The Players in "The Force"

Trent Lott, Scruggs's brother-in-law and onetime Republican majority leader in the U.S. Senate

Tom Anderson, Lott's longtime associate in Washington

P. L. Blake, a figure in their Mississippi network

Ed Peters, former district attorney in Jackson

Pete Johnson, former state auditor

The Political Figures Outside "The Force"

Jim Hood, attorney general of Mississippi

Danny Cupit, former Democratic chairman and influential Jackson attorney

Joe Biden, former U.S. senator from Delaware, now vice-president of the United States

The Judge

Neal Biggers, senior U.S. district judge in Oxford

The Wife, Mother, and Sister-in-Law

Diane Scruggs, Dick's wife; Zach's mother; Trent's sister-in-law

The Chancellor

Robert Khayat, leader of the University of Mississippi for fourteen years

"Abide in silence," the cloud-gatherer Zeus said, *"and obey what I say, for now all the gods of Olympus will be of no avail when I come closer and lay my invincible hands upon you."* His queen, Hera, was afraid, and she sat down in silence, wrenching her heart to obedience, and the gods in heaven were troubled in the House of Zeus.

—Homer's *The Iliad*

PREFACE

A long with much of Oxford, I was savoring the news that Ole Miss had secured the services of football coach Houston Nutt, five days after Thanksgiving 2007, when that headline was overtaken by a breaking story with greater significance. Rick Cleveland, a sports columnist for Jackson's *Clarion-Ledger* in town for Nutt's press conference, called me to say, "Your buddy's been indicted." I could find the first, sketchy details on his newspaper's website: Dick Scruggs had just been arraigned in federal court on charges of bribing a judge.

The news of the indictment of Scruggs, a take-no-prisoners trial lawyer of international repute, a power player in state and national politics, and a major benefactor of the University of Mississippi, was shocking. My initial reaction was similar to that of others who knew Scruggs. As John Grisham told *The Wall Street Journal*, "This doesn't sound like the Dickie Scruggs that I know. When you know Dickie and how successful he has been, you could not believe he would be involved in such a boneheaded bribery scam that is not in the least bit sophisticated."

In the two decades since Scruggs first drew blood from the asbestos industry and then brought Big Tobacco to its knees in litigation that produced hundreds of millions of dollars for himself and his clients, he had developed powerful enemies. At the time, he was locked in an epic struggle with his most formidable opponent to date—the American insurance industry—in a series of bristling lawsuits growing out of Hurricane Katrina. Though he had backed a few Republicans (most notably his brother-in-law, Mississippi senator Trent Lott), Scruggs was best known for his support of Democratic candidates. Upon learning of his indictment, there were celebrations in the corridors of chambers of commerce and Republican headquarters across the country.

Scruggs's indictment came while Mississippi was recoiling from Lott's announcement, only the day before, that he would resign from office. As a Republican leader in the Senate, Lott was one of the most influential men in Washington. If Lott's resignation and Scruggs's arrest were coincidental, it strained credibility.

As the investigation widened to draw in other important figures, the story grew even more intriguing. The chief U.S. attorney, Jim Greenlee, called it a "Greek tragedy."

In nearly forty years as a newspaper reporter, I had covered the civil rights movement, eight presidential campaigns, and numerous overseas conflicts. Even though I had retired at the conclusion of the 2000 election and become a member of the faculty at the University of Mississippi, it occurred to me that this might be the story of my lifetime.

Two months after the first arrests in the case, with a trial quickly approaching, I dropped Dick a note telling him of my interest in writing a book. "I appreciate that you have to be guarded in anything you say regarding the case, but at some point I would hope we could talk about it," I wrote. "I still remember your candor and cooperation when we first met ten years ago and I was working on a story for *The Boston Globe* that dealt with the Luckey-Wilson case." Ten years later, the repercussions from that case were factors in Scruggs's current dilemma. In the intervening years, Dick and I had both moved to Oxford, and I had gotten to know him better.

A couple of days after I sent him the note, he called. It was a gray and wintry Sunday. My wife and I were on our way to a Super Bowl party to watch the local hero, Eli Manning, lead the New York Giants to the NFL title. Scruggs was a big football fan, and we talked a bit about the game that would begin in a couple of hours. Then he said, "I got your letter."

"Hey, Dick," I told him, "I've always operated on the presumption of innocence" as a journalist dealing with defendants in criminal cases.

"Hell, I do, too," he blurted. But his laugh carried no humor. He said he was reluctant to talk about the case now. Maybe at some point down the road.

Oxford is a small town, and we saw Dick and his wife, Diane, at a dinner party a few days later. No one mentioned his case, though it hovered over the table conversation like a spectral presence. Afterward, I got a note from him. "Although you don't need my 'permission' to write on this sordid affair, I just don't feel right about the appearance of exploiting it." Since he grew up in a south Mississippi county adjacent to my childhood home, he attributed his sense of awkwardness to: "Maybe it's a Lincoln County thing?" To put me off further, he added, "Enjoyed Saturday night at the Boones' with you and Nancy. A book needs to be written about how you got Nancy to fall for you."

Without any assurance that Scruggs would ever talk on the record with me, I began my book project, following newspaper and magazine accounts, interviewing individuals involved in the case, gathering court documents, collecting information that had never been made public. Drawing on old Mississippi connections, I interviewed dozens of people on all sides of the ugly conflict.

Meanwhile, the Scruggs story went through several convulsions over the next few months.

It became increasingly apparent to me that this was a remarkable story of personal treachery, clandestine political skullduggery, enormous professional hatred within the legal community, a zealous prosecution—all with ramifications that extended to high levels in Washington.

In the summer of 2008, Dick's only son and junior law partner, Zach, who faced prison himself, began to talk with me. He spoke, for hours, of the villainy he felt the federal government had committed during its investigation. He talked, too, of many other things.

One day Zach and I went to lunch, and Dick joined us. It became clear that Dick now wanted to give me his perspective. We began a series of long interviews. Sometimes at his home, sometimes at mine. One day, he sat in our living room and talked, while I took notes, from midmorning until evening. He made many jocular asides, but as darkness began to gather us in gloom, he sighed and said, "My life is over." He and Zach and others with whom I talked went off to prison. I made visits to them in confinement. I continued to talk to others: prosecutors, defense attorneys, judges, lawyers, political leaders, academic lions, close friends of Scruggs as well as implacable enemies. I found that I had tapped into an extraordinary outpouring of emotions. In the spring of 2009, Scruggs was returned to the Lafayette County jail in Oxford to appear before a grand jury, and I got together with him again. As I was leaving the room where we met, he folded his hands and asked, "When all this is over, are you going to be able to tell me how I got mixed up with these guys?"

I have tried.

In the summer of 1992, a time when fortune first began to bless him with riches, Dick Scruggs received a disturbing call from his close friend Mike Moore, the attorney general of Mississippi. Moore reported that he had learned of a plot against the two of them by members of a political network that had been dealing influence throughout the state for decades. The powerbrokers were said to be indignant over a lucrative arrangement between Scruggs and Moore that enabled Scruggs, a private lawyer in the Gulf Coast city of Pascagoula, to collect $6 million in contingency fees while representing the state as a "special assistant attorney general" in legal actions against the asbestos industry.

Scruggs and Moore, regarded by the old guard as upstarts, had succeeded after a similar plan by members of the network had failed a few years earlier because of a shortfall in state revenue. Among the members of the cabal, Moore told Scruggs, were State Auditor Steve Patterson and Ed Peters, the Hinds County district attorney with jurisdiction in Jackson, the state capital. These men and their allies not only were disgruntled over Moore's contract with Scruggs; they had determined it was illegal and planned to indict Scruggs—a move that would also serve to short-circuit Moore's climb to political prominence.

Despite his emergence as a leader in asbestos litigation and his alliance with the attorney general, Scruggs was still naïve in the practice of backroom politics in Mississippi. When he heard that he was likely to be indicted, fear ran through him like a fever. His head throbbed at the outrageousness of the accusation, and despair gnawed at his gut. He found himself frightened and unsure where to turn.

Scruggs knew that he faced formidable forces representing an amalgamation of old Democrats and new Republicans, the survivors and descendants of a mighty political apparatus once controlled by the late senator James O. Eastland. Working the phone, he reached out to other sources for help.

As a major donor to the state Democratic Party, Scruggs made a late night call to Jackson attorney Danny Cupit, an operative with broad connections in party affairs. "They're out to get me," Scruggs wailed, blaming his dilemma on hostile politicians and professing his innocence. To Cupit, it sounded as though Scruggs was weeping. He offered to make some calls on Scruggs's behalf.

Instinctively, Scruggs also phoned his brother-in-law in Washington, Republican senator Trent Lott. The lawmaker listened while Scruggs complained about the perfidy of the charges being prepared against him. Lott made no promises—for this seemed to be the work of squabbling Democrats back home—but he assured Scruggs he would do what he could.

Others provided counsel—recommendations of good criminal defense lawyers and expressions of support—yet Scruggs remained uncomfortable. And lately he had grown accustomed to comfort. He had recently become a man of consequence in Mississippi, even before his fortieth birthday, when he hit a big lick—as lawyers like to call any sizable fees won in damage suits. With his new wealth, Scruggs had bought a sailboat, a luxury car, an airplane, a home with a view of the gulf, and he had begun to use his money to dabble in politics.

Scruggs seemed driven by a lust to become a winner, a characteristic often developed in childhood by smart but poor boys, and now he had to consider that the life he had built for himself and his family might be wiped out. An indictment could prove him unworthy for his wife, Diane, a local beauty who had been considered too regal for him when they were in high school. Criminal charges against Scruggs would also besmirch his son, Zach, on the threshold of his freshman year at Ole Miss, and the Scruggses' younger, adopted daughter, Claire.

Scruggs's downfall appeared to be coming at almost the same warp speed as his rise in the legal profession.

· · · ·

After treading in the backwaters of the state bar as a young lawyer specializing in bankruptcies, Scruggs had a breakthrough in the 1980s, after he devised an innovative way to attract a multitude of clients claiming to suffer from exposure to asbestos. In Pascagoula, the shipbuilding city where he lived, asbestos litigation had become something of a local industry itself. Thousands of workers had passed through the giant Ingalls Shipbuilding facility since World War II, producing countless vessels that helped keep the U.S. Navy afloat. Over the years, the work force at Ingalls had used asbestos to wrap the pipes, reinforce the boilers, and protect the engines of the ships they built. Eventually, it began to dawn on some of them that their jobs had come at a price: inordinate numbers of the shipyard workers were succumbing to mesothelioma, an illness that could be traced directly to handling asbestos.

Scruggs missed out on the first wave of damage suits filed in Mississippi in the 1970s in connection with asbestos. But after setting up a clinic in 1985 that provided free medical diagnoses for those who felt they might have contracted mesothelioma, he was able to enlist hundreds of clients. Then he figured out a way to consolidate these cases into one blockbuster lawsuit so ominous that the asbestos companies were willing to pay millions in settlements negotiated outside the courtroom in order to avoid the possibility of even greater losses in a trial.

By 1992, Scruggs stood out as a paradigm in his profession, a plaintiff's lawyer representing the powerless masses, whether they were humble shipyard workers in Pascagoula or ailing consumers bringing product liability complaints. Scruggs and his colleagues around the country called themselves "trial lawyers," and they thought of themselves as the new guardians of the American public, stepping into a vacuum created by a lack of government regulation. During twelve years of Republican rule in Washington, a time when Big Government had been turned into anathema, the teeth had been pulled from regulatory agencies. Big Business had been given an advantage, and it seemed that the only place to hold industry accountable was in the courts.

In the 1980s and '90s, the trial lawyers waged legal assaults on asbestos and tobacco, defective autos and dangerous chemicals, against careless physicians and deadly medications. In many cases, they won astronomical awards. They also earned a legion of enemies: boosters from chambers of commerce, rival corporate defense attorneys, Republicans protective of business interests, prosecutors suspecting legal malfeasance, even ordinary citizens simply appalled by the size of the judgments. But along the way, men like Scruggs became as rich as the captains of Fortune 500 companies.

Scruggs's success coincided with the ascension of his younger friend Mike Moore, another son of Pascagoula. Though separated in age by six years, the pair got to know each other in law school when Scruggs returned to the University of Mississippi after service as a navy pilot. They were a natural fit: bright, hustling, and progressive in their political views. In a state where many of their contemporaries had begun to embrace the Republican Party, Scruggs and Moore were Democrats.

Their relationship strengthened after the two men wound up back in Pascagoula, traveling in the same social circles and sharing many of the same interests. While Scruggs grew wealthy as a private lawyer representing working-class clients, Moore became known on the Gulf Coast as a crusading prosecutor.

After winning election as district attorney in Pascagoula, Moore tackled the entrenched system that gave unchecked power to county supervisors and encouraged petty corruption. At public expense, supervisors often paved lonely back roads or delivered gravel for friends; they awarded contracts in exchange for contributions and effectively sold zoning decisions.

The practices were common around Pascagoula, the seat of government for Jackson County, and throughout the rest of the Mississippi Gulf Coast. The region is close enough to New Orleans to maintain the same loose mores, the same tolerance for official wrongdoing that characterizes south Louisiana.

Mindful that energetic prosecutors from Thomas E. Dewey in New York to Jim Thompson in Illinois had parlayed the headlines they won in pursuit of corrupt officials into political dividends that made them governors, Moore built name recognition by challenging the Jackson County bosses.

One of them was the legendary Eddie Khayat, known on the Gulf Coast as "The Godfather" long before Francis Ford Coppola made his sequence of movies with that name. Not only was Khayat the president of the Jackson County Board of Supervisors, but he had long led the statewide association of supervisors, acting as chief representative for their interests in the state legislature. He was the ultimate insider, a fixture in the vast political constellation established by Senator James Eastland.

In Washington, Eastland held power as chairman of the Senate Judiciary Committee; he was noted for bottling up civil rights legislation and blocking the nominations of progressive candidates for federal judgeships. In Mississippi, the senator's organization had tentacles extending to every corner of the state, with contacts in all the county courthouses and well-placed friends in each community. The network teemed with unreconstructed segregationists. Though Eastland's acolytes—legislators, supervisors, sheriffs and other county officials, judges, businessmen, lawyers—were capable of delivering blocs of votes in any election, the organization did not function like a big city machine, rewarding political loyalty with patronage jobs. Instead, it operated as a confederation of individuals with common, conservative interests. Eastland's men gathered over coffee at local cafés to consider the merits of various candidates rather than holding regular meetings at political clubhouses. But ultimately they took their cues from Eastland, and following the Sphinx-like characteristics of the senator, who rarely made public speeches, they preferred to carry out their work in private.

It was Eastland who intervened when Eddie Khayat first faced indictment for income tax evasion in connection with a kickback scheme in the 1960s. The senator summoned Khayat to a rendezvous in his car, parked on a roadside in south Mississippi. Eastland was a laconic man, and he had just a few words for Khayat: Go plead nolo contendere, the equivalent of not contesting a criminal charge, but at the same time not admitting guilt. U.S. District Judge Harold Cox would take care of it, Eastland told Khayat. He should not worry about going to jail.

Judge Cox was Eastland's close friend. The senator had exacted Cox's nomination as a federal judge from President John F. Kennedy in exchange for Eastland's agreement not to block Kennedy's choice of a prominent black attorney, Thurgood Marshall, to serve on a federal appellate court.

Years later, after Hurricane Frederic ripped across the Gulf Coast in 1979, much of the landscape lay in tatters, and Khayat's constituents called for his services. As usual, he responded. He deployed county workers and public equipment to clear private property, repair private roads, and install culverts contrary to law. It was the old-fashioned approach to government, but the new district attorney, Mike Moore, found it unacceptable and was willing to confront the system.

Moore indicted Khayat on eight counts of misusing public property. By this time, Eastland had retired from the Senate and his organization was diffused. It still existed, but some of the hard-core conservatives looked to a rising young Republican—Trent Lott, a congressman who would soon become a senator—for guidance from Washington, while others still called themselves Democrats and huddled around old guard legislators. Khayat fought the charges for a while, but in the end, he agreed to plead guilty to a misdemeanor, paid nearly $80,000 in restitution for questionable expenditures, and resigned from the post he had held for more than three decades.

The case broke Eddie Khayat as a political leader in 1982, but it sent the district attorney to new heights. By the time he was thirty-five, Moore ran a statewide campaign to win election as attorney general. Looking lean and polished—in contrast to the old-school politicians of the state—he seemed on his way to becoming governor.

Emboldened by success, Moore—like Scruggs—was willing to test new methods of procedure, to challenge ingrained practices. After watching Scruggs beat the asbestos industry into submission, Moore decided in 1988, a year after his statewide victory, to appoint Scruggs "special assistant attorney general." He gave Scruggs authority to file claims against asbestos producers and distributors on behalf of the state.

At first, nothing appeared sinister about the pact. Operating with the official mandate from the attorney general, Scruggs presided over the legal end of a massive "tear-out" project in which asbestos was stripped from scores of public buildings, many of them on college campuses. In the name of the state of Mississippi, Scruggs filed lawsuits against manufacturers of the product and smaller targets, the companies that sold or installed asbestos, to recover the cost of the work. He won $8 million from W. R. Grace Co. alone, and reached settlements totaling nearly $20 million more from such companies as US Gypsum and Owens-Corning Fiberglas Corp.

Under the terms of his 1988 contract with Moore, Scruggs's law firm would be paid on a contingency fee basis, getting 25 percent of all the money recovered for the state. He would also be reimbursed for expenses out of the settlement funds from asbestos producers and distributors.

As money poured in for the state, funds were deposited into a trust account in Scruggs's and Moore's names at the Citizens National Bank in Pascagoula. To reimburse Scruggs for expenses submitted to Moore, funds were withdrawn from the same account. The arrangement may have disregarded a state law requiring settlement funds to be deposited into the state treasury. There was also a question of whether the attorney general had the authority to hire someone on a contingency basis without the approval of the legislature.

It might have been a mere oversight on the part of the two men from Pascagoula, but the moves by Scruggs and Moore did not escape the attention of powerful men in the state capital.

To some members of the old network, Scruggs was seen as an arriviste who had not properly paid his political dues and who deserved neither his state contract nor the title Moore had given him. Meanwhile, Moore was perceived as a brash newcomer, aggressive, excessively pious, and eager to leapfrog past others with stronger credentials waiting for their own chance to run for governor. If Scruggs was thought to be a bit too slick, Moore seemed a shade too virtuous.

Their critics, after inspecting Scruggs's audacious agreement with the attorney general, found several problems with the document and raised legal questions. Following the practices developed years before by Eastland, the old guard went about their business quietly, without any notice by the press.

The move to discredit Scruggs and Moore would not only diminish their stature, it would serve as retaliation for Moore's destruction of Eddie Khayat.

One of the principal figures in the effort was the state auditor, Steve Patterson, a man with political ambitions of his own. Overweight and inclined to enjoy long nights out on the town, Patterson unconsciously mocked Moore's Boy Scout image. He was a classic "good ole boy." Quick with backwoods bonhomie and raunchy jokes, Patterson encouraged friends to call him "Big Daddy," or, more symbolically, to refer to him as "Kingfish," a nod to the nickname of the late Huey P. Long, the populist leader of Louisiana. Patterson felt such a designation would accentuate his ties to the movers and shakers in his state.

Like so many men wedded early to politics, Patterson got his start delivering campaign leaflets and driving candidates around the state in the days when all local politicians were Democrats, albeit conservative ones. One job came directly through patronage; he operated an elevator on Capitol Hill in Washington, a position found for him by the other Mississippi senator at the time, John C. Stennis. Patterson later served as a foot soldier in the southern campaign of Jimmy Carter during the presidential race in 1976 and enlisted in the gubernatorial campaign of William Winter in Mississippi in 1979.

After Winter won election as the first progressive governor in the state's modern history, Patterson was given an office in the state capitol. But he clashed culturally with the bright, well-scrubbed aides surrounding Winter. Patterson was relegated to dealing with the county supervisors, political hacks, and job-seekers who infested the capitol. Winter's idealistic associates thought it a thankless, sometimes dirty task. Yet Patterson made the most of it before being eased out of Winter's orbit. He collected scores of political contacts—many of them from the remnants of the Eastland organization—and went on to become state Democratic chairman in the 1980s.

By this time, the Republican Party had made significant inroads into the old "Solid South" that had once delivered all of its votes to Democrats. The party of Lincoln had been reinvented by Richard Nixon's "Southern Strategy," a plan that made naked appeals to white conservatives fearful of the political rise of blacks recently enfranchised with the right to vote. As the South morphed into a base for Ronald Reagan, the GOP became attractive to many white Mississippians. In the face of Republican growth, Patterson worked with black leaders to preserve a viable Democratic Party in the state. At the same time, he managed to keep his bona fides with the old guard.

Eager to play in national politics, Patterson signed on in 1987 as a regional director in Delaware senator Joe Biden's first attempt to win the Democratic presidential nomination. After Biden's bid failed, Patterson refocused on the state level and won election himself, as state auditor of Mississippi in 1991. Officially, his responsibilities included oversight of bookkeeping in state agencies; the job also enabled him to peep into transactions involving public money.

He was in an ideal position to investigate the Scruggs contract. Besides, he was interested in running for governor and considered Moore a potential adversary. Patterson soon dispatched a team of agents from his auditor's office to comb through records on the Gulf Coast. They gathered evidence to be presented in a report issued by the state auditor. One document prepared for Patterson stated that "serious doubt exists as to the legality" of the asbestos agreement. Moore would be cited for "a singular lack of accountability." Scruggs would be implicated because his $20,000 contribution to Moore's reelection campaign in 1991 would be considered a payoff to Moore for the asbestos contract. Ultimately, both Scruggs and Moore could be subject to indictment.

To handle the criminal charges, Patterson's group found that Ed Peters, the district attorney in Jackson, was quite willing to present the information to a grand jury. A longtime associate of figures from the Eastland network, Peters could be counted on to prosecute their enemies or protect their interests.

Peters had a history of using the weight of his office to inhibit people—sometimes in the pettiest of ways. Years before, he had threatened Danny Goodgame, the editor of the student newspaper at Ole Miss, after *The Daily Mississippian* carried a story about price-fixing at local laundries. One of the Oxford laundries was owned by a family in league with the Eastland organization. Though Peters had no jurisdiction in Oxford, he summoned Goodgame to Jackson and informed the student that he could face criminal charges if the paper carried another irresponsible article.

Indeed, from the time he was first elected in 1971, Peters used the threat of indictment as a weapon to intimidate those who strayed from the path of the organization.

One evening in 1992, as Scruggs struggled to deal with the case Patterson and Peters were building against him, he received a telephone call at his home from a man named P. L. Blake. "I know what's going on, and I'm going to help you," Blake told Scruggs. "You need to come up and see me."

Blake was cryptic, but Scruggs understood the significance of his call. Blake's name was not recognizable in most households in Mississippi, but among the political cognoscenti he was regarded as one of Eastland's original agents who still had the ability to fix things. Blake had contacted him, Scruggs believed, at the direction of Scruggs's brother-in-law Trent Lott, who had assumed command of the state's conservative power structure after Eastland's departure from the scene.

Scruggs had first been introduced to Blake a decade before, by Lott's chief aide in Washington, Tom Anderson. Scruggs had been told by Anderson that there was "a friend up in the Delta" who needed help. Blake owned several thousand fertile acres in Mississippi and a group of grain elevators in Texas. But his empire faced bankruptcy and he needed assistance in filing Chapter 11 papers while trying to salvage much of his wealth. During this period, Scruggs handled mostly mundane bankruptcy proceedings. Still, he was fascinated by the intrigue of politics and eager to become an inside player himself.

Scruggs helped resolve Blake's financial problems, and while handling the bankruptcy issues, he became peripherally involved in defending Blake in a criminal case. Blake had been charged with offering officials of Mississippi Bank $500,000 in bribes in order to get $21 million in loans. Scruggs worked with Blake's criminal defense lawyer, a well-connected future Republican senator from Tennessee named Fred Thompson, to whittle down the felony to a misdemeanor. Blake pleaded guilty to the lesser charge and escaped jail. The hand of the Eastland ring was prominent in the disposition of the case.

Blake earned brief notoriety for the scandal, yet he remained an abiding mystery in Mississippi. No one knew how he had gained such wealth. By normal standards, he should have been the stuff of a Horatio Alger tale. He grew up in a tarpaper shack in a Tallahatchie County village in the Mississippi Delta and worked his way out of rural obscurity on the playing field at Mississippi State. Blake was a standout on State's undistinguished football teams of the 1950s and the leading receiver in 1959, with a total of six passes caught in an era of ground games and strong defense. For a while, Blake played pro ball in Canada before resettling in the Delta as a farmer.

Sometime in the 1960s he became prosperous, acquiring loans to buy property while assuming a semblance of importance in Greenwood as an officer in Eastland's army. Like his patron, Blake lurked in the background. When the legislature was in session, he could be seen patrolling the halls of the state capitol or trading messages after hours with officials in Jackson lounges. He did not seek public office; he did not openly support candidates. The general public had no idea that P. L. Blake represented power behind the scenes. Yet politicians knew he was one of the most important go-to guys in the state.

When David Bowen, a young Delta politician with a Harvard degree, decided to run for Congress in 1972, he was told that Blake's approval was essential to deliver the organization's support. Bowen got it and won the election. Thad Cochran was given the same advice in 1978 when he decided to run for the Senate seat Eastland had yielded: Call P. L. Blake. Cochran talked to Blake on the phone, asked for his help, and secured it. But the two men never melded after Cochran succeeded Eastland. Blake, like many members of the Eastland organization, moved to an alliance with Cochran's rival in the Republican Party, Trent Lott.

Despite his connections, Blake was seldom quoted and rarely photographed. He existed like some sort of enigmatic don in the Delta. Over the years, he bought more land, made substantial investments, lost much of it, yet still lived comfortably in a big house in Greenwood.

It was to this place that Blake summoned Scruggs in the summer of

1992. Though Scruggs had not seen Blake in years, he was familiar with his home. He had spent nights there in the previous decade dealing with Blake's problems. Now it was Blake's turn to reciprocate.

When Scruggs told his wife of the trip, Diane began to wonder what hold Blake might have over her husband, to summon him to travel three hundred miles to the Delta. To Diane, Blake should have been indebted to Dick; Blake, more properly, should have been the supplicant, rather than the one to hold court.

Diane had begun to wonder about some of her husband's associates outside the sphere of their friends in Pascagoula. In his rush to succeed, she believed Dick had taken untrustworthy partners into his law practice while consorting with others who seemed to her a bit crude and reaching. To Diane, the connections seemed out of synch with her husband's personality. Dick had always exuded a special charm, she remembered, even during their childhood days when he was a fatherless boy and she the daughter of a popular dentist. She became attracted to him after he developed manners that made him seem downright debonair in the years after he went away to college. By the time the two of them returned to Pascagoula as a couple, it was as though he were Pygmalion's Galatea, refined and acceptable to the local mavens. Yet for all of his social skills, Dick Scruggs now seemed drawn to men bearing the appearance of impropriety.

Despite Diane's misgivings, Scruggs flew in his private plane to Greenwood's small-town airport, where Blake met him. "You helped me a lot," Blake told Scruggs. "Now I'm going to help you." After they reached Blake's house in an upscale neighborhood, Scruggs was told to wait in the living room and relax. "Somebody's going to be here in about thirty minutes you need to talk to," Blake said.

Soon Scruggs was astonished to see Steve Patterson arrive. Blake greeted the state auditor warmly, but he also had a few scolding words. Waving in Scruggs's direction, Blake told Patterson, "This is chickenshit stuff. I want you to back off. If you want to go after somebody, go after somebody else." Patterson may have already gotten the message from others, because he did not object.

The case was effectively settled that night in P. L. Blake's living room. Patterson would not only write the district attorney a letter stating that "the auditor has found no evidence of criminal conduct on the part of Mr. Scruggs," but Patterson would also send a letter to Louisiana officials hailing Scruggs for "an outstanding job in [asbestos] litigation on behalf of the people of Mississippi." He recommended that the state of Louisiana hire Scruggs to serve as counsel on asbestos cases. For his part, Scruggs agreed to reduce his expense claims to the state by $63,000.

To cement the understanding, to form a new bond, Blake proposed that the three men go out for dinner at Lusco's, a venerable Greenwood restaurant that featured prime rib, pork chops, and pompano. With its private curtained booths and hard-drinking clientele, Lusco's was a throwback to Prohibition days, and one of the most popular spots in the Delta. The place sang with the clamor of good times. In drunken food fights, patrons occasionally lobbed rolls over each other's curtains or hurled butter patties to the pressed tin ceiling to see how long they might adhere there before falling on someone's head.

Lusco's represented a picture of joie de vivre, but Scruggs couldn't fully enjoy himself that evening. He had a sense of relief; the criminal charges would never materialize. Still, he had difficulty eating. His stomach knotted with tension as he reflected on the raw power he had just seen exercised.

Eastland was six years dead, but his organization lived on, still capable of fixing cases, blocking investigations, finding satisfactory solutions for political allies, and creating insurmountable obstacles for enemies. Scruggs suddenly felt as though he had become a "made man," like a character anointed by the Mafia. He was not exactly at ease with the role. Drawing from his memory of science fiction films rather than gangster epics, he thought a term from the 1977 movie *Star Wars* better described these people with whom he was dealing. They constituted, he thought, "the dark side of the Force."

CHAPTER 2

For all of the wealth and influence he accumulated later, Scruggs never outgrew his childhood nickname, Dickie. Though his name was Richard and he privately preferred to be known as Dick—it sounded more solid, more mature—he couldn't shake the diminutive. He had been Dickie as a boy, the mischievous kid, the product of a broken home who lived for a time with his uncle and aunt in the leafy South Mississippi town of Brookhaven. Friends continued to call him Dickie in junior high school, after he went to live with his mother on the Gulf Coast. The name stayed with him through years at military academies and followed him to Ole Miss. It even survived alongside the mocking term his fraternity brothers gave him for his preoccupation with developing a finely toned physique: Zeus.

Scruggs worked out compulsively at the campus gym, lifting weights and running through a daily regimen of exercises. One morning, after shaving in the common shower room at the Sigma Alpha Epsilon house, Scruggs patted his cheeks and said admiringly to the mirror, "You good-looking Greek god, don't you ever die." A classmate overheard him and instantly proclaimed him Zeus.

Scruggs might have been dubbed Adonis, for the vain and handsome character from Greek mythology. Or Narcissus, for that matter. But the boys at the SAE house knew little Greek beyond the alphabet, a requirement for initiation. So they stuck Scruggs with "Zeus," the king of the gods, and that name endured for decades among friends from his college days.

He was a handsome young man, and as he matured there remained something boyish about him, even as he flew navy attack jets off the decks of carriers in the Mediterrranean at the time of a Middle East War and international crisis of 1973.

He was a bona fide Baby Boomer, born in 1946, the year after World War II ended. There had been any number of dissolute young men drifting through the South during this period, and Dickie's mother, Helen Furlow, married one of them, Tom Scruggs, an attractive, hard-drinking ne'er-do-well from Texas. They christened their only child Richard Furlow Scruggs; the middle name came from Helen's more stable side of the family. The Furlows were respectable people in Brookhaven, and they took the boy to their bosom after Helen's marriage cracked, was soldered back together, then broke again. Dickie had no memory of seeing his father after the second divorce; he only remembered his mother getting a phone call that Tom Scruggs had died, somewhere out in Texas.

Years later, Dickie learned he had a half-brother, said to be living in Austin. When he found himself in that Texas city, he looked for an entry in the telephone directory for Leonard Coe Scruggs. When a young girl answered, he asked to speak to her father. There was a hesitation, followed by the voice of a woman. "This is Susie Scruggs, can I help you?" Scruggs identified himself and explained why he had called. "I'm sorry," she told him. "He's been dead ten years."

If he struck out with the Scruggses, he was nurtured by the Furlows. The boy and his mother lived for a time with the family of her brother, Bill Furlow. When Helen Scruggs moved to Pascagoula to take an office job at Ingalls shipyard, a position arranged for her by her classmate at Millsaps College, the Gulf Coast Godfather Eddie Khayat, Dickie stayed behind in Brookhaven with his uncle Bill's family. Though his elementary school playmates sometimes referred to him as the boy "who didn't have a daddy," Dickie never suffered the loneliness of an only child. The Furlows had three boys of their own, and they seemed to him as good as siblings.

Although Brookhaven, fifty miles south of Jackson, lay in Ku Klux Klan territory, a sense of innocence prevailed in Scruggs's early life. He had no knowledge of the murder of a black man, Lamar Smith, on the Lincoln County courthouse lawn in 1955 as Smith encouraged Negroes to vote. Nor was he aware of the rantings of a local segregationist judge,

Tom Brady, who wrote a widely distributed polemic "Black Monday," which excoriated the U.S. Supreme Court for its *Brown v. Board of Education* decision that struck down segregation in public schools. The racial tensions that roiled Mississippi had little impact on Scruggs until his college years, after he realized his family in Brookhaven was affected. The Furlows were known as "moderates," a designation for Mississippians who understood that segregation was wrong yet rarely challenged the system for fear of being socially ostracized. But after his uncle, who served on the town's board of education, voted in favor of a plan to begin integrating public schools to comply with a court order, he became the target of threats and vilification. Judge Brady's brother, Tullius, who had been one of Furlow's best friends and golfing companions, told him, "Bill, if you do this, I'll hold you personally responsible for the miscegenation of the races." He never spoke to Bill Furlow again. And some who did had only spiteful words.

Other than that bit of unpleasantness, Brookhaven evoked happy memories for Scruggs. He lived a sort of Tom Sawyer existence. Troublemaking for him consisted of slamming doors to wake napping neighbors, or trespassing through forbidden property during games of hide-and-seek. Facing prison a half century after his childhood, Scruggs remarked with dark humor that his "life of crime" had started in Brookhaven when he and a friend swiped a carton of empty soft drink bottles from the back of a diner and cashed them in for a refund in order to buy Cokes for themselves.

One incident was a bit more serious. After older boys in the neighborhood had picked on Dickie and a pal, the pair retaliated by setting fire to a cardboard fort their tormentors had built. The flames spread to a nearby garage, which burned to the ground. To curb his rambunctious nature, Dickie's guardians sent him an hour's drive away, to Jefferson Military Academy, near Natchez, to begin the fifth grade.

Drama had a way of pursuing him even then. Forty years before Hollywood made him a character in the movie *The Insider*, Scruggs took his place with dozens of other young Jefferson cadets on a meadow near the school, the set for John Ford's Civil War epic *The Horse Soldiers*. The cadets played the roles of Confederate schoolboys making a comic raid on Union forces commanded by John Wayne and William Holden.

In the seventh grade, Dickie moved to Pascagoula to join his mother. There was a mystique to the old Gulf Coast city. Around the time that French explorers made landfall in the region in the sixteenth century, two indigenous tribes, the Pascagoula and the Biloxi, were battling for control of the territory. When the Biloxi gained an upper hand, members of the Pascagoula tribe were said to have waded, hand-in-hand, into a river and drowned themselves en masse rather than submit to their victors. Both the settlement and the river took the name of the martyrs. The Pascagoula River became known as the "Singing River," and old-timers claim that on warm, quiet evenings the lamentations of the Pascagoula can still be heard, sad singing on the water.

In both location and milieu, Pascagoula lies far outside stereotypical Mississippi. Tucked into the southeast corner of the last low-lying county washed by the Gulf of Mexico, Pascagoula barely fits inside the state. The nearest metropolis is Mobile, Alabama, forty-two miles away. Pascagoula's lunch bucket population of shipyard workers—sons of immigrants from Slavic states and seaports in Lebanon and Greece and Italy; often men of Catholic faith or no faith at all—bore little resemblance to the farmers and small-town merchants, the earnest Rotarians and churchgoing Baptists, who characterize Mississippi in the minds of strangers.

Pascagoula has always been a rough working-class place. It swelled from a fishing village before World War II, mushrooming into a home for more than twenty-five thousand people. Its dominant industry—the largest private employer in the state—was Ingalls Shipbuilding. During the war, Ingalls produced dozens of ships on a breakneck schedule. The brisk pace continued afterward because of the power of the state's two senators, Jim Eastland and John Stennis (who became chairman of the Armed Services Commmittee), to deliver military contracts. Ingalls built destroyers and cruisers and nuclear submarines, feeding the local economy. And its work force was unionized, a rarity in Mississippi. The company was a huge presence in Pascagoula, and enormous steel gantries, the infrastructure of the shipyard, loomed over the coastline like a giant erector set.

But there was a deadly product used at the shipyard: asbestos.

Asbestos would turn into the scourge of Pascagoula, and decades later, it set in motion a series of bitter lawsuits, windfall fees for lawyers, contentious quarrels over the division of the spoils, petty feuds, charges of corruption, and an unbelievable outbreak of personal betrayals.

Scruggs would grow rich in Pascagoula, and he would meet many people who would have an influence on his life—the politicians Trent Lott and Mike Moore; his early mentor Robert Khayat the Godfather's son; and the girl who would become his wife. In Pascagoula, he would also take on as legal associates Roberts Wilson and Al Luckey, two men who would claim he had cheated them. They would pursue him through various courtrooms in the state across two decades.

But no one anticipated any of this when young Dickie Scruggs moved there in 1959.

Like other places of comparable size, Pascagoula was layered by class distinctions. The little city had three basic components: a white, working-class base tied to Ingalls; a smaller, poorer black population; and an elite group of doctors, lawyers, business owners, and shipyard executives.

Ordinarily, Scruggs and his mother would have been firmly grounded among the shipyard workers. Their undistinguished tract home was a bit roomier than the tiny two-bedroom "navy houses" in an adjacent neighborhood filled with Ingalls employees, but it couldn't approach the elegant mansions that graced the beachfront. In an environment where money determined the social pecking order, Scruggs would naturally have been cast among the children of the navy houses. Instead, using the force of his personality, he bridged the gap between the kids from his modest background and his affluent contemporaries who lived along the beach. He made that jump, in part, because his mother had a college education and knew the value of establishing a favorable impression. She was a stickler for high standards at home, insisting that her son not only study hard, but also practice good manners. He learned, for example, how to hold a fork properly, to consume his food like a gentleman, not to gobble. He addressed adults as "sir" or "ma'am." He knew that proper behavior might raise him above his unlettered schoolmates. As a result, Dickie began to infiltrate the more privileged young crowd from the beach and prosperous Washington Avenue.

In the ninth grade, Dickie Scruggs was assigned, by the alphabet, to the same homeroom as Diane Thompson, the daughter of Dr. Perry Thompson, a successful dentist. Scruggs found her especially pretty, but didn't dare ask for a date. She lived in a big, comfortable home just off the beach, and her social standing intimidated him. But like the Montgomery Clift character in the 1951 movie *A Place in the Sun,* he aspired to someday rise to her company of friends.

Their homeroom teacher turned out to be the Godfather's son, Robert Khayat. Recovering from an illness that disrupted his professional football career with the Redskins, Khayat had returned home to Jackson County to take a temporary position as an assistant coach and instructor. Knowing that his father had gone to college with Scruggs's mother, the athlete took a special interest in Dickie. The boy showed little promise in spring football practice; he was enthusiastic, but not blessed with talent on the playing field. In the homeroom, however, he struck Khayat as exceptionally wholesome and refreshing, a boy with an engaging grin. There was a mutual attraction. The boy admired Khayat; he felt a bit awed by his presence. In a way, Khayat, eight years older, represented the big brother Scruggs never had. Dickie called Khayat "Coach." He used the honorific for decades, until the time that they were both grandfathers and two of the most prominent men in Mississippi.

In the early 1960s, as Scruggs yearned to move beyond the world of navy houses to the beachfront, he cultivated new interests. He wanted, desperately, to escape the occupation of a mechanic or a pipefitter that seemed destined for so many young people in Pascagoula. Sports, especially football, offered a means to excel, but he realized that his physical abilities would never make him a star in conventional athletics. Still, he wanted to be a winner, so he began to swim, taking up the sport with religious zeal, and he discovered that this was an area where he could compete with the best.

Otherwise, his was a normal boyhood. He liked to hang out with other teenagers at Edd's Drive-In, wondering about far-off places. He was delighted to be invited to informal sock hops and dressy dances. It all seemed removed from Ingalls and other critical issues of the day. His boyhood coincided with the revolution of rock 'n' roll and the first stirrings of the civil rights movement. But if the youngsters living along Pascagoula's beachfront thought of black people at all, they thought of Fats Domino, Chuck Berry, and Little Richard.

Just as he had been oblivious of racial problems in Brookhaven, Scruggs and his friends paid little attention to the upheaval in the state. In 1962 he went with his uncle, Bill, to an Ole Miss football game in Jackson that was highlighted by a halftime speech by Governor Ross Barnett, braying of his love for the segregationist tradition of Mississippi. Barnett delivered his message at the height of his confrontation with President Kennedy over the admission of the first black student to a white school in Mississippi: James Meredith at Ole Miss. Scruggs had been unimpressed by the governor's demagoguery; in fact, the boy thought little of the crisis, not even the next day, when the campus erupted in a riot that claimed two lives and left hundreds injured. Before it was over, the federal government had deployed thousands of troops and U.S. Marshals to ensure that Meredith was allowed to enroll.

The Pascagoula newspaper, *The Chronicle*, had been more passionate in its objections to the Mississippi insurgency. Owned by an irascible native of New Orleans named Ira Harkey, the paper ridiculed Barnett as a false prophet. In one editorial, Harkey wrote:

> A pall of contradiction covers our state as if every one of us had developed schizophrenia . . . there is the call upon the United States of America not to send marshals into our state to enforce the law. How can we make such a demand without appearing devoid of all sense? . . . Gov. Barnett knows full well how laws are enforced when the lawless are defiant . . . In a madhouse's din, Mississippi waits. God help Mississippi.

For challenging orthodoxy in Mississippi, Harkey was awarded a Pulitzer Prize. But he received few honors in Pascagoula. After he was effectively driven from town by boycotts and social shunning, he wrote that he had been left with only one ally: Claude Ramsay, a union organizer at Ingalls who then served as state president of the AFL-CIO. Ramsay, said Harkey, "was the only one of Jackson County's 54,317 persons who came publicly to The Chronicle's defense."

The beachfront set in Pascagoula had other priorities.

To ensure that her son did not fall in with undesirable companions during his impressionable years—Pascagoula had its share of youthful rogues—Helen Scruggs managed to scrimp and save enough from her family budget to send her only child to Georgia Military Academy for his final two years of high school. Troubled that his grades had fallen and unsure of the fatherless home, she was willing to sacrifice personal comforts in order to find a better educational environment for her son. At the academy, Dickie competed on the swim team and found that his studious classmates nourished his own determination to go on to college.

In the autumn of 1965, three years after the campus had been rocked by the desegregation crisis, Scruggs enrolled at Ole Miss. Despite the upheaval, the school had a pull on young people in Mississippi. It was the oldest educational institution in the state and, at that time, the only university offering a strong liberal arts curriculum and a law school. For anyone interested in building connections, Ole Miss served as a valuable starting place. To those attracted to politics or the law, the school seemed essential to their curriculum vitae. Virtually every member of the state's political and social leadership had ties to the school.

Although Ole Miss was nestled in Oxford, a remote North Mississippi town served by no interstate highway, it drew many high school graduates from the Gulf Coast, three hundred miles away. It was a natural destination for Dickie Scruggs.

As a freshman, he plunged into the social life of Ole Miss. He pledged SAE, a popular fraternity, where bonds were formed that would last a lifetime. The SAEs were more noted for rowdy parties than high scholarship. (The janitor doubled as the most notorious bootlegger on campus.) But the fraternity, like several other social groups at the school, generated an interlocking network throughout the state. The governor at the time, Paul B. Johnson, Jr., had been an SAE. Though William Faulkner would have been horrified to hear his name invoked during rush, he, too, had been an SAE at Ole Miss.

One of Scruggs's pledge brothers was a classmate from Yazoo City, a witty, folksy fellow named Haley Barbour. In keeping with the tradition of assigning nicknames, the portly Barbour was called Whale. Decades later, Scruggs and Barbour would be antagonists in opposing camps. Scruggs would lead a national assault on Big Tobacco while Barbour would act as tobacco's chief lobbyist in Washington; later, Scruggs would be locked in political battles with Barbour, a Republican governor of Mississippi. But the friendship formed at the SAE house, a columned version of an antebellum mansion, enabled them to keep their relationship civil through all the years.

In fact, all of Ole Miss, which was then a small school with an enrollment of a few more than five thousand students, served as a kind of fraternal organization. Ole Miss was seen by its detractors from rival colleges in the state as a country club, a finishing school for the sons and daughters of the old planter class, a refuge for aristocrats and pseudo-aristocrats. The criticism was a bit false, for Ole Miss was merely the mother school in a poor state; nevertheless, the place exuded a sense of elitism. The school and its progeny embraced each other, long after graduation, and its alumni association included those in the top ranks of every business and profession in the state.

To begin his own climb to prominence, Dick Scruggs chose a track different from that of most students: Navy ROTC. A military affiliation never hurt in the South, where the armed services were honored. Even though students on campuses elsewhere in the country were beginning to turn away from the Vietnam War, the military was respectable at Ole Miss. But Navy ROTC? When Scruggs revealed that he had signed up with the navy, his fraternity pals thought him a bit weird. He was told that Navy ROTC was a course taken only by Yankees, a description for anyone from outside the South, or by those defective in judgment. ROTC was mandatory for every male student during his first two years at any public land-grant university during this period, but most of the freshmen chose the more conventional army or the air force.

There were few navy guys at the SAE house; to take that route seemed like joining a rival fraternity. Scruggs roomed with Johnny Morgan, who was annoyed by some of the navy routine. On weekday mornings Morgan and Scruggs were sometimes awakened by Ray Mabus, a serious student and navy cadet, shouting, "Commander Scruggs! Are you ready to report for duty?"

(Two decades later, Mabus would be elected governor of Mississippi. After an interval of another twenty years, he would become President Barack Obama's secretary of the navy. Morgan was a nephew of Ira "Shine" Morgan, an Oxford businessman whose political ties to the infamous senator Theodore G. Bilbo led him to alliances with conservatives across the state. Scruggs's roommate went on to become president of the Lafayette County Board of Supervisors. The poor boy from Pascagoula had an uncanny way of gravitating toward political power.)

The navy beckoned Scruggs because of the opportunity for flying lessons. From his high school days he had a romantic concept that grew out of his exposure to pilots based at a Gulf Coast naval air station. In Scruggs's mind, navy pilots invariably attracted beautiful girls. Moreover, he liked the idea of flying, of soaring away from earthly problems, of being in control of his own fate in the skies. There was an element of daring in flight, and Scruggs tended to be bold. His classmates' idea of risk might involve a chance to draw an inside straight in poker. Scruggs took a different approach. He would eventually fly perilous military missions and, without qualm, negotiate his way past dangerous thunderstorms as a civilian pilot. (Later, when he could afford it, he took up deep sea diving at a time when most of his contemporaries were slowing to more sedentary pursuits.) He learned to fly, at navy expense, at the little Oxford airport. As his junior year approached at Ole Miss, he signed on for two more years in advanced ROTC. It appeared to be a decent option for him. With the war in Vietnam demanding more and more manpower, the draft loomed after graduation. This way he could earn forty dollars a month in the meantime and continue flying.

In the summer of 1968, that tumultuous moment in America history that followed summers of free love and free speech in California, Scruggs was sent to San Diego for a training cruise on an aircraft carrier. The experience transformed him. The son of conservative Mississippi collided with the libertine culture of Southern California. More significantly, the pilots he had only watched from a distance on the Gulf Coast became his running mates, his role models. They had swagger and savoir faire. Many of them were between assignments in Vietnam, veterans of combat missions and imbued with courage. He saw firsthand the magnetism of a navy lieutenant with wings. The pilots, Scruggs thought, were like omnipotent gods to women; even more alluring than Greek gods.

The boys at the SAE house might think Navy ROTC a joke, but to Scruggs it became a religious calling. After graduation in 1969 he won his commission, another step toward becoming a full-fledged navy pilot.

Scruggs returned to Pascagoula that summer, on leave from flight training at a navy installation in nearby Pensacola. For the first time he felt comfortable with his standing in the community. He had an Ole Miss degree, a set of college friends who held the promise of influence in towns across the state, and, finally, a navy officer's self-confidence. No one would ever have described Dickie Scruggs as shy, but as a boy he had understood the limitations of his middle-class background. His gracious table manners, his infectious smile, his native intelligence—all had assured him some acceptability by the kids with homes on the beach. Still, he had known he didn't completely belong there. Yet.

And he had always considered Diane Thompson unapproachable. Until now. Scruggs encountered her at the post office in Pascagoula. They had a brief conversation. He was mailing a letter to a former girlfriend; he discovered Diane was in the process of breaking up with her boyfriend. Emboldened, he asked for a date. She said no, but did so politely. She thought he was attractive, but in high school he had run around with a crowd different from her own, and they had gone separate ways to college.

Diane attended the University of Southern Mississippi in nearby Hattiesburg. It was not Ole Miss, but for many young people in South

Mississippi, it was the school of choice. She continued to occupy a place in the proper circles of Pascagoula. The Thompsons were members at the Longfellow House, a private club with swimming facilities and a golf course along the waterfront, and the estate was considered tonier than the local country club.

A few years earlier, Scruggs would never have been tempted to ask her out, and certainly not to try again if rebuffed. But he followed up with a telephone call. Diane's rejection was so pleasant this time that Scruggs bantered with her. "If I get the same response the third time I ask you, I won't call again," he said. The third time, she broke a date to accept.

The relationship became so serious that a year later Dick—she always called him Dick—and Diane contemplated eloping to Matamoros, Mexico. He was stationed in Texas, near the border, where they could easily slip away and make their union official. It would qualify Scruggs, as a married man with a dependent, for more pay. Later, they could have a formal wedding ceremony back home in Pascagoula, for appearance's sake. Diane considered the proposal, but decided against it.

The next year, Lieutenant (junior grade) Scruggs married Diane Thompson in a ceremony at the Presbyterian Church in Pascagoula. He also acquired a brother-in-law, Trent Lott, who was married to Diane's sister, Tricia, and just beginning to establish his political career.

Scruggs flew an A-6, a medium-range attack jet that carried an imposing load: twenty five-hundred-pound bombs. There were two men in the crew: the pilot and a bombardier-navigator. As the war in Southeast Asia wound down, Scruggs was transferred to Virginia Beach. Then his squadron went to sea, joining other navy units on the USS *Roosevelt*, an aircraft carrier serving as a base for bombing practice over forlorn islands in the Caribbean.

The assignment resulted in a reunion. One of the pilots from another squadron was Charlie Nelson, a fraternity brother from Ole Miss who'd grown up in a small South Mississippi town near Brookhaven. Like Scruggs, Nelson had disregarded the wisdom of other SAEs and become a navy pilot, flying an F-8 Crusader. In their spare moments, the two men reminisced about the "old days" at Ole Miss, which were not so old but seemed so far away. It was good to see someone from home. For fun, they punctuated their conversations with frat boy expressions such as "Phi Alpha!" (the SAE war cry) or "Hotty Toddy!" (the opening line of the Ole Miss cheer).

In the air, Scruggs loved the sensation of shrieking through Caribbean skies as bright as lapis lazuli. And the catapult off the flight deck, hurtling forward at blinding speed, was far more thrilling than a carnival ride. Life was daring and good.

Then the adventure darkened. One day, as Scruggs circled above the *Roosevelt*, waiting for permission to land, he heard a commotion over the radio in his cockpit. Disembodied voices shouting, "Eject! Eject!" Followed by more cries. "Plane in the water!" Scruggs continued to circle, avoiding the mishap below. Peering down, he could make out a disturbance in the water off the carrier. After landing, he learned that Charlie Nelson's Crusader had malfunctioned on takeoff. As it pitched into the sea, Nelson was able to eject himself from the cockpit but was killed on impact with the water. Divers quickly recovered his body, and preparations were made to send it back to Mississippi.

The next day, Scruggs waited in his A-6, in line for launching, when another plane veered out of control on takeoff and disappeared into the Caribbean. This time, the pilot failed to escape the aircraft. The *Roosevelt* maintained its march through the sea; maneuvers would continue, without a break. In a conversation between Scruggs and his bombardier, seated next to him, the men expressed fear that they might be the next victims of a faulty catapult. Through the layers of his flight suit, Scruggs could feel a chill. But he had a mission to complete, and he carried out the takeoff.

Over the course of his assignment on the *Roosevelt*, Scruggs would see the carrier lose seven more planes. Two other pilots would die. By the autumn of 1973, the *Roosevelt* joined a U.S. fleet in the Mediterranean. Its presence in Middle Eastern waters coincided with the outbreak of the Yom Kippur War between Israel and its Arab enemies, Egypt and Syria. For a few days, it appeared that the Jewish state, America's close ally, might be overrun. The *Roosevelt*'s jets were deployed to fly reconnaissance missions over the Holy Land. As the United States rushed supplies to Israel, Scruggs flew escorts for heavier aircraft. When it seemed that the world's superpowers, the United States and the Soviet Union, might be drawn into the conflict, the *Roosevelt* moved toward Turkey. Flight plans included targets in Eastern Europe and the possibility of deploying nuclear weapons.

At the end of October, tensions eased. But "Zeus" Scruggs, at the age of twenty-seven, no longer felt the invincibility of the gods. For the first time in his life, he had been seriously confronted by mortality.

CHAPTER 3

After flying a navy jet, the practice of law seemed tame. Yet Scruggs enrolled in law school after the service, completed his studies in the requisite three years, and embarked on a career path similar to that of many of his contemporaries. An argument could be made that law attracted too many talented young Mississippians. Instead of expending their ideas on entrepreneurial projects or investing in businesses that might create jobs and wealth in an impoverished state, the best minds of each generation invariably chose a traditional course of law. But Scruggs had no interest in anything routine; if he played the profession for all it was worth, he believed, life would become glamorous and riches would eventually accrue to him.

To his delight, the freshly minted attorney was recruited by one of his childhood political heroes, William Winter, to join a Jackson law firm featuring some prominent names in the profession: Watkins, Pyle, Ludlam, Winter, and Stennis. Since his election to the legislature in the post–World War II period, Winter, fifty-four, had been a leader of an outnumbered "moderate" faction in the state Democratic Party. Scruggs remembered, as a boy in Brookhaven, attending an old-fashioned political rally where Winter, alone among all of the candidates for public office, spoke with clarity and common sense while others babbled of the dangers inherent in *Brown v. Board of Education*. That year Winter won election as state tax collector, campaigned to abolish his own office on the grounds that it was unnecessary, then was elected state treasurer. By the 1960s, he had developed a following among Mississippians who recognized that segregation not only was doomed but represented a hindrance to economic progress. This was not yet enough to get him elected governor—he lost in bitter campaigns in 1967 and 1975—but he retained his role as the leading white spokesman for racial equity in Mississippi, and Scruggs had long considered himself one of Winter's political followers.

While serving as lieutenant governor and preparing for another campaign for governor, the candidate got to know Scruggs at the Ole Miss law school, where Winter was an active alumnus. Scruggs worked on a couple of Winter's projects and impressed the older man with his outgoing personality and his commitment to changing the status quo.

After graduation, Scruggs signed on with Winter's firm and moved his wife and their two-year-old son, Zach, to Jackson. But the practice of humdrum bankruptcy hearings and pedestrian civil disputes soon had him chafing at the bit for more action. Meanwhile, Winter reduced his own stake in the firm as he mobilized for a third race for governor, leaving Scruggs at the mercy of the firm's managing partner, an easily irritated former judge named Arnold Pyle, whose nickname, Red, matched his temperament. After a meeting with some of the firm's clients in which Pyle belittled Scruggs's work on their behalf, Scruggs followed his boss into his office, grabbed his shirt, and told Pyle he would "whip his ass" if he ever talked that way again. One of Scruggs's best friends, his colleague Bill Reed, was shocked by his behavior, which Reed considered out of character—until he remembered that Scruggs was only a few years from a flight deck. Scruggs was fired that afternoon.

He would be vindicated later when other young lawyers in the firm mutinied against Pyle and forced his ouster as their boss. But by that time, Scruggs had made a lateral move to another well-known Jackson firm with a shorthand name, Watkins, Eager, which was often confused with Watkins, Pyle, Ludlam. Yet his duties there were no more rewarding. Watkins, Eager was a conservative firm with a list of blue-chip clients that included banks and insurance companies. Scruggs was not inspired.

The firm entrusted Scruggs with one case that left him bittersweet memories. He was dispatched to rural Holmes County to defend a power company that had been sued by a customer whose home had burned down after an electrical malfunction. Scruggs felt he had the facts on his side: the plaintiff had had several appliances drawing power from a single extension cord when the fire broke out. But Scruggs failed to reckon with the caprices of a backcountry jury and the persuasive powers of a local lawyer, Don Barrett, representing the single mother whose family had lived in the home. The plaintiff was black, and so were most of the members of the jury. They responded to Barrett's oratory with approving murmurs, as though they were members of a congregation stirred by a fevered sermon. The jury awarded the plaintiff $15,000 in compensation for her loss and added another $50,000 in punitive damages for good measure. Out of his element, Scruggs felt he had been rolled, an experience he likened to a mugging, and he called his drive home to Jackson that day "the longest sixty-mile ride of my life." But he felt a grudging admiration for Barrett, his courtroom rival. There had been something winning about Barrett's populist assault on the utility company.

When he decided upon law, Scruggs had not bargained for the grunt work given to young associates at big-time firms. Nor did he relish the prospect of defending insurance companies in every nickel-and-dime, slip-and-fall case filed in circuit court. He had dreams of greater glory, and he thus began cultivating an Alaska Indian tribe in an exotic civil case involving a food services contract at a distant military installation. It seemed out of Watkins, Eager's territory, but Scruggs liked to freelance. And he felt underappreciated for his work with another client he handled for the firm, Frigitemp Marine Corporation, a subcontractor at the Ingalls shipyard in Pascagoula.

He decided to challenge his superiors. He asked for a meeting with Bill Goodman, the managing partner of the firm, and explained that his Frigitemp connection had brought in a lot of money for Watkins, Eager. He was working for a salary at the time, earning a bit more than $15,000 a year. "If I don't get a good raise," he threatened, "then I'm going to have to leave."

Goodman closed the folder on his desk, looked at his young associate, and said, "Dick, we're sure going to miss you."

Thirty-four years old and out of work, Scruggs returned to Pascagoula in 1980.

Because of the presence of the shipyards, Pascagoula retained much of the frontier spirit that had characterized the place when he left there sixteen years earlier to go off to Ole Miss. In a rural state dependent on agriculture and dominated by a belief in religious fundamentalism, it was still a blue-collar union town with bars to match a hard-drinking clientele. The city had none of the moonlight-and-magnolia aroma of the Old South, few traces of an aristocracy built on the fertility of land in the Delta. Instead, Pascagoula looked out onto the uncertain mysteries of the Gulf of Mexico.

Before Scruggs made his decision to go back to Pascagoula, he had to convince Diane that it was the right step to take. She was reluctant to return to the place where she was known as "Dr. Thompson's daughter," without an identity of her own. "My claw marks are going to be all the way down Highway Forty-nine," she told her husband, referring to the route they would take from Jackson to the coast. But she acceded to the move, as she did to most of Dick's decisions.

From the time they had married, Diane held a series of jobs to help support their family. She handled loan closings for a law firm in Virginia, where their son, Zach, was born in 1974, while Scruggs was wrapping up his navy career. She had secretarial duties at academic offices at Ole Miss during his law school days. After she developed a serious health problem—she suffered from Crohn's disease, an intestinal disorder—her work in Jackson was sporadic. But the couple needed her income, and she went from one temporary job to another when she was able to do so.

Once the Scruggses were back in Pascagoula, Dick opened a law office of his own while Diane held a series of piecemeal jobs to help keep their bills paid. They renewed friendships with classmates from their school days and joined a group of doctors and lawyers who formed a subset of striving young professionals. In 1980, Pascagoula held out the prospect of hard work and little promise of sudden wealth. For some of the lawyers, the struggle was so difficult that they hung out at the Jackson County courthouse, hoping a judge might assign them to represent indigent defendants. The jobs paid $300 a case, and for these lawyers, this enabled them to pay their own bills.

Most of these local attorneys could be traced back to the Ole Miss law school. Their ranks included Raymond Brown, a former quarterback at Ole Miss. Brown had been the most valuable player in the Rebels' 1958 Sugar Bowl triumph over Texas and a defensive back for the Baltimore Colts the next season in the classic overtime NFL championship contest with the New York Giants—"the greatest game ever played."

There were younger, upwardly mobile guys in the crowd, too. Mike Moore had just been elected district attorney, and Lowry Lomax, who had given up pharmacy for law, was destined to become a successful trial lawyer himself. Scruggs forged a lasting bond with both men.

For a few months, the Scruggs family lived in the home of Diane's father before they were able to buy a house on Columbus Avenue, in a distinctly middle-class neighborhood with an unappealing view of the shipyard. They spent weekends in a predictable social pattern. On Friday nights, young couples and their children gathered at the Singing River Yacht Club, an unpretentious A-frame on the water, for the weekly "steak night," where members would grill their own selections of beef, washed down with cocktails and wine. Saturdays were given over to picnic expeditions to Horn Island, one of the barrier isles a dozen miles offshore.

One of the more talked-about escapades of the period involved two attorneys, slightly older than Scruggs, who had moved to Pascagoula after law school, carrying with them their reputation as gregarious frat boys with a penchant for fun: Joe Colingo, who had already attained notoriety in the pages of *Rolling Stone* for representing two Ingalls workers who swore they had seen UFOs, and his pal George Shaddock. The pair had been barhopping one evening when their car, moving erratically, was stopped by a state trooper. While Shaddock feigned a heart attack, Colingo explained that he needed to rush his passenger to the hospital. With a police escort, they arrived at the emergency room, where they summoned a friendly physician to administer a "life-saving" shot to complete the ruse.

The zany incident represented, as much as anything, the zeitgeist of the Singing River crowd. The lawyers, all still relatively young, were waiting for the big lick. For some of them, it would soon come. In the meantime, nothing would get in the way of a good time.

The political "moderates" in Mississippi won a rare victory when William Winter took office as governor in 1980. It pleased Scruggs, but he already had a contact in high places, and it was ironic that his brother-in-law Trent Lott occupied an ideological corner diametrically opposed to Winter. From the time he took interest in politics Lott stamped himself a staunch conservative and became one of the early Republican converts in the state. Family considerations proved to be an essential ingredient for the friendship between the Republican, who had been elected to Congress in 1972, and the Democratic lawyer.

Aside from wives who were daughters of Dr. Perry Thompson, Lott and Scruggs had a couple of other things in common. Both had moved to Pascagoula as boys, the only children produced in troubled marriages. Lott's father, who was drawn to the Gulf Coast by a job at Ingalls, had stayed with his wife and young son. But he drank heavily and earned barely enough to keep his family in one of the humble navy houses in a working-class neighborhood.

Lott was five years older than Scruggs. He, too, went to Ole Miss as an undergraduate and eventually emerged from Oxford with a law degree. Not many other entries in their résumés are alike, but the two men shared one important characteristic: they were both boundlessly ambitious.

At Ole Miss, Lott joined a fraternity, Sigma Nu, that would become pivotal to his future. The Sigma Nus were more egalitarian than many of the social clubs on campus; the group opened its arms to freshmen with few connections, making it possible for someone from an unmonied background like Lott to win acceptance. The Sigma Nus carried a combative complex about them and relished their nickname, the Snakes. Most of the brothers were given nicknames. Lott was known as Gap, for the space between his teeth. The Sigma Nus believed they functioned alone, arrayed against the rest of the wealthier, established fraternities on a campus where Greek life seemed as important as a bachelor's degree. But to those outside their house, the Snakes seemed a touch too "gung ho," a military expression left over from World War II to describe those overly enthusiastic.

The Sigma Nus were the most politically active house on fraternity row, with brothers running for practically every student office available. Cheerleaders were elected at Ole Miss, so Lott wound up a cheerleader for some of the most successful football teams in the school's history. The Sigma Nu house bred cheerleaders. One of Lott's good friends, Roy "Rah Rah" Williams, served as a cheerleader before going home to Pascagoula to practice law and join the Singing River gang. Another frat brother, Guy Hovis, led cheers with Lott and became a featured singer on *The Lawrence Welk Show*, a musical program that attracted millions of elderly, stay-at-home viewers on Saturday nights. After the show ran its course, Hovis returned to Mississippi to take charge of Lott's state office in Jackson.

There seemed to be no end to the Sigma Nu hunger for political success. But when Lott ran for president of the student body in 1962, he suffered the only electoral defeat in his career. He was beaten by the son of the head of Mississippi Power and Light Co., a candidate backed by most of the other fraternities. While the Phi Delts, Kappa Alphas, SAEs, and Sigma Chis ganged up against him, Lott realized, in retrospect, that he had failed to mobilize the "independents" on campus who could not afford Greek organizations or who disapproved of the fraternities' sophomoric high jinks. He would never again neglect the constituency of the aggrieved, white working class.

As the war in Vietnam intensified, hundreds of young men from Ole Miss, including Lott's future brother-in-law, enlisted in the military. Lott supported the war wholeheartedly, but he managed to avoid the service. He claimed four student exemptions while at Ole Miss and won a final 3-A classification from the draft board when he graduated from law school. The dispensation was granted "by reason of extreme hardship to dependents"—his wife and mother.

After law school, Lott began parlaying his Ole Miss connections. One was an influential state senator named George Payne Cossar who doubled as a lieutenant in Senator Jim Eastland's political apparatus. Cossar represented the Tallahatchie–Carroll County region, where the Lott family lived before moving to Pascagoula. More important, Cossar was an enthusiastic Sigma Nu who still made impassioned pleas during rush each autumn, exhorting freshmen to join the brotherhood. He had three sons in the fraternity with Lott.

Lott also had an uncle, Arnie Watson, who served the same area in the legislature. At public events, Watson preferred to recite a pledge of allegiance to the old Confederacy rather than to a government based in Washington.

But Lott's most important entrée to politics turned out to be the Gulf Coast's veteran congressman William Colmer, another nominal Democrat affiliated with the political network overseen by Eastland. Lott took a job out of law school as Colmer's administrative assistant. When the old man decided to retire before the 1972 election, he gave Lott his blessing to succeed him. But Lott surprised his benefactor, and many of his friends, by running as a Republican. It was an easy decision for him; it came at the height of President Richard Nixon's efforts to lure erstwhile Southern Democrats, upset over the Democratic Party's commitment to civil rights, to an increasingly conservative GOP. Lott felt at home with Nixon's policies. Besides, it was good politics in Mississippi, tying himself to a Republican standardbearer who won his greatest majority, 87 percent, in the congressional district that would elect Lott as its representative to the U.S. House of Representatives for the first time.

By the time Scruggs moved back to Pascagoula, Trent Lott had become the darling of the archconservatives in the state. With the retirement of Senator Eastland in 1978, a power shift took place. Members of the Eastland network, layered into the political infrastructure of every county, needed a new leader who could bring patronage and appropriations from Washington, and most of them felt more comfortable with Lott than Eastland's replacement, the freshman senator Thad Cochran.

No matter that Lott, as well as Cochran, had abandoned the Democratic Party for the Republican. Those belonging to Eastland's camp were Democrats in name only. Like Eastland, they called themselves Democrats for old times' sake—and to maintain party affiliations that preserved Eastland's seniority and ensured largesse from Washington. But the Mississippi conservatives had effectively broken with the national party long ago. For some, the rupture occurred in 1948, when the Mississippi delegation walked out of the national Democratic convention rather than accept a plank in the party platform that deplored segregation. Mississippi supported a Dixiecrat ticket that year that included the state's governor, Fielding Wright, as a running mate for the renegade presidential candidate Strom Thurmond of South Carolina. For younger members of the Eastland apparatus, the final schism came in 1964, when a Democratic president, Lyndon B. Johnson, engineered passage of the Civil Rights Act, while a Republican, Barry Goldwater, who opposed the legislation, carried the GOP banner that fall. Goldwater was buried under LBJ's national landslide, but he won more than 80 percent of Mississippi's votes.

Thad Cochran actually voted for Johnson in 1964. But as the Democratic president pushed the federal government toward his "Great Society" and encouraged a quicker fall for segregation, Cochran felt the thrust went too far and too fast for Mississippi. He drifted toward the Republicans. In 1968, he served as state co-chairman of Citizens for Nixon with Raymond Brown, the Pascagoula lawyer. Four years later Cochran ran as a Republican and won an open U.S. House seat—the same year Lott claimed Colmer's office.

The two new GOP congressmen never bonded, in spite of some shared background. Four years older and a member of a different fraternity, Pi Kappa Alpha, Cochran had been a cheerleader at Ole Miss and active in campus politics. The pair overlapped in Oxford; Cochran obtained his law degree while Lott was an undergraduate. But they were two different personalities.

From the beginning of his career on Capitol Hill, Cochran appeared easygoing, and courted friendships on both sides of the aisle. Lott was stridently partisan, and no issue better demonstrated this approach than his fight-to-the-last-ditch defense of President Nixon during Watergate, when Lott served as a junior member of the House Judiciary Committee.

Their attitudes were reflected back home, too. Cochran built a following among the wealthier, business-oriented voters flocking to the GOP. Lott attracted a coarser element, the hard-core segregationists and hardshell Protestant true believers. Cochran personified the Chamber of Commerce; Lott epitomized the all-white Citizens' Council, a Mississippi organization dedicated to the fight against *Brown v. Board of Education*, the Civil Rights Act of 1964, and the Voting Rights Act of 1965.

When Eastland retired, Cochran moved quickly to declare interest in the Senate seat and locked up support before Lott could act. Just as he nursed old grudges from his losing campaign for student body president, Lott never forgot that he had been preempted by Cochran. His rival might take over Eastland's office, but Lott began to assume control of Eastland's organization.

There was no formal passing of the torch. The Eastland apparatus existed outside of party lines and had no structure. It was composed of a motley assortment of interests, its most influential members local lawyers and judges who gave the organization a patina of legality. In Mississippi, all judges were elected, and they were as attuned to politics as the lowliest constable.

The Eastland organization may have lost its long battle against racial integration, but it survived to represent the interests of conservative white Mississippians. It was capable of finding jobs for the faithful, of making such irritants as minor criminal charges and traffic tickets disappear from court dockets, of promoting sympathetic candidates for public office, and of throwing up roadblocks to progressive ideas or any piece of legislation deemed too liberal.

For the Eastland crowd, it was a fairly smooth transition to Lott. He had proper manners. Despite his carefully groomed appearance—he had creases pressed into the blue jeans he wore when he went native, and he kept his hair styled—Lott seemed at home with the best of the good ole boys. He talked their talk, and he voted their way in Washington.

After he entered politics, Lott tended to surround himself with fellow Sigma Nus who could be trusted. He made it a rule to restrict his Capitol Hill internships to boys from his fraternity at Ole Miss, and at the top of his staff he preferred Sigma Nu alums to help watch over his interests. When he first took office, Lott appointed Tom Anderson, class of '68 at Ole Miss and a Sigma Nu, as his administrative assistant in Washington. Anderson had been a banker in Gulfport, and he possessed the loyalty and discretion that made him an ideal associate for Lott.

Anderson took charge of the new congressman's Capitol Hill office, imposing a strict dress code and issuing orders to other staff members with the discipline of a martinet. He was not the most popular figure in the office, but he became known as Lott's alter ego, and constituents soon learned that if they were unable to reach Trent, it was just as good if they could talk to Tommy.

Anderson proved vital to Lott, helping him bridge the distance between the nation's capital and Mississippi. He performed duties privately that the congressman avoided publicly, cutting deals, extending favors, and exerting pressure. It didn't take long for Lott and Anderson to fall into the folkways of the political apparatus back home, and when it came time to inherit the Eastland organization, they were ready. Under Lott and Anderson, the Sigma Nus formed a new subdivision of the old network that would grow through the years. At the same time, they knew to stay in touch with the veteran insiders, and one of the valuable contacts they inherited was Eastland's quiet operative, a former Mississippi State football player and Delta farmer named P. L. Blake.

Blake once described himself as a "plunger and promoter," but basically he claimed to be a planter. "I've been involved with farming during my childhood from sharecropping," he said in a 1985 deposition, "and had the desire of probably a lot of young people that was raised in the rural areas of someday owning a farm."

Court documents indicate that some of the earliest loans to finance his land purchases came from the Hancock Bank in Gulfport. Tom Anderson worked for the bank at the time, before joining Trent Lott's staff. The president of Hancock's mortgage operation was Kent Lovelace, a former running back at Ole Miss who had played against Blake in college and become his friend. Lovelace formed Dewitt Corporation, the real estate investment company that Blake took over in the mid-1970s as he began acquiring more than five thousand acres of farmland.

Blake held no political portfolio, but his association with Senator Eastland enabled him to obtain government loans easily as he built an agricultural empire. Some of his transactions proved to be as puzzling as the mystery about him.

Though Blake invested heavily in agriculture, buying farmland in North Mississippi, he dabbled in other ventures. In 1970, he served as a front man for the purchase of an American Basketball Association franchise that had been operating in New Orleans. Though he posed as the team's owner, Blake said later, "I don't think I put any money in it." The Louisiana Buccaneers were moved to Memphis, where the club became known as the Pros. Their coach was Babe McCarthy, who had guided Mississippi State to a couple of Southeastern Conference basketball championships in the years Blake played football there. But after signing Ole Miss ace Johnny Neumann to a deferred $2 million contract, the Pros faltered. Nearly five thousand Tennesseans invested in five-dollar shares in an attempt to save the franchise, but the league had to take over operations of the club within a year. The team was sold in 1972 to Charles O. Finley, the iconoclastic owner of the Oakland A's.

In another sporting gesture, Blake bought the Fighting Bayou Hunting Club in the little Delta hamlet of Schlater, a well-known venue for duck hunters. During shooting season, the club attracted a number of prominent Mississippians to its grounds, and Blake nurtured his connections there.

But Blake's primary investments were in agriculture. It was no coincidence that the Farmers Home Administration loan program looked favorably on Blake while Eastland was in office. Eastland owned an extensive cotton plantation in the Delta, and over the years he had been instrumental in preserving a system of federal subsidies to cotton farmers while helping to dictate farm policies in Congress.

By the time Eastland left office, Blake's political bona fides were so secure that he held on to his Farmers Home Adminstration connections. In fact, they may have been strengthened by Ronald Reagan's victory in 1980, for Lott became the Reagan administration's favorite son in Mississippi. Even though Cochran, a Republican senator, outranked Lott, the congressman scrapped and clawed to claim credit for every pork barrel project in the state, for the right to dispense patronage and to name federal judges. He came into conflict with Cochran on some issues, and often Lott prevailed with the Reagan White House.

The Reaganites remembered that Lott had been with them in their near-miss run for the GOP nomination against President Gerald Ford in 1976, while Cochran had not. Four years later, with Reagan closing in on the White House, Lott tried to wrest control of the state Republican Party from Clarke Reed, the state GOP chairman who helped deny Reagan the 1976 nomination by delivering the Mississippi delegation to Ford. The Mississippi votes proved decisive, and like elephants, Lott and the Reaganites never forgot. Once in power, they took care of their friends.

In 1982, Jim Lake, a lobbyist who had worked as Reagan's campaign press secretary, helped Blake win a government contract to store grain in elevators Blake had acquired in Texas. Tom Anderson also offered assistance. "He found out the routes that we had to go through, the procedures that we had to go through" to obtain a license to store grain, Blake said after questions were raised about the contracts. In 1984, the U.S. Department of Agriculture found Blake's firm, PLB Grain Storage Corp., in default on a contract after PLB could not account for one million bushels of government-owned corn that had disappeared.

Blake also ran into trouble when audits prepared by the inspector general of the Department of Agriculture determined that the Farmers Home Administration had failed to uphold agency regulations by making loans, intended for struggling farmers, to wealthy planters. The Gannett News Service followed up with a series of articles, and one of them featured P. L. Blake. The news report found that Blake, the sole stockholder of Dewitt Corporation, ostensibly a modest farming operation in Mississippi, owned several subsidiaries, including the Texas-based PLB Grain Storage Corporation, a catfish farm in Mississippi called Quiver River Plantation, a catfish processing plant known as Cupid Corporation, and a rice-growing operation in the name of Delta Rice Farms.

According to court papers, Dewitt's 1977 tax returns had listed assets of just over $3 million. But by 1983, its assets had grown to more than $42 million. Blake's grain enterprise in Texas appeared especially profitable. Since 1980, the federal Commodity Credit Corporation had paid Blake's company more than $17 million to keep surplus government-owned corn. The grain was stored in elevators once owned by a famous Texas con artist named Billie Sol Estes, who swindled investors and the government out of millions of dollars in the early 1960s by using nonexistent stores of cotton and anhydrous ammonia fertilizer as collateral for loans. Estes became so notorious that he appeared on the cover of *Time* magazine in 1962.

Blake, in applying for his own farm loans in Mississippi, made no mention of his investment in Texas. The Gannett article reported that Farmers Home had first heard from Blake in 1975 and "found him so persuasive it has loaned him money 'to make ends meet' every year since then—$11 million in all." Although the federal loan program requires borrowers to disclose all assets and income, Blake never listed the PLB operation in Texas. As a result, he qualified for loans designed for farmers in financial stress and unable to get conventional credit.

After reporters began to ask questions in Washington, Tom Anderson called Blake to warn him of the news service's probe. In a rare interview at his Greenwood home, Blake insisted to the Gannett reporters that his business was "still struggling our asses off and trying to make ends meet." He said he had intended to notify Farmers Home of his Texas holdings in the coming year. "I feel like I've done to the best of my ability of being honest. I never stole a soybean. I never stole a bushel of rice. Everything I've done has been reported and aboveboard."

Gannett's 1983 article noted that Blake "had friends in high places." One of those was Mississippi lieutenant governor Brad Dye, a major political figure in the state who grew up in the Eastland organization. Dye was said to earn at least $2,500 a year for serving on an "advisory board" for Blake's Dewitt Corporation. ("I've asked his help in a lot of things," Blake later said in a deposition.)

The news story identified another contact as Mark Hazard, an Eastland protégé who served as state director for Farmers Home Administration from 1977 to 1981, a period when Dewitt received most of its loan money.

After Hazard left, the state office was run by a Republican appointee named Pete Perry, who told the Gannett reporters that Anderson had made repeated calls to the agency on Blake's behalf. (Perry was later fired, but he kept his keys to the Farmers Home office. An agency employee discovered Perry inside the office one Sunday night, going through papers. P. L. Blake's file was found lying open on a desk.) Anderson, for his part, acknowledged that he "may have made a call on behalf of Mr. Blake in the past." Lott merely confirmed that he knew Blake. "He's been up here [in Washington] a time or two," the congressman said.

Outraged by the Gannett series, Blake sued *The Clarion-Ledger*, a Jackson newspaper that published the stories, for libel. The articles affected his mental health, he claimed, "probably the same way of a private on the battlefield of a war, anticipating the next barrage." Blake demanded $40 million in damages. In a decision upheld by the state supreme court, a district judge delivered a summary judgment in favor of *The Clarion-Ledger*. The newspaper used as its defense the ultimate weapon employed by the press in libel cases: the stories were true.

Despite his reversals, Blake's web of alliances grew stronger.

Later in the decade, Lott and Anderson called on Scruggs to help steer Blake through his bramble of financial difficulties, including bankruptcy by the Dewitt Corporation and the criminal case involving bribery at Mississippi Bank. In the latter, Blake escaped a prison sentence by pleading guilty to a misdemeanor in federal court. He was put on probation and ordered to pay $1.5 million in restitution, ending a long ordeal that lasted several years.

Along the way, Blake and Steve Patterson, who had once worked at Mississippi Bank, became close associates. That was obvious to Scruggs from the manner in which they disposed of his problems at Blake's home in 1992. Newspapers looking into Patterson's activities as state auditor confirmed the Blake-Patterson friendship. After obtaining records of Patterson's state-owned telephone through the Freedom of Information Act, *The Clarion-Ledger* reported that Patterson had made an inordinate number of private calls to Blake.

Although Scruggs began to do business with both men after their dinner at Lusco's, his friend Mike Moore was skeptical. Like Diane, Moore was uncomfortable around the pair. He knew of the federal criminal charges in Blake's background, but he was more troubled by Scruggs's association with Patterson. Though Patterson had shared a place on the ballot with Moore as a Democrat and also held state office, the attorney general carried a grudge dating back to Patterson's role in the 1992 plot to undermine Scruggs and Moore. When an opportunity arose to retaliate in 1996, Moore never hesitated to gather evidence related to a variety of improper transactions traced to Patterson's office. To avoid indictment, Patterson resigned his public position.

Nevertheless, both Patterson and Blake continued to prosper. Still a major player in the old organization, Patterson went to work as a "rainmaker" for a well-connected North Mississippi lawyer, Joey Langston, where he was able to use his influence with state politicians.

Blake also retained the vestiges of wealth. His home on Bell Avenue in Greenwood covered nearly seven thousand square feet and featured a swimming pool and a huge stone fireplace. He, too, stayed active in the politics of the conservative alliance.

When, in 1989, Tom Anderson ran for the congressional seat Lott had vacated to go to the Senate, Blake contributed to his campaign and turned over his $1 million Cheyenne twin-engine turboprop to fly Anderson around the district. The Democratic Congressional Campaign Committee filed an ethics complaint against Anderson for failing to report eighteen flights on Blake's plane. Though the district invariably supported Republican presidential candidates by wide margins, Anderson lost the election by thirty points.

According to Blake's testimony in a deposition taken during the newspaper litigation, he also loaned his plane to Brad Dye, during his campaign for reelection as lieutenant governor, and paid for flights for Trent Lott.

In November 1993, after Blake helped head off Scruggs's indictment in the asbestos case, Scruggs began to make significant loans to Blake. At first he gave him $15,000 a month, but those payments then increased to $25,000 a month. The loans were unsupported by any collateral, other than Blake's signature on a note and his promise to keep Scruggs informed of political developments. By 1994, Scruggs's income had reached such proportions that he felt he would never miss the money. He didn't mention the arrangement to his wife because he knew she would be troubled that he was now investing in "the dark side of the Force."

CHAPTER 4

Scruggs was in a position to dole out money in large amounts because his breakthrough theories on asbestos litigation led to massive concessions by the industry in the 1980s.

He had tackled the issue relatively late, a decade after other attorneys had begun winning big settlements. The asbestos industry first came under serious attack in the 1970s, with lawsuits against Johns Manville and other giants. Ron Motley, a flamboyant trial lawyer from Charleston, South Carolina, who called Johns Manville "the greatest corporate mass murderer in history," took his offensive to Mississippi. He won $1 million in federal court in Biloxi in 1982 for a client suffering from asbestosis after years as a sheet metal worker at Ingalls Shipbuilding. Mississippi attorneys also began cashing in on the assault, and some of the most successful included Danny Cupit, the Jackson lawyer who later came to Scruggs's rescue, and Gulf Coast attorneys Paul Minor and Lowry Lomax.

Scruggs did not make a major move until the mid-1980s, but it proved to be a profitable one. His skills as a trial lawyer were never based on courtroom pyrotechnics or densely articulated legal briefs. Instead, he seemed to have a genius for determining strategies, developing a line of attack, and assembling a coalition to carry out his plans.

With asbestos, Scruggs devised a way to consolidate thousands of claims into one case, breaking a logjam of individual lawsuits stacked ahead of him in federal court. First, he collected hundreds of clients by establishing a clinic where a pulmonologist diagnosed asbestos-related illnesses and pronounced patients fit to become plaintiffs. Then he was able to get cases filed in state courts, rather than federal, by naming local asbestos distributors as co-defendants. Finally, in a daring gamble, he had an idea to lump all of the plaintiffs into one case. Even though Mississippi had no legal provision for class action, Scruggs took advantage of an opening in the law that enabled him to consolidate cases with "common issues." The strategy behind the approach was based on Scruggs's plan to link a few strong cases with hundreds of lesser claims. He intended to set up a trial situation in which it would be possible for a jury to find the asbestos manufacturers and distributors liable for multiple damages, a verdict that could force corporate defendants to pay untold millions to thousands of claimants. If, however, a jury ruled for the corporations, all would be lost for every one of Scruggs's clients.

In the end, the industry blinked. Faced with the prospect of staggering losses, the asbestos corporations settled with Scruggs before the case went to trial.

Dick Scruggs, who had strived for years to move up and out from his middle-class milieu in Pascagoula, became a rich man.

He began to acquire the accoutrements of wealth. He bought a single-engine propeller-driven plane, but soon graduated to a Lear-jet. An avid sailor, he expanded his fleet from an ordinary sailboat to yachts. Remembering the time when he and his college roommate, Johnny Morgan, drove to the coast in Scruggs's Corvair—a car branded as a death trap by Ralph Nader—while milking leftover gasoline from hoses at service stations along the way, Scruggs traded his Mercedes for a Bentley. Even his friends thought the purchase a tad ostentatious. In 1991, a beachfront mansion owned by Johnny Walker, who had operated a small Pascagoula shipyard, went on the market following his death. Scruggs bought it and moved his family to the city's most elegant neighborhood.

While lavishing millions on an extravagant lifestyle, Scruggs shared his fortune with others. He poured funds into the Boys' and Girls' Clubs in Pascagoula, organizations that existed to help youngsters on the edge of poverty and trouble, in straits similar to his own as a boy. He bought the antebellum Longfellow House (so called because the author of the epic poem *Evangeline* was thought to have stayed there) and turned it over to the city for use as a public reception hall. Quietly, he paid the doctor's bills and college tuition of people he barely knew. Scruggs's contributions, friends felt, represented a throwback to his youth. At times he seemed haunted by his experiences as an only child in a single-parent home, by memories of financial insecurity, as if he could ensure that others avoided hard times with the wave of his checkbook.

Despite his generosity, he wound up with enemies. One of them was a former partner, Roberts Wilson.

Scruggs and Wilson began working together in 1984 on asbestos litigation and formalized their relationship a year later as partners in an enterprise called Asbestos Group. Though it started under the same roof as Scruggs's law office in Pascagoula, Asbestos Group was a separate entity designed to deal with claims against the industry. Scruggs and Wilson each had client lists of potential plaintiffs and thought they could be more effective by pooling their interests.

It proved to be a mismatch. Both men were graduates of Ole Miss law school, but there the similarities ended. Wilson was a son of the Mississippi Delta, overweight and a bit rumpled. Because his given name had an *s* at the end, Roberts, he was known at law school as Bobs. Scruggs, meanwhile, felt at home on the Gulf Coast, exercised regularly, and dressed fashionably. His nickname at school had been Zeus.

Wilson felt that Scruggs took advantage of his client list. Scruggs deplored Wilson's frequent absences from the office.

Diane Scruggs warned her husband from the beginning that the partnership would not work. After the Scruggses first returned to Pascagoula, Diane filled in as a temporary secretary in Wilson's law office and acquired a distinct distaste for him. As she anticipated, the pair's disagreement made its way into a rancorous legal dispute. After Wilson threatened to sue Scruggs for stealing his clients, Scruggs responded with a letter in February 1992. "Suffice it to say," he wrote, "that our styles are different and incompatible."

To Wilson's warning that litigation between the two would lead to a "public airing of our finances," Scruggs replied, "I can only interpret your statements as a threat to attempt to destroy us both . . . Frankly, a public airing would be embarrassing to me only in the sense that our colleagues in the bar would learn how much you have received from your association with me. Notwithstanding, I will seek appropriate safeguards from such disclosures should you attempt to 'poison the well.'"

Predictably, the argument led to lawsuits and countersuits that dragged on for the better part of two decades, like Dickens's endless *Jarndyce v. Jarndyce* in *Bleak House*.

The dispute between Scruggs and Wilson had a nasty by-product. Alwyn Luckey, a young partner in Scruggs's firm in Pascagoula, was given a minority share of the Asbestos Group in 1988. Scruggs fired Luckey in 1993, but because Luckey still owned 25 percent of Asbestos Group, he sued Scruggs to recover money he claimed was due him.

The contentions by Wilson and Luckey that Scruggs had cheated them became the first public accusations that Scruggs had a tendency to shortchange his associates. Over the years, Scruggs would become the subject of numerous lawsuits and quarrels involving the distribution of funds and the methods he used to get reimbursements for expenses. In some cases, he wound up alienating former partners. Along the way, he developed enemies who nurtured their hatred of him with the dedication of biologists cultivating a strain of poison to eradicate pests.

Though it seemed relatively insignificant at the time, Luckey's claim would escalate with each passing year. So would Wilson's demands, especially after Scruggs grew richer from tobacco litigation. Scruggs's former partners argued that he had used money that was rightfully theirs to help finance his tobacco initiative. As a result, they said, they were entitled to a piece of the tobacco spoils.

The lawsuits got uglier. In one affidavit, Mitchell Tyner, a former associate of Wilson's, testified that he overheard Wilson and Luckey conspiring against Scruggs in 1993, when they decided to retain a hard-nosed trial lawyer, Charlie Merkel, to represent them. Wilson fought back with a legal complaint charging that Tyner and Scruggs had a "secret financial arrangement" to obtain "confidential proprietary information" about Wilson's new firm.

While Scruggs's legal battles with Wilson and Luckey degenerated into a mess of lawsuits, the acrimony escalated into clashes involving millions of dollars.

At the time the legal challenges arose, however, they seemed only a minor irritant to the good life Scruggs was enjoying.

Even though Scruggs had assured himself of enough wealth to retire and settle nicely into middle age, he remained restless for new challenges.

He followed developments in a heavily publicized lawsuit in North

Mississippi against American Tobacco Company. Don Barrett, the law-yer who had outmaneuvered Scruggs early in the latter's career in the trial involving the electric company, was representing the family of a man whose death from lung cancer was blamed on cigarettes. The first trial, which took place in 1988 in Barrett's hometown in Holmes County, ended with a divided jury. After a mistrial was declared, Barrett was stunned. The cancer victim, Nathan Horton, was a local black man, and the trial had taken place in a predominantly black county. Barrett had felt he held home court advantage.

Though the tobacco industry declared victory, Barrett was unwill-ing to drop the case. Especially after his firm had been contacted by a local businessman who had been hired by American Tobacco as a "jury consultant." In a call tape-recorded without his knowledge, the businessman told Barrett's brother how the tobacco industry had influenced the jury through payments to friends and relatives of the jurors.

To rig the jury, Barrett later charged, tobacco interests paid fifty dol-lars an hour to local black leaders to serve as "consultants." They were expected to sit in the courtroom on the side of American Tobacco and to make nightly calls to the jurors' homes. African American churches were blessed with sudden gifts. In one instance, the cousin of a juror was freed from jail, with bail money provided by the tobacco repre-sentatives; he appeared in court the next day, sitting with the tobacco "consultants."

Barrett and other trial lawyers in Mississippi realized that if they challenged Big Tobacco, they were confronted with an enemy willing to pay a heavy price and committed to any technique short of outright bribery to fight off the litigation.

In 1990, shortly before the second trial was to start, courthouse of-ficials discovered that a metal box containing the names of prospective jurors had been forced open overnight, with papers strewn on the floor. But it took a pretrial publicity kit circulated in the black community by Barrett's firm to force a change in venue. The packet of material included comments by Louis Sullivan, a black member of President George H. W. Bush's cabinet, criticizing "unworthy efforts of the to-bacco merchants to earn profits at the expense and well-being of poor and minority citizens."

The trial was shifted to Oxford. After three weeks, a jury required only six hours to render a verdict. American Tobacco was found liable for Horton's death, but no financial award was given to the plaintiffs.

Afterward, jurors said they were not inclined to reward Horton's family because it had been his choice to smoke the fatal cigarettes.

If a successful assault was to be made against tobacco, new strategies were needed. Three years later, an idea emerged from the mind of a Mississippi Delta lawyer, Mike Lewis.

The mother of Lewis's secretary was dying in a Memphis hospital. After visiting her and seeing how this forty-nine-year-old woman— once a three-pack-a-day smoker—had been ravaged by illness, Lewis grew angry. The long hospitalization had exhausted her medical insurance and now was sapping her family's resources. To pay her bills, she had to turn to Medicaid, a government program offering health coverage for the indigent. Before she would die, it would cost the state and federal governments more than $1 million.

Ending a visit with her one day, Lewis, who had come to loathe the tobacco industry, had a thought before the hospital elevator reached the ground floor: If the lawsuits against tobacco failed because the plaintiffs had chosen to smoke, why not sue in the name of the state, which was forced to pay medical bills for heavy smokers through its Medicaid program?

After discussing his concept with his wife, Pauline, who practiced law with him, Lewis decided to call the state's attorney general, Mike Moore. Though the Lewises had both attended law school with Moore at Ole Miss, they were not sure he would be receptive. They were pleased when the attorney general liked the idea and asked to hear more. In a few days, the Lewises went to Jackson to elaborate on the unorthodox proposal to use the state of Mississippi as a plaintiff to recover costs the public had borne because of tobacco-related health problems. After hearing more details, Moore became enthusiastic and encouraged them to run the theory past Dick Scruggs, another law school classmate.

Scruggs was found in Greenville, a river city in the Delta, assisting Barrett in yet another losing battle with tobacco. This time a jury would reject the suit against American Tobacco on the grounds that the victim's death was unrelated to smoking.

But before Scruggs and Barrett suffered another disappointment, they met with Mike and Pauline Lewis in a room in an undistinguished highway hotel after a court session. Scruggs and Barrett were still charged with adrenaline from their courtroom clashes with the tobacco lawyers, and they became even more energized as Lewis explained his concept that provided a legal basis for an attack on tobacco in the name of the state of Mississippi. All four lawyers left the meeting with a fresh sense of resolve, united in an initiative that would eventually lead to unimagined riches for all of them. But within a few years, their personal bond was destined to be broken.

A few months later, in October 1993, Scruggs invited a small group of trial lawyers to a meeting in New Orleans to consider early steps in the offensive. With Moore's approval, Scruggs had become the de facto leader of the group, a role he enjoyed because he liked to assemble teams to brainstorm critical litigation. And the tobacco wars were so imposing that the effort would require legal and financial contributions from a number of players.

Scruggs and Moore were seeking commitments of support, but they also wanted to discuss strategy. On the agenda for the meeting in a private conference room at the Royal Sonesta Hotel in the French Quarter was a presentation by a man unknown to most of the lawyers: Dick Morris. Scruggs knew him as an innovative political consultant and pollster whose clients included President Clinton and Trent Lott.

A political switch-hitter, Morris had been involved in Lott's 1988 campaign to win a Senate seat and had helped defuse the populist attacks of Lott's Democratic opponent Wayne Dowdy. The Democrat had a mantra that he bellowed at every stop in the pronounced drawl of South Mississippi: "Ah wanna mess up his hair!" Lott prided himself on his appearance, and every hair on his head seemed held in place by lacquer. Morris advised Lott to loosen his image and accentuate his blue-collar background with a series of television spots. Lott's campaign succeeded.

Scruggs respected Morris's track record, so he hired him to conduct surveys in four separate counties in Mississippi to determine a site to file the suit against Big Tobacco. Unfortunately for the group, Morris reported that none of the locales seemed sympathetic to their issue. Opinion was sharply divided among potential jurors over the merits of the case. Even though a majority of the respondents expressed a favorable view of the state's position, it would not be enough to win over three fourths of the members of a jury, the number needed for a successful verdict in civil cases.

The Mississippi lawyers were discouraged by Morris's report, but undeterred in their determination to follow through with a lawsuit somewhere.

Scruggs had invited several Gulf Coast lawyers with experience in asbestos cases to the 1993 exploratory meeting, but he also included two Jackson lawyers who were quiet forces in the Democratic Party in Mississsippi, Danny Cupit and Crymes Pittman. Both men had been helpful in extricating Scruggs from his dilemma over asbestos contingency fees in 1992, and Scruggs saw this as a way of repaying them for that assistance.

Driving back to Jackson that evening, Cupit and Pittman talked about the wisdom of investing in the tobacco case. Cupit, already wealthy from his own asbestos lawsuits, was dubious. It was a risky endeavor. The tobacco industry appeared too powerful an adversary for a handful of Mississippi lawyers.

But Pittman was intrigued by the proposal. His mother, a smoker, had died from lung cancer. He thought it would be worth the investment to take up the fight against the tobacco companies.

"I'm in," he announced to Cupit.

"I think it's a harebrained idea," Cupit replied. "It doesn't have a chance of succeeding."

In casting about for favorable venues, several of the lawyers visited Smith County, a backcountry outpost southeast of Jackson with a reputation for producing fine hunting dogs and delicious watermelons. Outside Mississippi, Smith County was known, if at all, as the home of the National Tobacco Spitting Contest. The irony was not lost on Scruggs.

There were other factors that made Smith County attractive. The jurisdiction was effectively ruled by Eugene Tullos, a lawyer in Raleigh, the county seat. Smith County was one of those places where one man could wield disproportionate authority without holding public office. Tullos got his law degree at Ole Miss while Scruggs was an undergraduate, and in the three decades since that time, he had built a power base appreciated by attorneys around the state. Crymes Pittman, who had family ties to Smith County, liked to try cases there. With a predominantly white, working-class farming population, the county's jury pools were invariably filled with men and women who could be expected to side with underdog plaintiffs in lawsuits against business interests. And it was especially helpful to plaintiff lawyers if Tullos made it known that he supported their case.

Scruggs and Don Barrett had not forgotten the lessons learned in Holmes County a few years earlier, when Big Tobacco bought the jurors' goodwill. In Smith County, however, it would be possible to deliver a preemptive strike. Scruggs talked with Tullos and felt he had laid the groundwork for a suit there. The trial lawyers would take the tactics used by Big Tobacco in Holmes County and turn it on them elsewhere. By bringing Tullos into his fold, Smith County would be wired for the plaintiffs before the tobacco interests could move in with big money and consultant fees.

But the Smith County gambit died after the plan was revealed to Mike Moore. After listening to Scruggs and the other lawyers outline the proposal, Moore balked at the chosen venue. He told them, "Gentlemen, the attorney general of Mississippi isn't going to do this."

Despite his misgivings about Smith County, Moore did not lose enthusiasm for the tobacco offensive. He convened regular meetings in his office, and the number of interested lawyers was whittled down to a dozen or so. The group knew they faced a deadline to file their suit before June 30, 1994, when a new state law would take effect that would have a negative impact on their claim.

They also realized the venture would require a private financial commitment. To finance the project, they calculated that a 10 percent stake in the Mississippi lawsuit would require an investment of $30,000 a year until the litigation was completed. If they lost the suit, the financial cost would be significant for each of them.

Nothing was certain about the litigation, and to buck up their spirits, the attorney general employed a motivational tactic. Moore emulated a nineteenth-century performance by Col. William Travis, the commander of Texas troops at the Alamo, who drew a line in the sand of the besieged garrison and called upon his followers to step across it if they were willing to fight on. With his foot, Moore drew a figurative line in the blue shag carpet of his office and asked if the lawyers in his group were truly dedicated to the fight. The lawyers in the room grinned at Moore's act, but pledged their support.

As they plotted into 1994, word of the plan to use Mississippi's Medicaid program as the fulcrum for their lawsuit spread among politicians in the state, and it did not meet with unanimous approval.

One day, as Scruggs and Barrett conferred with Moore, the attorney general paused to take a telephone call from Charlie Capps, a legislator from Bolivar County. During his political career, Capps had progressed from serving as sheriff during the civil rights era to the chairmanship of the House Appropriations Committee. He was a legacy of the school of Delta politicians affiliated with Jim Eastland, and over the years he had ascended through that network to a position of power.

Capps had thirty years' seniority, in age and public office, over Moore, so he had no reluctance to deliver a blunt message to the attorney general. As Capps spoke, Moore thought to share the conversation with his guests. He put Capps's diatribe on speakerphone.

"I want you to know that the state is not going to pay for a single telephone call," Capps sputtered. "The state is not going to pay for a single pencil. Not even a sheet of notepaper will be paid by the state for this doomed lawsuit."

After Capps had hung up, Moore looked at his group. "Okay, guys," he said, "You can see how much help we're going to get from the state."

Scruggs reflected on the situation. The dark side of the Force is going to screw us again, he thought. The old network, in which his own brother-in-law had become an integral part, was still capable of gumming up the works. With tens of thousands of black voters now enfranchised, the old guard no longer held total control of the state, but they could thwart progressive legislation, defeat political adversaries in many places, and throw up obstacles to initiatives such as the anti-tobacco lawsuit.

Scruggs called P. L. Blake and told him, "We don't want a rear-guard attack by this group." He promised to pay Blake "to keep his eyes and ears open."

For good measure, Scruggs called Steve Patterson, who had become a political connection for him after Blake brought them together two years earlier. Scruggs wanted Patterson to stay on top of things, to serve as a back channel, passing on information quietly. Between Blake and Patterson, two major operatives in the "Force," Scruggs believed he could be assured of advance warning of attacks, and of some measure of protection.

Because of his experience as a "special assistant attorney general" in the asbestos cases, Scruggs knew of one vulnerability that needed fixing. He asked Blake to find someone to take care of a bit of legislative legerdemain. Blake said he knew the man for the job: Pete Johnson.

While men such as Blake wormed their way into Eastland's political network, Pete Johnson was born into it. He was a grandson of Governor Paul B. Johnson, who appointed Eastland to a vacant Senate seat in 1942, and the nephew of another governor, "Little Paul"

Johnson, Jr., who served for one term in the 1960s, while Eastland was at the peak of his power.

Pete Johnson had run for Congress twice, unsuccessfully, in a predominantly black Delta district, but he used his ties to his family's political organization to win election as state auditor in 1987. Of course, he knew P. L. Blake. Anyone active in politics in the Delta knew Blake and understood that he had behind-the-scenes influence. In the post-Watergate period, Johnson referred to him as "Mississippi's Deep Throat," because Blake operated in the shadows and seemed to know so much.

In March 1994, a couple of years after an unsuccessful bid to follow his relatives as governor, Johnson got a call from Blake. By this time, Johnson had switched parties and become a Republican. No matter. Most of the old guard had gone over to the GOP, too, and Blake was now closely allied with Trent Lott.

"Dickie needs your help," Blake told Johnson. Scruggs wanted to draw on Johnson's experience as state auditor and his contacts in the legislature to arrange passage of an amendment that would eliminate the problem that had exposed him to indictment in 1992. He wanted to be sure that future contingency fees for lawyers representing the state would be legal. "Are you willing to talk to him?" Blake asked.

"Sure," Johnson replied. Not only had he known Scruggs as an undergraduate at Ole Miss, but Johnson was married to Scruggs's cousin.

Blake drove Johnson to a rendezvous with Scruggs at a restaurant at the Jackson airport. On the way, he told Johnson that the Pascagoula lawyer was willing to pay him a $10,000-a-month retainer.

After Johnson sat down with Scruggs, he was told of the plans for the Medicaid initiative on behalf of the state. The lawyers who took part in the action against tobacco, Scruggs said, needed Johnson to determine what changes were necessary in state law to ensure that they could be paid contingency fees.

Johnson was glad to be involved in the effort, and he left the meeting with the impression that Scruggs had promised him a $5,000-a-month retainer for two years—less than Blake mentioned, but a nice bonus nonetheless. More alluring, Johnson believed, was a cut of Scruggs's share in any settlement Mississippi might get out of the litigation. Afterward, he would swear that Scruggs had given him assurances of 10 percent, a figure that would eventually amount to a king's ransom.

. . .

Johnson was not a registered lobbyist, but he knew the legislators who mattered. He discovered that a bill relating to Medicaid had already cleared both houses of the legislature and now rested in the hands of a conference committee, where any differences between the House and the Senate would be resolved.

Johnson needed help from inside players on the conference committee. He thought of Roger Wicker, a state senator from Tupelo. Wicker was a logical contact. Though he never advertised the affiliation, he was one of those who made up the new generation's core of the old Eastland network. He had earned his political spurs as a member of Lott's congressional staff—headed by Lott's chief acolyte, Tom Anderson—and was now in his second term as a legislator. Of course, Wicker had also been a Sigma Nu at Ole Miss.

At Johnson's urging, Wicker slipped seventy-three words into the Medicaid bill. In one essential passage, the language authorized the state to "employ legal counsel on a contingency basis." The measure passed with little notice.

Only a handful of legislators were aware of the changes written into the bill. State senator Robert "Bunky" Huggins of Greenwood was one of them. A veteran of the legislature, Huggins counted P. L. Blake as both his constituent and his contemporary. As a committee chairman with oversight of health and welfare, Huggins had a major role in the conference committee. The night the bill became law, Huggins sidled up to Danny Cupit at a bar in Jackson with a message: "Tell Patterson we got the deal done."

Later in the decade, Scruggs talked with Michael Orey, who was writing a book about the tobacco wars called *Assuming the Risk*. Scruggs was candid. "There were people who had political connections, that I'm not even at liberty to tell you who they are, that had to be touched, that had to be talked to, that had to be given a stake in [the litigation]." He said he relied on clandestine consultants. "These guys have lots of friends and connections with legislature. These are people who are lobbyists, but they're not really registered lobbyists. It's really sort of the dark side of the Force."

He estimated that he paid these people over $500,000.

Actually, it was much, much more.

CHAPTER 5

For much of his life, Scruggs had risen to the dare, taken up the challenge, so when Don Barrett told him of a mysterious man who might possess damaging information about Brown and Williamson Tobacco Corporation, Scruggs was intrigued. He agreed to join Barrett in Jackson for a meeting with Merrell Williams, who was driving down from Louisville, Kentucky, in the heart of the tobacco kingdom.

Their meeting at a deli just off I-55 in March 1994 triggered mutual suspicion. Scruggs thought Williams flaky and unclear about this mission. Williams feared that Scruggs—about Williams's age but considerably more composed—was an undercover FBI agent.

Williams had reason to be careful. For some time he had been locked in a legal battle with Brown and Williamson, and details of his plaint against the company had already appeared in newspapers. A few years earlier, while working as a paralegal at a Louisville law firm representing the tobacco giant, Williams had copied hundreds of pages of documents that he believed would reveal a secret campaign by the tobacco industry to hide the deleterious effects of their product. He had leaked some of the papers to investigative journalists and anti-tobacco activists. Thus far, the recipients had been unwilling to use the material because it was stolen. When Williams moved to sue Brown and Williamson for what he perceived as deceit, the corporation countered with its own threat to have him prosecuted for blackmail.

As he considered his options, Williams contacted Barrett, a central figure in the well-publicized tobacco trials in Mississippi. Though Williams had a personal history as a wanderer, he had spent a lot of time in the state. As a boy, he spent vacations at a family cottage on the Gulf Coast. After graduating from Baylor University, he taught drama at local colleges in Jackson before obtaining a Ph.D. in Colorado. Unbeknownst to either man, Williams's peripatetic life had intersected with Scruggs's several times. Williams had performed in summer theater productions in Pascagoula, opened an English-style pub in Oxford at the time Scruggs was winding up law school, and knocked around at different jobs along the Gulf Coast after Scruggs returned there.

Although Scruggs was bemused by Williams at their first meeting, he agreed to help him relocate. The furtive air about Williams and the explosive potential of the Brown and Williamson papers appealed to Scruggs. It was another instance in which Scruggs found himself tugged by the excitement of operating in the shadows while at the same time exploiting an opportunity to obtain an edge over his adversaries. Dealing with Williams represented a high-stakes gamble, but it could prove to be worth the risk.

Once ensconced back on the Mississippi coast, subsidized with "loans" from Scruggs and working in a job arranged by the Pascagoula lawyer, Williams told him of the documents stored months ago with a friend in Florida. In mid-April, a few weeks after their first encounter in Jackson, Scruggs used his plane to fly Williams to Orlando to pick up the contraband material. The documents were packed, like so much typing paper, in small boxes, about three reams in all.

Scruggs realized that he was engaged in activity that was probably illegal. He was indirectly paying for stolen property. Since the papers came from a law firm, it was privileged material that had been copied and sneaked out of the office. But he knew that his adversary in the coming conflict had deep resources and a record of disregarding rules, and he felt he needed all the ammunition available to him.

For the 1,500 pages Williams provided, Scruggs would eventually buy Williams a house and a car, and pay him more than $2 million.

The same spring that Scruggs obtained the Brown and Williamson documents, the state of Mississippi girded for battle with Big Tobacco. At least Attorney General Mike Moore did. The governor, a conservative Republican named Kirk Fordice, wanted nothing to do with the lawsuit, and allied himself with the old political guard working to thwart Moore.

The attorney general's coalition of trial lawyers was not blind to the political implications. Though the issue might be argued in a court of law, they knew politics would help determine the outcome. So they weighed a number of factors before deciding how to proceed.

Mississippi judges, from the county level to the state supreme court, are elected, and there are often sharp distinctions between those who frown on product liability suits and those who generally sympathize with plaintiffs in civil cases. To the Moore-Scruggs group, it became important to find the right venue. There was another consideration. If the pollster Dick Morris's data indicated difficulty in winning a jury verdict, it would be better to submit the suit to a chancery court, where there are no juries and where judges rule on issues of law and equity.

In late May 1994, the case to recover damages from Big Tobacco for Mississippi was filed in chancery court in Pascagoula, the home of Moore and Scruggs.

Later, the governor, who despised Moore and his cadre of trial lawyers, filed his own lawsuit before the state supreme court in an attempt to block the litigation.

Political war broke out over tobacco in Mississippi, and hostilities soon spread across the country as Scruggs and Moore lined up attorneys general in other states to turn the case into a national issue.

For Mississippi, Moore would serve as the public official representing the state's interests, while Scruggs would emerge as the principal voice for the plaintiffs. They worked in tandem, backed by the investments of others in the group. Ultimately, a dozen law firms, including those of Scruggs, Barrett, and Mike Lewis, who had conceived of the approach, signed on for a joint venture. They called themselves the "Health Advocates Litigation Team"—HALT for short. With 25 percent, Scruggs held the biggest share, followed by Ron Motley from the redoubtable South Carolina firm of Ness Motley, the only partner outside Mississippi. Other than Scruggs and Motley, no shareholder controlled more than 10 percent.

As the offensive began, it became clear that more infusions of cash would be needed. In their enthusiasm to take the battle across the country, Scruggs and Moore ran up budget-busting bills with their travel expenses. Scruggs also tended to take initiatives without informing others in the partnership. His investment in Merrell Williams was one of them.

Scruggs's practice of making lone decisions for the partnership annoyed some of his associates. His freewheeling style and his propensity to make secret side payments to people such as P. L. Blake also ate into his own resources.

For all of his fortune built on the ruins of asbestos, Scruggs was no longer able to keep up with expenses for this new venture, so he went to David Nutt, a prosperous attorney in Jackson, and made an arrangement to assign half of his prospective income from the HALT project to Nutt in exchange for a commitment of $2.5 million to support the litigation. Nutt would ultimately reap a staggering return on his investment. Even though Scruggs would negotiate Nutt's share downward, Nutt would wind up getting $17 million a year for the next quarter-century from Scruggs's allocation.

As Mississippi's case against Big Tobacco moved forward in 1995, another Brown and Williamson whistleblower came to Scruggs's attention. Jeffrey Wigand, a disaffected biochemist who had formerly been in charge of research and development at the company, was convinced that the tobacco industry was deliberately jacking up the impact of nicotine to hook consumers on their product. Fired earlier after a dispute with his boss at Brown and Williamson, Wigand remained dependent upon the company for health insurance and had signed a confidentiality agreement that posed a problem for him. But he harbored anger at the industry, and in the months after he left Brown and Williamson, a producer for CBS's *60 Minutes* named Lowell Bergman began to draw information from him. Among Wigand's allegations, he charged the company with deleting damning material from its own documents and he accused the chief executive officer of committing perjury in testimony before Congress.

By cooperating with the television network, Wigand exposed himself to retaliatory action by the company. He needed legal defense, so Scruggs was called upon. As in the Williams case, the unfolding drama and corporate warfare fascinated Scruggs. After meeting with Wigand that fall, he agreed to represent his interests at no charge.

Knuckling under to legal threats from Brown and Williamson, CBS killed its *60 Minutes* exposé featuring Wigand. Unhappy over the network's decision, someone leaked the information to *The New York Times* and other newspapers. Wigand became a cause célèbre.

Scruggs not only offered Wigand his services pro bono, but he also spent thousands of dollars to hire a San Francisco private detective, Jack Palladino, to develop counterintelligence against Brown and Williamson after the company released a lengthy, unflattering dossier it had compiled on Wigand. Scruggs also developed a lasting friendship with Bergman, even though the *60 Minutes* piece remained unseen.

To ensure that Wigand's critical remarks gained wide circulation, Scruggs called upon Wigand to give a pretrial deposition in connection with the Mississippi case. Wigand flew to Pascagoula and stayed at Scruggs's beachfront home, where private guards were deployed to protect the star witness. In a circus-like atmosphere, Wigand appeared the next day in a courtroom filled with members of Moore's Mississippi team and lawyers representing the tobacco industry. The deposition was punctuated by frequent legal spats, and Wigand's testimony ratcheted up the offensive against tobacco.

(A few years later, director Michael Mann would turn the Wigand affair into a popular movie, *The Insider*. Al Pacino had the role of Lowell Bergman; Russell Crowe portrayed Wigand. Moore played himself. Scenes were shot at Scruggs's beachfront mansion, but Scruggs's voice was deemed insufficiently southern for Hollywood's purposes. He speaks in a clear and precise manner, in the style of a newscaster who doesn't betray a regional background. Scruggs's part was given to Colm Feore, a Canadian actor who appeared in the film as a dashing aviator-attorney in dark glasses, speaking with a distinct southern accent.)

Wigand's testimony, based on his experiences at a high level in the industry, gave credibility to the case against tobacco. While Mississippi pursued litigation in state court, the fight took on wider proportions, and the major battleground shifted to Washington.

With the strength of other states behind them, Moore and Scruggs were working to increase pressure on the industry and force surrender. As a goal, they envisioned a national settlement so vast in its sweep that it would involve hundreds of billions of dollars. But it would require congressional action that would, among other things, ensure the tobacco companies' protection against future lawsuits based on health issues.

In the fall of 1995, Scruggs called upon his best contact in the nation's capital, his brother-in-law, the second-ranking Republican in the U.S. Senate. He told Senator Lott of a possible breakthrough against tobacco. The Liggett Group, a traditional name in the tobacco trade, seemed to be considering a settlement. The company's share of the market had been reduced over the years, and the prospect of an expensive legal struggle projected further losses. Scruggs hoped to use Liggett's weak link in tobacco's united front to strike for greater concessions. He solicited Lott's help.

The tobacco issue did not thrill Lott. As a deeply conservative, pro-business lawmaker, he was philosophically opposed to the profession of trial lawyers and the idea of mass torts. Over the years, he had become friends with many of the chieftains in the tobacco industry. But like his brother-in-law, Lott enjoyed swimming in political back channels and consummating deals behind closed doors. There could be something in it for him. A business connection. A political IOU. The satisfaction of brokering an important agreement.

The process would introduce Scruggs to the Washington branch of the Mississippi network he thought of as "the dark side of the Force," a consortium of political interests led by Lott and his principal factotum in Washington, Tom Anderson. Although he no longer had a place on the congressional payroll, Anderson continued to handle affairs for Lott. Among Mississippians in Washington, he was regarded as Lott's "hatchet man."

Lott and Anderson served as Scruggs's entrée to men with connections to the tobacco industry, to Washington operators who could prove helpful when Scruggs decided to pounce.

After Liggett settled with the anti-tobacco forces in March 1996, others in the business appeared to be looking for the best way out of their dilemma. Steven Goldstone, the chief executive officer of RJR Nabisco, the parent company of R.J. Reynolds, floated a trial balloon in an interview with the *Financial Times* of London. The tobacco industry did not have "such a fight-to-the-death mentality that it would ignore eminently reasonable solutions," Goldstone said. Though Reynolds would not follow Liggett's course, he said, the CEO clearly opened the door to compromise, speaking of "legislative, executive, political, social and other sources" that might come together to resolve the issue. That was, of course, the way things worked in Washington, through legislative, executive, political, and social means.

At Lott's suggestion, Scruggs hired Anderson and his associate John Sears, a well-known Washington political figure, to serve as intermediaries to the tobacco industry.

After seventeen years as Lott's chief of staff on Capitol Hill, a span interrupted by a stint as American ambassador to a collection of

Caribbean islands during the Reagan administration, Anderson became head of Team Washington, Inc., an operation that held the franchise for a chain of Domino's pizza outlets in the area and delivered free pizza to friendly Republican congressional offices.

Over the years, Lott and Anderson managed to keep each other comfortable. Lott and his son Chet invested in Domino's pizza parlors themselves, while in 1995 Team Washington paid for a five-day excursion to Aspen for the senator and his wife that attracted the interest of journalists. Anderson could afford to operate on the same level as his old boss because he had been able to accumulate great wealth and an estate in horse country outside Washington. Like so many former congressional aides, Anderson had become a classic insider in the commerce of the nation's capital.

But Sears had more political pull. He had served as a White House lawyer under President Richard Nixon and went on to become the national campaign manager for Ronald Reagan. Though he led Reagan to the brink of the Republican presidential nomination in 1980, Sears was overthrown during a campaign makeover by Reagan. Still, he retained celebrity as a Republican insider. His Notre Dame degree helped extend his social circle to some Democrats, and journalists enjoyed his company at long liquid lunches in Washington's better restaurants.

Though both Anderson and Sears had separate offices in Washington, they were partners with a prominent figure in Florida's Jewish community named Joel Hoppenstein, in an enterprise called The Developing Markets Group. The firm had stationery indicating an office on Van Ness Street in Washington.

Hoppenstein's curriculum vitae listed him as a lawyer specializing in structuring financial transactions. In one deal, Hoppenstein and Sears were involved in the sale of a Red Sea resort, built in disputed Sinai territory when it was controlled by Israel, to the Egyptian government after the land changed hands following the Camp David Accords.

There was never any formal mention of him, but P. L. Blake turned out to have a silent role with The Developing Markets Group.

Without the knowledge of his partners in the Mississipppi team, Scruggs met with Anderson and Sears in the spring of 1996 to discuss inroads to the tobacco industry, explorations that might include a meeting with the RJR Nabisco CEO Steven Goldstone, to feel him out about a settlement.

There were contacts between Sears and Anderson and the tobacco interests, but apparently the only fruit the meetings produced turned out to be a distasteful quarrel between Sears and Scruggs over millions of dollars Sears claimed to have been owed for his services.

Scruggs and Moore operated more openly in Washington with another powerful Republican, Senator John McCain of Arizona. McCain was not only one of the biggest champions of the anti-tobacco effort in Congress, but he held a position as chairman of the Senate Commerce Committee. He and Scruggs, both former navy pilots, struck up an easy friendship that led to an invitation for Dick and Diane Scruggs to spend a weekend with McCain and his wife, Cindy, at their home in the Arizona desert. More important to the campaign against tobacco, McCain allowed Scruggs and Moore to set up a war room inside the Capitol Hill offices of the Commerce Committee.

His access to working space in the halls of Congress, coupled with the knowledge that other Capitol Hill doors were opening to him, put Scruggs in his element. He loved politics, and this seemed infinitely better than doing business with the rinky-dink operators back in Mississippi. Still, some of those old relationships proved helpful to him in Washington. Especially those with P. L. Blake and Steve Patterson.

In the years since Scruggs escaped the clutches of the dark side of the Force, he had learned how to navigate Mississippi politics. To keep his initiatives afloat, he knew it was necessary to establish links with some of the same people who had once plotted to indict him. There was something a bit louche about these connections, Scruggs realized, but consorting with rogues was far more fascinating than wallowing in the drudgery of bankruptcy law.

Patterson, who had worked a decade earlier on Joe Biden's failed attempt to win the Democratic presidential nomination, opened doors to the Delaware senator. It was important to win support among Democratic liberals such as Biden, who generally opposed Big Tobacco but were skeptical of any settlement—such as the one Scruggs seemed to be forging—that might immunize the tobacco industry against future lawsuits.

It helped that Scruggs agreed to Patterson and Blake's suggestion to hire the senator's brother Jim Biden as one of those assigned to the "legislative, executive, political and social" campaign in Washington on behalf of the anti-tobacco team. Before the struggle ended, Scruggs would pay thousands of dollars—he was never sure exactly how much—to Jim Biden's lobbying operation, Lion Hall Group.

. . .

Scruggs courted other Democratic allies at the highest levels in Washington. At the White House, he felt Vice-President Al Gore would be a strong advocate. Gore's sister, Nancy, had died from lung cancer after years of smoking, and her widower, Frank Hunger, was an acquaintance of Scruggs who had been a lawyer in Mississippi before coming to Washington to take over the civil division of the U.S. Department of Justice.

The Mississippi team had another connection to Gore, through David Nutt, the Jackson attorney who had come to their financial rescue. Nutt hosted a private dinner for the vice-president at his Mississippi home and invited members of the HALT group to come discuss with Gore their anti-tobacco litigation.

At the same time, Trent Lott helped arrange secret White House meetings for Scruggs. Though the Senate leader of the opposition party, Lott was in regular contact with President Clinton's chief of staff, Erskine Bowles, crafting compromises before congressional issues blew into political crises.

Negotiations between anti-tobacco lawyers, industry representatives, and political leaders seemed to be making progress. Scruggs, who had never been gifted as an orator in an actual trial, preferred out-of-court settlements and, in August 1996, felt that the various sides were on the verge of an acceptable plan. It would cost the tobacco interests billions of dollars in payments each year to a settlement fund, but it would protect the industry from future lawsuits.

The deal was set back by a story in *The Wall Street Journal* that described specific provisions of the proposal and reported that "formidable opposition" to the plan was developing. Scruggs felt the information had been turned over to the newspaper by a California congressman, Henry Waxman, the ranking Democrat with oversight on the issue in the House. Waxman was a staunch critic of tobacco, and another of the Democratic liberals unwilling to give immunity to the industry.

Scruggs felt betrayed. Early in the struggle against tobacco, he and Mike Moore had entrusted Waxman with the Brown and Williamson papers provided by Merrell Williams. And Scruggs had shared with Waxman a draft of the prospective settlement.

Negotiations got back on track, but nearly another year would be needed to complete the deal.

By the spring of 1997, thirty-nine other states had joined Mississippi in the campaign against the tobacco industry. With Moore and

Scruggs handling the case for the coalition, a series of private talks were held with industry attorneys. It was high drama, albeit behind closed doors. To ensure privacy, the meetings took place in out-of-the-way hotel conference rooms around the country.

On June 20, an agreement was finally reached. Over a twenty-five-year period, Big Tobacco would pay out $368 billion to compensate for health costs related to smoking. The industry would also submit to tougher regulations and put an end to much of its advertising. In exchange, tobacco would no longer face massive class action suits, eliminating the danger of crippling punitive litigation in the future. When Moore announced the settlement, he called it "the most historic public health agreement in history."

But the agreement still needed congressional approval.

Anxious to resolve the dispute, the tobacco industry began to make a separate peace with the various states. An agreement was reached within two weeks with Mississippi that gave $3.4 billion to the state.

For the members of HALT, this represented the ultimate big lick. They had risked their own money to represent the state at a time when state officials—other than Moore—were unwilling to challenge Big Tobacco. And the fees that they reaped did not come directly out of the state's windfall, but were assigned by independent arbitration panels.

For the next twenty-five years, each of the Mississippi attorneys who had signed on for the fight would be paid millions of dollars. A 10 percent share in HALT, such as those held by Crymes Pittman and Mike Lewis, would be worth roughly $140 million.

Scruggs's big lick would be even bigger, for he had a greater share in HALT and was involved in additional litigation on behalf of Florida, Texas, and others. Tobacco was settling with these states, too. The total amounts coming to Scruggs seemed incalculable. Some news accounts had him getting as much as $848 million, leading to descriptions of him as a billionaire. The lick was never that big, but far more than most Americans would earn in a lifetime.

Looking back on the period a few years later, Scruggs would tell a friend, "The money was obscene. Nobody thought we'd make money like this. It was a frenzy."

Even though the national settlement, announced with great fanfare in 1997, broke down in Congress the next year, the victim of legislation that had become top-heavy (tobacco's liability had grown to more than $500 billion), the industry had been dealt a severe blow, and Scruggs had been given a title: King of Torts. It complemented his college nickname, Zeus, king of the gods.

But the crown did not rest easily on him.

Instead of enjoying his riches in comfort, he was forced to fight rearguard actions to protect his interests. During the four-year struggle over the tobacco litigation, Scruggs agreed to assign various percentages of his eventual payout to others. Some of the promises were sealed with nothing stronger than a handshake, leading to bitter quarrels over disputed terms. Later, questions would arise about payments to agents of the dark side of the Force.

No better example of the curious deals and money frenzy exists than Scruggs's agreement with a prominent North Mississippi trial lawyer named Joey Langston.

Less than two months after the tobacco interests began to reach agreements with various parties to the conflict, Scruggs was alarmed by an article in *The Wall Street Journal* that touched on a problem that could wreck the process. The story reported that Ron Motley, one of Scruggs's chief partners in the tobacco fight, had been sued for $1.5 billion by a former client in Jones County, Mississippi. The plaintiff was the widow of a small-town barber named Burl Butler who had died of lung cancer after a career of inhaling smoke in a barbershop dense with the discharge of cigarettes. Initially, Mrs. Butler had been represented by Motley, who had boasted of the suit's unpredecented nature—the first to claim that death had been caused by secondhand smoke. After Motley emerged as one of the lawyers involved in a settlement that would spare the industry from suits such as Mrs. Butler's, she accused him of undermining her interests.

The Butler case had been valuable to the members of HALT. The judge in Jones County who presided over the case was considered sympathetic to the plaintiffs and had allowed Motley a great deal of leeway to obtain tobacco industry documents through a legal process known as discovery. To Scruggs, the Butler case had become a "discovery engine," providing much detail and information to the plaintiffs.

The new conflict had the potential of jeopardizing any settlement with tobacco because it might affect an agreement on immunity.

The Butler case had taken a strange turn. Instead of representing the widow, Motley had been sued by her. Handling Mrs. Butler's suit was a Jackson lawyer named Shane Langston. His sister, Cindy, though associated with another law firm, was also a member of the new Butler legal team.

To see if the affair could be resolved, Scruggs turned to the Langstons' brother Joey. Scruggs knew Langston as a successful attorney who had maintained his father's practice in the little town of Booneville while his siblings had gone off to more urban locations. Scruggs didn't know Langston well, but he recalled sending a few asbestos cases his way after Steve Patterson, who now worked with Langston, asked for the business. Scruggs felt he was in position to seek a favor.

"This is going to be a big stink," Scruggs said of the suit against Motley when he called Langston. Invoking the brotherhood of trial lawyers, Scruggs added, "It takes away our high ground."

Langston agreed to see what he could do. If he was successful, Scruggs promised to assign 3 percent of his take from tobacco toward a settlement of the Butler disagreement. (According to Langston, Scruggs had made a commitment to him earlier for a 3 percent "contingency" cut of anticipated fees from the tobacco initiative.) The conditions were vague, but some of Motley's share of the tobacco money would also go to resolve Mrs. Butler's complaint.

Langston traveled to Jackson to meet with lawyers representing the various parties. He found himself shuttling between different floors of a building, carrying offers back and forth. One of the sticking points was Scruggs's promise of 3 percent, which had not been sealed with a signature. After some discussion on the phone, Scruggs agreed to meet with Langston at a familiar setting, P. L. Blake's home in Greenwood, to sign the papers.

A settlement was reached, and the case was sealed by a judge in Jones County, with details of the arrangement kept secret. The deal would lie smoldering for nearly a decade until it was revived in another dispute between Scruggs and an erstwhile friend and associate. This time the antagonist would be Joey Langston.

Diane Scruggs had long been troubled by some of her husband's associates. Coming from a privileged environment, the daughter of a prosperous dentist and the wife of a successful attorney, she detected in Dick's associates' character scents of raw greed and uncultured manners that were almost Snopesian in their dimension.

Langston's effort to horn in on Scruggs's tobacco money represented an early warning sign to her. She resented Langston's grasping style— she felt he had been slow to repay a significant loan, $2 million from

Scruggs that Langston described as an "advance" on expenses in Fen-Phen cases. Though Diane considered Langston something of a charlatan, she felt even more uncomfortable in the presence of his associate Steve Patterson.

From the time he sought to indict Dick in 1992, Diane had an aversion to Patterson. She thought him, at best, a boor. She recoiled when Langston and Patterson visited the Scruggses' skybox at Ole Miss football games, glad-handing Dick and Diane and their guests during halftime breaks. To the elegant Diane, the two men seemed relentlessly on the make for money.

When she complained to her husband, Scruggs brushed off her objections. He liked to invoke an old maxim: Keep your friends close and your enemies closer. He laughed at Diane's objections and asked her not to say anything unpleasant in public.

She dutifully kept a smile in the men's presence, but it was difficult. Diane had questions about P. L. Blake, too. He was something of an enigma. Though she saw him no more than two or three times throughout the years, she recognized his deep voice when he telephoned, and he called Scruggs's home often. He was invariably cordial and seemed to be watching out for the Scruggses' interests. (When the planes crashed into the World Trade Center towers on September 11, 2001, he was the first to call to make sure the Scruggses were watching television.) After learning that Scruggs paid Blake thousands of dollars a month, Diane wondered exactly what services he provided. And why would Dick respond to Blake's summons to come to his home in the Delta to settle business? "If I were working for somebody, wouldn't it be presumptuous for me to tell the boss to come meet with me?" she asked her husband. "It sounds like the tail is wagging the dog."

Scruggs laughed at her questions, explaining that Blake had valuable political connections.

While various claimants nibbled at Scruggs's share of the tobacco initiative, solidarity among members of the HALT venture unraveled. Pauline and Mike Lewis were troubled over Scruggs's tendency to take center stage. He had rushed around the country piling up heavy expenses while making unilateral decisions. Sometimes he seemed to be taking the initiative in uncharted directions. Without consulting with his partners, he spoke for them in public forums and television interviews.

The couple felt Scruggs was taking all of the credit for Lewis's groundbreaking idea. To the husband-and-wife team, Scruggs's conduct amounted to theft of their "intellectual property." Acting independently, he had used Lewis's concept—designed for Mississippi—and applied it in cases where he represented other states outside the scope of the HALT alliance. As a result, Scruggs made millions more than the others in the group.

Though the Lewis firm's share of the Mississippi settlement was $140 million, they never forgave Scruggs for his handling of the case. They concluded that he was nothing more than a megalomaniac, and they joined the ranks of other Scruggs partners who believed they had been chiseled by him.

There were other, more bizarre demands on Scruggs's tobacco funds.

Pete Johnson, the former state auditor who had fixed the legislation to approve contingency fees for outside counsel in state cases, claimed that Scruggs had failed to live up to his agreement to pay him 10 percent of his tobacco fortune. There was nothing on paper, but Johnson insisted he had Scruggs's word.

Scruggs had paid him $5,000 a month for several months after Johnson got the language inserted in the Medicaid bill, but then cut him off. Before Johnson could reach an understanding with Scruggs, he became gravely ill with a liver malady. Johnson moved with his wife, Scruggs's cousin Margaret, back to her Delta home in Clarksdale—he thought to die. He decided to spend his final days fighting Scruggs, summoning enough energy to drive more than three hundred miles to Scruggs's office in Pascagoula in order to confront him. Johnson languished in Scruggs's waiting room all afternoon and never saw him; he figured Scruggs had escaped through a back door. Still, Johnson persevered.

Johnson obtained a liver transplant in 1996. (Scruggs says he helped get Johnson to Texas for the operation; Johnson insists Scruggs offered no such assistance.) Restored to better health, Johnson sought vindication with a lawsuit, asking for $140 million, which he understood to be 10 percent of Scruggs's share of the tobacco money. The suit never got traction.

Finally, in 2001, P. L. Blake called Johnson with instructions to come to his home in Greenwood. For years, Johnson had known Blake as a spoke in Eastland's wheel; any message from Blake carried authority. So Johnson made the hour-long drive through the cotton fields of the Delta, then sat and listened as Blake told him to give up his lawsuit. It was folly, Blake said. To settle, Scruggs was willing to pay him $100,000. Johnson decided to accept. Blake closed the deal by writing Johnson a check that day for $100,000 from his own account.

The same year, coincidentally, Johnson was appointed chairman of the federal Delta Regional Authority, a Republican patronage position that could be traced to Trent Lott. With the job, Johnson got a spacious office in the abandoned chambers of a federal judge in the post office in Clarksdale, where he proudly displayed the hardwood walking stick his grandfather "Big Paul" Johnson, the governor of Mississippi, had once used to cane a political enemy.

There were others. An anti-tobacco activist named Richard Daynard also sued Scruggs and Ron Motley. A law professor at Northeastern University in Boston, years before the Mississippi Medicaid litigation Daynard had founded the Tobacco Products Liability Project to discourage smoking, and had served as a consultant in the case.

In a 2000 lawsuit, Daynard contended that he had made a handshake deal with the two lawyers who agreed to pay him 5 percent of any tobacco fees they collected.

Scruggs dismissed his claim, saying that Daynard was "a bit more mercenary than people think he is."

But Scruggs yielded in the end. Each quarter, Daynard began to get $100,000 from Scruggs's tobacco account.

A particularly nasty dispute grew out of Scruggs's arrangement with The Developing Markets Group, the partnership held by John Sears, Joel Hoppenstein, and his brother-in-law's associate Tom Anderson. Even though Scruggs channeled millions of dollars through the group, they clamored for more. And details of where the money went were murky.

Following the successful conclusion of the tobacco case, Scruggs met several times with Anderson and P. L. Blake to adjudicate issues. Though Scruggs professed later that he was "not sure what DMG is," it seemed clear to him that Blake had an interest in it. Because of the long relationship between Anderson and Blake, Scruggs assumed the pair had a formal business association. But after an argument broke out over fees, Anderson insisted that Blake was not a part of DMG.

Nevertheless, according to court documents, some of Scruggs's early payments to Blake were routed through DMG. Scruggs agreed to pay the group $15 million for their services, plus another $1 million a year for the duration of the tobacco settlement. Blake got $10 million, which amounted to two thirds of the initial payment to DMG, and was guaranteed additional payments from Scruggs of almost $2 million a year. Blake's $50 million understanding with Scruggs was breathtaking.

Charles Merkel, an attorney who delved deeply into Scruggs's finances in connection with another lawsuit, found evidence that $10 million to Blake had originally been routed through Scruggs's friend Joey Langston before finding its way into Blake's hands. Merkel was unable to reconcile those payments with documents showing that Blake got the money via DMG.

In an attempt to determine how Blake used the money, Merkel succeeded in winning a subpoena for records of Blake's account at a Greenwood bank. But U.S. District Judge Allen Pepper sealed these documents against wider inspection. Pepper was a prime example of Lott's Sigma Nu network. Back at Ole Miss, Pepper had roomed with Lott and sung with him in a quartet, called The Chancellors, that still performed at Sigma Nu reunions four decades after their graduation. Scruggs attributed Pepper's elevation to the federal bench by President Clinton in 1999 as a thank-you to Lott for the Mississippi senator's refusal to join other Republicans in pressing for Clinton's impeachment and ouster a few months earlier.

How the pieces of Blake's tobacco money were distributed would remain cloaked in secrecy. When Scruggs was asked, during a 2004 deposition, what Blake had done to earn the money, he gave few insights: "Mr. Blake for many, many years had been a confidante of politicians in high places," Scruggs testified. "I think Senator Eastland was his principal contact, but he made numerous contacts because of the power of Senator Eastland. He knew lots of people, and he was the best person I could come up with to be a listening post for us on any sort of effort . . . I trusted his advice and his ability to advise us on political forces that might derail our litigation . . . We spoke almost daily for several years."

For instance, Scruggs explained, during the tobacco wars, Blake had suggested that Scruggs approach Senator Fred Thompson, who had represented Blake during his earlier troubles in Mississippi. Blake also recommended that Scruggs "make contact with the Lion Hall Group of which Senator Biden's brother was a member—or maybe his brother's wife was a member."

Blake's explanations, in a separate deposition, were even more feeble. He said he provided Scruggs with pertinent newspaper clippings.

While Blake got $10 million, the remaining $5 million in Scruggs's original outlay went directly to DMG. In addition, Scruggs passed through the group a curious $4.3 million for Americans for Tax Reform, a conservative lobbying organization dedicated to fighting taxes. Its president was Grover Norquist, an influential figure during the rise of the far right in the Republican Party. *The New Yorker* once quoted Norquist as saying that an ideal government would be one cut "down to the size where we can drown it in the bathtub."

Scruggs's contribution seemed totally out of character for a man fast acquiring a reputation as an ardent Democrat and advocate, as a trial lawyer, for the working class. When asked years later about the strange gift, Scruggs said it was given to fight a proposed "confiscatory tax" on tobacco fees.

After Michael Kranish, a reporter for *The Boston Globe*, obtained in 2006 a list of donors to Americans for Tax Reform, he found two startling entries from Scruggs's home state. The Mississippi Band of Choctaws gave Norquist's group $1.5 million to oppose a proposal to tax profits at Indian casinos. Scruggs's $4.3 million contribution also showed up. He told the reporter the payment had been made to fight Republican legislation "aimed at essentially de-funding the Democratic Party by penalizing trial lawyers." No matter that he had given millions to a right-wing activist, Scruggs said. "There is an expression," he said. "'If you need a thief, take him from the gallows.'"

Later, after Scruggs became ensnared in questions about some of the payments he had distributed from his tobacco largesse, he said he sent the money to Americans for Tax Reform at the behest of Anderson's group, DMG. He explained that he made the donation to establish a "negotiating position" with DMG as he sorted out the claims made by the DMG partners. Scruggs complained that the Washington group sought more than 20 percent of the fees his firm expected to get out of the tobacco initiative.

Scruggs balked at going beyond the $15 million he delivered to DMG in the months after the tobacco money began coming in. He was reluctant to pay any more to Hoppenstein, who, Scruggs said, "seemed to be taking far more credit for the result than I thought was justified."

In 2000 the bickering with Sears became even more intense. After Sears sent Scruggs a letter in January suggesting that the Mississippi lawyer might be close to committing "fraud" and a violation of "federal criminal laws" by failing to honor a DMG claim, Scruggs responded with a blistering letter of his own.

He told Sears he had learned that his highly touted meetings with

RJR officials were no more than "non substantive, courtesy meetings that lasted for only minutes." Though Sears purported to be close to the tobacco industry, Scruggs wrote, he had, in fact, been "excluded from the loop" during negotiations. Despite Sears's minor role on behalf of the anti-tobacco team, Scruggs said, he had been told that Sears actually "wanted $2 billion from the industry for 'putting the deal together.'" Since the tobacco industry refused, Scruggs said, Sears turned to him. Though annoyed, Scruggs offered to settle with Sears and Hoppenstein.

Sears wrote back that Scruggs's response seemed to apply only to him and Hoppenstein. "As you know, there are four of us involved." The other two, presumably, were Anderson and Blake. In a subsequent letter, bristling with anger, Sears told Scruggs, "Nobody is blackmailing anybody and I resent the charge."

Scruggs finally came to terms with Sears and Hoppenstein. Each man began to get $250,000 in quarterly payments out of Scruggs's tobacco allotment. Blake's cut was even greater. He began to draw $468,000 each quarter from Scruggs.

In addition, Scruggs sent separate quarterly payments of $375,000 to Tom Anderson. Inexplicably, the money was paid by Scruggs personally, rather than out of his Delmas Capital account, which had been created to distribute the tobacco money. (Scruggs's office in Pascagoula was located on Delmas Avenue.) After being questioned by one of his financial advisors about the method of paying Anderson, Scruggs began wiring the money to Anderson in the name of Bainberry LLC. Throughout the first quarter of the twenty-first century, the money will be disbursed to Anderson: $1.5 million a year from Scruggs's tobacco revenues.

Once all of the claims and assignments were factored into Scruggs's tobacco income, he was left with less than a third of it. On a schedule of payments that began at the time of the settlement and will continue through 2025, roughly $1.6 billion will go to Scruggs's legal operation. His total reward, adding up over the years, will amount to $500 million. David Nutt, who helped bankroll the tobacco initiative, will get a similar amount. The remaining $600 million will be distributed to others.

While he tried to stamp out these calls on his checkbook, which seemed to be breaking out like brushfires on the prairie, Scruggs continued to fight off the old lawsuits filed separately by his former associates Roberts Wilson and Al Luckey. Neither would go away. And since the actions were first filed, their claims had grown. Both Wilson and Luckey were calling for a slice of the tobacco money, too, arguing that Scruggs had used the asbestos money due them to fund his tobacco initiative.

The demands were wearing Scruggs down. "Success has many followers," he lamented a couple of years after the tobacco settlement. "People were coming out of the woodwork" making unjustified claims.

At night, he found himself possessed by terrible dreams. In them, he scattered the symbols of his wealth in the streets and let his tormentors pick through the debris. He said he was resigned to live on what they left behind.

Politics had been embedded in Scruggs's psyche since boyhood. Although his family did not belong to the ranks of the bitter-end segregationists, when he attended old-fashioned rallies in South Mississippi he had found the oratory of the demagogues absorbing. There was something fascinating about these homespun politicians—something repellent and, yet, wild and alluring. Their pursuit of public office seemed as much a sport as football. And Scruggs realized, as he grew older, that the machinations of public policy also served as a game involving long-term strategies, short-run tactics, lots of money, and private persuasion. Though he never ran for office himself, Scruggs loved the competition, and he became a big-time player.

His early efforts in Mississippi were innocent, the stuff of moderate reformers: supporting such candidates as his former boss William Winter, who was elected governor in 1979, and his Ole Miss classmate Ray Mabus, who won the office eight years later. Both Winter and Mabus were progressive Democrats. So was Attorney General Mike Moore, one of Scruggs's closest friends.

But Scruggs had learned from his 1992 brush with the old guard that politics were not played out on a field of fairness, with referees maintaining order. To win—and Scruggs became obsessed with winning—he knew that he had to consort with rascals, and that he had to employ grit and guile to prevail.

He also recognized that many things could be done simply with money.

Following the election in 1991 of Kirk Fordice, a hard-bitten conservative, as the state's first Republican governor since Reconstruction, the trial lawyers in the state were faced with a belligerent adversary in high office. Fordice had made his own money in construction. With his crude manners, he would never be mistaken for a plutocrat. But he was a businessman holding a businessman's values and a contempt for liberals, Democrats, and trial lawyers. He thought them synonymous.

Much of Mississippi shared Fordice's beliefs. A growing resentment of the plaintiffs' bar was fired by the escalating judgments they were winning, with corresponding increases in insurance premiums. The first stirrings of a national movement called "tort reform"—a campaign to control costly class action lawsuits and to rein in the power of trial lawyers—began to quiver in the state.

To protect their position, the lawyers saw a need to create a political arm. Danny Cupit, the most politically active attorney among those who had made millions in asbestos litigation, had become disgruntled with the work of the Mississippi Trial Lawyers Association. He felt that decisions being made by the organization were dictated by attorneys who had little at stake in the struggle and who had failed to raise significant funds to wage the coming fight over "tort reform." The subject came up one night in 1994 during a leisurely dinner in New Orleans between Cupit and another like-minded Mississippi lawyer, John Grisham, whose novels with legal themes were beginning to attract national attention. As a former Democratic legislator, Grisham was no stranger to state politics, and he had a suggestion: Why not create a political action committee?

The idea took form shortly afterward at a breakfast at Primos Restaurant in Jackson between Steve Patterson, the state auditor at the time, and an out-of-work political consultant named Jere Nash. Both were seasoned Democratic operatives. Patterson had been state party chairman before winning statewide office, and Nash served as chief of staff for Governor Mabus. Patterson's connections to the "dark side" went back two decades. Nash seemed more of an idealist, a former state director for the "good government" advocacy group Common Cause, and one of the few liberals active in Mississippi politics. They seemed an odd pair. Neither man held a law degree, but both had natural ties to the trial lawyers through the Democratic Party. Importantly, Scruggs—who would be the political action committee's first president—knew them both and trusted their political judgments. Even Patterson's. With Scruggs's approval, Nash wound up as director of the committee.

For financing, the committee asked for $5,000 contributions from at least one hundred lawyers around the state. Scruggs, Cupit, and a few others gave much more. Bill Liston, the lawyer who had helped prepare charges against Scruggs two years earlier, was a key supporter, along with David Nutt and Gulf Coast attorneys Paul Benton and David McCormick—who would all go on to make fortunes with Scruggs in the tobacco venture. Other activists included Grady Tollison, Joey Langston, and Joey's brother, Shane, all of whose names would resonate across the state fourteen years later as Scruggs's empire came under siege. A Jackson lawyer named Johnny Jones, who became deeply involved in the future struggle against Scruggs, thought of a whimsical acronym for the group: ICEPAC. It would serve as shorthand for Institute for Consumers and the Environment Political Action Committee.

Rather than have individual lawyers randomly putting a $500 contribution behind a friendly legislative candidate in their home district, the committee planned to channel much larger donations—big enough to sway the outcomes—to targeted races. Nash would analyze the records and reputation of candidates around the state and recommend who should be supported. To get ICEPAC's endorsement, the candidates were required to pledge their opposition to "tort reform" efforts. Those favored by the committee would be blessed with contributions of $40,000 or more from the pool of money raised from the trial lawyers. If elected, the candidates would be expected to honor their commitment.

ICEPAC was successful in the 1995 legislative races, and its influence grew in the statewide elections of 1999 after its members, suddenly flush with millions of dollars from the tobacco settlement, poured hundreds of thousands of dollars into Mississippi races where once a few thousand might have made a difference.

Scruggs was not content to rely on ICEPAC. He relished his position as a powerbroker in other statewide races, though his enthusiasm was tempered somewhat by his naïveté. One day, as he marched with other lawyers toward the capitol on a lobbying expedition, he had to ask on which side of the building lay the state senate. His Democratic contemporaries were leery of his relationship with Trent Lott, who had become Senate majority leader. In a crunch, they feared, Scruggs would prove unreliable.

But the days immediately after the tobacco settlement were a heady time for him. Not only was *The Insider* playing in theaters across the country, but he was being saluted in print as the scourge of unscrupulous business interests.

A lengthy 1999 profile in *Newsweek* magazine, which Scruggs clipped and framed for his office wall, described him as a modern-day Robin Hood, "a master at marshaling the forces of fellow attorneys against industries that he believes betray the public trust." The article went on: "Using a web of high-powered political connections and a keen sense of what plays on Wall Street, Scruggs embodies the class action lawsuit gone thermonuclear, a new weapon hovering over corporate America."

To extend his influence in the political sphere, Scruggs handed out millions of dollars to candidates who spanned a spectrum of loyalties. He predictably supported the Democratic candidate for governor Ronnie Musgrove with financial backing in 1999. (Four years earlier, he had guaranteed a $75,000 loan from a Pascagoula bank to Musgrove's campaign for lieutenant governor.) Scruggs also provided new contributions and help for others on the party slate. But in the independent style he demonstrated during the tobacco fight, passing out money with abandon, he strayed from the norm in the Democratic primary in 1999 to choose an unusual candidate for lieutenant governor, an important office. (Under law, the lieutenant governor effectively controlled the state senate, with authority to appoint committees and set the legislative agenda.)

The logical choice for progressives that year was Grey Ferris, a two-term veteran of the senate and a leading champion of public education. His brother, William Ferris, was one of the state's most respected visionaries: the founder of the Center for the Study of Southern Culture at Ole Miss before becoming President Clinton's chairman of the National Endowment for the Humanities.

But Scruggs's "dark side" had another candidate: a thirty-six-year-old woman named Amy Tuck, who was masquerading as a populist Democrat. P. L. Blake arranged a lunch at Nick's, a popular steakhouse in Jackson, to introduce her to Scruggs. Afterward, Blake convinced him that to succeed in Mississippi, one needed to fish in waters away from "the elites" such as Ferris. Scruggs quietly agreed to "loan" Tuck $500,000 for her campaign. She defeated Ferris in the Democratic primary and went on to win the election.

Tuck proved to be one of the poorest political investments Scruggs ever made. Two years after taking office, she switched parties to become a Republican and helped lead "tort reform" to passage. Both she and Scruggs were embarrassed when details of the $500,000 arrangement, which Tuck had not repaid, were made public. Democrats were furious after learning that Scruggs had financed a closet Republican.

Scruggs, however, remained philosophical. Tuck was emblematic, he said, of a maxim he attributed to Earl Long, who inherited the political machine his brother, Huey the Kingfish, created in Louisiana: "You don't buy politicians; you just rent 'em."

Although Mississippi had developed a reputation as a plaintiff's paradise by the turn of the twenty-first century, Tuck's political betrayal was symptomatic of the problems that the trial lawyers began to encounter there.

For a time in the 1990s, it seemed as though power had been transferred into the hands of this new breed of swashbuckling advocates. Scruggs acted as the prototype, but there were scores of others who also suddenly got rich. With the fortunes they accumulated through litigation, they represented new wealth in a poor state, and they were willing to use their money to stave off "tort reform" in the legislature, elect friendly judges on the local level, and keep a majority of sympathetic justices on the state supreme court.

But in exercising their strength, some of the more zealous lawyers overplayed their hand, triggering a public reaction against their attempts to establish fiefdoms where plaintiffs could run amok. After ensuring the election of congenial judges in Jefferson and Claiborne counties, two predominantly black jurisdictions in southwest Mississippi, the courts in those areas became venues for many mass tort suits. Outlandish judgments of millions of dollars resulted from cases of dubious merit.

Much of the litigation was initiated by lawyers outside the councils of Scruggs and his friends. Realizing that the bonanza might prove counterproductive, Scruggs worried about some of the decisions coming out of these courts, where friendly juries and complicit judges ensured big victories for plaintiffs. Aided by state laws that allowed nonresidents to join a Mississippi plaintiff in a single blockbusting suit in a favorable venue, unscrupulous lawyers took advantage of the situation. Their rush toward these targeted courts grew increasingly unseemly and fanned the "tort reform" reaction.

Abuses also ran rampant in cases related to the diet drug Fen-Phen. Staggered by the prospect of thousands of claims growing out of a report that Fen-Phen patients were susceptible to heart valve disease, American Home Products Corporation, the maker of the product, agreed to put up $3.75 billion to compensate those who had taken the drug. A federal investigation found that dozens of bogus claims, amounting to millions of dollars, had been filed in Mississippi by people who had never actually used the drug. Some of those making false claims were eventually sent to jail, but only one attorney in the state was convicted of fraud.

While the Fen-Phen scandal played out, lawyers brought fresh claims against the medical community through malpractice suits against doctors and hospitals. At the same time, there seemed to be a rise in the number of personal injury cases resulting from automobile accidents. To attract clients, lawyers resorted to billboards complete with leering pictures of themselves and a convenient 800 number to call. The legal profession, once so staid that advertising was thought unethical, began to assume a rapacious air. Meanwhile, Mississippi's reputation as a plaintiff's heaven worsened in business circles.

At first, Scruggs tried to laugh off the unflattering image. Occasionally he introduced himself as "the nefarious, ambulance-chasing Dick Scruggs." But for the trial lawyers, the analogy pairing them with Robin Hood began to fade. A former judge in Jackson who had sympathized with their work complained privately. "The public was willing to accept petty larceny," he said, "but they gagged at grand larceny. The trial lawyers got greedy. They were not content with half-million-dollar verdicts. They sought more and more."

Business interests that were being hammered by litigation mounted a counteroffensive, tagging the Mississippi courts as "judicial hellholes" and "the jackpot justice capital of America." The U.S. Chamber of Commerce and the Republican Party began putting up huge amounts of money of their own to arrest the power of the plaintiffs' bar, and Mississippi was turned into a war zone where the clash for control of its legislature and its court system consumed millions of dollars and had national implications.

The most public fight took place in the legislature, where business interests mobilized support for "tort reform" with horror stories of physicians moving out of the state, driven away by onerous premiums for malpractice insurance.

The Medical Assurance Company of Mississippi, which wrote much of the malpractice coverage in the state, raised its rates dramatically, and other insurers withdrew from Mississippi altogether. Seizing the issue, proponents of "tort reform" juxtaposed the portrait of a kindly family doctor confronted by a predator, the trial lawyer.

While Mississippi provided a Ground Zero for the clash between Big Business and the plaintiffs' bar, lawyers across the country were being beaten into retreat by adverse publicity concerning "judicial hellholes." After market research found an overwhelmingly negative reaction to the term *trial lawyer*, the Association of Trial Lawyers of America, the lobbying organization known for years by its acronym ATLA, changed its name to American Association for Justice.

In conservative Mississippi, a natural constituency already existed to support moves to check the power of the trial lawyers, who were perceived as liberals and partisans of an unpopular national Democratic Party. The drumbeat for change intensified in a campaign, orchestrated by the U.S. Chamber of Commerce, to demonize the trial lawyers in Mississippi.

ICEPAC lost its hold on the legislature while the Scruggs-sponsored lieutenant governor, Amy Tuck, went over to the business interests. Even Governor Musgrove, a Democrat favored by the plaintiffs' bar, capitulated in the face of the "tort reform" movement by approving legislation in 2003 that established ceilings for damages awarded in malpractice cases.

The next year, a new Republican governor, Haley Barbour, Scruggs's SAE pledge brother at Ole Miss, advocated even more sweeping changes in laws to restrict the trial lawyers. Tighter caps were imposed on judgments in all types of litigation, and favorable trial venues became less accessible for plaintiffs.

A related struggle taking place at the same time did not get as much notice, but it was no less important and just as rancorous: a bruising, expensive conflict for control of the state supreme court.

Though seats on the supreme court were won by election, there had been little passion involved in the process. Voters rarely showed much interest in determining who served on the court, and the justices themselves were not well known. Oddly enough, during the period that Mississippi was being transformed from a Democratic state to a Republican one, the supreme court wound up with a majority that tended to side with plaintiffs.

The trial lawyers enjoyed this advantage, actively recruiting candidates and backing their campaigns with big contributions. One judge received a letter from a prominent lawyer that put the trial lawyers' desires quite bluntly. Support our interests and it will put money in your pocket. He thought: They want to make sure we know we are being bought.

On the other hand, attorneys who represented corporations and defended businesses in civil actions—the natural rivals of the plaintiffs' bar—had been gripped by lassitude for years. They could be seen at the country clubs after hours, shedding their three-piece suits for golfing outfits. They had little interest in dirtying their hands in the combat of local politics. As a result, they ceded the supreme court to the trial lawyers for a number of years.

All of that began to change. Nationally, the American Medical Association and other professional organizations founded a lobby called the American Tort Reform Association to challenge the work of the trial lawyers. On top of their effort, the U.S. Chamber of Commerce and the Republican Party trained its guns on Mississippi. To counter the pocketbooks of the newly rich lawyers, business groups poured hundreds of thousands of dollars into the state, concentrating on winning back the supreme court.

Scruggs threw his own money and influence into the fight, but some of his efforts appeared erratic to those trying to maintain a majority in favor of the trial lawyers. In one instance, after a vacancy occurred on the court, Scruggs prevailed upon Governor Musgrove to appoint George Carlson, the uncle of Amy Scruggs, the lawyer's daughter-in-law, to fill the seat. Musgrove had intended to name Richard "Flip" Phillips, who had the backing of most trial lawyers, until Scruggs intervened. In other cases, Scruggs's political confidant P. L. Blake encouraged him to stay out of court races where candidates of the "dark side" were involved rather than fund candidates whom he might ordinarily favor.

After the U.S. Chamber of Commerce invested more than $1 million in one set of state supreme court contests, the majority was reversed. Big Business had regained the upper hand by the time its ally, Haley Barbour, became governor.

A Jackson attorney, Alex Alston, was troubled by the ensuing drift.

In a 2008 opinion piece published in *The Clarion-Ledger*, the biggest newspaper in Mississippi, Alston made an argument that reverberated in legal circles in the state:

> If you are a victim of personal injury, malpractice or corporate fraud, you have almost no chance of having a jury verdict in your favor affirmed by the state supreme court.
>
> In the past the supreme court rarely overturned a jury verdict, especially if it was based on a dispute over a factual issue. That day is gone. During the past four and one-half years, according to my research, an astonishing 88 percent of all jury verdicts in favor of the wronged victims have been reversed by the state supreme court.
>
> But what about the jury trials won by defendants, in which the victim takes an appeal to correct an error? Here, again, the numbers are staggering.
>
> Over the same four and one-half-year period, a plaintiff's success rate in reversing a jury verdict for the defendant is an astonishing zero.

With Big Business now entrenched in power on the state supreme court, John Grisham, an erstwhile compatriot of the trial lawyers, grew so distressed by the spectacle of electing judges that he set his 2008 novel, *The Appeal*, in Mississippi, loosely basing the plot on a real campaign to unseat a justice. In Grisham's book, the villain is the CEO of a corporation who wants to buy a pivotal supreme court seat to be sure that a pro-business majority on the court will hear the company's appeal of a $41 million verdict awarded to a woman who lost her husband and son to cancer caused when factory runoff poisoned a town's drinking water.

Though Democrats still counted on Scruggs in most statewide races, his political interests could no longer be categorized. Much of what he did he did in private. It was assumed that he did business with Trent Lott, but Scruggs's alliance with P. L. Blake, one of the most stealthy of Lott's political confederates, was largely unknown. Few knew that his former adversary Steve Patterson also helped coordinate Scruggs's spending as he dabbled in the "dark side."

Public interest groups in Washington attempt to track campaign contributions, but it was hard to follow Scruggs's money trail. He took unusual steps in his choice of candidates, and channeled some of the donations through family members to political committees designed to circumnavigate disclosure guidelines.

In 2000, instead of supporting Vice-President Al Gore in his race for president, Scruggs directed $250,000 to Gore's opponent, George W. Bush. Scruggs was limited in what he could give Bush directly, so he passed the bulk of the money through the Republican National Committee. It was Scruggs's form of retaliation to Gore. Despite Gore's long record of opposing the tobacco industry, Scruggs felt the vice-president had helped scuttle the national settlement in 1998 in order to keep the issue alive for his 2000 campaign.

The next year, Scruggs returned to the form expected of him. He quietly furnished much of the money to finance a campaign led by his hero, former governor William Winter, to change the state flag. Mississippi was the last state in the Union to feature the Confederate battle flag in its own banner. The Stars and Bars, used by the Confederate Army, had occupied a corner of the Mississippi flag since 1894. But during the civil rights movement, the battle flag was adopted by the Ku Klux Klan, giving the symbol a certain infamy. Saying that the Mississippi flag might best be relegated to a museum, Winter and other progressives wanted to replace it with a new flag. Despite Scruggs's backing, the effort failed in a statewide referendum.

In the early part of the new millennium, Scruggs would have a hand in many other elections. But none would better serve as a precursor to the events that later convulsed the legal world than his involvement in a bitter 2000 race for a seat on the state supreme court between Oliver Diaz, a Gulf Coast favorite of the trial lawyers, and Keith Starrett, whose candidacy had the strong support of the Republican Party and the U.S. Chamber of Commerce.

Though the election was decided that year, it would take the rest of the decade for the contest to unwind, spinning through federal investigations and indictments, charges of political prosecution said to be instigated by officials at the highest levels of the U.S. government, the selection of a federal judge, allegations that Senator Lott intervened to save his brother-in-law, and the tarring of the reputation of several judges and lawyers.

CHAPTER 7

Following the death of Mississippi Supreme Court justice Michael D. Sullivan in February 2000, it became clear to a small group of influential trial lawyers that they needed to rally quickly behind a candidate to recommend to Governor Musgrove to fill the open seat.

Their choice was William Myers, the chancery judge in Pascagoula who had presided over the first Medicaid-tobacco litigation. In telephone calls with his colleagues, Dick Scruggs argued that Myers would be compatible with their interests. He had proven open to the plaintiffs during his handling of the tobacco case without appearing too one-sided. Scruggs felt he would be politically acceptable.

But when Scruggs, Danny Cupit, and a formidable Biloxi lawyer, Paul Minor, met with Musgrove in the governor's office within days of Sullivan's death, Musgrove resisted their choice. Picking Myers, the governor said, made him uncomfortable. It would subject him to criticism that the appointment had been dictated by Scruggs, the leader in the tobacco case and a major donor to Musgrove's campaign.

The lawyers were prepared with a fallback position if their recommendation failed. Their second choice was Oliver Diaz, another Gulf Coast figure who already sat on the state court of appeals.

Diaz's name had been promoted by Minor, whose success in asbestos and tobacco litigation was almost as legendary as Scruggs's. He had scored big licks in asbestos cases before Scruggs made his breakthrough, and as a partner in the HALT group, Minor had enjoyed a share in the settlement that amounted to about $140 million.

Minor was often compared to Scruggs. They were friends, the same age, who practiced on the Gulf Coast. Both had admirable military backgrounds, Minor as a decorated veteran of the Vietnam War; Scruggs as a navy jet pilot. Together they owned a condominium in Biloxi as investment property. And they had just returned from an adventurous trip to New Zealand, arranged by Scruggs, to cheer on the dashing American sailor Dennis Conner in the America's Cup competition. Scruggs offered his yacht as a hotel for his guests; it also served as a floating hospitality suite for Conner's wealthy supporters to watch the races. As their wealth and renown grew, Minor and Scruggs enjoyed this ability to hobnob with celebrities as much as they relished their influence to sway political decisions.

Back home, Minor was also known as one of the principal benefactors of local Democratic candidates. Like Scruggs, he tended to operate as a lone wolf in dispensing his largesse rather than coordinating it through party functionaries. Many of Minor's beneficiaries were considered, by Mississippi standards, liberal.

Minor's political leanings could be traced directly to his father, Bill Minor, a respected newspaperman who had been reporting on the Mississippi scene since the days when Jim Eastland was a freshman senator. For more than a half century, the elder Minor had assailed demagogues and alerted his readers to the unfortunate consequences of racist policies. During the civil rights movement, visiting correspondents invariably sought out Bill Minor for guidance and perspective on Mississippi matters. In 1997, he had been the first recipient of the $25,000 John Chancellor Award for Excellence in Journalism, an honor given annually to courageous reporters.

The son, Paul, had become something of a celebrity in Mississippi, too, though in a different field. And unlike the gregarious Scruggs, Paul Minor exuded an air of arrogance and superiority. Sometimes his brusque behavior was burnished by alcohol. Minor did not hold his liquor well. His bristling, aloof manner often offended others, even his close associates, and it would work against him when trouble descended.

Yet he was persuasive in presenting to the governor the case for appointing Diaz. Though Diaz was considered plaintiff-friendly, he had served in the legislature as a Republican, and it was thought that this should spare Musgrove from partisan complaints.

Musgrove agreed to make Diaz his interim appointment. For consolation, the governor put Scruggs's choice, Judge Myers, into a state court of appeals seat being vacated by Diaz.

After their meeting with Musgrove, Minor and Scruggs went to lunch. As they walked into the restaurant, Minor used his cell phone to deliver the good news to Diaz. Before ending the conversation, he passed the phone to Scruggs, who added his congratulations.

Over their meal, Minor and Scruggs mused about their latest thrust of political power. They had succeeded in putting their man on the state supreme court. But only for a few months. In November, Diaz would have to run for a full eight-year term.

Four of the court's nine seats were up for election that fall when the U.S. Chamber of Commerce flooded Mississippi with money and a massive campaign of television commercials, the greatest involvement ever by outside forces in a state supreme court election.

The Chamber's candidate in the race against Diaz was Keith Starrett, a South Mississippi lawyer with strong ties to the Republican Party. Though judicial candidates do not run with party designation, it was no secret that Starrett was favored by the GOP. Following the first round of voting, which essentially produced a standoff between candidates favored by the plaintiffs' bar and those perceived as pro-business, in late November Diaz and Starrett wound up in a runoff that provoked a new wave of spending by business interests.

To meet the threat posed by the U.S. Chamber of Commerce, Minor guaranteed an $80,000 loan to Diaz and urged Scruggs to do the same. Scruggs was told the money was needed to finance the purchase of TV time for Diaz to offset a million-dollar blitz on Starrett's behalf. He was given a private screening of Diaz's ads at the Green Oaks Bed and Breakfast, operated by Diaz's wife, Jennifer. Convinced of the soundness of the campaign, Scruggs agreed to guarantee another $80,000 loan from Merchants and Marine Bank of Pascagoula, where he did much of his business.

Diaz narrowly won the election with 51 percent of the vote to retain his seat, but an altogether different battle was just beginning that would keep him suspended for much of the term.

The Republican Party had regained control of nominations to the federal judiciary with George W. Bush's victory in 2000. So, by the next year, the Bush administration was able to offer some solace to the Mississippi GOP and its business constituency, still smarting from Diaz's election and the loss by the party's nominee for a congressional seat, Dunn Lampton. It appeared to fit into a national plan. As GOP theoretician Ben Ginsberg observed, "Republicans began to wield the RIP (revelation, investigation and prosecution) weapon against Democrats."

In a move approved by the state's two Republican senators, Trent Lott and Thad Cochran, Lampton was named U.S. attorney for the southern district of Mississippi. And Lampton, along with the representatives of the Public Integrity Section of the U.S. Department of Justice, soon launched an investigation of Democratic activities, looking into loans that had been given by trial lawyers to candidates for state judgeships. After news of an investigation of Minor and Scruggs was leaked to *The Clarion-Ledger* in Jackson, Democrats quickly noted that Lampton and Starrett were childhood friends and that Minor had once won a substantial judgment against one of Lampton's relatives. It was also obvious that Minor's father had long been the scourge of the Republican Party in Mississippi. Scruggs, of course, had his own Democratic credentials.

Well before the investigation resulted in indictments, the probe was being denounced by Democrats as a Republican witch hunt.

Scruggs was accustomed to guaranteeing loans for political candidates—and in some instances, never being repaid. Minor had a similar history. In 1996, before Steve Patterson was drummed out of the state auditor's office, Minor wrote Scruggs about a debt owed by Patterson. "Trustmark demanding payment from me on the note that I guaranteed on Steve Patterson in which you said I would not have to pay," Minor said in a somewhat jocular letter. "I realize you have been looking for an opportunity to retaliate for my recommendation on Copytel stocks, but this is not funny. Seriously, do you know whether Steve Patterson has raised any money and can retire this note or are we stuck with it?"

A few years later, there were problems with the Diaz loan, but Scruggs was not particularly upset until his friend Attorney General Mike Moore called in 2002 to tell him of the investigation. "You've got some explaining to do," Moore said, and he set up an appointment for Scruggs to speak with the U.S. Attorney's Office in Jackson.

Scruggs told the prosecutors of complications involving the transaction. The note, which had been signed by Jennifer Diaz instead of her husband, had not been repaid. After the couple split following the election, she had demanded that Oliver Diaz's name replace hers on the note. This created a legal question, Scruggs said, because state law prevented a sitting justice from raising money to retire an old campaign debt. When he discussed the difficulty with Minor, his friend suggested staging a fund-raiser to pay off the debts owed to them. No fund-raiser was held, and Scruggs appeared stuck with the loan. Exasperated, he paid it off himself.

"I was kinda in a catch-22," Scruggs later told a grand jury. "I couldn't help raise the money to pay it, but if I paid it off myself, then I was in violation. But I owed the money. So what do you do? So I just paid it off, rather than try to pass the hat, which I felt like it was too late to do."

In July 2003, two months after Scruggs was called before the grand jury—and four months before Republican Haley Barbour would challenge Governor Musgrove in statewide elections—the U.S. attorney announced the indictments of Diaz, his former wife, two other state judges, and Minor in connection with loans. Scruggs was not indicted.

During his grand jury testimony, Scruggs was asked about other loans arranged by Minor that had ensnared the two other Gulf Coast judges named in the indictment, Wes Teel and John Whitfield.

Scruggs said he loaned $27,500 to Teel, a chancery judge, at Minor's request in February 2000, to help bail the judge out of "some financial emergency of some sort."

"For whatever reason, either Paul didn't have the money or didn't want to guarantee the note or give him the money, loan him the money," Scruggs testified. "He wanted me to do it, I said: I'll do it, but only with a promissory note, and I want to be paid back."

Scruggs said he had never appeared in court before Teel and knew of no cases Minor had pending before the judge. "Generally speaking," he said, "trial lawyers don't go into chancery court very often."

Teel's loan was paid back within two months, he said.

During his grand jury appearance, Scruggs was also asked about a $100,000 note that Minor held for Whitfield, a circuit judge who routinely heard civil litigation. Scruggs testified that Minor had asked him to substitute his name for Minor's on the note. He inferred from their conversation, Scruggs said, that Minor "had a case before the judge or something coming up that would have looked bad . . . I think the reason he called me was because he didn't think it was proper."

Scruggs refused, he said, because "I just was not going to play that game. I did it for Teel before because I didn't think Paul would have many cases, if any, in chancery court. But I knew he had a lot of cases in the circuit court," where Whitfield presided.

Scruggs asked the prosecutors to let him elaborate on his answer. "The main reason I didn't guarantee that note, that $100,000—whatever it was—note that Paul asked me to guarantee for Judge Whitfield, was because I didn't want to make Paul's problem my problem. I didn't want to get involved in that transaction.

"Another reason is," he continued, "I thought I'd get stuck with it financially. Paul sometimes doesn't pay his debts and I didn't want to have to look to him or the judge for that money."

Scruggs testified without seeking immunity, which meant that he left himself open for possible prosecution on anything he said. The prosecutors seemed satisfied that Scruggs had been truthful. Minor's defense attorneys, inspecting Scruggs's secret testimony later, also concluded that nothing he said had been particularly damaging to Minor.

But intimations of a broken friendship were apparent.

Near the end of Scruggs's three hours before the grand jury, Lampton, the federal prosecutor, asked about Minor's reputation as a "judge maker." Scruggs might have been describing himself with his answer.

"Paul aggressively plays the political game," Scruggs said. "He thinks he has to do that, I think, to counter organizations like the chamber of commerce that come in with large sums of money and try to influence elections, judicial and otherwise. The governor's race is one of those places, and when vacancies occur on the bench the governor is the one that makes the appointment for the interim seat."

Minor often leaned on Democratic governors "to appoint people who were trial lawyer–friendly or consumer-friendly," he said. "I have never heard Paul characterize himself as a 'judge maker' or words to that effect. But he does—everybody knows that he is very active—and he is not the only one. There are lots of lawyers who are active on both sides of the aisle in asking the governor to make judicial appointments. Paul plays it—you know—is very aggressive in doing that."

Minor and Scruggs were no longer speaking to one another at the time of Scruggs's testimony. But differences over loans had not been responsible for the breach. Their long relationship had been ruptured by a very personal incident.

Several of Minor's friends, including Scruggs, had become increasingly worried about his heavy drinking. Minor slurred words after a couple of glasses of wine, and his condition deteriorated when he went beyond social consumption. He had barely escaped serious injury in two auto accidents attributed to alcohol—once when he drove himself off the road.

Scruggs had grown alarmed during their America's Cup trip to New Zealand, when Minor stayed drunk for the first three days of the journey. One evening Minor woke from a jagged afternoon nap on the yacht insisting that it was 8:00 a.m. It was actually twelve hours earlier.

Later, in the summer of 2002, following an incident at Minor's beach house in Destin, Florida, Scruggs was asked by Minor's friends to talk with him. Minor had cut his nose after falling at a party, and there were fears that he would eventually hurt himself badly.

After consulting with a former partner of Minor's and another Gulf Coast lawyer, a recovering alcoholic who had undergone treatment, Scruggs brought in a representative of the state bar association who dealt with lawyers with drug and alcohol problems. Once an appointment was lined up at the Betty Ford Center, a well-known California clinic offering rehabilitation from drug and alcohol dependency, the group arranged an intervention.

Scruggs and two others went to Destin to discuss their concerns with Minor, persuading him to check into the clinic. Accompanied by his wife, Minor boarded a plane Scruggs made available for the trip to Rancho Mirage. They got as far as the clinic when the intervention went awry.

When Scruggs called the center to make sure that Minor had checked in, he learned that Minor had departed. He reached Minor, who told him there was no reason to check into the facility on a weekend. He assured Scruggs he would do it on Monday. He never did. That was the last Scruggs heard from Minor.

Minor, like many targets of an intervention, was resentful over the action. He broke off communications with his old friend.

A year later, as he came under investigation, Minor charged that Scruggs was being protected by Senator Lott, and his attorneys argued that the case against Minor was the latest example of political prosecutions encouraged by Bush's White House.

CHAPTER 8

Despite the riches that came with the tobacco settlement, Scruggs seemed afflicted with a sequence of vexing problems that began to engulf him.

His share of the tobacco settlements gave him an annual income projected at $20 million over a twenty-five-year period. But the good life it should have brought him was spoiled by contentious events that took place outside the courts of law.

He had been exceedingly generous to his hometown of Pascagoula, providing local charities with large gifts. Yet his most visible donation, the purchase and restoration of the antebellum Longfellow House for use as a community reception hall on the beach, had become the source of a squabble almost comic in its ferocity. Scruggs had bought the 150-year-old mansion for $200,000 in 1993 with money he had accumulated in asbestos litigation, and during the decade he spent another $1.2 million to have it renovated. His wife, Diane, personally supervised the work of craftsmen as they installed expensive woodwork and fine glass to return the building to its former grandeur.

Instead of winning gratitude, however, the project aroused resentment among neighbors of the Longfellow House. Foremost among the opponents were Joe Colingo, a Pascagoula lawyer who had been retained by R.J. Reynolds during the tobacco battle, and Terry Carter, the head of the local chamber of commerce. Colingo bore a particular dislike for Scruggs. Eight years older than Scruggs, he was part of the Singing River crowd that had once frolicked on boozy weekends. But they had become rivals in the tobacco case, and there was another reason for antipathy. Colingo's wife, Johnette, had grown up in the beachfront home that the Scruggs family now occupied, and it was annoying to see Scruggs ensconced there. Carter, meanwhile, served as the voice for business interests in Pascagoula; thus, he had obvious motivation for his animosity toward the anti-business trial lawyer.

After the old house was reopened in 1997, objections by Colingo, Carter, and others led the Pascagoula City Council to impose limits on outdoor functions at the site. Scruggs not only challenged the legality of the decision, but also chose other ways to get even. He bought a home in the upscale neighborhood where his opponents lived and encouraged a rumor that he intended to move his housekeeper into it. He also built a concrete wall, nine feet high, in the rear of the Longfellow House property, which blocked his adversaries' view of the Mississippi Sound.

The spat, which festered for more than a year, reached a critical mass in the spring of 1999 upon the occasion of the wedding of Scruggs's niece Tyler Lott, the daughter of Senator Lott. One afternoon, as workmen prepared outside lighting for the reception, they were startled by the landing of several dog turds that had been pitched over the wall. Peering over the obstruction, workers saw Carter, the chief of the chamber of commerce.

"What in the hell do you think you're doing?" one of them shouted.

"Fuck you!" Carter retorted, and shoveled another load of dog shit over the wall.

The workers reported the incident to Scruggs, who filed charges against Carter. In response, Carter claimed it was an accident, that he had meant to fling the considerable droppings of his St. Bernard elsewhere. He was fined $170 for malicious mischief and forced to write a note of apology to Scruggs: "I deeply regret and sincerely apologize," he said, "for the unfortunate incident involving the dog poop shoveled from my yard . . . My conduct was inappropriate as a good neighbor."

But the shenanigans didn't end there. Two days after the dog shit episode, electricians at the Longfellow House experienced a visitation. A Jeep Cherokee with several passengers drove onto the property and an argument ensued about noise from a radio being used by the workers. During the verbal exchange, the driver of the Cherokee pulled a pistol and, according to one of the workmen, threatened "to kill every fucking one of you." As workers cringed behind trees, the foreman used his pickup for cover and feverishly punched digits on his phone. First 911; then Scruggs's number.

"Mr. Scruggs," he wailed, "I'm running out of trees to hide behind."

The driver of the Jeep was identified as Colingo. The passengers included his wife and his son-in-law, Dr. Mark Lyell, whose home had lost its water view when Scruggs built the wall.

The electricians filed charges against Colingo. In a countermove, Colingo pressed charges against the workers, claiming that their menacing behavior had put him "in fear of imminent serious bodily harm." Scruggs threw his weight behind the electricians, hiring an acoustics technician to determine if the radio had really been a nuisance and a private investigator to look into Colingo's record. He also asked for an injunction to prevent Colingo from coming to the Longfellow House, and underscored this action by placing armed guards on the grounds.

To save the dignity of the Lott wedding, one of Colingo's law partners and Attorney General Mike Moore intervened. Colingo agreed to apologize, and the reception finally took place, amid great gaiety, without further interruption.

As a goodwill gesture, Scruggs invited Colingo and Carter to lunch. He dismissed the misunderstanding as an example of the unruly Gulf Coast life that a local editor, Ira Harkey, once described as conduct befitting "sons of the beach." But Pascagoula was too small a place to mend a feud. And a long account of the incident in *The Wall Street Journal*, headlined "Mississippi Madness," provoked snickers across the nation and did nothing to soothe hard feelings.

Scruggs's overreaction to the Longfellow House disagreement and his impulse to hire technicians, investigators, and security forces regardless of cost were typical of his freewheeling style. Faced with a problem, he tossed money at it. He gave away thousands of dollars to friends, with no thought of ever being repaid, and he became the most conspicuous of consumers, buying vacation homes and yachts and jets and fancy automobiles with the recklessness of a Saudi prince.

Much of his spending had commendable purposes, however, and a lot of it was done anonymously. After a childhood friend from Brookhaven asked for help in reducing his credit card bills, Scruggs dispatched an accountant to check on the situation. When it was found that the friend owed $90,000, Scruggs covered the debt.

He paid for field trips for schoolchildren and established scholarships for college students. He supported virtually every charitable organization in the area. Once, after hearing a tale of woe from a Pascagoula waitress, serving him lunch, he sent his secretary back that afternoon with a $1,000 check for her.

In a startling act of generosity, he telephoned his high school homeroom teacher, Robert Khayat, who had become chancellor of the University of Mississippi, and said, "Coach, Diane and I want to give you forty million dollars."

Khayat was stunned by the offer, one of the largest gifts ever offered to the school. Scruggs left it to Khayat's discretion to see how the money would be used. Khayat was pursuing a Phi Beta Kappa chapter for Ole Miss, so he recommended raising salaries for the liberal arts faculty. Scruggs agreed to send $1 million a year for the twenty-five-year life of the tobacco distribution, and he asked his friend David Nutt, who was sharing the tobacco wealth, to give another $5 million.

Scruggs admired Khayat, the son of the late Gulf Coast "Godfather." He was pleased over Khayat's stewardship of their alma mater, his ability to transcend political differences in the state in order to unify the school's alumni base. He was also proud of Khayat's eloquence in East Coast settings, where the chancellor defied the southern stereotype of bigotry and ignorance. His former coach seemed well on his way to restoring the school's reputation, tattered by the desegregation crisis in 1962 and handicapped by the state's poverty, and Scruggs wanted to help.

He created a $100,000 scholarship fund in honor of Diane's cousin Andy Mullins, one of Khayat's deputies. He set up another scholarship program for children of Ingalls's employees stricken with asbestosis. He gave $1 million to the athletic association and served as chairman of a drive to raise funds to build an indoor practice facility for the football team and a similar building for basketball. He pledged another $5 million for the construction of a new law school. He even gave the school possession of Longfellow House, which was worth $3 million when it was sold for tax purposes.

Though Scruggs did not ask for the honor, Khayat unilaterally named the music department the Diane and Dick Scruggs Hall and renamed an adjacent building Nutt Auditorium.

During their talks about money and Ole Miss, Khayat became aware that Scruggs was effectively operating out of control. As happy as he was over the gifts to Ole Miss, he was concerned for his friend. Scruggs seemed to be squandering his fortune, spending some of it rashly. Khayat thought he knew of just the man to rescue him.

Rex Deloach was a certified public accountant who had been Khayat's savior at Ole Miss, helping the chancellor extricate the school from financial distress a few years earlier. Deloach was the same age as Khayat, but came from a different environment. He had grown up in the impoverished Delta community of New Africa and gone to college not at Ole Miss but at Delta State and Memphis State. Despite his lack of pedigree, Deloach became managing partner of the Memphis office of Arthur Andersen, a national accounting giant. He retired before the company's ruination, and moved with his wife, Ruthann Ray, another accountant, to an estate of woods and rolling meadows outside Oxford. He had expected to spend his retirement years riding horses from his stable or traveling to faraway places—until Khayat implored him to come work at Ole Miss.

Acting as the university's chief financial officer, Deloach became known to some departmental potentates as Doctor No. He did away with personal domains controlled by various bureaucrats and consolidated control of the school's budget in the Lyceum, the administrative headquarters. The managers of campus stores and food services were replaced, and the businesses began to turn a profit. With construction stalled on a new business school, Deloach helped Khayat appeal to a prosperous donor for $16 million to ensure completion of the project.

Khayat regarded Deloach as a financial miracle worker. To repay Scruggs for his generosity to Ole Miss, the chancellor wanted to introduce the lawyer to Deloach, thinking he could stabilize Scruggs's books.

Their first meeting was not a propitious one. Khayat invited Dick and Diane to dinner at the chancellor's home with Deloach and his wife. However, the date was a Saturday night after a basketball game in Oxford between Ole Miss and Kentucky, and Scruggs changed his plans. He and his wife dropped by the Khayats' for a half hour of cocktails and chitchat, then left to take Ashley Judd and her boyfriend to dinner at City Grocery, a fashionable restaurant on Oxford's Square.

Scruggs had always been a bit starstruck. He had gotten to know Hollywood actors Al Pacino and Russell Crowe during the filming of *The Insider* at his Pascagoula home, and he became acquainted with Judd through his nephew Chet Lott, an investor in Kentucky pizza parlors. Knowing the actress was a rabid Kentucky basketball fan, Scruggs sent his jet to Kentucky to bring her party to the game.

But he followed up Khayat's suggestion later by inviting Deloach to Pascagoula to have a look at the operation of his law firm. When he arrived in the summer of 1999 the accountant was appalled by what he saw. Although Scruggs's law partners were fixed for life with income from the tobacco settlement, the firm was hemorrhaging money with a payroll of more than fifty people—paralegals, secretaries, runners—all who had little to do. The excesses at Scruggs's firm were so obvious that one partner joked about erecting a sign for passing motorists: "Honk If You Don't Work for Dick Scruggs." Some of the lawyers came in no earlier than noon, checked their messages, and departed early.

Scruggs had taken up a somewhat indolent lifestyle himself. He and Diane took frequent vacations to exotic locations. Deloach discovered that Scruggs owned a racing sailboat and three yachts, fully crewed, at far-flung ports around the world. The gem of Scruggs's fleet was the 120-foot-long *Emerald Key*, recently refurbished at great expense and docked in the South Pacific, served by a crew of seven awaiting Scruggs and his guests for the America's Cup competition off New Zealand. Scruggs also owned the 112-foot *Claire Elizabeth*, named for his daughter. The boat was based in the Bahamas, where Scruggs had bought a home to replace one he used to own in Key West. The smallest of his yachts was a mere ninety-one feet long. It was used for cruising the waters off Pascagoula and was valued at $6 million.

To get to his destinations, Scruggs owned one jet outright and held one third interest in two others.

While Deloach was in Pascagoula, inspecting Scruggs's books, his host asked him to come to the Longfellow House. When the CPA arrived, he found Scruggs, decked out in a seersucker suit and a sporty straw hat of the type once fancied by southern gentleman, seated in a new Bentley convertible, sales price $300,000.

Scruggs was finding all sorts of ways to spend his millions.

The law firm needed radical surgery, so Deloach recommended a form of triage: Scruggs should clean house, fire all of the unproductive lawyers and staff members, and pare the office down to a handful.

Characteristically, Scruggs did not want to deliver the bad news. For all of his litigation prowess and his recent tiff with Colingo and Carter, he often shrank from confrontation. Psychologists associate a childhood spent in stormy or broken households with an adult reluctance to engage in unpleasant arguments. When Scruggs avoided personal clashes, as he often did, he seemed to fit the drugstore psychoanalysis of a "child of an alcoholic parent." Whatever the reason, Scruggs went off to the South Pacific to follow the chase for America's Cup on the high seas and left the dirty work to Deloach.

Among those who were there, it became known as the "Mardi Gras massacre," and Deloach, tall, thin, and looking the part of a bloodless accountant, earned a new nickname, T-Rex the Grim Reaper.

He began the day by meeting with the firm's newest hire, a young lawyer named Sid Backstrom, whose childhood had been as checkered as Scruggs's. Backstrom's parents divorced when he was four, and he lived with his mother in Cajun country in South Louisiana through her turbulent remarriage to a musician-carpenter. Backstrom's father, a graduate of Ole Miss law school, wound up a respected judge in Pascagoula. Backstrom graduated from LSU and chose to attend law school there because he expected to practice in Louisiana, where the Napoleonic code still prevails in legal matters.

He was an intern at a Baton Rouge law firm when he first saw Scruggs, who flew over from the Mississippi coast to complete a piece of business in 1994. Because of his asbestos settlements, Scruggs already had a reputation as a corporation slayer, and the Baton Rouge lawyers were atwitter over his presence. Appearing knowledgeable and courageous, Scruggs lived up to his advance billing. Impressed, Backstrom told his father of the visit, and the judge responded, "Oh, yeah, he's the real deal."

Backstrom hoped he might find a place with Scruggs, and after he practiced for a few years in New Orleans, his father made the connection for him. Judge Backstrom often saw Scruggs at lunch in Pascagoula, and the judge learned of a possible opening for his son in the firm.

Young Backstrom came to see Scruggs several times, but it was not until the fourth visit that Scruggs suddenly asked, "Are you coming to work for me?" He offered a salary of $75,000 and a percentage of any awards Backstrom might be involved in winning. Though the terms were vague, Backstrom's hiring was sealed with a handshake. He felt Scruggs was an honest man, and he and his family moved to the Gulf Coast in the summer of 1999.

Less than six months later, Deloach appeared in Backstrom's office at the start of the morning. "I'm here for Dick to let everybody know they're retiring today," Deloach told him. "You are not. You can keep your stuff here, but I want you to leave the office right now. If you say anything, you're gone, too."

Eleven lawyers, including some of Scruggs's close friends, were purged that day, along with fifty support personnel.

When Scruggs returned from New Zealand, he rehired a few people. But his firm had been reduced to a core including him, his loyal secretary Charlene Bosarge, Backstrom, and a couple of clerical assistants.

Another significant change soon took place in Scruggs's life, but few knew of it. In May 2000 he underwent back surgery for a herniated disk. A second operation followed in June. To deal with the pain, he was given a prescription for Fioricet. Scruggs found that the drug not only relieved his discomfort but infused him with an extraordinary sense of well-being.

Because Fioricet was a barbiturate rather than a narcotic—Scruggs was allergic to narcotics—he rationalized his use. He began to take the pills often, even after the pain from the surgery had ebbed. His intake of ten to twelve pills a day increased; he began to rely on the drug.

To satisfy his craving, he asked his employees to obtain prescriptions in their names. The drug would be ordered impersonally, online through bulk distributors, and turned over to Scruggs.

When the drug took hold, Scruggs's cares receded. After the turmoil of asbestos and tobacco, Fioricet delivered a feeling that all was well.

Scruggs was approaching his sixtieth birthday, and he entertained the thought, as many aging men do, of moving on to something new. One grand possibility seemed within his reach: to become an American ambassador. He had the right political connections. He had supported the new president, George W. Bush, in 2000, and his brother-in-law, now the Senate majority leader, was one of the most influential men in Washington. Scruggs could count on bipartisan help, for he often hedged his bets and usually gave more to the Democratic Party. Because of his jet-set travels and professional experience overseas, he felt worldly enough. He was at ease with the rich and powerful, and with his charm he felt he could represent his country better than some of the boobs who were given ambassadorial appointments to reward their political contributions.

His desire to become an ambassador grew as strong as his earlier yearnings to make the big lick. South America became the heart of his ambassadorial affections; he even settled on Ecuador as his next home. Surely, he figured, Trent Lott could deliver that for him. After all, Lott had arranged for Tom Anderson to serve as ambassador in the Caribbean during the Reagan years.

With the title, Scruggs could enjoy the honorific "Ambassador" for the remainder of his life. It was an attractive thought, and the appointment seemed certain.

Scruggs began taking Spanish lessons. Confidently, he purchased a sixteen-seat Gulfstream, a luxury jet with the capacity to fly from the Gulf Coast to Quito without refueling. He even chose the figures to be painted on its tail: DS 368. The numbers referred to the $368 billion the tobacco industry had put up to settle their case. The DS, he said, did not stand for Dick Scruggs, but for "dollar signs."

At the beginning of the Christmas season in 2002, Lott attended a one-hundredth birthday party for Senator Strom Thurmond of South Carolina. Before abandoning the Democratic Party and becoming a talisman for the "Southern Strategy" that lured segregationists into the Republican Party, Thurmond had been the presidential candidate of the racist States' Rights Democratic Party, known as Dixiecrats, in 1948. Mississippi was one of four Deep South states to give Thurmond its electoral votes. In the flush of the moment, more than a half-century later, Lott toasted his ancient colleague and remarked, "I want to say this about my state. When Strom Thurmond ran for president, we voted for him. We're proud of it. And if the rest of the country had followed our lead, we wouldn't have had all these problems over all these years."

In the ensuing storm of criticism, Lott gave up his position as majority leader within two weeks, and Scruggs's dream of becoming an ambassador died.

South America was no longer an option. But the time had come, Scruggs thought, to leave Pascagoula. For all of his childhood memories and current friends, the place had become too close for comfort for him. His friend George Shaddock, a local lawyer, knew of animosities that Scruggs had stirred, and he had warned him, "Get out of town. You've got a target on your back." A desire for a change of venue, a clean plate, played into Scruggs's thinking.

He wanted his son Zach to join his law firm, and he realized that Zach's wife, Amy, opposed living on the coast. Even though her hometown, Jackson, and Pascagoula occupied the same state, the cities were worlds apart. The Gulf Coast beat to a different rhythm, celebrated a culture that sometimes seemed indifferent to the pressures of ordinary life.

Oxford represented an obvious compromise. Dick and Diane already owned a condominium on University Avenue, a couple of blocks from the campus, and were often joined there by Zach and Amy. They had been spending more and more weekends in Oxford, attending Ole Miss sporting events. They found that Oxford offered concerts that played nowhere else in Mississippi, and that many of their friends were also moving to the thriving college town in North Mississippi. The Scruggses' close friends from their Pascagoula days, Marla and Lowry Lomax, planned to build a permanent home in Oxford, and many others had weekend places near the campus. In the years since Dick had attended law school, residential sites in the town had exploded into some of the hottest properties in the Deep South. The prices were driven by hundreds of alumni, nearing retirement age and prosperous beyond any belief they might have dared imagine in college, who wanted to come home to Ole Miss.

The amazing migration, which began in the 1990s, transformed the town. Though it was still known as William Faulkner's home, it was no longer Faulkner's town. The farmers who peddled produce on the square, their country contemporaries who whittled idly on cedar sticks in the front of the courthouse, the Gothic characters who peopled Faulkner's novels—all were gone, replaced by newcomers who had far more than a dime in their pocket. The feed-and-seed and hardware businesses, the five-and-dimes, the turn-of-the-century pharmacies with soda fountains, had given over their storefronts to trendy shops featuring apparel for students. City Grocery retained its name, but it had been converted into a restaurant offering New Orleans cuisine, a menu so impressive that its owner would win a prestigious James Beard Award. Square Books occupied a corner once held down by Blaylock Drugs, and it had grown into one of the preeminent independent bookstores in the country; its owner, Richard Howorth, was the town's mayor. A progressive Democrat, Howorth personified Oxford's unique character in the otherwise conservative hills.

The public schools were happily integrated, and none of the private "seg academies," such as those sponsored by fundamentalist churches and flourishing in other locales in the area, had gained a foothold in Oxford. Bars, forbidden by Prohibition laws when Scruggs had enrolled as an undergraduate, were open in many spots around the square, and after the sun went down, the town throbbed with the sound of rock bands and folk singers. There was something very satisfying in sitting on the balconies of the bars on the square and sipping a cocktail in the company of friends from college days.

Dick and Diane talked over the idea of relocating to Oxford with their daughter, Claire, who would attend Ole Miss. For Zach and Amy, the decision to make the move was an easy one.

In many ways, Zach was more familiar with present-day Oxford than was his father. Though he had been born in Portsmouth, Virginia, while Scruggs served in the navy, Zach had lived in Oxford as a small boy and, more recently, as an undergraduate and law student. He knew all about life on the square, for he had occupied the same second-floor apartment looking out on the courthouse that football player Eli Manning later rented. Amy liked the idea of returning to Oxford because she, too, had attended Ole Miss.

Zach spent most of his childhood on the Gulf Coast, moving with his family from their first, crowded quarters in his grandfather's home to a modest house in a blue-collar neighborhood before stepping up to a nicer area. Even before Dick Scruggs became wealthy, he displayed a tendency to shower others with material possessions. One day Zach came home from school and discovered his bedroom bare. His father had given away his son's bed, desk, chair, and chest of drawers to a boy from a poor home who had been helping the Scruggses with odd jobs.

It was not until Zach reached the fifth grade, on a day that Dick Scruggs first drove home in a Mercedes, that the boy suspected he had become a child of privilege. His suspicions were confirmed after he overheard his father telling Zach's grandmother Helen of the financial success that asbestos litigation was bringing him. Zach was thrilled when he heard his father say, "I'm going to be a millionaire." The next year, the asbestos windfall brought the family their first private plane. Trips to faraway places became a reality for them instead of a distant dream.

When Zach grew older, he was able to enroll in a private school in nearby Mobile. He graduated from high school there, removed from some of the problems that afflicted the public schools in Pascagoula.

There was little doubt that Zach would go to Ole Miss, but he followed a slightly different path from that of his father. Instead of pledging SAE, he joined Sigma Nu, the fraternity of his uncle and the campus home for many Pascagoula boys. The Sigma Nus were unabashedly political, regularly running brothers for campus offices. Zach liked that. In his senior year he ran for "Colonel Rebel," the popularly elected equivalent of "Mr. Ole Miss." He failed to win, but the loss did nothing to dim his interest in politics.

Zach had a close relationship with his uncle Trent, and he found Republicans appealing. Lott, whose male aides tended to be Sigma Nus, gave his nephew an unpaid position one summer in Washington, and Zach grew intoxicated with the political air he breathed there. After graduation, he returned to Washington and worked for a year on the staff of a North Mississippi Republican congressman, Roger Wicker, an Ole Miss Sigma Nu, a protégé of Lott's, and an increasingly important part of the state's conservative network.

But Zach's personal politics began to change in law school, when he became disillusioned over Republican attacks on Attorney General Mike Moore, who was like an uncle to young Scruggs. The GOP's negativity pushed him closer to his father's Democratic views.

After graduating from law school, with cum laude honors and a spot on the *Law Journal* staff, Zach took a job with a Jackson law firm to begin his own five-year plan for himself and his family. A son, Jackson, was born just before Christmas 2002, and a daughter, Augusta, would follow in a couple of years. Zach intended to spend the time in Jackson gaining experience in different phases of law practice, but there had always been an understanding that he would someday join his father's firm.

Even though he was nearly a decade removed from undergraduate school, Zach retained the appearance of a guileless sophomore. He had his mother's delicate features and a habit of sweeping from his forehead a fall of hair worn moderately long, in the style favored by fraternity boys at Ole Miss.

Zach plunged into the practice of law, yet continued to be drawn to public service. He was bright, energetic, and ambitious, and after being approached by prominent Democrats, he entertained notions of running for office. They suggested that Zach become a candidate for secretary of state, a position that might serve as a stepping stone to higher things. But Moore felt the move would be premature for his young friend, and he counseled against it. There would be a better time, he suggested.

Even though he had moved away from the Republican Party, Zach valued the advice of his uncle Trent, who also discouraged him from mounting a statewide campaign at an early age.

His life seemed in order. But after only three years at the Jackson firm, Zach ended his apprenticeship to join his father as a junior partner in Oxford.

Before making the move, Zach already had the opportunity for firsthand criminal defense work under the tutelage of his father's friend Joey Langston. In 2002, he had gotten a message from the skilled Booneville attorney: Would Zach be interested in assisting in the defense of two Lee County deputy sheriffs charged in federal court with the death of a suspect in a sensational shoot-'em-up near Tupelo? Of course he would.

Had the case not been so tragic it could have been an episode in *The Dukes of Hazzard*. It started at a routine Fourth of July roadblock when a motorist refused to hand over his driver's license for inspection. Instead, Billy Ray Stone produced a gun, suspecting that the officer could see that his passenger in the work truck was a woman who had been assaulted, kidnapped, bound with duct tape, and stuffed into the well between the dashboard and front seat. A shot was fired and a chase ensued, with bullets flying in the summer night. Stone wrecked the truck, and his hostage was killed in the melee, but he managed to escape into the woods. After a manhunt, he was cornered in a country outhouse. He died in a climactic confrontation, but not before fatally wounding the Lee County sheriff, Harold Ray Presley, a second cousin of Elvis.

Sometime well after the dust had settled, the federal government brought criminal charges against two deputies, saying that Stone had actually been beaten to death after his capture. Since the state had no interest in prosecuting its own deputies, the U.S. Attorney's Office invoked the same charges—deprivation of civil rights—that the federal government relied upon in the 1960s to bring suspects to trial in racial murders.

It would be an interesting experience for young Scruggs. He joined Langston and two members of another firm famed for criminal defense work, Steve Farese and his cousin Tony Farese, in preparing for a trial. The case was moved by the government to the U.S. District Court in Greenville, in the Delta, where a predominantly black jury would be expected to frown upon a pair of white deputy sheriffs from Mississippi's hill country accused of stomping someone to death.

As they worked over the list of prospective jurors, the defense team hired a knowledgeable woman from the Delta to aid them in learning about each individual. Facetiously, Langston dubbed her "Madame

Cleo," a mystical soothsayer who would ensure that the defense found the proper jurors. Though the tactic of vetting jurors is standard practice for any trial preparation, Langston's reliance on the wisdom of Madame Cleo happened to converge with the prosecutors' concerns about the composition of juries in cases involving Langston. Their suspicions intensified after the two deputies were acquitted.

During the week-long trial, Zach fraternized with his older colleagues, sat in on all strategy sessions, and handled the cross-examinations of several witnesses.

Langston had the front page of the Tupelo newspaper bearing a banner headline—NOT GUILTY—framed and gave it to young Scruggs. He added his own inscription, "Zach, Great Job! Your friend, Joey." The memento hung on the wall of Zach's office for the next six years.

Oxford was running over with lawyers. Some settled there after law school. Others were attracted by the college town's cultural advantages and shifted their practices in mid-career. Still others, on the cusp of retirement, opened offices after choosing to spend their latter years among the memories of their student days.

The glut of attorneys fostered a carnivorous atmosphere. Jealousies and hatreds developed within the legal profession, and it was not too far-fetched to compare the environment to that of a lobster trap where creatures crowded into a small space begin to tear limbs from the bodies of others.

With so many attorneys, there also existed a shortage of space. One prominent lawyer, Grady Tollison, owned a large corner office with balconies overlooking the courthouse, while others were reduced to offices in back alleys or to working from their homes.

Scruggs wanted the best spot available, so he paid $695,000 for a second-floor location in an older building on the square. A popular café, Ajax, occupied the street level and lent the address some panache. The place had a funky atmosphere and a down-home menu featuring plate lunches of meat loaf and pork chops. A bar in the front was braced by the dining area, where the acoustic tile ceiling had been pierced by hundreds of toothpicks blown there through drinking straws by patrons. Ajax had been Eli Manning's favorite café when he played quarterback at Ole Miss. The visiting novelist and poet Jim Harrison spoke of its virtues in *The Raw and the Cooked*, a book about his eating experiences. "I was saved by the Ajax Diner on the Square," he wrote, "a southern-soul-food restaurant that is always crowded, where

I was soothed by five vegetable dishes: potato salad, black-eyed peas, butter beans with beef gravy, turnip greens with smoked pork, and, grudgingly, broccoli."

Before Scruggs took possession upstairs, the space held a warren of apartments for students. To turn it into something more worthy, he invested hundreds of thousands more in renovation. When that work spun toward the million-dollar mark, he again called upon Rex Deloach for help, this time to supervise the renovation.

Scruggs wanted nice art, so Deloach put him in touch with a gallery in Memphis. He bought a few still lifes in the range of $25,000 each and was loaned others. Scruggs told the gallery owner he wanted to know more about paintings, so she sent him an expensive book, designed to grace coffee tables, extolling art. Scruggs read it for a day, then lost interest in the subject.

When the office was complete, it gleamed with polished wood wainscoting. The floors were adorned with Oriental rugs, and the furniture was of the finest quality. The Scruggs Law Firm, 120A Courthouse Square, Oxford, stood out like a showpiece.

The Scruggses, père et fils, relocated their families to neighboring houses on a stretch of road north of town, where they planned to live until they could find bigger and more comfortable quarters for themselves.

The move to Oxford seemed to have worked. A bit of resentment lingered in the old community over Scruggs's wanton spending, but the Scruggs family had essentially been assimilated into Oxford as part of the surge of alumni coming home. When asked, Scruggs invariably responded with handsome checks for local causes. They were putting down new roots. Dick and Diane found land just south of the campus, a large, wooded lot harboring deer and other wild game, where they planned to build a vast home that would shelter them the rest of their lives.

At the end of 2004, Dick felt that most of his problems had been resolved. Everything seemed secure, as warm and satisfying as a fever dream induced by drugs. But the next year, Scruggs's life would begin to go haywire.

Diane Scruggs began to notice a change in her husband's behavior. Always a gregarious personality, he started to withdraw from social invitations. Apropos of nothing, he made startlingly weird remarks. Some days he would be driven home from work by his staff members and go to bed early. He blamed it on headaches, and he used that malady as an excuse to expand his search for medication.

He called various doctors asking for prescriptions for Fioricet. When the physicians were reluctant to give him carte blanche access to the drug, he discovered it could be ordered quite easily via the Internet. Unexplained notices—"It's time for your prescription to be refilled"— began showing up on the Scruggses' home computer. Diane learned the magnitude of Dick's orders when she inspected an itemized credit card statement and saw a troubling number of shipments listed.

Concerned over her husband's altered personality, Diane concluded that it was drug-induced. She called Dick to a "come to Jesus meeting" to discuss his problem with her. He agreed to stop using the drug. Instead, he became adept at hiding the tablets from her. He mixed them with the contents of an Excedrin bottle. After being awakened, night after night, by the noise of Dick rattling the bottle, Diane determined he was trying to fish out his Fioricet.

In the mornings, he seemed fine. But in the afternoons and evenings, he relied more and more on the drug. He insisted it was essential to his livelihood.

Scruggs looked for new issues to exploit. He felt he found one in the operation of nonprofit hospitals. Arguing that these institutions tended to overcharge uninsured patients and failed to devote an appropriate percentage of revenue to charity cases, Scruggs led a series of class action lawsuits by a team of trial lawyers across the country. More than four hundred nonprofit hospitals, many of them functioning under the umbrella of religious denominations, were targeted in roughly fifty separate suits. Though the cases spanned the continent, from New York and Illinois to California and Texas, Scruggs acted as the mastermind for the attack from his small office in Oxford. The effort won him greater approbation as an advocate for the little man, as the scourge of bottom-line values. After the suits were filed. *Time* magazine characterized him as "corporate America's worst legal nightmare."

Scruggs enjoyed the company of reporters and served as his own press agent, winning favorable coverage for his initiatives. While some lawyers were reticent and reluctant to talk openly, Scruggs gladly flew off in his private plane to Washington simply to meet with journalists to promote interest in his suits against the nonprofit hospitals.

But the initiative stalled early in 2005. A federal judge not only dismissed a suit filed by Scruggs against New York Presbyterian Hospital and the American Hospital Association, but she also rebuked him for an "orchestrated assault on scores of non-profit hospitals, necessitating the expenditure of those hospitals' scarce resources to beat back meritless legal claims." Other federal courts refused to hear his cases.

Undaunted by the setbacks, Scruggs announced the opening of a "second front" to be conducted in state courts. He vowed to hold the hospitals accountable, under state laws, for "consumer fraud, breach of contract, deceptive business practices, unfair and predatory debt collection practices, and breach of usury limits." It was vintage Scruggs, employing strong words and drawing upon his ability to attract press attention. Yet the "second front" proved no more productive than the first.

Scruggs won minor victories. And even his critics conceded that the offensive forced hospitals to change policies. There were fewer attempts to extract payments from poor people for bloated bills, increased instances of charity care for the indigent, and tighter vigilance by the Internal Revenue Service over the nonprofit nature of these institutions.

Still, a big lick never occurred. And Scruggs, who boasted a couple of years earlier that he only went after "primary kills"—the figurative lions and tigers ("I don't want to get there after the antelope has been brought down," he told *Chief Executive* magazine)—he came out of the nonprofit venture without a head to mount.

While the promise of his initiative against the hospitals withered, Scruggs continued to be hounded by the lawsuits filed by two former partners—the cases that would not go away. The action had grown out of Scruggs's handling of fees won in the asbestos litigation, the source of his first major triumph, and had persisted for years, from the time of his first clashes with Roberts Wilson and his firing of a young associate named Al Luckey.

After countless delays and shifts in venue, Wilson's and Luckey's separate suits against Scruggs crystallized in the hands of a single lawyer, Charles Merkel of Clarksdale, who was every bit as headstrong and stubborn as Scruggs.

Although they wound up as implacable enemies, as determined in their hatred of each other as Sherlock Holmes and Professor Moriarty, Merkel and Scruggs had similar backgrounds, coming from little Mississippi towns to obtain Ole Miss degrees in the 1960s. Five years older, Merkel was studying at the law school by the time Scruggs enrolled as a freshman. Merkel created a bigger splash on campus, graduating magna cum laude from law school. But in the ways of the sports-addicted school, he created a more lasting name for himself there through baseball.

From the time he was a child in Leland, a Delta town advertising itself on a welcoming road sign as the home of 5,000 NICE PEOPLE AND A FEW OLD SORE HEADS, Merkel had been passionate about baseball. Though no major league franchise was closer than St. Louis, the Delta had three teams in the old Cotton States League, a Class C association of big-league farm teams. In the days before television, the Greenwood Dodgers might draw as many as a thousand spectators to a game with the Clarksdale Planters, an hour's drive up U.S. Highway 49. One of the products of the league was Ryne Duren, whose wildness later terrified the American League. Duren's bottle-thick eyeglasses and thirst for alcohol compounded his control problems, provoking quakes of fear from opposing hitters and making him a memorable relief pitcher for the New York Yankees, Merkel's favorite team.

There was something refreshingly competitive about the sport in the post–World War II period, and if there was no game in the Delta, the air crackled with radio dispatches of bigger contests in places such as Boston and Brooklyn. Like so many boys his age, Merkel played makeshift games, using marbles and sticks in lieu of balls and bats, all the while dreaming of a career in the sport. He came closer than most, starring as an infielder for the Ole Miss Rebels. He played shortstop, next to the All-American third baseman Jake Gibbs, who wound up with the Yankees. But it was Merkel's aging collection of Topps baseball cards that ultimately drew him wider recognition, in a coffee table book, *Smithsonian Baseball: Inside the World's Finest Private Collections*, published in 2005, the year his feud with Scruggs reached new heights.

Merkel was known in legal circles as smart and tough. His self-confidence touched some as conceit. His nickname at Ole Miss was Self. But no one dismissed him as an unworthy adversary. Early in his career, he was linked to some of the sharpest minds in the practice of law in Mississippi, in a partnership with three others who would later have major roles in Scruggs's life: Jack Dunbar, Robert Khayat, and Grady Tollison. After that union broke up, Merkel established a law firm in Clarksdale specializing in plaintiffs' cases. Years later, Merkel and Cocke would be cited by a trade publication as among the "super lawyers" in the Mid-South.

Once he was retained to represent Luckey, Merkel began pursuing Scruggs as relentlessly as Arthur Conan Doyle's fictional detective tracked Moriarty. Said Sherlock Holmes of Moriarty: "A criminal strain ran in his blood, which, instead of being modified, was increased and rendered infinitely more dangerous by his extraordinary mental powers." Said Merkel of Scruggs: "I have nothing for him. On a scale of one-to-ten, I'd put Dick Scruggs at about a two." Merkel recognized that Scruggs was cunning, bold in his gambles, and especially astute in attracting favorable publicity. But he burned over the belief that Scruggs was essentially a scoundrel.

For more than ten years, the two men waged a legal war. Merkel insisted that Scruggs owed Luckey millions of dollars in dividends from a joint asbestos litigation project. Scruggs refused to pay. As a result, Merkel put Scruggs through a series of grinding depositions, testimony taken outside a courtroom for use in a prospective trial, where they clashed over issues both petty and significant. They addressed each other in mocking, sarcastic tones, and occasionally the volleys between the two men grew so loud that others would threaten to leave the room.

Contending that Scruggs had used income from the asbestos victories to finance the tobacco triumph, Merkel argued that a "constructive trust" existed that would extend Luckey's claim against Scruggs to his tobacco earnings. In an effort to find how Scruggs had expended the tobacco money, Merkel probed a Rube Goldberg–like flow chart showing the circuitous route that Scruggs's payments took. Merkel's questions eventually revealed P. L. Blake's $2 million-a-year arrangement with Scruggs. Merkel deposed Blake, too, and extracted from him the laughable explanation that he had earned the income through such chores as sending Scruggs newspaper clippings.

The psychic battering troubled Diane Scruggs. She worried that the lawsuits by Luckey and Wilson were undermining her husband's health and mental alertness, and contributing to his growing dependency on drugs. She grew to loathe Merkel, whom she considered tactless, and she feared that his persistent hounding of her husband had a deleterious effect outside the hearing rooms. She urged Dick to bring the cases to an end. But Merkel's bargaining position asked for $60 million from Scruggs, and it was difficult for Scruggs to countenance the thought of paying anything at all.

Scruggs had retained a succession of attorneys during the spasmodic life of the litigation, and as it neared a climax he chose Jack Dunbar, an old lion of the Mississippi bar, to lead his defense. For nearly a half century Dunbar had gathered accolades. He was past president of the Mississippi Bar Association and once a finalist for president of the American Bar Association. Lists of best lawyers in the land invariably included him. Though Scruggs could have hired the most high powered advocate on the East Coast, he felt he needed to go no farther than Dunbar's office, a few steps from Scruggs's on the Oxford Square.

A native of the Delta, Dunbar had been valedictorian of his law school class at Ole Miss in 1957 and started his career as a young partner with the fiery Clarksdale lawyer Charlie Sullivan. Their law firm prospered because both men were smart and effective speakers. Shortly after they opened their office, Sullivan began to entertain political ambition. He ran for governor in 1959, on a platform that called for putting an end to Prohibition in Mississippi, and finished a surprising third. His opposition to Prohibition cast him as a reformer; in fact, Sullivan was quite conservative, and his candidacy had been surreptitiously supported by Senator Eastland to siphon votes from a moderate in the race. The Machiavellian move helped elect Ross Barnett governor and bring calamity to the state with Barnett's defiance of Supreme Court integration orders. Sullivan's true colors as a tribune of the right emerged the next year when he ran on the Constitution Party ticket as a symbolic candidate for president of the United States. For those efforts, Sullivan won eighteen thousand votes in Texas.

Though Dunbar enjoyed war-gaming political strategy with Sullivan, his own politics were far more progressive. As a young man, he had a variety of other interests, appearing in community theater productions and socializing outside the country club crowd. When civil rights activity caused upheaval in Clarksdale later in the 1960s, Dunbar served as a public voice of reason.

By the time Sullivan died in a plane crash, Dunbar had made a professional alliance with others, moved to Oxford to head the offices of a prestigious firm, and identified with the interests of the national Democratic Party. His views generally dovetailed with those of Scruggs. Dunbar had been offered a piece of the HALT initiative against tobacco, but decided not to make the investment, missing out on the big lick. Still, he had been successful throughout his career and had earned the adjective *avuncular* that is often applied to wise old lawyers.

To help fight off Luckey, Scruggs hired others. Dunbar would be in charge, but attorneys from several firms were added to Scruggs's team. They included Johnny Jones, the Jackson lawyer active in ICEPAC, and Joey Langston, who worked out the settlement on the secondhand smoke case. Langston brought with him his own associate, an earnest young lawyer named Timothy Balducci.

In June 2005, twelve years after Luckey's lawsuit was first filed, the two sides began to put an end to it in a trial in Oxford before Jerry Davis, a federal magistrate. Davis was first approached about hearing the case—which had been stuck on the docket without any action—during a chance encounter with Merkel at the Denver airport. Dunbar, knowing Davis as an impartial figure, was amenable to the idea. But first, details had to be worked out. Both sides wanted to close proceedings to the public. Davis refused. If a trial took place, it would be open and would follow normal guidelines for federal court, he told them. Luckey and Scruggs agreed. They also decided to accept Davis as the final voice; neither would appeal his verdict.

Dunbar convinced Scruggs that a trial without a jury had tactical advantages. The logic of a judge would prevail over the emotions of a jury, and it was felt that a strong case could be made against Luckey's conduct while associated with the Asbestos Group. But Dunbar knew Scruggs was exposed on one point. Luckey had been given 25 percent of the stock in Asbestos Group, and his ownership position had never been reconciled by Scruggs. Before the case went to trial, Scruggs's team presented arguments before a focus group to get their soundings. One member of the group, a retired sociology professor at Ole Miss named Vaughn Grisham, kept raising the point in discussions. "What about the stock?" Grisham asked. "What about the stock?"

Scruggs never considered Luckey's side of the argument. Taking the same position he had held since the day he fired Luckey, Scruggs refused to make a settlement and went into the trial convinced that he would win.

The trial opened with an exchange that illustrated the intimacy of the Mississippi legal community, where virtually everyone knows one another, regardless of age. Judge Davis informed the lawyers that court would recess early the coming Friday because he had tickets to an interleague game in St. Louis between the Cardinals, the baseball team he had followed for most of his life, and the Yankees. "If anybody else has got a ticket, I'll see you in St. Louis," he said, making a play on the name of the 1944 movie musical *Meet Me in St. Louis*. Turning to Merkel, Davis added, "I can't miss the Cardinals and the Yankees. I hope you're going to make it, Mr. Merkel."

"I might do that, judge," Merkel said.

Not all of the dialogue in the courtroom was as pleasant—especially the snarls between Merkel and Scruggs.

Scruggs was prepped beforehand by his counselors. They submitted him to a barrage of hostile questions and helped him fine-tune his answers. They advised him to maintain a steady bearing, to be civil and respectful while on the stand. Arrogance, they told him, would tarnish the image he should seek to present.

Scruggs performed well in his first morning of testimony. But his lawyers were disturbed by the change they noticed in his approach in the afternoon. After lunch, he became cavalier in his responses to Merkel. He traded subtle insults with his rival. Pleased with himself, Scruggs smiled overconfidently. He adopted an air of bravado that sometimes resulted in remarks damaging to his own case.

Watching him change from focused witness to ad hoc antagonist, Scruggs's close friends suspected the cause of the transformation.

During the lunch recess, he had washed down several doses of the medication he called "happy pills."

During nearly two weeks of testimony much of the background for the case was revisited. Scruggs had hired Luckey, a fresh graduate of the Ole Miss law school, to go to work for his Pascagoula firm in 1985. Within months, he assigned the young lawyer to the Asbestos Group, the in-house corporation formed by Scruggs and Roberts Wilson. Over the next few years, Luckey was given increasing shares in the business; at the time Scruggs fired him in 1993, he owned one-quarter interest in Asbestos Group.

Scruggs took action after members of his staff reported that Luckey had asked them to backdate as many as fifty medical reports of clients in order to qualify for awards processed by the Center for Claims Resolution, which dealt with asbestos claims. "The girls refused to comply with his instructions," Scruggs testified. After checking into the complaints, Scruggs invited Luckey to a restaurant at the La Font Inn, the site of many business conversations in Pascagoula, to avoid an ugly scene in his office. Scruggs refused to accept Luckey's explanation that no problem existed, even though his associate told him "none of the reports had left the office." He discharged Luckey that day.

"We were in the middle of the mother of all trials," Scruggs said, referring to a mass tort case involving asbestos. "Mr. Luckey had just committed an incredibly unethical act." When Merkel smirked at Scruggs's observation, Scruggs snapped, "You can laugh if you want to, if you think it's a laughing matter."

Scruggs said he was astonished when Luckey approached him after his dismissal and asked for $14 million in compensation for his interest in Asbestos Group. He called Luckey's figure "utter fantasy."

"Mr. Luckey was entitled to nothing after he ceased work," Scruggs said. "Do you pay salary to people that don't show up for work?"

Merkel had a caustic response. "So you were judge, jury and executioner." But even as he parried with Scruggs, Merkel knew the charges of tinkering with the records hurt Luckey's case.

During his own testimony, Luckey's credibility suffered further damage. On cross-examination, Dunbar led Luckey through a seemingly benign discussion of his handling of asbestos cases. With no warning, Dunbar confronted Luckey with copies of medical reports, bearing his initials, that had been altered. The witness had no explanation.

For a moment, it looked as if Luckey was lost. Judge Davis, a heavy-set, imposing figure, seemed visibly troubled by Luckey's testimony. Shortly afterward, he ruled that Luckey was not entitled to any of Scruggs's tobacco money. Asbestos money was still on the table, but Scruggs felt encouraged by Davis's body language.

Merkel, who had been using $60 million as a settlement figure, cut his negotiating position in half. Scruggs had never been willing to settle at any cost; now his position hardened because he felt his sacking of Luckey had been vindicated.

Dunbar and Rex Deloach, Scruggs's financial advisor, celebrated with a drink the night after Luckey's testimony was complete. They, too, sensed that Scruggs was on the verge of winning. Deloach raised his glass in tribute to Dunbar. "They ought to charge admission to see a cross-examination like that," Deloach said.

But as Merkel had observed during negotiations outside the court, it didn't matter if someone was an ax murderer. If they owned 25 percent of a corporation, they were entitled to 25 percent of its value.

As the case wound toward a conclusion, Scruggs faced a strange diversion. One of his own attorneys, Joey Langston, began to pressure him for more money from the tobacco settlement. It involved the 3 percent share of his income that Scruggs had promised in 1997 to resolve the dispute with the family of Burl Butler, the barber who died of cancer. Langston, who brokered the agreement involving his brother, Shane, and Ron Motley, claimed that Scruggs had not calculated the "three points" accurately. Langston complained that Scruggs had used the net amount, a smaller figure, as a basis to determine the 3 percent rather than relying on the larger, gross amount. Langston said he was raising questions at the insistence of members of the Butler family. He warned that they were ready to sue for a greater payout.

Scruggs was perplexed by the demand. He thought the ploy was, at best, crass. Deloach was outraged. He did not trust Langston. Despite the attorney's well-groomed appearance, the accountant considered him "slick and greasy" and out to get more money for himself. Deloach met with Langston twice to explain the calculations. Unwilling to accept Deloach's figures, Langston sent his associate Tim Balducci to Oxford to negotiate the issue.

In a July 8, 2005, letter, Langston wrote Deloach: "You have offered no suggestion on how to resolve the outstanding issues. Regardless,

I must get answers for Mrs. Butler and her present attorney as he continues to call me with questions and seeking answers." Mrs. Butler's "present attorney" was Langston's brother.

Scruggs responded with a brief note, saying, "I believe that we have fully complied with all undertakings regarding these fees over the last seven years." Nevertheless, he promised to listen to Langston's "concerns."

Deloach was more blunt in his own letter to Langston. "I am not aware of any errors in calculating the fees," he wrote. "In the fall of 2004, your CPA audited the accounting and calculations. Following the audit, you advised me by telephone that there were no suggested changes."

Doubting Langston's claims about the 3 percent misunderstanding, Deloach did some homework of his own and discovered that Langston was keeping most of the money for himself. As the disagreement intensified, Langston insisted that he was originally designated as the sole recipient of the 3 percent—which eventually amounted to more than $4 million a year. The Butler family was given a one-third share as a result of the negotiations hammered out later in Jackson and sealed in P. L. Blake's living room in Greenwood, Langston said. Deloach found that Langston's brother, Shane, took his own contingency fee from the Butler share, leaving the barber's survivors with about 20 percent of the $4 million.

When Scruggs learned of the division of the "three points," he reproached Joey Langston for the way the funds had been distributed. Langston said Scruggs always knew of the way the money would be split, but Langston dropped his bid to get more.

Diane Scruggs was indignant after hearing of Langston's action. Though she kept abreast of her family's finances through regular meetings with Deloach, she had never been privy to Scruggs's handling of the tobacco money. This peek at one example of Scruggs's side deals astonished her, and she wondered how her husband tolerated relationships with people like Langston.

Inexplicably, Scruggs kept Langston as his lawyer and his friend.

On July 20, Judge Davis issued an eight-page opinion. He found that Scruggs "had adequate grounds to terminate" Luckey's employment and denied Luckey's constructive trust claims, which would have led to Scruggs's tobacco money. But on the fourth page of the judgment, the tone of the decision began to change.

"The court finds that Scruggs' position concerning Luckey's status within Asbestos Group to be unreasonable and in conflict with existing law," Davis wrote. He added that Scruggs's refusal to pay Luckey's fees was "frivolous" and constituted "a breach of fiduciary duty entitling plaintiff to prejudgment interest" on the money due him.

Davis ruled that Scruggs owed Luckey $13.7 million. Nearly half of that figure represented interest that accrued during the long dispute. In addition, Scruggs was ordered to pay nearly $4 million in attorney's fees and expenses: $4 million to Merkel, his nemesis.

Scruggs was staggered by the judgment. Not that he was incapable of paying such a figure; he had the resources to do that. But the magnitude of his loss to two of his bitterest rivals ate at him. Scruggs was so consumed by enmity toward Merkel, Luckey, and Roberts Wilson that he was prepared to go to extreme lengths to prevent another judgment like this.

He walked down the hall of his office suite, pitched the order onto Zach's desk, and expressed incredulity that Davis could have reached this decision. He quickly began to develop second thoughts about the wisdom of submitting the case to the magistrate. He wondered how Davis could have come down so hard against him.

Years before, in 1998, he had seen Davis at one of Mississippi's premier social events, tailgating among thousands in the Grove before an Ole Miss football game. Davis, who had long experience in the federal court system, mentioned that he was interested in an open federal judgeship. Scruggs called his brother-in-law to see if he might submit Davis's name to the Clinton administration for consideration. Trent Lott quickly dismissed the idea. He told Scruggs that Davis was a partisan Democrat, too liberal for his tastes. (Lott didn't tell Scruggs, but the senator intended for the nomination to go to his old college roommate and Sigma Nu brother Allen Pepper.)

Scruggs wondered if Davis's decision represented retaliation for Scruggs's failure to deliver a judgeship. Scruggs's post-trial doubts were reinforced after local lawyers said he should have known Merkel and Davis were good friends. Later, thinking back on the critical ruling, Scruggs remembered a conversation at a restaurant with Oxford lawyer Grady Tollison that especially irritated him. Tollison enjoyed baiting people, even his friends—and Scruggs was no friend—so he did not miss the opportunity to question Scruggs's judgment. "I was surprised you took that case to Jerry Davis," Scruggs recalled Tollison saying. "You know, he and Merkel go way back. They go to baseball games together."

The rumor of Merkel and Davis hobnobbing at baseball games may have been conceived during their repartee at the beginning of the trial. Though both men were ardent baseball fans, they had never gone to a game together.

Scruggs smoldered over the judgment, but he paid. After his checks were sent, Luckey had them reproduced. He also made a copy of the glowing *Newsweek* article that had been headlined "Who's Afraid of Dickie Scruggs?"—the same piece that Scruggs had framed and put on the wall of his office. Using the checks and the *Newsweek* piece, Luckey designed a montage that he framed and sent to Merkel. It wound up on Merkel's wall, too; his own big game trophy.

With the success of Luckey's lawsuit, Merkel took charge of related litigation, the old Roberts Wilson suit against Scruggs involving millions of dollars Wilson claimed from their joint venture in the Asbestos Group.

After years without movement, the Wilson case now loomed ahead for Scruggs. He felt beset by a rash of misfortune and found resonance in the biblical testament of Job, the prophet who lamented, "I have no peace, no quietness; I have no rest, but only turmoil."

The setbacks in July bled into August, and the wound to Scruggs festered. He was angry with himself, and the balm of his drugs did little to comfort him. He would be sixty the next spring, and he began to think about pulling back from his law practice. It would be a radical step, but suddenly the thought had appeal. When he drove out to Deloach's country estate to discuss the idea with his financial advisor, Scruggs was struck by the pastoral beauty of the place. Deloach owned many acres of fields and forests, and the road to his home cut through a landscape as tailored as a fairway at Augusta National. Scruggs had construction work under way on his own mansion in town. The time seemed favorable for him to put a halt to his frantic pace.

"You've got to get me out of law," he said when he sat down with Deloach. "Clear me out of my practice and set something up for Zach and Sid," his son and the associate he'd brought with him from Pascagoula. With millions of dollars of income assured each year for another two decades, Scruggs was fixed for life. He was ready to turn the Scruggs Law Firm over to the next generation.

Deloach said the transition could be accomplished without a great deal of difficulty. But he was unable to move on it right away. Deloach and his wife were leaving the next week on a trip to Greece.

"Why don't you and Diane come with us?" Deloach suggested. They could talk about the future there, and do it around the splendor of the Aegean Sea.

Another nice thought, Scruggs said. But there was no time to put together such a grand trip on such short notice. They would talk about it again, he said, when Deloach returned.

A few days later, on the morning of Saturday, August 27, Scruggs received a telephone call from Pascagoula telling him that his mother had died. Helen Scruggs had been in failing health for some time, and bedridden at her home, a couple of blocks from Scruggs's beachfront house, since suffering a bad fall. Still, the news came as a shock to her only child.

Dick, more heavily medicated than usual, and Diane flew to the coast, where they were joined by Zach and Amy, who had been in nearby Gulfport for a wedding. Their duties were sad ones as they prepared funeral arrangements. By contrast, the late summer day was glorious, with clear skies and little wind, weekend weather that ordinarily lured thousands to frolic in the gulf waters. But something ominous was out there, beyond the Mississippi Sound and the barrier islands.

The storm was already hurricane-strength and had been given a name: Katrina. Its course was unpredictable, but projections pointed it toward New Orleans, one hundred miles to the west. Landfall was two days away, but close enough for apprehension. Pascagoula had endured great hurricanes before: Camille in 1969 and killers before the weather service designated names for the storms. The Mississippi coastline was regularly battered by seasonal blows, so residents knew to keep their vigilance.

Early Sunday morning, Scruggs woke his son. "This thing's heading our way. We've got to board up."

A look at television news confirmed his report. On the screen, Katrina had grown into a monster, a spinning red mass that seemed to occupy much of the gulf between the west coast of Florida and New Orleans. The Scruggses, accustomed to the drill over the years, began to gather portable items of value—pictures and antiques—and moved them to Helen's home, a comfortable ranch house. It was built close to the ground, but high water had never gone that far inland in previous storms. At the Scruggses' house, furniture was moved upstairs or away from windows. Storm shutters were sealed, and sandbags placed at the foot of doors. They pitched outdoor furniture into the water of the swimming pool to prevent the deck chairs and chaise lounges from being blown away.

A visitation in Pascagoula to mourn Helen's passing was canceled. Her body was sent ahead to her family's old home in Brookhaven, a two-hour drive north. She had wanted to be buried there, and services would be rescheduled once the storm had passed.

By noon, Pascagoula was under an evacuation order. Scruggs learned he had until 2:00 p.m. to leave. At that time the airport would be closed, and his plane would be grounded. Moving quickly, the Scruggses fit themselves and as many friends as they could into the jet and were airborne for Oxford.

Shortly before dawn on Monday, Katrina struck land in the marshy bayou country south of New Orleans, near the mouth of the Mississippi River, then caromed toward the Mississippi coastline like a billiard ball. By that point, those who had fled their homes and those who had stayed could do nothing other than hope.

Scruggs followed the situation from his home in Oxford, depending on television and sporadic cell phone calls from friends and family members who had stayed behind. First came word that Trent Lott's lovely beachfront home, less than a mile from Scruggs's place, was gone. Then it was the home of their good friends and neighbors the Bosios: gone. The home of Diane's brother, Perry Thompson: gone. Then Scruggs's own home: parts of it still standing, but basically, gone.

Unsatisfied with its carnage on the coast, Katrina came churning inland, crippling the city of Hattiesburg, ninety miles north of Pascagoula, and then wiping out trees and electricity in Jackson, nearly two hundred miles from the coast. To Scruggs, the storm seemed to be chasing him. Still not spent, Katrina struck Oxford at nightfall, uprooting towering old oaks and forcing many residents to resort to candlelight. For emphasis, a tree fell on a guest house at Zach and Amy Scruggs's home.

Two days after Katrina, Scruggs obtained permission to fly his family south for his mother's graveside service in Brookhaven, where heavy debris—felled trees and sheets of corrugated tin—lay scattered throughout the town. A small group gathered at the cemetery, members of the Furlow family and a few close friends. Scruggs was too emotional to speak. Instead, Zach spoke for the family.

Afterward, they reboarded Scruggs's jet and flew into Pascagoula, where Zach had left his car behind at the airport. The scene resembled a war zone. Helicopter rotors beat noisily in the air, and armed guards were posted at intervals on the way into town.

They found the devastation they anticipated along the beach, but realized the damage went much deeper into Pascagoula. Helen's house, which had remained dry through previous storms, had taken on five feet of water in the surge, and it reeked with the smell of decay—dead fish and animals. After hearing reports of looting, Dick and Zach armed themselves with handguns and shotguns and went about salvaging what was left in their homes. Mud caked Helen's place. At Scruggs's home, damage was much worse. Two wings of the mansion, as well as a guest house and small gym in the rear, had been washed away.

As he picked through the wreckage along the coastline, Scruggs encountered many old friends faced with a similar task. Their mutual plight pulled him, spiritually, back to Pascagoula.

He began a ritual that he carried out daily for several weeks. Each morning he loaded his plane in Oxford with provisions for the survivors and flew to Pascagoula with food and cases of bottled water and beer. Seeing the need for generators, he bought out the supply at the Oxford Wal-Mart and ferried them to Pascagoula for distribution. Sometimes Scruggs used both his nine-seat Citation and the more spacious Gulfstream; when he did, he flew as co-pilot because he had only three pilots on his payroll. He became a one-man relief agency, and the little Pascagoula airport, named Trent Lott International, took on the appearance of a third world waystop as people clambered around the planes to get the goods Scruggs was handing out. Each evening, he returned to Oxford, sometimes overloading his planes with passengers who wanted to flee the scene.

The work made him manic. One morning, when he was told that the Gulf Coast air space was off limits because of a visit by Vice-President Dick Cheney, Scruggs told his pilots, "Fuck 'em. We're flying in. They can shoot us down if they want to."

His obsession intensified after some of the Katrina victims told him in early September that insurance companies were already denying their claims for the loss of their homes. Citing fine print in the complicated policies, representatives of the insurance companies pointed out that coverage existed for wind but not for water. And much of the coastal damage was being attributed to the storm surge.

Just when he had contemplated retirement, a new cause had come

to him, a new target, one even more vast and powerful than the tobacco industry, one of America's giants: the insurance industry. Scruggs
felt energized again. His appraisal of the insurers mirrored his attitude
toward the ban on use of Dick Cheney's air space. Fuck 'em. We're
flying in.

He would see them in court. And he would forge another alliance,
just as he had done to carry out his wars on asbestos and tobacco. To
combat the insurance industry, he would create a new entity, and this
time he would give it his name and that of one of the greatest natural
disasters in the history of the country. He would call it the Scruggs
Katrina Group.

CHAPTER 10

To form his new attack group, Scruggs called on his comrade from the tobacco battles, Don Barrett, and the man who financed much of that initiative, David Nutt. He also invited a couple of new faces into the venture. One of them was Johnny Jones, a Jackson lawyer who had served on Scruggs's defense team during the Luckey trial.

Jones charmed his way into the group with a beguiling email to Scruggs less than three weeks after the storm: "Cupit tells me that you guys are getting together a class action or other consolidated action against insurance carriers for denying claims for Katrina damage. He tells me that he attended a meeting with you guys on that topic. I told him I knew he was lying since I knew you guys would call me if you were looking for a real lawyer in Jackson . . . Do you want to get mixed up in more litigation with overweight and overpaid lawyers? . . . Cupit? Say it ain't so." He signed it simply, "Johnny."

Jones's swipe at Danny Cupit, his old friend, was good-natured, but it succeeded in winning him a position in the unit Scruggs was developing.

Papers formalizing the Scruggs Katrina Group were drawn up within two months, with Nutt's firm putting up the first $1 million to handle expenses for the organization. SKG began to attract clients through advertisements and word of mouth, and before long a map of the Gulf Coast in Scruggs's office was decorated with pushpins representing the properties of hundreds of clients. It looked like an exhibit in a war room.

Scruggs, as usual, engaged in a bit of freelancing that his partners knew little about. A few months after he targeted the insurance indus-try, he received a tip concerning some potentially explosive evidence from a friend of his chief secretary, Charlene Bosarge. The source was the mother of Corri and Kerri Rigsby, two sisters who worked as claims adjusters on the Gulf Coast. After learning about "some hanky-panky going on" from her daughters, she told Bosarge, "Dickie needs to know what these girls are doing." Scruggs met with the mother, then with her daughters, and grew enthusiastic over what they told him. State Farm, they said, had been doctoring reports on Katrina damage in an effort to absolve the company of responsibility. The Rigsby sisters turned over a couple of documents indicating that engineering reports to determine the cause of damage had been changed from "wind" to "water."

Scruggs enlisted the sisters, who were working for an Alabama firm that investigated claims for State Farm, to cooperate with him. Over the coming months, he would come into possession of roughly a thousand pages of confidential State Farm files.

Scruggs excitedly described the women to his associates as "insiders" who were in a position to cripple an adversary in the same way that Merrell Williams and Jeff Wigand had damaged the tobacco industry's credibility. But he was also mindful of the legal jeopardy involved, and in an attempt to justify his arrangement with the Rigsby sisters, Scruggs hired them as "consultants," with annual salaries of $150,000 each.

He employed the documents against State Farm, and to maximize pressure on the insurance company, he had much of the information passed to the U.S. Attorney's Office for South Mississippi and to the state's new attorney general, Jim Hood, who was elected in 2003. (After holding the office for sixteen years, Mike Moore had given up his po-litical career to return to private practice.)

The Rigsby sisters would become central figures in a complex series of lawsuits and countersuits that eventually ensnarled Scruggs in a criminal contempt citation by a federal judge. But not before their evidence helped persuade State Farm to surrender on one set of claims.

Throughout 2006, the Scruggs Katrina Group fought and negotiated with State Farm before finally reaching a tentative agree-ment near the end of the year that promised to bring nearly $90 million for a set of clients and another $26.5 million in fees for the five law firms involved in the action.

But an argument broke out over plans to divide the fees, and two relatively unknown lawyers—who had helped represent Scruggs in the Luckey trial and hoped to build on the association—wound up on opposing sides of the dispute. Johnny Jones and Tim Balducci were both native Mississippians and products of the Ole Miss law school, but had little in common other than a stake in Scruggs. They were separated in age by more than a decade and had contrasting interests and temperaments. Though working in the same profession, they traveled different tracks. Yet each had a critical part in a case that would send tremors across the country's legal community. In fact, without them the whole drama would never have occurred.

Jones was bookish and had a background that carried, by Mississippi standards, a whiff of the bohemian life. The product of a freethinking household in Jackson, Jones was one of a handful of white schoolchildren who stayed in the city's public schools during the desegregation era. His mother taught English at Millsaps College and belonged to a cadre of liberal women who shared with their neighbor, the author Eudora Welty, an interest in literature and an allegiance to the national Democratic Party.

When schoolbuses filled with new black students pulled up in front of Bailey Junior High, an Art Deco landmark on North State Street, at the beginning of the fall semester in 1970, most of Jones's classmates withdrew. He felt like a guinea pig, thrown into an unprecedented social experiment. Scores of prominent white Mississippians had passed through the corridors of Bailey over the years; suddenly Jones found himself in a distinct minority at the school.

A few blocks away, at the socially fashionable First Presbyterian Church, plans for a private, alternative school, Jackson Prep, were drawn up for those who felt dispossessed by the events at Bailey and elsewhere. "First Pres," as the church was known in Jackson, rivaled the nearby First Baptist Church for power and rigid conservatism. Later, the congregation would lead a breakaway movement from the mainstream denomination and help form the new, theologically right-wing Presbyterian Church of America (PCA).

Jones and his mother were never part of the religious axis—First Baptist and First Pres—that dominated politics in the state capital. As Episcopalians, they subscribed to the teachings of their own minister,

John Jenkins, who encouraged racial reconciliation in a city torn by a decade of sit-ins, Freedom Rides, the assassination of civil rights martyr Medgar Evers, and a police fusillade at Jackson State that killed two black students. The Joneses also admired William Winter, a lay leader at the more progressive Fondren Presbyterian Church. Because Winter's life would be distinguished by his long struggle to save public schools in Mississippi, it was no coincidence that Jones had been attracted to him for many of the same reasons that had led Scruggs to Winter's law firm.

After graduation from Murrah High School, once the seed ground for Ole Miss freshmen and now predominantly black, Jones lasted only a year in Oxford. In Jack Kerouac style, he went on the road. He painted houses in Austin at a time when the Texas capital was a refuge for the outlaw musicians Willie Nelson and Waylon Jennings. He spent a year at Millsaps, then returned to Ole Miss and finally graduated, two years late, in 1977. He went west again, worked a night shift in a canning factory in the Pacific Northwest, spent an obligatory amount of time in San Francisco, and wound up tending bar at Old Faithful Inn in Yellowstone Park. He then drifted back to Mississippi, met his future wife, and settled down.

His mother's friends, knowing of his fondness for English and history, got him a job with the state archives. Jones went through a phase that prepared him for a task awaiting him: writing legal briefs. He worked on an oral history project that enabled him to interview some of the state's literary giants, including Shelby Foote and Walker Percy. The interviews were considered so artful that they were published by the University Press of Mississippi.

In 1981, Jones and his wife moved to Oxford, where he enrolled in graduate school. Serendipitously, he arrived in the university town around the same time as two legendary Mississippi figures, the literary equivalents of Willie Nelson and Waylon Jennings, wound up there.

Willie Morris, a native of Yazoo City and author of *North Toward Home*, had returned from years as an expatriate writer and editor of *Harper's* magazine in New York to join the Ole Miss faculty. Barry Hannah, a brilliant craftsman of stories anthologized in many American collections, had also come to Ole Miss, to teach creative writing after losing his tenured position at the University of Alabama for displaying a pistol in class. Heavily fueled by drink, Morris and Hannah were at once friends and rivals, and they spent late hours almost every night in an off-campus coffeehouse with admiring students like Jones serving as their courtiers.

To put some order in his unfocused life, Jones opted for law school and obtained a degree when he was thirty. Returning to Jackson, he clerked for a federal district judge, Tom S. Lee, and worked for a while in Danny Cupit's firm during the asbestos frenzy.

He carried on a knockabout practice for years and had no illusions that Scruggs was hiring him for his talent when he was asked in 2004 to join in the defense against Luckey. The case had been transferred at one point to Judge Lee's jurisdiction, so Scruggs fell back on an old tactic: he retained Jones to make sure his side had a face familiar to the judge.

Scruggs's own interests and politics meshed with those of Jones, and the older lawyer enjoyed the younger man's company. Though Scruggs reacted bitterly over the loss of the Luckey case, Jones had no qualms about inquiring if there might be a place for him in the Scruggs Katrina Group.

Tim Balducci had also served as a junior member of Scruggs's defense team in the Luckey case, but he took a route far different from that of Jones to get there. Born in Shelby, a little town in cotton country not far from the Mississippi River, Balducci belonged to a well-known family. Like many others in the area, the Balduccis could be traced to a tribe of Italian immigrants who left Ancona province on the Adriatic Sea a century earlier to settle in the rich farmland of the Mississippi Delta. They labored in agriculture, boasted of their skills in making whiskey—illicit at the time—and served as pioneers in introducing the Catholic Church to the region. As their numbers increased, the Italian Americans became a significant force in the community, producing outstanding athletes and a corps of merchants, physicians, and tradesmen. Balducci's father was a banker. Though some Old World customs were retained—Shelby had a bocce league—the Italians were effectively assimilated into the local community, and many became Protestants in the process.

Tim Balducci never strayed far from home. He attended Delta State University, located a few miles from Shelby. After graduation, he went to law school at Ole Miss. His grades were good, and he seemed bright enough, striking some of his classmates as a quick study and eager to learn. Others thought him ingratiating. Once, he approached his instructor in a poverty law class to assure her that the course had been a touchstone for him, revealing truths about the poor that he had missed all his life. She dismissed his comment as arrant bullshit; after all, Balducci had grown up in Bolivar County, where two thirds of the people were black and one third of the population lived below the poverty level.

In many ways, Balducci was a quintessential good ole boy, a regional description for those who might choose hunting and fishing over books. A law degree did not rule anyone out of the good ole boys' club. There is nothing inherently antiintellectual about a good ole boy. Plenty of lawyers readily accept the designation. But good ole boys prefer telling jokes and outlandish tales over having serious discussions. Good ole boys dare to be uncouth and poke fun at high manners. They favor informality: Caterpillar caps, blue jeans, and boots. They devote Saturdays to NASCAR rather than the Metropolitan Opera. Despite his Italian surname, Balducci fit right in with the Bubbas.

Good ole boys are essentially friendly, and Balducci realized that flattery and a willingness to learn from his elders could be tools as he climbed through the legal profession. Following law school, he had a modest practice in a couple of small-town firms in North Mississippi. To augment his income, he worked as a public defender in Oxford and nearby Holly Springs, representing indigents who faced criminal charges.

During this period, he became acquainted with circuit judge Henry Lackey, who presided over many of the cases. Balducci made the most of the relationship. He called Lackey, who was a generation older, his "mentor" and described their friendship as a warm one. As he said later of Lackey, "He took me in his court, taught me the practice of law from the bench, showed me my mistakes, congratulated me on my successes, counseled me on my failures. We became close friends, not just in a professional sense, but more in a personal sense. I really looked up to him."

After attracting attention as a hustler, Balducci was hired in 2000 by Joey Langston to return to the law firm where he'd spent the first year of his career. While Balducci may have thought of Judge Lackey as his mentor, he considered lawyers such as Langston and Dick Scruggs role models.

At the end of 2006, after the Scruggs Katrina Group's settlement with State Farm, the lives of Jones and Balducci would take radically different directions.

For Jones, bad news came in a telephone call on December 6. Scruggs told him that he could expect to receive a check for $1 million for his work on the Katrina cases. At first, Jones thought: This is great. It would cover his expenses and compensate for his work over the past year, and the money would come just before Christmas. Then he asked, what about his share of the $26.5 million fee coming to the group from the State Farm settlement?

"Well," Scruggs said, "you won't get any more money out of this settlement."

Jones felt his stomach heave. He was being cut out of the deal.

Scruggs tried to allay Jones's distress. "This is the first one, Johnny, and we are going forward, and we've got other settlements coming in. We think we can get the same thing that we got from State Farm out of Nationwide and Allstate combined."

Scruggs said the million-dollar payment to Jones was something that others in the Katrina alliance had decided they "can live with." He added: "Johnny, this is the first one. It's a proposal, you know." There was no malice in Scruggs's voice, no tone of dominance by an older partner. He sounded almost casual, as though a few million dollars here, a few million dollars there, amounted to little in the greater scheme of things.

But to Johnny Jones, fifty-one at the time and still in search of the big lick, the words were devastating.

"Dick," he said, "I don't want to say anything right now. We've been friends for a long time. But this doesn't make me whole. Just let me shut my big mouth and think about this."

It was the last real conversation the two men ever had.

Around the same time, thirty-eight-year-old Timothy Balducci had grown dissatisfied with Langston. Just as Scruggs had served as "special assistant attorney general" two decades earlier in the asbestos cases, Balducci had held the same title as a member of Langston's firm. In a move that would later cause controversy, Langston had been given a mandate by Attorney General Jim Hood to recover unpaid taxes for the state from the bankrupt Mississippi colossus MCI/WorldCom. The effort collected over $100 million for the state treasury and won a $14 million legal fee that Langston split with the Louisiana firm that came up with the idea to sue MCI/WorldCom.

Like Johnny Jones, Balducci was disappointed over his failure to get a substantial share of the fee. "I didn't get paid shit out of it," he told one friend. Actually, Balducci had been disgruntled for some time over Langston's distribution of the money pouring into the little law office in the northeast Mississippi town. He felt that Langston was keeping virtually all of the spoils for himself and leaving little for his subordinates.

Balducci found a partner in his complaint—Steve Patterson, the former state auditor who had been working as a "rainmaker" at Langston's firm for a decade. Tommy Cadle, a Booneville lawyer, once said admiringly of Patterson, "Hell, he not only makes it rain, he makes it storm." Patterson had been hired because of his connections. Years after he had been forced out of public office, he kept reappearing in a narrative of behind-the-scenes politics in Mississippi. He seemed to have limitless contacts, from former governors to current U.S. senators. He knew valuable sources in courthouses across the state, and had maintained his friendships with players in the old Eastland network. Despite his move against Scruggs in 1992, Patterson and Scruggs now consulted with each other on politics and inside deals.

One hundred pounds overweight, Patterson had the appearance of an Edwardian actor, his bloated face crowned with wavy brown hair. With his jowls, he would never be mistaken for a matinee idol, but he excelled in bringing business to Langston. And he, too, had begun to feel underappreciated.

Balducci and Patterson became close while working at the Langston firm, and they commiserated with one another over slights they felt they'd suffered at Langston's hands. They envied Langston for his wealth, and they resented his attempts to exploit some of Patterson's connections.

A few years before, Patterson's old friend Senator Joe Biden of Delaware had come to Mississippi to attend an Ole Miss football game. Instead of Patterson, it had been Langston who got to parade Biden around North Mississippi, showing off the visiting senator like a prized possession. Driving in Oxford on game day, Langston stopped to shout at friends, "I want you to meet a good friend of mine. I've got Senator Biden here with me." Later, Langston escorted Biden to Dick Scruggs's stadium skybox to impress the group there. Though the Georgia Bulldogs vanquished Ole Miss that day, Biden left with a favorable impression. The parties in the Grove, a wooded area on campus where tens of thousands of fans fraternize on football Saturdays, were grand, he thought.

Privately, Balducci and Patterson talked of striking out on their own, using Patterson's connections for themselves to start a new superfirm. They believed they could persuade Dick Scruggs to lend his support. If Scruggs were willing to join them in any kind of legal initiative it would give them the imprimatur they needed to become a legitimate big-time operation.

The pair intended to call their firm Patterson and Balducci, but Patterson held no law degree, and the state of Mississippi demanded that founding partners of legal firms have such qualifications. Instead, they chartered the operation in Washington, D.C. Later, as their preparations evolved, they allowed themselves, in their wildest dreams, to consider a more powerful name: Patterson, Balducci and Biden.

While Balducci was thinking expansion in North Mississippi, Johnny Jones saw his situation deteriorating. From the time he had been invited to take part in Scruggs Katrina Group, Jones had counted on its potential to deliver his struggling firm out of its everyday practice and into a world already enjoyed by other partners in the group.

Jones and his colleagues in the firm of Jones, Funderburg, Sessums, Peterson and Lee worked out of an old mansion on North State Street in Jackson, not far from the state capitol. The building had all of the elegance of Tara after the Civil War. Boards creaked. A draft pushed through the halls on chilly days. Painted surfaces were chipped and peeling. There was little that looked illustrious about the place, but Jones and his associates knew that everything could change with one big lick.

Jones felt he was a full partner in the Katrina enterprise. From the inception of the agreement until well into 2006, he worked practically full time on the SKG project. As a writer whose reputation extended beyond the bar association, he was entrusted with preparing the briefs.

Under the contract, Nutt provided the bankroll. Scruggs served as "lead counsel." Dewitt "Sparky" Lovelace, a Florida lawyer with Mississippi family connections to P. L Blake, would provide expertise on "adjuster retention," while Don Barrett, the fiery veteran of the tobacco wars, was given responsibility for developing witnesses.

Barrett had doubts about Jones from the start. He had never heard of the Jackson lawyer, and when he asked Scruggs why he wanted to bring Jones into the group, Scruggs replied, "He's a great writer." Barrett remained unconvinced.

If Scruggs Katrina Group struck it rich, the terms of the agreement called for Nutt to recover his investment and take 35 percent of any net fee. The remaining 65 percent would be split among the remaining partners through a formula based on *Model Rules of Professional Conduct* and on each partner's contribution to the successful litigation. Agreement by four of the five parties was necessary to decide precisely how much each partner would receive.

In the first blush of the news that State Farm had settled, Jones's firm projected an infusion of upward of $5 million. With those hopes dashed, Jones began to look for a way to get a greater share of the money. Less than a week after Scruggs's telephone call, Jones served notice on the Katrina Group that he would hold them in breach of contract. A series of snarling exchanges ensued, threats that soured the Christmas season and spilled over into the new year.

Jones asked Jack Dunbar, the Oxford lawyer who had spearheaded the defense of Scruggs in the Wilson and Luckey cases, to intercede informally and offer his services as a mediator. Dunbar held the respect of both Jones and Scruggs, and he agreed to see what he could do to resolve the dispute. But after talking with Scruggs, Dunbar realized there were other belligerents in the case who made a compromise unlikely. Don Barrett was adamant that Jones should be rebuffed.

Meanwhile, Balducci and Patterson broke with the Langston Law Firm at the end of 2006 and established their own office in Patterson's hometown of New Albany. It seemed a curious place to build a super law firm. New Albany lay halfway between Langston's base, thirty miles away in Booneville, and Scruggs's office in Oxford, and no highway fancier than old four-lane U.S. 78 served the town. New Albany had tenuous fame as William Faulkner's birthplace, but the writer's family had moved to Oxford a century earlier. The place was best known, if at all, as simply a pleasant little southern town, a remote county seat in the hills of northeast Mississippi.

Patterson had lived there as a child and had moved back a few years before, causing folks to wonder how he had acquired his money after he bought a house for $300,000 and spent at least that much more renovating it. Balducci had moved his wife and twin sons there, too, and paid handsomely for a new home.

There was nothing modest about their venture. They hired a few young associates fresh out of law school, and found several attorneys around the state willing to lend their names to the firm's letterhead as "of counsel" in exchange for $1,000 a month. After Patterson and

Balducci rented the office of a retired judge, Rodney Shands, they hired him to serve "of counsel" as well. Through the association with Shands, they sought to develop some local credibility. But they stirred indignation with their audacity.

When a young woman introduced herself to a local lawyer, Thomas McDonough, as an employee of the new "Patterson-Balducci" firm, McDonough observed that no such firm existed because Patterson lacked a law degree. Patterson responded with a letter to McDonough.

> I am not a lawyer and have never claimed or desired to be one. I am just an old worn out politician who is trying to make a future for my son. I am a member of a Washington, D.C. based group that bears my name and my son will soon be a member of a New Albany firm that will bear his name. The irony is I don't claim to be a lawyer and you do! Piss ants often try to disrupt picnics, but rarely do. Be assured you will not disrupt mine.

Patterson's letter set off a volley of correspondence to the arbiters of ethics with the Mississippi Bar Association. Stephen Livingston, president of the Union County Bar Association, noted that a $10,000 campaign contribution to Attorney General Hood had been attributed to "Steve Patterson, New Albany lawyer." Livingston also noted that a defendant had claimed in city court that he had hired Patterson as his attorney. He submitted further evidence that a "Patterson Balducci Law Group" was advertising in Gulf Coast newspapers to attract clients, urging victims of Hurricane Katrina, "It's not too late to take action against your insurance company!"

Livingston told the state bar association, "We are not trying to ruffle anyone's feathers, but we would like for the Mississippi bar to look at this matter and advise whether or not there is any unethical conduct occurring."

Balducci responded with his own "Dear Steve" letter to Livingston. "It appears that someone has recently stolen some of your firm's letterhead and has mailed a series of crazy, accusation-filled letters about me and my firm to the Mississippi bar." In language steeped in sarcasm, Balducci praised Livingston "for your Solomon-like wisdom, which is tempered only by your relentless hunger for justice, which abides you always as our chosen Leader."

Livingston dismissed it as a "smart aleck" letter. When he mentioned the controversy to his friend Judge Henry Lackey that summer, Balducci's mentor merely smiled and assured Livingston, "It's all going to work out in the end."

When Jones walked into a showdown meeting with the Scruggs Katrina Group on March 2, 2007, there was a perceptible coolness in the surburban suite of Nutt's firm. Based on conversations he had had earlier, Jones believed that Nutt would support him. And Scruggs did not seem aggressively opposed. But he discovered that Barrett would preside over the meeting, and it was apparent that Barrett was bristling over Jones's threat to sue.

Barrett had tried to replace Jones earlier, hiring his own brief writer, Jeff Schultz, for $10,000 a month. During one clash, Schultz called Jones a "greasy redneck." Jones, on the other hand, considered Barrett the real redneck in the group, a hick from the hills posing as a prima donna. If a closing argument had been needed in any trial, Jones said at one point, "you couldn't have wedged Dick and Barrett out of that."

Barrett was annoyed that Scruggs had offered Jones $1 million in the first place. It was another instance, he thought, of Scruggs acting without the approval of partners in the venture. But he was especially angry over the tone of Jones's emails that held out the threat of a lawsuit.

To Barrett, a rough-and-tumble son of Lexington, a town on the edge of the Mississippi Delta, Jones represented the elite culture of Jackson. Jones might consider himself an erudite fellow, but Barrett wrote him off as a pissy-assed whiner.

At the outset of the tense meeting, Barrett told Jones that the group had $22 million ready to distribute that day, and that two checks had been cut for Jones.

One check represented 6 percent, or a bit more than $1 million. "You can take that," Barrett said firmly. "If you take it, we've got the check cut, and we can go about our business. We can be out of here. We can continue working, and you can continue working on the litigation, and we'll reassess the future. We'll act like this didn't happen."

A second check had been written for 3 percent of the $22 million, Barrett said. "I don't think you're entitled to three percent. You're certainly not entitled to six percent. But we have two checks for you. If you don't take the first check, then the group has voted to kick you out and to pay you three percent."

He demanded an answer from Jones "before you leave this room."

Jones asked about the possibility of sending the disagreement to arbitration.

"Nothing to arbitrate," Barrett said. The agreement among the prin-
cipals of the Scruggs Katrina Group was clear: a member could be
removed by the vote of supermajority of four others in the venture.
"Only thing to arbitrate is: you signed this thing right here saying we
could kick you out on a four-to-one vote."

If the case came to arbitration, Barrett said, "I would ask: 'Is that your
signature?' That's what I would say to the arbitrator. And you would
be out on your ass."

Jones was sitting next to Scruggs, whose silence seemed as cutting as
Barrett's remarks. Jones felt that after working with Scruggs for more
than two years he was being consigned to Barrett's wrath.

Jones turned to David Nutt, who he felt would be sympathetic.
Nutt volunteered no support. "Johnny," he said, "I know you think I'm
betraying you. I know you think I fucked you." Nutt said he had been
told "some things" about Jones, some "stuff that I'm not going to get
into" that convinced him the offer to Jones was fair.

Jones and one of his partners, Steve Funderburg, asked if they could
confer with other members of their firm.

Barrett cut him off. "No," he said. "You can call them from here. We'll
leave the room and you can talk to them on the speakerphone right
here. But we want an answer before you leave."

Funderburg appealed to Nutt. Surely, Funderbug said, he and Jones
could consult personally with their partners. In spite of Barrett's objections, Nutt said he thought that would be all right.

Funderburg turned to Scruggs. "Dickie," he asked, "do you have a
problem with it?"

Speaking for the first time, Scruggs said, "No, I think you're entitled
to go talk to your partners about this."

But Jones sensed that he and Funderburg were outnumbered. He
picked up his briefcase and prepared to leave, struggling to express his
disappointment. "I thought we were really going to come here to talk
about how we could resolve this," he said. Instead, he said he had been
subjected to a "muscle job" by Barrett.

Scruggs, who seemed passive during the argument, finally spoke
up as Jones and Funderburg walked out of the room. It was apparent
that the two men had alienated the other members of the group. "You
shouldn't be surprised," Scruggs told Jones.

Driving from the meeting, Jones got a speeding ticket. At home late that afternoon, he wandered around his yard in a deep funk. For the first time in his life, he felt terribly deceived.

His partner agonized over their ouster through the weekend. On Sunday afternoon Funderburg composed an angry email, which he sent to "Mr. Scruggs." Funderburg wrote of his pride in having helped represent Scruggs in the old disputes over fees. "I felt you were a fair man and that Wilson and Luckey were accusing you of vile conduct to get money." Then his tone changed as he addressed the action by Scruggs Katrina Group. "You went along with it. I have looked in the mirror all weekend and tried to figure out how I could be so stupid."

Funderburg was just warming up. He continued:

We DEFENDED you when people said you were greedy, or were a back-stabber, or a liar, or anything else. Good lord, we trusted you as a friend. Well . . . good job. You have developed a good routine. It worked. But go to your grave knowing that you have shaken my belief in everything I hold dear. I did not believe that people like you really existed. I am ashamed and will always be ashamed of having defended you and protected you. You are a man without honor and you should know that about yourself. You betrayed your friends without even a phone call. You never even tried to work it out with John or me. You just sat there and let Barrett do the talking. Whether you believe it or not, neither Don Barrett nor David Nutt would have stayed up nights worrying about you. I doubt they give a damn about you or your family. You all deserve one another.

Meanwhile, Johnny Jones contemplated his firm's options. He had asked Jack Dunbar to seek mediation, and that had failed. Arbitration had been ruled out. He decided his last resort was a lawsuit.

He turned to Danny Cupit, because, as he said later, he didn't want to retain a lawyer "who would light the fuse and let it blow up."

Cupit explained that he was not in a position to sue Scruggs. Instead, Cupit suggested another name to Jones: Grady Tollison. Others might be timorous about challenging Zeus, the King of Torts, Cupit told Jones, but Tollison would not hesitate to take on Scruggs.

CHAPTER II

Grady Tollison was known around Oxford as a man with strong opinions, opinions expressed so forcefully that he antagonized acquaintances and sometimes exasperated his friends. He held a Manichean view of the world in which he placed himself on the side of light and set his adversaries in the fields of darkness. Over the years, he developed a reputation for tenacity in the courtroom and righteous indignation in private conversations. He often broke the peace of social gatherings with shouts and sneers as he vented his rage. Tollison could be obnoxious. But no one denied that he was a damned good lawyer and a robust advocate for any client.

In 1994 he defended the embattled state insurance commissioner, George Dale, after Dale had been indicted on charges of giving preferential treatment to Blue Cross and Blue Shield of Mississippi in exchange for campaign contributions. Federal charges against Dale were dropped.

During one of the more curious criminal proceedings in the state in recent memory, Tollison's firm also defended Lewis Nobles, president of Mississippi College, a Southern Baptist institution steeped in fundamentalist doctrine. Nobles was accused by the school of embezzling $3 million and charged by federal authorities with using the money to pay for prostitutes. When Nobles's office was raided, agents found

$27,000 in cash, pictures of naked women, and a bottle of strychnine nestled with biblical treatises. Nobles fled. After the FBI tracked him down to a trysting spot in a San Francisco hotel, he gulped down poison in an attempt to kill himself.

Tollison reveled in high-profile criminal defense cases, but he was also known as a hard-hitting plaintiff's attorney. Though he rarely acted as if he were a candidate in a popularity contest, his colleagues thought enough of his abilities to elect Tollison president of the state bar association. As one of his contemporaries said of him, "Grady's got a good mind. If he had any kind of Dale Carnegie training he'd be a hell of a fellow."

For such an unusual character, it was not surprising that Tollison arrived at the practice of law through an unorthodox fashion. He was the product of a white working-class neighborhood in Memphis, one of the first to be taken over by blacks as the city's population shifted. His father had been a soldier in Ed "Boss" Crump's political machine, an organization that had so many votes locked up in Memphis that its influence extended throughout Tennessee. So the son came by Democratic Party politics naturally.

While Elvis Presley, a kid who transferred from Tupelo, Mississippi, was matriculating at Humes High School, Tollison was attending Southside High, another gritty public school across town. Both young men had their own ways to break out of their backgrounds.

Tollison enrolled in a small, prestigious liberal arts college, Southwestern at Memphis, now known as Rhodes College. He played football, and it is easy to picture him on the field while crowds of a few hundred followed low-stakes contests with the likes of Sewanee and Millsaps. He was short and bulky, built as strongly through the chest as a bulldog. Tollison was a natural lineman, and a good one. But he excelled in academic work, too. He won spots in honor societies and a listing in *Who's Who in American Universities and Colleges*.

In 1962 he enlisted in the Marine Corps, spent three years in their service, and reached the rank of sergeant. It is easy to imagine him there, too.

In 1965 he was hired as head football coach at the new Coahoma County High School in Clarksdale, Mississippi. During the struggle over desegregation in the Delta, CCHS had been created as a school that would be open to blacks. Segregationists were willing to sacrifice the school's "purity" in order to try to preserve an all-white status at other public facilities in Clarksdale. In the throes of the desegregation process, a certain esprit developed among members of the CCHS faculty. They were willing to accept the challenge of integration and make it work. Tollison was comfortable with the situation. His political views as a progressive Democrat were maturing. After moving to Clarksdale, he asked to be introduced to Aaron Henry, a local druggist who was one of the most formidable civil rights figures in the South, and he identified with a tiny coterie of white liberals in the town.

When Tollison expressed an interest in law school, it seemed odd that the most conservative bank in Clarksdale agreed to sponsor him. But the arrangement enabled Tollison to burnish his curriculum vitae. At Ole Miss, he became editor of the *Mississippi Law Journal*, a position reserved for the best law student, and he followed up with the highest grade point average in his graduating class. Instead of returning to Clarksdale to become a trust officer in the bank, Tollison stayed in Oxford to help establish a beachhead there for a prominent Clarksdale law firm that included Jack Dunbar and Charlie Merkel. Tollison's performance was so impressive that within a few years he joined the masthead of Holcomb, Dunbar, Connell, Merkel and Tollison.

He also plunged into Democratic politics in the state and served on a biracial delegation from Mississippi to a Democratic National Convention. Tollison was expanding his horizons.

The firm attracted some interesting names, including an Ole Miss superstar, Robert Khayat. After giving up his professional football career, Khayat had joined the law school faculty before leaving the academic setting to go into private practice with Tollison. In a smart commercial investment, the two men bought the most conspicuous building on Oxford's square, a three-story structure known as the Thompson House, and rented office space to their own law firm. But there was a rupture in the relationship between Tollison and Khayat, who left the firm and sold his interest in the building to Tollison. And after Dunbar moved from Clarksdale to Oxford to take over as head of operations there, an unpleasant break occurred in the friendship between Tollison and Dunbar, too. Tollison left to start his own firm, and sued Dunbar on the way out.

Tollison lost the security of belonging to a successful shop full of lawyers, but he held a trump card: the old Thompson House. Just as Oxford had begun to acquire a reputation as one of the most attractive locales in Mississippi, Tollison groomed the old building, which had

once housed a hotel, into a eye-catching office and turned the upper
floors into chic living quarters for himself.

His firm prospered and grew. Tollison offered positions to family
members, in-laws, and promising newcomers just out of law school.
But the board by the front door listing associates in the Tollison Law
Firm had to be updated frequently to account for the divorces and
disagreements that changed the cast of characters inside. In one tragic
episode, a prominent Oxford businessman climbed to the second-floor
balcony of Tollison's office before dawn one day and shot himself to
death.

One figure remained at the firm through all its turnovers: Tollison's
son Gray. He proved to be a major asset. Gray was not only quick-
witted, like his father, but far more easygoing. People liked Gray Tollison. They elected him state senator from Oxford's district in 1995. In a
legislature blighted by many burned-out bulbs, young Tollison quickly
rose in respect, and he began to be mentioned as a possible gubernatorial candidate for the Democrats someday.

When Johnny Jones took his grievance against Dick Scruggs and
the rest of the Katrina group to Grady Tollison after the bitter meeting
in Jackson in early March, he could not have found a more enthusiastic
counsel.

Tollison had never particularly liked Scruggs, even though Scruggs
had provided financial support to Gray Tollison's campaigns and had
cashed an IOU with Lieutenant Governor Amy Tuck to ensure that
the young state senator got a coveted committee assignment. The older
Tollison did not like Scruggs's swagger, and he felt that Scruggs was
naïve in his dealings with Mississippi politicians.

Scruggs sensed Tollison's resentment. In spite of his contributions of
thousands of dollars to Democratic candidates and his support of the trial
lawyers' political arm, ICEPAC, Scruggs felt he had never been truly
accepted by Tollison and his Democratic pals. He knew they considered him a closet Republican. After all, Trent Lott was his brother-in-
law, and Scruggs had occasionally sided with Republican candidates.

There was one particular apostasy that grated on Tollison. When
Susan Collins, the moderate Republican senator from Maine, came to
speak at Ole Miss, Scruggs helped sponsor a fund-raiser for her. It was
in gratitude for Collins's vote in a Republican caucus that gave back a
leadership position to Lott. But that was not enough of an excuse for
Tollison.

In the four years since Scruggs had moved to Oxford, Tollison's bitterness had only grown. Though known as one of the top trial lawyers in the state, Tollison had never been a participant in any of Scruggs's big licks. Instead, Tollison had built his own practice in Oxford. And he curried a name for himself by hosting elaborate parties for a panoply of important visitors from around the state following Ole Miss football games. He also sponsored Democratic fund-raisers at the Thompson House, which offered guests a sweeping panorama of the Oxford square.

When Scruggs arrived, it was as though the town was not big enough for both of them. While the Tollison Law Firm held down a spot on the northern corridor out of the square, Scruggs bought office space on the west side of the square and underwrote a costly renovation that transformed the upstairs space from dingy student apartments into an elegant suite. Scruggs even built a large balcony that overlooked the old courthouse and peeked around the corner at Tollison's office. If the four sides surrounding the Oxford courthouse were represented on a Monopoly board, it was as if Scruggs had come in and seized Park Place and Boardwalk.

Within a few months, Scruggs had supplanted Grady Tollison as the Big Dog Democrat in Oxford. High-octane receptions were being scheduled at the Scruggs Law Firm. In 2004, Scruggs fêted the Senate Democratic leader Tom Daschle at a lunch in his office. Many of the movers and shakers in Mississippi's community of trial lawyers were on hand to deliver campaign contributions to the national Democratic cause. John Grisham came from Charlottesville, Virginia, where he spent most of his time, to introduce Daschle and lend the event a measure of pizzaz. Tollison attended the gathering, but grumbled privately that it was he, not Scruggs, who had arranged for Grisham to be there, because Tollison once represented the novelist's father.

Tollison's disposition was not helped when the rear of the Thompson House buckled and began to collapse a couple of years later, leading to the condemnation of part of the building. Unsightly barricades had to be put up along North Lamar Avenue to ensure that bricks did not fall on passersby. It seemed that townspeople were laughing at Tollison's distress and, at the same time, sucking up to Scruggs, who showered local charities and causes with substantial contributions.

Tollison's animosity boiled to the surface at a meeting in Columbus, Ohio, involving a number of lawyers sorting through distribution of some of the tobacco funds. After an earlier meeting in the same city, Scruggs had given Tollison a ride back to Oxford in his private jet. Things were not so cozy at a later get-together. Tollison felt that Scruggs had been working, without authority, to change the terms of the agreement among the anti-tobacco lawyers and had claimed false credit for hammering out a compromise. He confronted Scruggs in the hallway of the Ohio courthouse where negotiations were taking place. Reverting to the harsh discipline he had learned in Marine training at Parris Island, Tollison yelled at Scruggs, "Do you understand what fiduciary duty is? Do you!" Other lawyers involved in the case, huddled in a nearby conference room, were astounded when they overheard the outburst.

When Scruggs flew home that night, he did not invite Tollison to join him, and Tollison, who had been counting on the ride, had to spend the night ingloriously in an airport hotel and catch a commercial flight back to Memphis the next day.

Less than two weeks after he had been banished from the Scruggs Katrina Group, Johnny Jones and Tollison, newly retained, prepared to file suit against Jones's erstwhile partners. It was a labor that inspired Tollison to rhetorical heights. He quickly whipped up a harsh eighteen-page attack portraying Scruggs and others as greedy and deceitful. He wrote, "The facts in this case show reprehensible conduct" by the Scruggs team. Though four firms in the group were all listed as defendants, Scruggs stood out as the obvious target.

Marshaling material provided by Jones, Tollison itemized no fewer than 130 points. He charged that "Scruggs and Barrett conspired among themselves and others" to set Jones's allocation "at a ridiculously low figure." During three months of arguments that had gone on since Scruggs's December telephone call, Jones had been subjected to a campaign "to bully and cajole" him into accepting less than his fair share, the suit contended. "These intentional, egregious acts were intended to cause and did cause extreme distress" in Jones and members of his firm.

Jones's suit demanded 20 percent of the fees collected by Scruggs Katrina Group—a claim that would be worth roughly $5 million—plus 20 percent of fees the consortium might be awarded in the future. In addition, it called for heavy punitive damages against Scruggs and Barrett to "deter such conduct in the future" and to serve "as an example to others that such conduct would not be tolerated."

. . .

On March 15, 2007, Tollison took the papers to file at the Lafayette County courthouse, across the street from his firm. He also carried a one-page attachment he had prepared in advance. That page contained an "order" to put the lawsuit under seal for four days, giving Tollison authority either to unseal the complaint by the afternoon of March 19 or to dismiss it altogether. On the single sheet, Tollison had left blank places for a docket number, a date, and a signature by a circuit court judge.

He encountered Judge Henry Lackey at the circuit clerk's office. As one of only three judges in the district, Lackey was well known to members of the bar in Oxford. Tollison's relationship with the judge was cordial, but not close. Because of the informality of the court system, Tollison effectively chose Lackey to preside over the Jones case when he asked him to sign the document sealing Jones's complaint. Tollison explained that the lawsuit contained derogatory comments about lawyers and suggested that it might best be kept secret from the public. As Lackey would describe it later, Tollison told him "he hated to hang out our dirty wash in public."

In Mississippi, where judges are short-staffed, it is not unusual for attorneys to prepare an order for a judge to sign—if the language is satisfactory. But in this case, the order given to Lackey provided Tollison with a trigger to use against Scruggs and his co-defendants: the threat that the complaint would be made public in four days.

Lackey signed the order. It was the first time he had ever put a case under seal.

With the judge's order in hand, Tollison unleashed a parallel action. He sent the Scruggs office a copy of Jones's suit along with a two-paragraph letter. "The complaint is currently under seal by order of the court at our request as a courtesy to you," Tollison wrote. "Unless this matter can be resolved by Monday, March 19, at 4:30 p.m., we will move the court to unseal the complaint and will move forward."

Scruggs recognized Tollison's ploy immediately upon reading the letter. It represented the same kind of threat Scruggs had used during litigation many times himself. With such a tactic Scruggs, drawing on his many contacts with the press, was able to ensure that unfavorable publicity fell upon his adversaries when they refused to come to a settlement.

Unless he agreed to settle the Jones case, Scruggs knew his own name would be sullied this time. Well aware of Tollison's growing antipathy toward him, Scruggs simply ignored the letter.

The next move was Tollison's. On the morning of March 28, an article by the Associated Press appeared in *The Clarion-Ledger*, a Jackson newspaper that circulated throughout the state. Under a bold headline, the story began: "A Jackson law firm has sued millionaire trial attorney Richard Scruggs for allegedly withholding money it claims it was owed for working on Hurricane Katrina insurance-related litigation."

On the same day that the Associated Press article on the Jones lawsuit appeared, Steve Patterson and Tim Balducci showed up, unannounced, at the Scruggs Law Firm. The pair had completed their break with Joey Langston and were trying to build a caseload that would sustain their new firm. To show they were serious, they intended to establish an Oxford branch, renting a small office once used by Scruggs on the square. But Patterson and Balducci said they had come to see Scruggs about another matter: a product liability case in Kentucky that involved defective masks for coal miners.

Through Patterson's political contacts, their new firm had landed a piece of the legal action with lawyers planning to file suit on behalf of the Commonwealth of Kentucky. Patterson and Balducci believed it would enhance their standing if Scruggs joined them, for his role in the tobacco wars was well known in Kentucky. Scruggs had already made one trip to Kentucky with Patterson to get a feel for the case.

When Patterson and his partner arrived in the reception area of Scruggs's firm that Wednesday morning, there seemed nothing unusual about setting up an impromptu meeting. The two men were frequent visitors to the office. They gathered around a long table in a conference room with Scruggs, Zach, and Sid Backstrom, and their talk eventually turned to the issue featured in *The Clarion-Ledger* that morning.

The conversation changed forever the lives of those five men.

After disposing of questions about the Kentucky case, Patterson spoke up: "By the way, I saw where that bullshit lawsuit of Grady Tollison's got assigned to Henry Lackey. Y'all need to hire Tim. Nobody has a better relationship with Henry Lackey than Tim. He's like a son to him." Balducci nodded in agreement.

Zach liked the idea. Although another Oxford firm was already representing Scruggs, he proposed hiring Balducci as an additional attorney of record in the case.

Balducci responded that it would not be necessary to retain him formally. "Let me just go and talk to the judge. Let him know I'm on the case. I have to go down there anyway. We'll see what the judge says."

Everyone at the conference table agreed on the plan. Balducci would ask the judge, as a personal favor, to send the case to arbitration. Though no one asked Balducci to offer anything to Judge Lackey, there was an underlying recognition that his mission was unethical. He had been asked to make a request, outside the court, to a judge to issue a favorable ruling for Scruggs. It is a practice known by an archaic term: earwigging. And Balducci knew he risked the loss of his law license by doing it.

Despite that possibility, Balducci telephoned Judge Lackey and asked if he could drive down to Calhoun City to see him. The older man was fond of the young lawyer, and he agreed to a meeting that afternoon. Lackey seemed to be a sympathetic figure. He had helped Balducci through some rough patches early in his legal career. But he was curious about Balducci's urgency. He wondered if Balducci's law practice was struggling, if he might be seeking more public defender cases to augment his income.

Lackey had the appearance of a fatherly country judge. With his shock of white hair, soft drawl, and courtly manners, he seemed eminently approachable—on any legitimate matter. But there was nothing in his background to indicate that he would be amenable to a bit of judicial chicanery.

For virtually all of his seventy-two years, Lackey had lived in Calhoun City, which really wasn't a city at all, but an out-of-the-way town with a population of about eighteen hundred. Only forty miles lay between Oxford and Calhoun City, but the two were worlds apart. The little town's most distinctive feature is a humble square, which motorists on State Highway 9 must circumnavigate. Lackey was born there, left to attend Mississippi College, then returned to help run his family's Ben Franklin dime store. Several years later, he enrolled in the Ole Miss law school and received a degree in 1966.

Like most of the residents of Calhoun City—which was named for the ninetieth-century South Carolina demagogue John C. Calhoun—Lackey was a religious man and a conservative. He described himself as a "deepwater Baptist" and served as a deacon in the local Baptist church. He also followed state politics closely and was one of the early Republican converts in the days when Democrats were held responsible for civil rights legislation and the GOP became a refuge for disaffected white Southern voters.

After a quiet career as a small-town lawyer, Lackey was appointed circuit judge in 1993 to fill a vacancy by Governor Kirk Fordice. He won subsequent elections without opposition and had served on the bench ever since, presiding over criminal and civil cases. He handled a couple of trials that attracted press attention. One involved a lawsuit against the University of Mississippi brought by a former football coach, Billy "Dog" Brewer. A couple of Lackey's rulings struck the Ole Miss lawyers as strange. He disallowed evidence submitted by the school to support its decision to fire Brewer for committing NCAA violations. Though Brewer's dismissal was based on interviews with individuals familiar with the football program, the judge disallowed the material as hearsay. Later, Lackey instructed the jury that a burden of proof rested on the defendant, Ole Miss, rather than the plaintiff. Brewer claimed vindication when he won a $250,000 judgment.

But publicity and controversy rarely followed Judge Lackey. In short, Henry Lackey hardly fit the profile for a man who might dispense an illicit favor for Dick Scruggs.

Lackey seemed jolly as he ushered his young friend into his personal office. He called his visitor Tim. Respectfully, Balducci addressed him as Judge. Lackey inquired about Balducci's twins, and after other pleasantries, he learned that Balducci had left the Langston firm to start a practice in New Albany.

After a few minutes, Balducci got to the point. "Judge, I want to tell you the main reason why I came down here. While I was practicing with Joey Langston I made some mighty good friends, and I made some mighty good money practicing with them." The "friends," he explained, were the members of the Scruggs Katrina Group. And now they were under attack in a lawsuit before Judge Lackey. "Some scurrilous allegations" had been made against them in the case that Grady Tollison had filed, Balducci said, and his friends were being unfairly abused. "I only want them to be treated properly," he said, and suggested that Judge Lackey could accomplish this by disposing of some of the worst allegations in a summary judgment and sending the remainder of the case to arbitration.

Balducci acknowledged that he had "an interest in the outcome" of the case, even though he was not officially representing Scruggs. If Lackey would be willing to rule favorably, he said, it would "be an advantage to me," implying that it would set Balducci in good stead with Scruggs.

When Balducci mentioned Scruggs's name, he set off a soundless electric charge in the room. In recent years, few names had been more frequently mentioned in legal circles than Scruggs, and the judge could hardly believe it had come up in this context.

Dickie Scruggs was the very antithesis of Henry Lackey. Scruggs was known as the primary benefactor of the Democratic Party in the state; Lackey was a staunch Republican. Scruggs exuded wealth and fame; Lackey lived a middle-class existence and served in relative obscurity. Scruggs was cosmopolitan; Lackey was country. Although Scruggs lived only a few miles away, the judge had never met the man. Yet there was something distasteful about him. Lackey considered Scruggs a ruthless man who threw his weight around.

One example leaped quickly to mind, concerning Lackey's friend George Dale, the state insurance commissioner. Lackey and Dale had served on the board of trustees of Mississippi College. In the Baptist fashion, Lackey referred to him as "Brother Dale." At the time, Dale was the target of a campaign by Scruggs to drive the insurance commissioner from office. The judge thought it outrageous. Only three days before, the Scruggs Katrina Group had bought full-page advertisements in Mississippi newspapers to ridicule Dale, who was up for reelection later in the year. The ads had gone beyond the bounds of normal criticism, resorting to an ugly caricature of Dale branded with pink lips and a slogan, "Lipstick on a Pig."

And now Scruggs had the temerity to send an emissary, the judge's own protégé, to fix a case.

Before he left Lackey's office, Balducci put out another idea. For their new firm, Patterson and Balducci were hiring older lawyers— some had held public office as judges or prosecutors—to act "of counsel." Their names would be listed on the firm's letterhead to give it weight. Balducci told Lackey that when the judge decided to step down from the bench, the firm would be honored to enlist him in that capacity.

As he sorted out the conversation later, Lackey concluded that the offer of the "of counsel" position represented the quid pro quo necessary to make Balducci's visit a crime.

Baffled and offended, the judge felt ill after the meeting. A couple of days later, he happened to see Kent Smith, a lawyer who had once practiced with Balducci. Lackey told Smith about the visit and asked, "What kind of character flaw do you think I have exhibited that would make Tim believe I would do something like this?"

Lackey felt he needed to talk with others. He called a fellow judge, Andy Howorth, who happened to be one of Johnny Jones's closest friends. Howorth encouraged Lackey to report the overture to authorities. Lackey also discussed the situation with Lon Stallings, a local assistant district attorney. Stallings said his office did not have the capability to pursue the case properly. Stallings also said there might be a problem in taking it to the next level, the state attorney general's office, because he understood Attorney General Jim Hood had been threatened with defeat in the 2007 election unless he sided with Scruggs in connection with SKG's State Farm case.

Lackey was incensed over the power that Scruggs held over public officials, and he wondered where he might turn. On the morning of April 11, two weeks after his meeting with Balducci, the judge telephoned his old friend John Hailman, a prosecutor in the U.S. Attorney's Office in Oxford, and told him, "Something's come up and I really need to see you."

Hailman was an interesting character, an honest-to-god Renaissance man who made his home in Oxford years before it became a Renaissance community. He had come south from Indiana to play baseball and basketball at Millsaps College and wound up, after a youthful, circuitous journey, speaking French fluently and acquiring an appreciation of wine so sophisticated that he once wrote on the subject for *The Washington Post*. He developed these talents almost by accident. As a college student Hailman decided he needed some savoir faire after being rebuffed by a Delta girl, he set off for Paris to study at the Sorbonne. Instead of returning home after his year abroad, he stayed to work as an English-French interpreter for Air France. On trips to London, he began spending spare time watching trials in courtrooms at the legendary Old Bailey, and he grew intrigued by law.

He graduated from Ole Miss law school in 1969 after working part time for legal services programs that were thought by many Mississippians to be the instruments of left-wing devils. Then he clerked for two years for a federal judge overseeing school desegregation cases in the state before he took a job in Washington with John C. Stennis, the more moderate of Mississippi's two U.S. senators. When Stennis was shot and wounded by a gang of thieves, Hailman spent days at the old man's side at Walter Reed Army Hospital in Washington, listening to Stennis rail at the slowness of the federal investigators while he helped the senator prepare for the trial of his alleged assailants. When prosecutors convinced one of the defendants to testify against the other two men charged in the case, a tactic that resulted in guilty pleas for all, Hailman thought for the first time that he might like to be a prosecutor himself. That opportunity arose when he was lured from a faculty position at the Ole Miss law school to join the local U.S. Attorney's Office in 1974. He signed for a two-year stint. By the time Judge Lackey called him, Hailman had been there thirty-three years. He was chief of a criminal division with twenty lawyers, but planned to retire in a few months.

Hailman had known Lackey for years. He prosecuted some of Lackey's clients before Lackey became a judge, but that did not damage their relationship. Both men were easygoing, natural storytellers who enjoyed each other's company. Once Hailman had taken a small delegation from the justice ministry of Oman, visitors attired in ceremonial robes and turbans, to visit the judge, and Lackey entertained the group with folksy observations about the American judicial system. More recently, Hailman had been notified by security personnel about a curious package Lackey had left for him. Upon inspection, Hailman found that it was a fruit jar filled with homemade blackberry wine. The bottle bore a phony label of "Appelation Controlee," with the claim that the contents had been pressed by virgins and bottled by Baptists.

When Lackey came to Hailman's office at lunchtime, the two men talked of wine and legal affairs for nearly twenty minutes until Lackey, visibly agitated, changed the subject.

"John, I hardly know how to begin, but there's something really serious that's bothering me. I'll tell you right out: a lawyer I've been like a father to came to me and offered me a bribe."

Lackey described his relationship with Balducci, then gave his account of the meeting with him.

"John, I wanted to do two things—to throw up and to take a shower. Normally I'd lose my temper, but I was so shocked I didn't do anything. Tim talked on and on. Finally, I had to say something, so I told Tim: 'The case is new. I need to read the pleadings.'"

Lackey asked if the conversation with Balducci merited attention as judicial bribery.

Just as Lackey had been struck by the potential enormity of the case when Scruggs's name was mentioned, Hailman immediately realized the gravity of what Lackey was telling him.

Hailman assured Lackey that he had done the right thing to report the meeting.

As soon as Lackey left the building, Hailman walked down the hall to the office of the man who would soon take his place as head prosecutor, Tom Dawson. Hailman closed the door behind him and said, "You're not going to believe what I just heard."

Dawson proved to be receptive to allegations against Scruggs. When Scruggs had moved to town a few years earlier, Dawson and Hailman had figuratively rolled their eyes. They knew of Scruggs for his exploits as a plaintiff's attorney, and they felt that he and some of his associates had been skating on the edge of illegal activity with judges and juries. Unsure of exactly what they had on their hands, the two prosecutors set up another meeting with Lackey. If there was to be a case, there had to be evidence.

"Henry," Hailman instructed the judge, "it's important to remember things that happened. Balducci may claim you misinterpreted what he said. Write down now everything you remember each of you saying. And don't go to another meeting or take another call without a tape recorder."

He asked the judge if he was willing to wear a wire.

Lackey sighed. "Absolutely," he said, adding, "I knew you'd ask that. I feel horrible." He expressed the hope that Balducci might back off.

Hailman persisted. "Play this out," he told Lackey. "You can't let it drop." He instructed the judge about the rules regarding entrapment, how it was permissible to lay down bait but improper to entice someone to seize it. "Don't get cute. Don't question too much and scare them off," Hailman warned. "Just let him do what he's going to do."

The prospect of dealing with a case that might implicate Scruggs stimulated all kinds of sensitivities in the U.S. Attorney's Office in Oxford. First of all, it raised concerns about Scruggs's brother-in-law, one of the most influential Mississippians in Washington. Though Trent Lott's relations with the Bush administration had been strained in the years since the White House had greased his slide from power in the Senate, he still had plenty of Republican markers to play. There had been suggestions that federal prosecutors in the Southern District of Mississippi had failed to indict Scruggs in the Paul Minor case because of the inhibiting presence of Lott in the background.

At the top level, the office of U.S. attorney is inherently political, chosen by the president, and acting at the behest of political allies in each state. Jim Greenlee, head of the Oxford office, had been nominated for the job by Republican senator Thad Cochran. Though Cochran and Lott were not close, they generally worked together to find mutually acceptable candidates when vacancies occurred for federal judgeships and U.S. attorneys in the state. Thus, Greenlee had been dependent upon Lott's approval when he was selected. It was not well known, but Greenlee was part of the extensive political network that could be traced back to Lott's Sigma Nu house at Ole Miss. Those outside the Sigma Nu sphere laughed at Lott's allegiance to his college club; it seemed sophomoric for a senator. But it was a very real factor in Lott's decision making, and Greenlee's background on fraternity row at Ole Miss had been helpful.

As soon as Hailman and Dawson took the news of Lackey's visit to Greenlee, the case was plunged into a thicket of bureaucratic infighting and personal antagonisms that divided the offices of the U.S. attorney and the FBI in Oxford.

Greenlee had worked in the office's civil division before he was tapped for promotion. After the political move, he became a subject of scorn among some of the assistant attorneys who considered their jobs a career opportunity and served for years regardless of which party held power. They felt they had earned their positions because of their talents and not through their political connections. Greenlee's mannerisms, which were sometimes petulant, also grated on them. Behind his back, the prosecutors called him Queeg, a reference to the mad captain in *The Caine Mutiny*.

Despite Greenlee's relationship with Lott, he authorized an investigation of the senator's brother-in-law. But it would have to involve the FBI, and this created another problem.

·   ·   ·

A serious schism had developed between the U.S. Attorney's Office and the local FBI that threatened their ability to work together. The two units responsible for bringing federal cases to trial had simmering differences over both policy and procedure. A more vituperative argument between personalities also existed.

The bureaucratic clash grew out of post-9/11 activites, when the U.S. Attorney's Office in Oxford plunged into President Bush's war on terrorism with enthusiasm. In 2003, Greenlee developed a "Convenience Store Initiative" that targeted scores of Arabs and Muslims operating small gas station–food stores in North Mississippi. To conduct the investigation, Greenlee's office called upon representatives of the Drug Enforcement Administration (DEA), the Internal Revenue Service's criminal investigation division, and the Bureau of Alcohol, Tobacco and Firearms (BATF). But agents assigned to the Oxford FBI, considered the key investigatory unit in the region, wound up feeling left out of the loop.

To the consternation of several agents, they discovered that some of their undercover contacts in the Arab-Muslim community, shopowners who had been cooperating in investigations, had been drawn into the dragnet. Many of the convenience store owners were actually American citizens with Palestinian or Yemeni backgrounds. Though some were believed involved in the sale of Sudafed and other medical products that were used to manufacture illegal methamphetamine, the increasingly popular drug known as crystal meth, few were considered potential terrorists.

After learning more about Greenlee's initiative, the FBI agents were angered further when they found that the names of many suspects had been provided to the federal prosecutors by the police department in the small town of Byhalia, whose source was a lone and dubious "confidential informant."

Acting on the source's information, nearly eighty grand jury subpoenas were issued to the Arab Americans. The convenience store owners suffered other adversities. The U.S. Attorney's Office called for tax investigations of many individuals who had never been suspected of any illegal activity.

Arguments ensued between the FBI and Greenlee's office, and the FBI agents eventually challenged decisions made by three men who would later have critical roles in the Scruggs case: Greenlee, Hailman, and Dawson.

In a confidential report drafted in September 2004 by Hal Neilson, the supervisory senior resident agent in charge of the Oxford office, and endorsed by four of his agents, the U.S. Attorney's Office in Oxford was accused of deceit and excessive zeal. Neilson's report said, "It was determined through conversations with DEA and IRS-CID agents that the only individuals targeted by the CSI (Convenience Store Initiative) were of middle eastern descent and the only apparent nexus for investigation was ethnicity."

According to the document, when the FBI pointed out, in one meeting with the prosecutors, that the initiative had ignored federal "restrictions regarding the targeting of U.S. citizens," Hailman had waved off the claim and said these restrictions "did not apply" to the U.S. Attorney's Office. The report, which was sent to FBI director Robert S. Mueller, also compained that Dawson had tried to base a grand jury probe on a preliminary DEA inquiry that never resulted in a formal investigation.

"Out of an abundance of caution and in the interest of insuring the civil rights of U.S. persons," the Oxford FBI agents asked for legal guidance "regarding this situation."

The report lay fallow for months.

In the meantime, the U.S. Attorney's Office opened its own investigation of Neilson, the top FBI agent in Oxford, in connection with his role in a partnership that owned a building that became the local office for the bureau. Although no formal charges were brought against Neilson at the time, he was accused of hiding his financial interest in the building.

Neilson's supervisors subsequently took him off several high-level cases. In March 2006, Neilson filed a second report with the special agent in charge of the FBI in Mississippi appealing for personal safeguards through provisions of the federal Whistleblower Protection Act.

Knowledge of the feud was quietly confined to the FBI and the federal prosecutors, who had their own office across town. But it simmered.

The dispute would be deepened by the handling of the Scruggs investigation, and ultimately the two offices would become locked in a miniature version of the nuclear age theory of "mutually assured destruction," in which fear of retaliation prevents one power with nuclear capability from deploying atomic arsenals against another. In this case, Neilson was being secretly threatened with indictment at the same time he was prepared to level charges of misconduct against the prosecutors. Yet neither side seemed ready to pull the trigger.

. . .

Determined to keep the Oxford FBI office in the dark in the Scruggs case, Greenlee, Hailman, and Dawson drove to Jackson to meet secretly with the state supervisors of the FBI.

While bypassing the Oxford FBI, the prosecutors were taking the explosive case to FBI personnel in another federal court district where agents had investigated the Paul Minor case and were still smarting over the failure of the U.S. Attorney's Office in Jackson to seek an indictment against Scruggs.

The Oxford prosecutors explained that they wanted "absolute operational security," an undercover effort that would prevent the Oxford FBI from knowing about an investigation in their own backyard. This was, after all, a case involving a lawyer with a national reputation whose brother-in-law was a powerful U.S. senator.

The Jackson FBI unit detailed Bill Delaney, an agent who had already been working on a criminal case in North Mississippi involving a failed beef processing plant that had cost the state more than $50 million. During the course of the investigation, Delaney had become a familiar figure in the U.S. Attorney's Office in Oxford, so it was thought no one would suspect a thing.

Later, two other federal prosecutors, Bob Norman and David Sanders, would be brought into the investigation, along with other FBI agents.

For several months, utter secrecy was stressed. Since the investigation needed a code word, Dawson decided to call it Operation Benchmark. Despite these efforts, word of an investigation involving prominent figures raced up and down Justice Department channels between Mississippi and Washington. Although Operation Benchmark was never formally compromised, its secrets had begun to seep out.

In the beginning, it seemed that Operation Benchmark was being governed by Murphy's Law, the old proposition that if anything can go wrong, it will, indeed, go wrong.

Using his own equipment, Judge Lackey tried to record a telephone conversation with Balducci in April, but failed to capture anything other than his own preamble, in which he introduced himself, gave the date, and explained whom he would be talking with on the tape. Otherwise there was static and an unhelpful silence.

Bill Delaney had technical skills and state-of-the-art acoustical devices developed at the FBI center in Quantico, Virginia, so he utilized his own know-how. Delaney met several times with Lackey and established rapport with the judge. At his request, Lackey initiated another call to Balducci—which was successfully recorded—to say that a hearing had been set in the Jones case. Lackey pointed out that he had not yet seen any language from Balducci that could be included in an order. (A document like this was important to begin developing a criminal case.) Balducci told Lackey the Scruggs Katrina Group had decided not to seek a summary judgment in the case and preferred that the case be sent to arbitration. Following the judge's wishes, Balducci said he would fax a proposed order compelling arbitration.

(Murphy's Law would reassert itself. Though the prosecutors believed the original text of that order came from Scruggs's partner Sid

Backstrom, they could never find a trace of the document in the memory of Backstrom's computer.)

On May 4, the investigation finally picked its first fruit. It came in a brief call in which Lackey acknowledged that he had received Balducci's draft.

"That was just some thoughts, ideas, and suggestions that I thought I'd put on paper," Balducci said. "To see if His Honor thought that would look like something he might be interested in."

"It does," Lackey said. "It looks good." He suggested that Balducci meet with him the following week.

Delaney was hiding nearby when Balducci arrived at Judge Lackey's office, and the FBI listening devices were up and running. Lackey betrayed nothing of the trap that had been set; he carried off the deception as if he were a veteran from the cast at Old Vic playhouse. He even had a cheery greeting for Balducci: "Tim-o-fus!" Lackey liked to toy with names. Sometimes he called the younger lawyer "Baldooch," attempting to put an Italian flourish on his pronunciation. The judge occasionally gave odd twists to his own name: "Lacking Style" or "Lackenstein."

The pair began with a rambling conversation about the legal profession in Mississippi. Though his practice was largely based on plaintiffs' cases, Balducci fell back on his ingratiating manner with the conservative judge by criticizing excesses by the plaintiffs' bar. He described a period when he represented clients in the Fen-phen litigation as "probably the worst time of my life practicing law," and observed that abuses by others in the handling of these cases had led to the move to put limits on damages. Lackey grunted his approval.

Balducci bubbled enthusiastically about the progress of his new firm. Without repeating his offer to give the judge "of counsel" status, Balducci talked of his efforts to line up others. So far, he said, he had enlisted several former judges and public officials and found office space in Oxford.

So many attorneys were moving to Oxford, the judge said, "It's gonna be Lawyersville."

Eventually, it was Lackey who turned to the heart of the matter: the order compelling arbitration in the Jones case. "I'm convinced this thing is going to go to the Supreme Court," Lackey said.

Balducci said he doubted the case would go that far because Johnny Jones was "posturing" for a settlement. The Jackson lawyer was "in a bad way" financially, he claimed. "He's doing back channels, trying to do everything he can to get this thing settled and try to get 'em to pay. And they've offered him a damn big pot of money, and, you know, right now he won't take it."

"What kind of offer have they made him?" Lackey asked.

"They've offered him three million."

"Good lord!"

"They've offered him three million dollars. He wants six."

"What created the rift between them?" the judge asked. "Did Jones just not work?"

Balducci minimized Jones's contribution to the Scruggs Katrina Group. "I guess it sounds like I'm being an advocate when I say this, but, shit, he's the only one that ain't happy." He characterized Jones as a lawyer who "always had a real inflated idea about his own value and worth. His pride in authorship of writings and things like that."

He suggested that Jones had no real claim. When the Katrina group was formed, Balducci explained, "They said, look, we're gonna go sue the shit out of State Farm and whoever else ain't paid" on the Gulf Coast. "We don't know if we're going to be successful or not, and we don't know whose contributions are gonna be the most successful. We don't know if politics is gonna be the most important, if elbow grease is gonna be the most important, if finance in the litigation is gonna to be the most important, if dumb luck's gonna be. What we're gonna do, the five firms sitting here, we gonna agree, at the end of the day, we're gonna split the money up rather than trying to set percentages on the front end. These five law firms agreed: We'll see when the money hits, and we'll decide. And if four out of five of us agree on it, then that's fair. That's what they did."

Lackey prodded him with monosyllables. "Yeah . . . Yeah."

"So anyway, at the end of the day, when the Katrina group sat down and said: You know, here's what we think, Johnny. We think you're entitled to X percentage, and he went off the reservation. He just said: No, hell no. That's not enough. I'm not gonna take that. Then he started all this business about suing under the agreement."

Balducci continued: "I don't know what you think from looking at it. But, hell, I think the agreement's pretty clear that it ought to be arbitrated, judge. What do you think?"

"It does," Lackey agreed. "It looks like that's what they agreed to." Referring to Balducci's proposed draft of an order, Lackey laughed and said, "I'm not questioning your ability to put it on paper."

"Listen," Balducci responded, "that's just something to look at."

For the first time, Lackey embraced the idea of issuing the order on behalf of Scruggs.

"If they are satisfied with this order . . ."

"Yes sir."

"Are they?"

"That is perfectly in line with what their best-case scenario is," Balducci assured him.

"I want to be certain that you're gonna get credit where credit is due."

A grateful Balducci gushed thanks. "My relationship with Dick is such that he and I can talk very privately about these kind of matters, and I have fullest confidence that if the court is inclined to rule in favor, everything will be good."

The judge offered a note of caution. "You're confident that our conferences are . . ."

Balducci finished the sentence for him. "Yes sir. I'm one hundred percent confident that everything is in confidence."

Lackey asked if Don Barrett, one of the members of the group, knew about the approach Balducci had made. Lackey knew Barrett slightly. "Barrett knows nothing about any of this," Balducci told the judge. "The only person in the world outside of me and you that had discussed this is me and Dick. They ain't but three people in the world that have had this conversation, and two of 'em are in this room."

Balducci elaborated on his relationship with Scruggs. "He and I— how shall I say it—over the last five or six years, there are bodies buried that he and I know where they are. And my trust in him and his in mine, I'm sure are the same."

Lackey laughed. "Well, that's good."

After a few minutes, as Balducci prepared to go, he talked of his pride in his twin sons, and of the way things seemed to be working out for him professionally. "I'm having a great life right now, judge. I'm blessed, I tell you."

"That is so good, Tim."

As soon as Balducci departed, Lackey called the FBI agent. "William," the judge said, "this is Lackey. The fella has just left, and it's interesting what he said. I'm not sure of your opinion what's the next step I should take."

The FBI wanted Lackey to pursue his talks with Balducci. His ex parte contact with the judge had been improper, but stronger evidence was needed to establish a criminal case. Lackey tried a couple of times to call Balducci and failed to reach him. The judge persisted. When he finally found Balducci, he announced himself as "Lackenstein" calling.

Balducci apologized for failing to return the judge's earlier calls; he seemed to be cautious about pushing the case further.

But Lackey had been instructed to link Scruggs more firmly to the request. So he told Balducci, "You know, I never have been involved in anything like this and I guess I just need reassurance."

"Yes sir."

"I know you told me this, and I'm satisfied with it," the judge said. "But I just want to hear you say it again, I guess. You and Scruggs the only ones know anything about this?"

"Absolutely, judge," Balducci replied, repeating that only "three folks in this world know that I've even seen you. And it's me and you and him. And that's it."

"Thank you," Lackey said. "That's good."

Suddenly, Balducci began to retreat. "Listen," he told the judge. "I don't want you to do anything you're uncomfortable with, either. It's one of those situations where, frankly, I think that the law's on our side, and I think probably had I never even approached you, we'd probably had the right result for us on this thing." Balducci stammered and told Lackey again, "I don't want you to do anything you're uncomfortable with. I mean it. I respect you too much for that."

Twice more, Balducci stressed that Lackey should do nothing if he felt troubled.

Still, the judge probed. He asked if Scruggs might someday use Lackey's involvement "for any other purpose."

"No, sir," Balducci said. "He ain't that way, and let me assure you, as I told you the other day: me and Scruggs, there's bodies buried along the roadside between the two of us, and even if he were inclined to such—he couldn't and he wouldn't."

"Well, it's been bothering me somewhat, and I just wanted to be sure that you and I was on the same page."

"Yes, sir. Well, listen again. I don't mean to make you uncomfortable. I certainly don't mean to do anything to make you uncomfortable or to bother you, and like I said, if it's not something that you feel right about then, you know, you do what your heart tells you."

Lackey was uncomfortable. That same day, he composed a brief letter recusing himself from the Jones case. Stating that the other two circuit judges in the district had declined to hear the case, Lackey wrote, "I find that it would be in the best interest of all parties if I also declined to sit, therefore we are requesting the Supreme Court to appoint another judge to hear this case." He faxed copies of the letter to lawyers on the two sides.

That might have been the end of the investigation. Just as Balducci had pulled back from his approach to the judge, Lackey wanted to wash his hands of the unseemly business. He even concocted a reason for pulling out of the case. He told Balducci that he had attended a reception and unwittingly had a conversation with an attorney from Grady Tollison's office, the firm that represented Johnny Jones. It was a lie, but the judge rationalized that Balducci had been lying, too.

Neither side in the Jones case expressed concern over Lackey's decision. Balducci appeared to have been relieved. When the judge told him that he had recused himself, Balducci repeated that he had never wanted to do anything to jeopardize his relationship with his older friend. "I don't want anything in the world to harm you," he said. "It would break my heart if I thought I had put you in a bad position."

Though no one else had been perturbed by Lackey's recusal, federal authorities were upset and determined to keep him actively involved. He was their key asset in the case. The FBI and the U.S. prosecutors felt they had a high-profile personality, Dick Scruggs, on the hook in an egregious attempt to bribe a judge, and they required Lackey's services.

The day after Lackey decided to recuse himself, he tried to call his friend John Hailman, but learned that the prosecutor was out of town. So he called Delaney to tell him the news. The following day the FBI agent was waiting in the judge's office when Lackey returned from lunch.

Delaney appealed to the judge to reconsider. The government had made a major investment in the case, he said, and would be prepared to follow through. But the government needed Lackey's commitment, too, to bring down the plot to pervert justice.

Lackey was not sure about continuing his role as undercover government agent.

When Hailman returned to Oxford in late May, he stopped by Dawson's office and found his colleague and Delaney slumped in their chairs, distressed that Lackey was no longer cooperating. Hailman said he would see what he could do. He called Lackey at his home that night, but the judge was sleeping and had told his wife not to wake him. The following day, Hailman talked with Lackey, who sounded confused. The judge repeated his bogus story about a tainted conversation with someone from Tollison's firm, but he told Hailman he felt he had made a mistake in recusing himself.

Hailman reinforced Lackey's will, rekindling his outrage over what he believed was Scruggs's attempt to subvert the Jones case. The judge was encouraged to renew his conversations with Balducci, to mention Scruggs's name, to lay down enough bait to trap the King of Torts. Before they finished their talk, Lackey agreed to maintain his role in the investigation. A few days later, he made a trip to New Albany to see Balducci.

Their friendship seemed secure. Over lunch at a café at the local livestock auction barn, Judge Lackey listened as Balducci and Steve Patterson and two others connected with their firm talked of the strides they were making. Afterward, Balducci drove Lackey to see their office. The younger lawyer was enthusiastic about his venture and the possibility that he could recruit older men to act "of counsel."

Balducci had no way of knowing it, but the judge was wearing an FBI body wire. Lackey recorded two hours of conversation with their target, but he picked up nothing incriminating. Balducci never mentioned the Jones case.

Murphy's Law still appeared to be at work.

The prosecutors urged Judge Lackey to persevere. On June 1, he met again with Hailman and Dawson. Afterward, Lackey made an entry in the journal they had asked him to keep:

> We finally decided that I should send the attorneys in the case a fax transmission telling them that after I had reconsidered the matter I had decided to get back in the case and let a little time expire to see if Tim would contact me again. I agreed to do that though I doubt he will because I just get the feeling that he realizes he crossed the line. I am sending the attorneys a fax this morning and time will tell if they are still interested in trying to influence me.

On June 4, he sent a formal two-paragraph message to the lawyers in the Jones case. "Gentlemen," he began. "After having time to review some of the cases dealing with recusal and giving consideration to my reason for giving you the previous notice of recusal I have determined that I am obligated to hear the matter . . . I apologize for any inconvenience my actions may have caused either of you."

While Judge Lackey wrestled with indecision over the case, the man who would turn out to be his prey, Dick Scruggs, was dealing with a number of other issues as the summer of 2007 approached, and Johnny Jones's lawsuit did not hold a high priority in Scruggs's mind.

The tone for the period was set when a federal jury in Jackson convicted Scruggs's friend Paul Minor and two state judges of charges that Minor had won favorable rulings in exchange for loans and lines of credit. Scruggs had been a reluctant witness in the case, and the decision marked the end of a protracted effort by the federal government. Earlier trials ended in hung juries, and one of the original defendants, state supreme court justice Oliver Diaz, was acquitted outright despite repeated attempts by the prosecutors to convict him of various charges.

Minor was sentenced to eleven years in prison. Scruggs was troubled by the harsh sentence, but by this time much of his attention focused on other legal, personal, and political pursuits. In retrospect, some of his adventures bore omens as heavy as Minor's conviction.

Even vacations turned perilous. In the company of friends, Dick and Diane had flown commercially because their vacation destination—the Maldives, an island nation off the coast of India—lay beyond the range of Scruggs's Gulfstream. The group planned a diving expedition in seas famous for exotic marine life and underwater majesty. Though Scruggs was drawn to water, his idea of a good time did not involve leisurely hours on the beach. He and Diane had taken up the sport in the years since their income enabled them to use their own boats to sail to favorable destinations. Though Diane qualified as a diver before Dick, he became an aggressive diver who plunged to daring depths, exposing himself to snags and sharks and other dangers. To him, it was far more exciting than mere swimming.

En route, Scruggs scheduled a stop in Southern California to deliver a commencement address at the invitation of Parham Williams, the dean of Chapman University's law school. When Scruggs was a young law student, Williams had been dean at Ole Miss and a progressive force on campus as the school struggled to free itself from the interference by segregationist politicians that nearly cost accreditation during the civil rights era.

Attracting the famed Scruggs was considered a coup for Chapman's law school, in only its tenth year, and more than two thousand guests attended. They heard a message about legal courage and commitment. The school posted one quote from Scruggs as "words of wisdom" on its website: "A lawyer's most precious asset is integrity. You must guard it carefully throughout your career. For it is like a match; once struck, it can never be relit."

Continuing west, the Scruggs party encountered near-disaster in the waters of the Indian Ocean. Jeff Fox, one of Scruggs's friends and an expert diver who had shared many excursions with him, suffered bends and lay near death for nearly two days in a decompression chamber miraculously located on a remote island within reach of their boat. Fox recovered, but Scruggs returned to the United States, sobered and somewhat shaken from the experience, to resume negotiations with insurance companies over Katrina claims.

On the last day of May, Scruggs flew from Oxford to Pascagoula to attend the funeral of Mike Moore's father. While there, the grieving Moore took him aside for a brotherly lecture concerning Dick's growing dependency on drugs. Scruggs's close friends had begun to recognize the problem.

There was also a political diversion on the trip. Scruggs landed in Jackson to meet briefly at the airport's private flight facility with Senator John McCain, his ally from the tobacco wars. Scruggs delivered thousands of dollars of contributions, including $16,000 from members of his family, for McCain's campaign for the Republican presidential nomination. In addition, Scruggs bundled contributions from other grateful lawyers who had profited from the tobacco initiative.

Though he felt a loyalty to McCain, Scruggs also planned to provide support to at least two Democratic candidates, Hillary Clinton and Joe Biden.

While federal investigators were secretly bearing down on him, these few weeks epitomized life in Scruggs's fast lane: transoceanic flights, a major speaking engagement, a brush with death, legal wrangles, and politics at the highest level.

Ever present in the background was the malevolent buzz from Katrina. Scruggs's relentless stalking of the insurance companies brought him into conflict with two statewide elected officials he once supported: Insurance Commissioner George Dale and Attorney General Jim Hood. Both men were running for reelection in 2007, and each felt his political career had been threatened by Scruggs.

The trouble with Dale was predictable. The commissioner had long been considered too cozy with the industry he oversaw. In the previous decade, he had been indicted for making favorable rulings for a health insurer to reward political contributors. At the time, Scruggs gave $5,000 to Dale's defense fund, and later the prosecutor dismissed the indictment. But Scruggs's view soured dramatically when it appeared Dale was siding with insurers in the dispute over Katrina claims.

A hundred days after Katrina struck, Scruggs had a contentious meeting with the insurance commissioner and his deputy, Lee Harrell. He told Dale that Gulf Coast people were now calling him "the commissioner for insurance rather than the commissioner of insurance." He pressed Dale to intervene on behalf of the Katrina victims.

"I want you to champion the cause," Scruggs told him.

"Dickie, I'm not going to do that," Dale responded, saying that some of the claims were not valid.

Scruggs became incensed after Dale called the post-Katrina imbroglio "a six-county problem" that would force insurance rates to go up in the state's other seventy-six counties. Dale and Harrell later insisted that Scruggs was angered because the commissioner refused to allow him to administer a $500 million settlement program to be established with State Farm money.

Whatever his reason, Scruggs left the meeting annoyed. A year later, his irritation boiled over. He felt that Dale took a laissez-faire approach toward the insurance industry, and Scruggs wanted an activist in the office. So he decided to try to drive Dale from the post he had held for eight terms. Before the 2007 campaign was finished, Scruggs committed hundreds of thousands of dollars to the effort. He retained a public relations firm to conduct an all-out assault on Dale that reached its peak in the full-page newspaper advertisement titled "Lipstick on a Pig." In a cartoon, George Dale's bespectacled face, painted with pink lipstick and given porcine ears, appeared on a pig's body with cloven feet. The beast, labeled "Georgie Dale," lounged in a tub, pampered by attendants at a "State Farm Beauty Salon."

Scruggs approved of the "Lipstick on a Pig" idea and paid for the ad, but did not see it before it ran. He thought the pig would symbolize State Farm and didn't realize that Dale's likeness would be used in the caricature. But he laughed anyway when he saw the finished product in the Sunday morning newspaper.

Diane Scruggs was not so amused. She thought the ad in poor taste, and she wondered about her husband's decision to underwrite the anti-Dale campaign. She felt Dick had been unduly impressed by his PR team from Washington. He had bragged of their talents. Some of his advisors were sophisticated practitioners of "black ops," he said, with experience overseas, working on contract for the U.S. government to destroy the credibility of foreign opponents. One of Scruggs's contacts appealed to him precisely because of the whispers about his agency's operations. The head of the group, John Rendon, had been profiled in *Rolling Stone* in 2005 as "The Man Who Sold the War" on Iraq. The article described Rendon as "a secretive and mysterious creature of the Washington establishment" who was "in charge of marketing" the war for the CIA and the Pentagon. Scruggs was intrigued by such credentials.

Dale was already under siege by the state Democratic Party for his endorsement of President George W. Bush in 2004. The Republican governor, Haley Barbour, guaranteed Dale that he would have no primary opposition if he chose to run for reelection as a Republican. But Dale felt confident. Once, he had been reelected despite an indictment, and he had always seemed to win handily. So he told Barbour he preferred to run as a Democrat, failing to reckon with Democratic Party officials who had struck his name from their primary ballot on the grounds of disloyalty. Dale sued to regain a place on the ballot, and a conservative state supreme court justice assigned his challenge to a judge expected to be sympathetic, Henry Lackey. But by the time the case was heard, Dale realized he would lose in the primary and asked permission to run as an independent. Judge Lackey approved Dale's original request and restored his name to the Democratic ballot but said he lacked the authority to give the commissioner independent status.

In August 2007, Dale was dumped, after thirty-two years in office, by Democratic voters. The victor in the primary, an African American candidate named Gary Anderson, benefited from big majorities in predominantly black counties. But Dale blamed his defeat on Scruggs and his "childish" and "hurtful" advertisement. He said he was also victimized by "push polls" underwritten by Scruggs that asked prospective voters such questions as: "Did you know that George Dale has been indicted for bribery? Did you know that George Dale has been in the pockets of the big insurance companies because all the money he takes is from the insurance industry?"

Scruggs's contretemps with Jim Hood seemed more surprising because the first-term attorney general was seen as the lineal descendant of Mike Moore and a beneficiary of Scruggs's generous support in the last election. Despite these connections. Hood was an independent character with a streak of stubbornness.

Before winning office in 2003 to replace Moore, Hood had been the prosecuting attorney in the same North Mississippi district where Judge Lackey held court. He was a bit rough-hewn. With his back-swept pompadour, Hood resembled a country singer, and his twang matched that image. But as a Democratic candidate, he won strong backing from the same wealthy constituency of trial lawyers that, with a few exceptions, had favored Moore for many years. Scruggs could count on access to Hood's office to pitch his case, but he could not always rely on Hood's agreement.

In the first weeks after Katrina effectively destroyed every dwelling that hugged the Mississippi shoreline between Pass Christian and Pascagoula, Scruggs and Hood took compatible courses. Outraged over the failure of insurance companies to settle claims of Gulf Coast residents satisfactorily, both Scruggs and Moore urged the new attorney general to take action. Hood shared their indignation over the insurers' position that the storm destruction had been primarily caused by a surge of water, which was not covered, instead of wind damage, which was included in the insurance contracts.

Hood convened a meeting in his office with Scruggs, Moore, and three other Democrats who had worked closely with the attorney general's office in the past: Danny Cupit, Crymes Pittman, and Bill Liston.

Scruggs came armed with a draft of a complaint he urged Hood to file. Hood asked Cupit to rework Scruggs's language, which resulted in a sweeping civil suit brought by the Mississippi attorney general against the insurance industry and the ambiguities regarding wind and water damage in insurance contracts.

As they left the attorney general's office, Cupit was startled by Hood's admonition that the five lawyers' work on the case should be pro bono—performed without pay for the public good. A few days later, he saw Scruggs, in a television interview, declare that he intended to bring action against State Farm on his own. Cupit wryly concluded that Hood wanted to volunteer Cupit's services pro bono while letting Scruggs collect fees. In fact, Hood was not entirely sure of Scruggs's motives, and he asked Cupit to help him monitor the developing struggle with the insurance companies.

At the same time, Hood had taken evidence given to him by Scruggs, the documents obtained by the Rigsby sisters while working as State Farm claims adjusters, and initiated a criminal investigation of the company. Grand juries were convened in two Mississippi counties, posing the threat of indictments against State Farm officials.

In a twist, the criminal proceedings became an obstacle to a multi-million-dollar settlement the Scruggs Katrina Group had been negotiating. State Farm was ready to settle 640 claims for $89 million, with another $26.5 million going to the lawyers' group. (The $26.5 million would become the source of contention with Johnny Jones.) But the company was unwilling to sign off on the agreement as long as the criminal case remained outstanding.

When Hood refused to drop his investigation. Scruggs grew apoplectic. In a move later characterized by his friends as an "afternoon decision" driven by a large dose of his painkilling medication, Scruggs offered to pay $500,000 to Steve Patterson and Tim Balducci to get the attorney general on board.

Scruggs figured the pair would have difficulty influencing the obstinate attorney general. Sure enough, Patterson and Balducci were able to arrange one inconsequential dinner, which Hood grudgingly agreed to attend, at a Jackson restaurant. They got nowhere with him. But Scruggs had actually hired the pair because he believed Patterson could use his friendship with Danny Cupit, Hood's advisor, to persuade Hood to drop the criminal investigation.

Scruggs and Cupit should have been natural allies. They were progressive Democrats, successful trial lawyers, the same age. Yet a profound level of distrust existed between the two men. Cupit considered Scruggs devious and quick to stray from a common cause in order to operate on his own. On the other hand, Scruggs thought Cupit part of a capital city cabal that disliked him. Because of his family ties to their political archenemy, Trent Lott, Scruggs felt Cupit's crowd had never fully accepted him as a real Democrat. The clique included the other advisors to the attorney general: Liston, the lawyer who had drawn up charges against Scruggs in 1992, and Pittman, a member of Scruggs's team in the tobacco litigation. Scruggs also knew Cupit was close to Grady Tollison, the Oxford litigator who was becoming one of Scruggs's fiercest antagonists.

But as he parsed through all of these associations, Scruggs had not forgotten that Cupit's circle sometimes widened to take in people like Patterson, who now worked with Scruggs on political issues. Scruggs also remembered that it had been Cupit who helped intercede, on Scruggs's behalf, with Patterson in the 1992 case drummed up by the dark side of the Force. To call upon that connection for help fifteen years later, Scruggs agreed to pay a half-million dollars.

Patterson and Cupit's relationship went back nearly forty years, to the time when they were young men involved in Democratic politics. Both men had served as state chairman of the party and worked together on legislative issues and other matters not so public. They were quintessential inside operators.

As Scruggs tried to wind up negotiations with State Farm, Patterson called Cupit regularly to promote Scruggs's position. Patterson acknowledged that Scruggs had assured him "a piece of the settlement"—even though Patterson was not a lawyer and, thus, was ineligible for any part of a contingency fee. He told Cupit, "Scruggs still thinks you're trying to elbow in on the fee." As a result, Scruggs didn't want to deal with Cupit directly, and he hired Patterson to be his middleman.

The dynamics of the State Farm case seemed to change from day to day, but the company's agreement with SKG was contingent upon Hood abandoning the criminal investigation. Scruggs grew emotional over the prospect of a rich settlement, calling for Hood to end the investigation, while telling State Farm that he could not control the attorney general. Meanwhile, Hood complained to associates that he was drawing "friendly fire" from the Scruggs group.

In one conversation with Patterson, Cupit instructed his friend to tell Scruggs to "cool his jets" while Cupit worked to get the attorney general out of the dilemma while retaining for Hood some measure of credit for resolving the State Farm case. Throughout the Christmas season, little progress was made.

In January 2007, Patterson warned Cupit that Scruggs was prepared to deliver an ultimatum to the attorney general. Unless Hood agreed to assure State Farm that there would be no indictments, Scruggs would fall back on a plan conceived by his public relations team. There would be a press conference, attended by several high-ranking public officials—including Senator Lott, who had sued State Farm himself—to endorse a settlement benefiting hundreds of Gulf Coast residents. The group would announce that only Hood stood in the way. The publicity could kill Hood's reelection chances.

The scenario was the subject of a heated discussion in a private room at the Jackson airport in January 2007, involving Hood, Scruggs, Patterson, and Joey Langston (Patterson's former employer who had strong connections to both the attorney general and Scruggs).

Two days later, on January 22, Hood drove to Memphis—the Republican governor had denied him use of a state plane—to meet with three high officials of State Farm. On the way, he talked by cell phone with his staff members about the status of the criminal investigation. He was told by one aide, who had been meeting with a grand jury in Pascagoula, that there was plenty of evidence to support the state's civil action against State Farm, but little to warrant criminal indictments.

During his Memphis talks, Hood first reached a settlement with State Farm on the state's civil case. The company agreed to pay $5 million to the attorney general's office as reimbursement for its expenses in the investigation and to set up an apparatus to deal with unresolved claims that could cost the company as much as $400 million.

Before he left the Tennessee city, Hood also informed State Farm that he would discontinue the criminal case.

This cleared the way for the final settlement of the 640 cases represented by the Scruggs Katrina Group, but the war between Scruggs and State Farm would continue to reverberate throughout the year.

A decade earlier, Scruggs had flirted with trouble by relying on whistle-blowers for information about the tobacco industry. The tactic won his character a role in the movie *The Insider*, but it also resulted in lawsuits and threats of prosecution for using material that had been copied and stolen from a law firm. He knew he had crossed a line and exposed himself to criminal charges, but he felt it was worth the risk.

In the case of the Rigsby sisters, Scruggs tried to inoculate himself against charges that he had purchased stolen material. Rather than buying documents, he hired the two women as consultants when they lost their jobs as adjusters with E. A. Renfroe and Company in Alabama. They were fired after they told their employers of a weekend in early June 2006 in which they downloaded hundreds of pages of computerized State Farm files in a "data dump."

They had come to Scruggs months earlier, and he knew he had dramatic material in his hands. He shared it with state and federal authorities, then the public. One of his gifts as a plaintiff's attorney was an ability to drive his message across to journalists. While others might be uncommunicative with the press, Scruggs invariably responded to interview requests and cultivated friendships with reporters. He often proved a reliable source for what is known in the trade as "good copy." Because he understood the tactics that worked with journalists, he was often able to plant useful stories in the hands of well-known, legitimate reporters.

Drawing upon his wiles, Scruggs set up interviews with the Rigsby sisters. One story struck a raw nerve with State Farm. Brian Ross, an ABC correspondent who had developed Katrina stories with Scruggs's assistance, featured the women in an exposé on the popular investigative show *20/20*. Wearing State Farm jackets on camera, the sisters accused the company of doctoring engineering reports.

A week later, the Renfroe company, which provided adjusters for State Farm, sued the Rigsbys in federal court in Birmingham. The case was assigned to a conservative judge who had been put on the bench by President Ronald Reagan in 1982. Judge William M. Acker was eighty years old but still active, and his views tended to reflect the farthest shores of the right wing in America.

Early in his tenure as a federal judge, Acker had been the subject of controversy when he was rebuked by a federal appellate court for his handling of a criminal case involving Alabama members of the Ku Klux Klan. The appeals court found that Acker had ruled improperly when he ordered the acquittal of a Klansman convicted by a jury, dismissed the indictment of another, and suppressed critical evidence against other Klan defendants.

In 2000, Acker summarily dismissed a First Amendment case brought by two students who said they were punished for refusing to say the Pledge of Allegiance because they believed it constituted "idol worship" and violated their religious beliefs. Five years later, he declared that he would no longer consider students from Yale Law School, his own alma mater, for clerkships because Yale had limited campus access for military recruiters.

After the Renfroe company, working in concert with State Farm, demanded the return of the stolen documents, Judge Acker obliged with a December 8, 2006, injunction ordering the Rigsby sisters and their attorneys to hand over the material and to cease disclosing information taken from the papers.

There were two loopholes in Acker's order. He excluded "law enforcement officials" from the injunction, and the order did not take effect for three days. In the interim, Scruggs called Jim Hood and had his set of papers sent to the Mississippi attorney general before the December 11 deadline.

Acker was outraged by Scruggs's action, and the mood of Scruggs's other adversaries darkened after they learned that his Katrina group had sponsored a television commercial on the Gulf Coast containing a double-barreled blast at Insurance Commissioner George Dale and State Farm. In the commercial, Kerri Rigsby told viewers, "I used to work for State Farm. I know firsthand how far they will go to avoid paying your claim. Take it from me, you need a lawyer, not the Insurance Commissioner's mediation program . . . Don't give in to big insurance."

In June 2007, Scruggs and his son, Zach, spent two days in Washington speaking individually with a bipartisan list of senators—many of them members of the Judiciary Committee—in favor of legislation to raise the salaries of federal judges. The informal lobbying—suggested by other Mississippi lawyers as a legitimate way to help the judges—served as an opportunity for Scruggs to renew his Washington contacts. On the way back to Mississippi, Senator Lott hitched a ride on his brother-in-law's jet. Although Lott had reached a settlement with State Farm in April over the loss of his home to Katrina, the senator was still steaming with indignation that was almost Democratic and populist in its intensity.

The day after Scruggs returned from his mission on behalf of federal judges, he was hit with a criminal contempt citation from Judge Acker for his "brazen disregard" of the injunction. There was further irony. Alice Martin, the Republican U.S. attorney for North Alabama who would be accused of political motivation in connection with the conviction of Don Siegelman, the former Democratic governor of Alabama, declined to prosecute Scruggs. Refusing to give up, Judge Acker appointed two Birmingham attorneys as special prosecutors.

Scruggs countered by hiring a prominent criminal defense lawyer from San Francisco, John Keker, to represent him. Keker had been recommended to Scruggs by Lowell Bergman, the former CBS producer whose work with tobacco industry whistle-blower Jeff Wigand had led to a friendship with Scruggs. Neither Scruggs nor Keker knew it at the time, but the association would lead to countless hours together in the coming months.

Judge Acker was not the only federal judge giving Scruggs difficulty. Over the past year Scruggs had been dealing with a succession of adverse rulings by U.S. District Judge L. T. Senter, who had been given jurisdiction over hundreds of Katrina-based lawsuits pending in Gulfport, Mississippi.

In one of Senter's crucial decisions, he effectively ruled that insurance companies were not liable for flood damage during the hurricane. After hearing a case brought by Scruggs on behalf of a Pascagoula couple, Paul and Julie Leonard, Senter limited their recovery to $3,000. The Leonards had sought $130,000 from Nationwide Mutual Insurance Company.

Senter, who heard the case without a jury, upheld the insurer's contention that water had caused most of the damage. His verdict was hailed as a major victory for the insurance industry. It was a setback for Scruggs, but he insisted he was pleased that Senter had upheld the insurance company's liability for any wind damage. "We didn't bring home the full measure of damages for the Leonard family," he said. "But they cleared a big path for all the other homeowners on the Gulf Coast."

Another Senter ruling made it more difficult for Scruggs to consolidate Katrina cases into mass tort actions. At one point, it appeared he would be forced to try each claimant's case individually, a task that could last a lifetime.

Still, Scruggs and other members of his Katrina group battled to reach mass settlements with the industry, and by the summer of 2007, they had succeeded in obtaining agreements with Nationwide, Allstate, and Met Life that covered several hundred other families on the Gulf Coast.

The pace was furious. To Scruggs, it now seemed inconceivable that he had ever contemplated retirement.

Through the summer of 2007, a time of languor and oppressive heat in Mississippi, there was little progress by the federal investigators in developing a case against Scruggs. The sun beat against the pavement in visible waves, and the courthouse square in Oxford seemed to lie stricken under the assault. Only a few hardy shoppers and laborers ventured outside for long periods. Air-conditioning had made the climate more bearable three quarters of a century after Faulkner (who privately deplored the modern contraption for "messing with the weather") had begun his short story "Dry September," with the words "Through the bloody September twilight, aftermath of sixty-two rainless days . . ." The fierceness of the season in the Deep South had not ebbed over the years.

Down the road in Calhoun City, Judge Lackey felt frustrated; he thought of himself "like a lost ball in tall weeds." He had effectively placed his life under the control of federal authorities. They had become his handlers, and he had been reduced to the role of spy. Yet there was little about the situation that seemed romantic.

The federal agents running the Lackey operation were discouraged, too. No incriminating evidence had been turned up since the judge had tried to take himself out of the case in May. They encouraged Lackey to keep trying. Finally, on the afternoon of August 9—less than forty-eight hours after the defeat of his friend, Insurance Commissioner

George Dale, in the Democratic primary—Lackey resumed his efforts. He placed a call to Tim Balducci and opened the conversation on a mirthful note.

"I'm looking for the piss ant," the judge began, making a joking reference to the dispute in Balducci's home town over Steve Patterson's lack of a law degree.

"Well, the piss ant ain't here right now," Balducci replied, laughing.

"You stirred up a wasp's nest."

"These sons of bitches stirred it up," Balducci said. "All I've done is respond to it. There's a lot of things I can take, and I can take all the slings and arrows, and I can take all the talking and the backbiting and all the gossiping around the courthouses. But when you haul off and start writing letters to the bar, and trying to get me in trouble with the way I practice my living and feed my children, that I take awful seriously."

As the judge had suspected nearly three months earlier, Balducci had no further interest in pushing for a decision from him in *Jones v. Scruggs*. It was time for the judge to revive the subject.

After a bit more banter, Lackey asked if Balducci was in a position to talk confidentially. Assured that he was, the judge asked, "You think Dickie wants this thing in mediation—I mean arbitration?"

"Yes, sir. That's his number one goal."

"Well, I just wondered if he wanted me to take care of it somehow."

"Yes, sir. That'd be terrific. If that's how you sees [*sic*] it after you've taken a look at it."

"I've got it in the bosom of the court now," the judge said. "I don't know him, and of course I trust you."

"Yes, sir," Balducci said, ever obsequious. "The only concern I think anybody had after the hearing was Johnny Jones blowing his snot bubbles and stuff. Everybody was afraid he might pull on somebody's heart strings. But, you know, I think this is one of those where it has the added benefit of being right. If you look at the agreement, hell, I think they're right. So all they want is for the thing to get kicked to arbitration."

"As long as they feel comfortable with that," Lackey said, "rather than in the court . . ."

"That's what they want."

"All right," Lackey agreed.

"That'd be terrific, judge."

The conversation constituted more improper talk with a judge. Still, there was no mention of a bribe, no quid pro quo, and until that was offered, no real crime existed.

Lackey's subsequent attempts to reach Balducci during the month failed. *This show has got to stop,* the judge thought to himself. *I have been living with this thing since March and I want to bring it to a head one way or another.*

To buck up Lackey's spirits, the FBI praised him for his value to the investigation, for bringing Balducci's overture on behalf of Scruggs to their attention. It was not the first time that Scruggs had been in the crosshairs of the FBI. They had been unable to secure an indictment against him in the Paul Minor case on the Gulf Coast, but they were prepared to try again. They encouraged Lackey to keep trying, too. It would be helpful, they said, if Lackey arranged another meeting with Balducci. And it would be decisive if money were mentioned explicitly. Otherwise, the case would go nowhere, and all of Lackey's agony over the past six months would have been for nothing.

Suddenly Lackey grew very uncomfortable with the role he had been playing. He was, after all, a god-fearing deacon, and the thought of asking for money flew against his nature. He didn't want to do it. And even if he did, he still privately hoped that his young friend might say that it had all been a terrible misunderstanding. Then that would be the end of it.

Lackey was ambivalent over continuing, but the FBI prevailed upon him to make one more effort. The judge called Balducci's office in New Albany and learned he was in Washington for a couple of days. He hung up, cleared his throat, and with fresh resolve prepared to pursue him further. Speaking into the FBI's recording device, Lackey set the stage:

"I could not reach Mr. Balducci on his phone at his office, was advised he was in Washington, D.C., and would not be back until Thursday, which is day after tomorrow. I'm going to attempt to reach Mr. Balducci on his cell phone, and, again, I'm going to attempt to make a recorded telephone call to him from my office number. The time is approximately three minutes until five p.m. on this, the eleventh day of September."

Instead of talking with Balducci, the judge got his cell phone's voice mail. Even as he spun one of the last strands in his web, Lackey could not resist another joke based on the recent news that Vice-President Cheney had inadvertently wounded a hunting companion.

"Baldooch," Lackey said, "I know you're running around those ivory towers. If you run into Cheney, tell him I'm going to pass on the duck hunt."

Then the judge became more serious. "I do need to talk to you about this matter that we're both concerned about. I've got something I want to run by you and see what you think about it."

A week later, Lackey finally found Balducci by telephone at his New Albany office. On a wry note, he inquired, "You made it back from the ivory towers?"

"I have," Balducci said. "I been up there tending to good government, judge."

They joshed with each other for a moment more, then Lackey lowered his voice and asked, "Are you where you can talk?"

"Yes, sir, I am."

"Well, I've got something to say to you, and it may shock you," the judge said. He sighed audibly and continued. "I've been thinking about this thing with Mr. Scruggs and them, and I want to help 'em any way I can." He drew a deep breath again. "I don't know what my future holds. I don't know how long I'm gonna be able to hang in here and do what I need to do. What I'm gonna say is what I've never said to anybody before. I want you to understand that because I trust you."

Balducci, who had been punctuating each of Lackey's sentences with "yes, sir" and "right," underscored the expression of trust. "You can. You well should, judge. This is, as I like to say, dead man stuff."

Lackey snorted a laugh and began to talk elliptically about his target. "I don't know him, you know, and I don't know what his reaction might be one way or the other." To be sure Balducci understood, Lackey added, "When I say 'his,' I'm talking about Mr. Scruggs." This introduced Scruggs's name to the FBI recording.

"Right," Balducci said.

"I know he is a very powerful man, and apparently extremely sharp. Sometime I'd like to meet him. But let me cut to the chase."

"Sure," Balducci said, who employed another idiom. "Put the corn on the ground."

"If I help 'em, would they help me?"

"I think, no question that would happen. Yes, sir."

"We'd have to work something out down the road," the judge said. "But I think that's absolutely in the cards."

"Listen," Balducci said, taking charge of the situation. "I'm the one that needs to handle that."

Fumbling for words, Lackey said he did not want Steve Patterson brought into the plot. He trusted only Balducci. He implied that some action needed to be taken soon because Grady Tollison was putting pressure on him to resolve the Jones case. "Talk to your man. Whatever you need to do. Holler back at me."

"I can tell you I know that I can get that done," Balducci replied quickly. "I mean, you wanna just leave that to my discretion? Or do you wanna give me some kind of ideas of what I need to do?"

"I'm not talking about a mountain," the judge said. "Just kind of help me over a little hump I've got."

"I gotcha."

"It's my making, my hump, and I can't blame anybody else but me." Suggesting that he had fallen into hard financial straits, he talked wistfully of his country practice of law, the job he had given up to become a judge.

"That's all part of the world," said Balducci. "I understand all of that, judge. And that's no problem." He said he would drive over to see Lackey before the week was out. If he could get a favorable ruling for Scruggs, whatever the cost, it might provide the binding for a stronger relationship between the Patterson-Balducci operation, in its infancy, and one of the most recognized trial lawyers in the land.

Listening to the conversation afterward, the federal prosecutors in Oxford felt a surge of accomplishment. This was the breakthrough they had worked toward for months. The old judge had laid down the bait, and his young friend had taken it.

The development was particularly satisfying to Tom Dawson. He had been contemptuous of Scruggs even before the investigation began. Now, with Hailman's retirement, Dawson's title as first assistant U.S. attorney effectively put him in charge. The sting operation had the potential to turn into the dream of any prosecutor: building an ironclad case against a famous figure.

A decade earlier, Dawson had been on the team of independent prosecutor Kenneth Starr during the Whitewater investigation that led to President Clinton. Dawson had been recruited from his job in Oxford to take a temporary position, and he spent eighteen months on the case. He helped edit the papers used in the impeachment, yet it was Starr and his chief deputies who got the headlines, and Dawson returned quietly to the U.S. Attorney's Office where he had spent most of his career. Now only a year from retirement himself, Dawson saw the Scruggs case as his crowning achievement.

"Zeus" ascending—a young Dick Scruggs, in flight gear, as a navy pilot.

"If I get the same response . . . I won't call again."—After being rebuffed in previous attempts to get a date with Diane Thompson, Dick Scruggs persevered and eventually married her.

"The King of Torts" and his court—Dick Scruggs (*seated, center*) surrounded by Democratic state office holders following 1995 elections. They include Lieutenant Governor Ronnie Musgrove, who would become governor (*seated, left*); Attorney General Mike Moore (*standing, far left*); auditor Steve Patterson (*standing, second from left*); and insurance commissioner George Dale (*standing, far right*).

The aftermath of the "Mardi Gras massacre"—The reconstituted Scruggs law firm, featuring (*from left*) Dick Scruggs, Sid Backstrom, and Zach Scruggs.

"To hobnob with celebrities"—On the high seas off New Zealand, Dick and Diane Scruggs host the sailing champion Dennis Conner on their yacht, *Emerald Key*, during the America's Cup competition in 2000.

"Commander for life."—U.S. Senator Trent Lott not only rose to become leader of Senate Republicans, he also presided over a vast network of his Sigma Nu fraternity brothers.

"This thing's heading our way"—Despite efforts to batten down his house against the storm, Scruggs saw his mansion on the beachfront in Pascagoula torn apart by Hurricane Katrina in 2005.

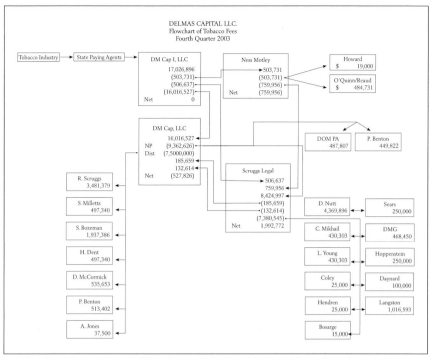

DELMAS CAPITAL LLC.
Flowchart of Tobacco Fees
Fourth Quarter 2003

| Tobacco Industry | → | State Paying Agents |

DM Cap I, LLC
17,026,896
(503,731)
(506,637)
(16,016,527)
Net   0

Ness Motley
503,731
(503,731)
(759,956)
Net   (759,956)

Howard
$ 19,000

O'Quinn/Reaud
$ 484,731

DM Cap, LLC
16,016,527
NP   (9,362,626)
Dist   (7,5000,000)
185,659
132,614
Net   (527,826)

DOM PA
487,807

P. Benton
449,822

Scruggs Legal
506,637
759,956
8,424,997
(185,659)
(132,614)
(7,380,545)
Net   1,992,772

R. Scruggs
3,481,379

S. Milletts
497,340

S. Bozeman
1,937,386

H. Dent
497,340

D. McCormick
535,653

P. Benton
513,402

A. Jones
37,500

D. Nutt
4,369,896

Sears
250,000

C. Mikhail
430,303

DMG
468,450

L. Young
430,303

Hoppenstein
250,000

Coley
25,000

Daynard
100,000

Hendren
25,000

Langston
1,016,593

Bosarge
15,000

Flow chart of tobacco fees—To follow the money distributed by Scruggs from tobacco litigation, one must navigate this complicated trail that leads (*lower right*) to quarterly payments of $468,450 to P. L. Blake (through DMG) and $1,016,593 to Joey Langston.

Claiming "reprehensible conduct" by Scruggs—Grady Tollison, a rival of Scruggs's with offices on Oxford's square, attended a press conference where Scruggs's indictment was explained.

"They believe I'm the weak link."—Sid Backstrom, who resisted early efforts by the prosecutors to cop a plea, heads toward federal court to plead guilty.

"So you were judge, jury, and executioner."—Charles Merkel, one of Scruggs's fiercest opponents, accused Scruggs of making improper and unilateral decisions that affected his former partners—and Merkel's clients.

Ghosts of Mississippi—Bobby DeLaughter, portrayed by Alec Baldwin as the hero in Rob Reiner's 1996 film dealing with the conviction of civil rights–era assassin Byron De La Beckwith, walks from federal court twelve years later following his own arraignment in a judicial bribery case.

"I'd cut my own throat for you."—Even as he assured Joey Langston and Steve Patterson that he would protect them, former Hinds County district attorney Ed Peters prepared to give evidence against them to federal authorities.

"A Greek tragedy."— U.S. attorney Jim Greenlee gave a classical description to his account at an Oxford press conference of Dick Scruggs's involvement in a judicial bribery case.

"A monster that we were dealing with."—State judge Henry Lackey, the key witness in the case against Scruggs, referred to him repeatedly as a "monster."

"You've had your chance to respond."— U.S. district judge Neal Biggers, who presided over much of the case against Scruggs, was known as "Maximum Neal"—even by his admirers—for his stern rulings.

"You would be out on your ass."—Johnny Jones, once a partner in Scruggs Katrina Group, was threatened with expulsion from the legal team and subsequently sued Scruggs and others.

"I've taken care of my problem."—Joey Langston (*left*) decided he had no choice but to plead guilty. After receiving a three-year prison sentence, he walked from the federal courthouse with his attorney Tony Farese.

"An embarrassed man."—Steve Patterson on his way to another court appearance in Oxford.

The Insider—On the set of Michael Mann's 1999 film, shot in part in the Scruggs's Pascagoula home, life imitates Hollywood as Scruggs, *60 Minutes* producer Lowell Bergman, and CBS correspondent Mike Wallace—all portrayed as characters in the movie—enjoy a laugh.

"This ain't my first rodeo."—Attorney Tim Balducci insisted that he had been involved with Scruggs in other scandalous activities.

A "childish" and "hurtful" advertisement— Insurance Commissioner George Dale blamed his defeat in the 2007 election on this full-page ad, placed in Mississippi newspapers by Scruggs.

"He has so much to offer society."— Robert Khayat (*center*), chancellor of Ole Miss, annoyed Judge Biggers when he suggested leniency for Scruggs (*right*). Before the case developed, the two old friends from the Gulf Coast met with a visiting Dan Rather on the Ole Miss campus.

"He knows a lot of people."—P. L. Blake, one of the stealthiest players in a political organization that has had influence in Mississippi for decades.

"Their family could not survive without him for a decade."—After urging her husband to plead guilty to a lesser charge rather than face the possibility of a harsh sentence at the end of a trial, Amy Scruggs, six months pregnant, hosted a farewell party for Zach before he left for prison. Their daughter, Augusta, plays at the left.

"I had to stand there . . . and take an ass-whipping."—On his way to sentencing in federal court, Dick Scruggs is accompanied by his chief attorney, John Keker (*left*), son Zach (*rear*), and wife, Diane.

He had grown up in Meridian, Mississippi, where his father served at a naval air station. Law had not been in his future plans when he attended Southwestern at Memphis and graduated from the University of Southern Mississippi. Dawson majored instead in chemistry, but took the law school admission test as a lark with his fraternity brother Sam Davis. They both wound up at the Ole Miss law school, and forty years later both were back in Oxford—Dawson as a federal prosecutor and Davis as dean of the law school.

Dawson's first job had been with the Meridian law firm of Tom Bourdeaux, one of William Winter's closest friends, and Dawson's first brush with serious politics came in support of one of Winter's campaigns. However, Dawson's personal politics grew more conservative over the years. Interviewed for a place at the U.S. Department of Justice during the Nixon administration, Dawson admitted that he had probably "lost a case in every court of record in Mississippi." His prospective employer liked that response, for he felt that good lawyers learned from losing. Dawson spent three years in Washington, specializing in white-collar crime, then came back to Mississippi in 1975 to take a job in the U.S. Attorney's Office in Oxford. Other than his Whitewater assignment, he had been there ever since. He liked the camaraderie, comparing it to a legal *M.A.S.H.* unit, where humor could be found in serious business.

Dawson preferred the role of the "bad cop" in interrogations. He could look intimidating, a bit like a character from the Old West. He was bald, but retained a fringe of long hair that fell close to his neck to complement a closely sculptured beard.

Even with the Scruggs investigation at an early stage, Dawson began preparing for the showdown. He kept separate files for a possible cross-examination of Scruggs or a closing argument at a trial. In his research, he uncovered an item he intended to use. It came from remarks Scruggs had made five years earlier during a panel discussion about legal venues. The event had been sponsored by Prudential Financial, and Scruggs delivered a lecture on his concept of "magic jurisdictions." Describing the convergence of politics and law and how it augured against impersonal corporations, he said:

> The trial lawyers have established relationships with the judges that are elected. They're state court judges; they're populists. They've got large populations of voters who are in on the deal. They're getting their piece in many cases. And so, it's a political force in their jurisdiction, and it's

almost impossible to get a fair trial if you're a defendant in some of these places . . . The cases are not won in the courtroom. They're won on the back roads long before the case goes to trial. Any lawyer fresh out of law school can walk in there and win the case, so it doesn't matter what the evidence or the law is.

Dawson savored the opportunity to challenge Scruggs in the courtroom. As he directed the investigation with deliberate timing, he wanted to be sure that every element was put in its proper place. And useful tidbits kept coming with almost every wiretapped conversation.

Despite Lackey's admonition not to talk of the situation with Steve Patterson, Balducci immediately told his partner of the judge's suggestion of a bribe.

"How much?" Patterson asked.

Balducci said he didn't know yet, but planned to meet with Lackey in a couple of days.

"Find out how much he wants," Patterson instructed his partner.

Fixing the case would be worth the risk if it succeeded in currying favor with Scruggs, because Scruggs represented the font of fresh infusions of money. Lackey's overture had come during a time of growing desperation over the future of their new law firm in New Albany. Though Balducci had spoken confidently to Lackey of the influential connections that he and Patterson had made, of the important names that had been lined up for the firm's letterhead, of his own satisfaction in reaching this plateau in his profession, he and his partner were in financial distress. Their money had virtually run out, squandered on private planes to impress others and payments to secure audiences with potential clients. Even the $500,000 that Scruggs had paid the two men, in $100,000 increments, over the summer for interceding with Attorney General Jim Hood was gone.

Law firms in Mississippi were oozing money. In the wake of the tobacco settlement, literally millions and millions of dollars circulated in the hands of a loose network of lawyers—so much money, in a poor state, that it was crazy. Patterson and Balducci had dreamed of cashing in on a bonanza through Scruggs, but it had not yet worked out that way. Meanwhile, the money that constituted their grubstake had seemed to vanish, and their operating funds were perilously low.

Still, the two men kept up an appearance of stability. Showing no signs of trouble, they flew to Washington and Jackson to make alliances with influence peddlers and lobbyists. They stayed in fine hotels and dined in expensive restaurants. They even traveled, in separate trips, overseas. If they were to share in Scruggs's windfall, it was essential to live like Scruggs.

Scruggs was their ultimate meal ticket. If he could be persuaded to lend his name to their initiatives, it would serve as a message to the world that Patterson and Balducci were members in good standing in the big leagues and legitimate players at the table when the big licks were divided.

So it was vital to stay in Scruggs's good graces, and against that backdrop, Balducci soon paid another call on Judge Lackey.

The conversation between the judge and his friend opened on a strange note. Patterson had undergone surgery the day before to reduce his weight, and Balducci described the procedure in clinical detail. Patterson's health was good, he said, but he had been "grossly obese" for years and hoped to lose one hundred pounds as a result of the operation. The doctors had cut the size of his stomach—"they pinch off a portion of it"—to ensure that he could not eat as much. On doctor's orders, Balducci's partner had been kept on a liquid diet for two weeks prior to the operation. The diet was necessary "to shrink your organs, to shrink your stomach, shrink your liver, your pancreas and your gallbladder and all that" so the surgeons "could get in there and maneuver easier."

"I'll be darned," the judge remarked, amazed at the wonders of modern medicine.

Balducci then waxed philosophical about the essence of law. He said he had once been given a piece of wisdom by Jack Dunbar, the Oxford attorney who represented Scruggs in the Luckey and Wilson cases. "Jack's sort of a scholar and a gentleman of the law, and he told me something that stuck with me. He said: 'The law typically is what it ought to be.' And, you know, I found that to be true."

"Yeah. Yeah," the judge agreed. Then Lackey offered his own curious parable.

"My father-in-law had this old black gentleman that worked for him. He was just like a member of the family, you know. Burley couldn't read and write, and it wasn't his fault. It was the system's fault because he was bright as he could be. They were feeding the hogs one day and Burley asked him, 'Mr. Henry, who named the hog?' And he said, 'Well, Burley, I don't know who named the hog. Why?' And Burley said, 'Well, whoever named him, named him just right 'cause he eats just like one.' "

The two men laughed. They were dancing around the purpose of their meeting, as though neither wanted to bring up an unpleasant subject.

Lackey eventually steered their conversation to the business at hand by thanking Balducci for coming.

"Shoot, Judge, I'm glad to listen," Balducci said, warming to his mission. "You and me, we tight now. There ain't no other way to put it now. We gonna figure out what we need to do here. Ain't no problem. I want you to tell me—because I understood what you said on the phone the other day. You're in a position where you need a little help. I wanna help. But I got to have some kind of parameter to operate in, Judge. I need to know where we are."

"What I need—and it may be more than Mr. Scruggs or whoever would even consider—but to get me over a hump, I need forty," Lackey said.

The judge had chosen the figure on his own. Forty thousand dollars was a substantial amount, but not outlandish. A favorable decision might save Scruggs millions, but the country judge was reluctant to call for a larger payoff for himself. To ask for a million in tribute would put him in the company of high-rolling trial lawyers who dealt with big money, and Lackey had no interest in joining their ranks. So he opted for a reasonable figure. In Mississippi, $40,000 was still more than many people earned in a year.

"You need it pretty soon?" Balducci asked.

Lackey said he faced a deadline for his debts in nine days, on October 1. If it were inconceivable to raise that much, he said, "I could probably get done what I need to get" with a partial payoff. "Then the remainder by the first of November."

Balducci told him it should be no problem, but he needed to figure out a way to get the money to the judge. "Are you gonna have to have it in cash?"

"I would like to have it, Tim."

"Just let me take care of it," Balducci said. "It's fine."

"I don't want a nickel from you," the judge said.

"That's not what it's gonna be. I'm gonna get you the help you need, and we gonna take care of it."

"To show my commitment," the judge said, "just bring me the order that he wants signed, and I'll sign it."

"That's fine. That's fine."

"I've been wishy-washy in this, and other things have been bothering me," Lackey said, moving their intimate talk to his thoughts of retirement.

"I wanna talk to you," Balducci said. "I wanna lay the corn on the ground. What are your plans, Judge? What are you thinking you're going to do? How much time you got left in your term?"

"Three years. But with my health situation, my defibrillator, and my pacemaker, I don't see me going to the end of the term."

Balducci indicated that he understood the politics behind Lackey's decision to resign. The judge would wait until the completion of the 2007 election, coming up in six weeks, in order to ensure that his place on the bench would be filled by an appointment made by Lackey's fellow Republican, Governor Barbour, who was gliding to reelection.

"I really haven't given that much thought, to tell you the truth," Lackey said. "I've been having more physical problems than I'd like to admit. It's impacting a lot of things, and I hate to be in this position."

The judge's words prompted Balducci to return to the idea of bringing Lackey into his firm. "I'm not encouraging you," the younger lawyer said. "I'm not doing anything. I'm not trying to sway you. I'm not doing any of that. I'm just asking, as I have said before. When you make the decision for yourself, for your health or for whatever reason—that you're tired of fooling with it and you're tired of living the rat race of it—when you make the decision to lay down that gavel, I want you to join our firm, if you will, of counsel." Balducci masked his financial difficulties. "We've got a great, great deal going right now."

Lackey considered the offer. "It would be fun," he said, "because you've got some fun people working with you."

During the early stages of the investigation, the FBI relied upon Judge Lackey to ensure that his telephone calls with Balducci were recorded and that sophisticated equipment installed in his office captured Balducci's visits on videotape. Now it was necessary to go a step further.

Four days after Balducci met with Lackey, Tom Dawson of the U.S. Attorney's Office applied for authorization for the FBI to begin intercepting all calls made over Balducci's cell phone. The request went to the senior federal judge for Mississippi's Northern District, Neal Biggers, and for the purpose of the prosecution the case could not have gone into better hands.

Biggers was seventy-two and had a reputation as a stern jurist. More important to the federal authorities, the judge had a background as a prosecutor himself. He had served as a county prosecutor in his home town of Corinth shortly after getting his law degree from Ole Miss in 1963, and he later served two terms as a district attorney in northeast Mississippi, handling myriad criminal prosecutions in a region with a long history of redneck gangsters. Corinth, a crossroads city that had been fought over in the apocalyptic Civil War battle at nearby Shiloh, lay on the Tennessee border, and a murderous band of bootleggers and gamblers had operated in the area for years. Just across the state line, Sheriff Buford Pusser, the hero of the movie *Walking Tall*, had flirted and fought with the mob before his death. Biggers was no stranger to thugs, and he had little sympathy for them.

There was another aspect to Biggers's record that would be helpful to the federal investigators. Before he became a federal judge, he had served for almost ten years as a state circuit judge—the same position that Lackey held—and he could be sure to be insulted and indignant at any attempt to undermine the sanctity of the office.

On September 25, Biggers signed an order authorizing the FBI to begin tapping Balducci's phone. Almost immediately, it produced results.

One of the first recorded calls involved an effort by Patterson and Balducci to make a name for themselves in Fred Thompson's campaign for the Republican presidential nomination. Hedging their bet on Biden, the pair funneled a sizable contribution to Thompson through a third party and wanted to be represented at an upcoming Thompson fund-raiser in the Mississippi Delta by Balducci's father, a banker in the area.

Patterson urged his associate to ask the elder Balducci to attend the event and "to look up Tommy Anderson and tell him who he is" by identifying himself as the father of Patterson's partner.

Patterson said he had just "talked to Tommy" and knew that Anderson would be with Thompson at the party.

In the years since Jim Eastland had passed from the scene, the dark side of the Force had become, if nothing else, bipartisan.

Before nine o'clock on the morning of Thursday, September 27, Patterson called his partner as Balducci, who had been up early, drove between Oxford and Calhoun City.

"Since you're stopping by there to see Dickie," Patterson said, there was something Balducci should know. "I mentioned very cryptically to P.L. one day last week that I had a pretty good problem that I had solved, and I was gonna go ahead and solve it." Patterson said he had asked Blake, "What should I do?" and Blake had replied, "Solve it, and if you need help, let me know."

Balducci told Patterson he planned to tell Scruggs that "I've taken care of something you and I have gotten handled, and I was gonna get you to talk to P.L. and let P.L. visit with him at some point."

"I've already done that," Patterson said. "P.L. doesn't know what it's about. He just knows the amount."

"What'd you tell him?" Balducci asked.

"Forty."

"So you didn't pad it?"

"No."

"Great job," Balducci said. "Way to go."

"Yeah," said Patterson. "I just told him the truth."

Patterson said he asked Blake, "Do I go ahead and take care of it or what?" And Blake told him, "Yeah, go ahead and take care of it." Patterson said he assured Blake, "We've already taken care of half of it."

Balducci, bearing $20,000 in cash and en route to Lackey's office, told Patterson that he would "reinforce that this morning." He added that he had already stopped by Scruggs's office "to pick up that thing Sid had gotten for me," a reference to the order Scruggs's associate was supposed to be preparing for Lackey. Balducci told his partner he would return to Oxford after meeting with Judge Lackey and talk to Scruggs.

"I'm gonna lead with this issue," Balducci said. Then he would ask Scruggs to make two calls that would serve as a blessing for their dream firm, the association they intended to call Patterson, Balducci and Biden.

The pair had become deeply involved in negotiations with Senator Biden's brother, Jim, whose wife, Sara, was a lawyer and could lend the Biden name to the law firm. They wanted to add other big names to their masthead.

"Mention Ieyoub to him," Patterson suggested, speaking of the former attorney general of Louisiana, Richard Ieyoub, whom Patterson had approached about lending his name to the group. "See what his reaction is. I think it'll be positive."

He asked Balducci if he had heard yet from another contact named Zeke Reyna, a Texas lawyer whom they were counting on to send $500,000 to buy a share of a mass tort case.

"The motherfucker never called me back."

A half hour later, Balducci was in Lackey's office. The judge observed that his visitor was "traveling mighty early this morning."

"Oh, man," Balducci said, "I got things rolling, rocking and rolling." He reported that Patterson was still sore from surgery. "He's being kind of a baby about it. I think he's playing up his sympathy thing." He said he had told Patterson "you better get your big ass up and rolling" because they had an important black-tie dinner to attend in Washington that weekend. It was an event where they planned to meet with members of the Biden family to try to enlist a prominent black minister from Boston, Charles Stith, as an associate of their firm. Stith had served as ambassador to Tanzania during the Clinton administration.

After more small talk, Lackey sighed deeply and opened the unpleasant subject. "Let me tell you," he said, "I don't want a nickel of your money, Tim."

"I know that, Judge."

"And if this is not coming back to you, if it's not Mr. Scruggs's money, I don't want a nickel of it because it's not gonna do Tim any good, and he's the one that I'm trying to help."

"Don't worry about that," Balducci told him. "All that's taken care of."

Lackey sighed again. "This is my first trip, and I know you think I'm a complete horse's ass."

"Absolutely not!" Balducci interjected.

"And I feel lower than whale shit, to tell you the truth," the judge continued.

"I'm just glad I'm in a position to help you, Judge," Balducci said and whispered conspiratorially, "This is between me and you—and just between me and you. There ain't another soul in the world that knows about this. Okay? And this is taken care of."

Lackey seemed bothered about the note of confidentiality, the absence of Scruggs's name in the agreement with Balducci. So Lackey said, "I would think Mr. Scruggs would have to know something."

"Here's how it works," Balducci replied, taking satisfaction in lecturing his mentor on the unsavory ways of the world. "Just so you'll have some understanding of how it works, there will come a time where I'll just sit him down in private and tell him that I solved a problem for him. That he had a problem that needed solving, and that he needs to take care of the problem that I solved for him. That's how that'll work. So don't worry about any of this."

"All right," Lackey said. But he still had concerns. "There's one other thing that I've heard about over the years, that when a substantial amount of cash is withdrawn, you have to sign . . ."

"This money didn't come from a bank," Balducci said. "Judge, I've been around long enough to know—and I've been involved in enough to know over time—that you always gotta have a slush fund."

"Yeah."

"You can't have gotten where I've gotten in my life at this point and not know that sooner or later things come up that you gotta take care of, and you need a slush fund."

Lackey asked to see a copy of the order that would send the Jones case to arbitration. Balducci produced the document, which he described as "pretty straight." Then he laid an envelope containing $20,000 in cash on Lackey's desk.

"Lord have mercy," the judge exclaimed.

"You good for a couple more weeks, right?" Balducci asked. The $20,000 represented half of the payoff to Lackey. He believed it would keep Lackey's debtors at bay until the remainder arrived.

"Let me ask you," said Lackey, "aren't no serial numbers or nothing traced on this doggone . . ."

"Absolutely not."

Lackey fretted again over the situation. To calm him, Balducci said, "This is just business, Judge. You're in a position to help me. I'm in a position to help you. There's no reason why we shouldn't help each other."

The judge listened as Balducci explained there was no urgency to issue the order. Then he spoke quietly. "Tim, you've always been special to me."

"I know, Judge. This doesn't affect our friendship. It doesn't affect the way I think of you and my fondness for you . . . It would break my heart if I knew that you were without options to get the help you needed," Balducci said. "You taught me how to practice law as much as anybody, so I owe you a great debt of gratitude."

Lackey felt it was necessary to bring up Scruggs's name again. "Whenever you tell Mr. Scruggs. Or Dickie or whatever. Dick—whatever I should call him. I don't know what I should call him. Don't even know how old he is. I know I'm older than he is because I'm older than dirt. But you tell him this is a first-time venture for me."

"He's not even involved at that level, Judge," Balducci said. "He's not involved in a direct manner. Doesn't want to be. Doesn't need to be."

Once again, it seemed as though an explicit connection to Scruggs was slipping away.

"Well, he's a powerful fellow, I know."

"He knows how things work," Balducci agreed. "You don't climb the mountain he's climbed without cutting a corner here and there."

"Yeah," said the judge. "All right."

"It will be fine because I will tell him, and he trusts me implicitly. Listen: this ain't my first rodeo with Scruggs."

. . . .

Lackey had another entry for the journal the prosecutors wanted him to keep.

"As Tim walked out of the office," he wrote, "I felt so forlorn and sad that our profession had come to this, that a young man of Tim's ability would be this cowardly and stoop this low at the behest of scum he is trying to help just so he can add another dollar to his pile."

Driving back to Oxford, Balducci got a call from Jim Biden. They talked about the two telephone calls they wanted Scruggs to make. In one, Scruggs would call Jim Biden and express his support for the Patterson, Balducci and Biden firm; ideally, he might even agree to have his name used on letterhead as an investor in joint ventures. Scruggs's name carried clout, not only in the South, but also in Washington. In the other call, Balducci said he would ask Scruggs to vouch for the group with Gabor Ondo, a Swiss attorney who might be helpful in securing lucrative international deals.

"That would be absolutely perfect," Jim Biden said.

Shortly before noon, as soon as Balducci left Scruggs's office in Oxford, he called his partner. They had an extraordinary exchange. Some of the people who knew them felt they were an unlikely pair, the slightly built Balducci and the grossly overweight Patterson, a modern Mutt and Jeff. But in this talk, they delivered a low-comedy routine worthy of Abbott and Costello.

After Patterson answered the call, Balducci had an instruction.

"Repeat after me: You're the man."

"I'm the man."

"No! I'M the man."

"Oh, you the man?"

"I'm the man."

"You the man."

"I'm the man. Say it one more time."

"You the man."

"There you go."

"You the man."

"Say it like you mean it."

"You the man!"

Balducci sounded exhilarated. "All right! Done! Handled! All is well!"

Patterson laughed. "What's done? And what's handled? And what's 'all is well'?"

"All of it," Balducci shouted.

"There's a lot to handle."

"I know."

"And there's a lot that ain't well," Patterson said.

Balducci refused to be discouraged. "Well, what I can tell you is from this trip this morning, all is done and all is handled and all is well. Top to bottom. Soup to nuts."

"Including Oxford?" Patterson asked.

"Yep. Everything."

"Calls made?"

"Calls are made. Everything's great. Follow-up has been done by me, just now, touching everybody."

"Was he aware of what we were doing?" Patterson asked of Scruggs. "Could you tell if P.L. had talked to him?"

"I asked him, and he said P.L. had not talked to him. I said, well, he's going to be giving you a call here soon."

"Okay."

Patterson asked about the two calls they wanted Scruggs to make. "Did he talk to Jimmy?" He was referring to Jim Biden.

"He left him a message. I was sitting right there and he left him the appropriate message. I mean, he took the pledge, put his foot on base. All nine yards."

Balducci said he had just called Biden to tell him of Scruggs's message.

Patterson wanted to know if Scruggs had talked to Ondo, the Swiss contact.

"He left him a message. I told Jimmy that he talked to him. But he actually left him a message."

"Good enough," Patterson said.

"Same thing."

"You da man."

"I'm the man."

"You the man."

Balducci said he would have lunch before heading back to New Albany. Patterson asked if he had heard yet from Zeke, the Texan with the money.

"Hadn't heard from the motherfucker."

The next afternoon, Patterson had a surprise visitor at his home. Joey Langston had been to see Scruggs earlier in the day and stopped in New Albany on his way back to his own home in Booneville. The encounter developed into an awkward conversation between the successful lawyer and Patterson, his former associate.

Patterson sensed that Langston was fishing for something when his visitor said he was troubled that his one-time colleagues Patterson and Balducci might be working behind his back. It would be bad for everyone's image, Langston said.

"Nobody's going behind anybody's back," Patterson told him. "We're all big boys and we can do business with whomever we want." He confirmed that he and Balducci had a "done deal" with the Bidens and planned to open an office in Washington.

That was not comforting news to Langston. He considered himself a key Mississippi connection to Senator Biden, even though it was Patterson who had originally introduced Langston to Biden. But Langston didn't want to betray his feelings, so he told Patterson, "That's fine. Have at it. I think you ought to."

The atmosphere at Patterson's house was thick with treachery, and the distrust intensified when the telephone rang. Patterson's wife, Debbie, answered. Both men could overhear her. "Oh, Mr. P.L., he's in the middle of a meeting. I'll have to let him call you back."

Having no inkling that she should handle the call with discretion, she hung up and called to her husband: "Mr. P.L. says he just got out of that meeting you told him to have."

Langston grinned. When he was in Oxford that morning, Scruggs had told him he was going to Birmingham later to see Blake, who had moved to the Alabama city. He wondered why Patterson had arranged the meeting between Scruggs and Blake. He worried that it was another instance of Patterson conniving behind his back, perhaps trying to sabotage Langston's relationship with Scruggs.

Patterson shrugged off the call with a lie. It was some bullshit bit of business, he told Langston, involving help for somebody's son-in-law.

Before Langston left, Patterson revealed a few more dimensions of the new firm of Patterson, Balducci and Biden. The information would give Patterson the appearance of leveling with his old boss, but it also had the effect of turning the knife. He told of contacts that had been made in Venezuela, and of an ambassador who was joining the team. "We're fixing to have some pretty big announcements," he said to Langston. "They'll be getting a lot of attention. We plan to do all the national business we can do. Where we can use Dickie, we're going to use him. And where we can use you—if there's something you want to bring to the table—we'll use you, too. We're going to all go make a lot of money, and if you want to do the same thing, then go to it."

Langston nodded sadly at the changed dynamics. Patterson no longer worked for him. "I can't do that without you," he said.

"Well," Patterson replied, "I ain't there anymore."

Although Patterson had promised Langston he would not tell Balducci about the conversation, he reported the details of their talk later in the day.

"The only thing Joey was saying was 'I don't want people thinking that we're being deceitful to each other,'" Patterson told Balducci. "And I said, 'Let me clear the air with you on that. I'll tell you everything I know.' And I did. Except I didn't tell him you were going to Switzerland." He laughed. Balducci was flying to Switzerland that weekend to try to tie up a contract with Gabor Ondo. Patterson added that Langston had said, "Please don't tell Tim" about their talk.

"Yeah, he don't want to piss me off so I don't hurt him on MCI," Balducci said, referring to the giant settlement Langston had helped win for the state. Balducci was still miffed over Langston's failure to give him a respectable cut of the multimillion-dollar fee.

Patterson had another thought. "I think, if Langston could, he'd kill the deal with Gabor, and try to put it together himself."

They speculated that Langston was also trying to wring information out of Jim Biden and the senator's son Hunter Biden.

Balducci's bitterness toward his former boss poured out. "I want Langston—if he hasn't figured it out already—I want him to get the message and understand that if he tries to fuck us, that I'll fuck him on MCI. The best thing for him to do is to get the fuck out of the way and shut up."

That same afternoon, Scruggs made a short flight to Birmingham in his jet to see P. L. Blake. There were issues he needed to talk over. One involved the pending criminal contempt charge against Scruggs in federal court in Alabama. He wanted to learn the temperature of the courthouse crowd in Alabama, to see if fault lines were developing in Judge Acker's action against him. Now that he lived in Alabama, Blake would know some of the right people. He could pass on intelligence to Scruggs. Blake was, after all, still being paid handsomely.

He and Blake met in a quiet room at the facility called the FBO, fixed base operation, by pilots flying private planes into the Birmingham airport. They had always been an odd pair, the debonair Scruggs and the gruff, laconic Blake, whose poor grammar spoke of the rural background he had never shed. Despite their differences, Scruggs enjoyed his conversations with Blake. In a way, their meetings were a throwback to Scruggs's daring days as a navy pilot when he devised a method to hurtle through the air undetected by radar. Blake was a guy, Scruggs thought, who always flew below the radar. He knew Blake was unvarnished and that not all his activities were taken from the Boy Scout manual. But he realized that Blake was a valuable asset. He epitomized Scruggs's vision of the dark side of the Force, and Scruggs always wanted these men on his side.

Near the end of their meeting, Blake told Scruggs that Patterson and Balducci—he called them "the boys in New Albany"—needed help. He suggested that Scruggs give them $40,000 and find some work to justify the payment. It was an elliptical conversation, as most talks were with Blake. Nothing was ever etched out clearly by him. But Scruggs agreed to furnish Patterson and Balducci the money. To him, $40,000 was relatively insignificant. He had thrown far more than that at problems in recent years.

Blake remained vague when he talked with Patterson later on the telephone. He told Patterson that the chat with Scruggs had gone well. They had talked of the new law firm being developed, and Scruggs volunteered that he would help Patterson and Balducci in any way he could.

"I think I've got your horse sold," Blake added. Patterson dealt in Thoroughbreds on the side. "I told him how much the horse would cost, and he said, 'That's no problem.'"

Blake said there would be nothing to worry about. He would be able to deliver Patterson "your money on your horse."

Listening to the recordings of the conversations between Patterson and Balducci, the federal authorities decided to broaden their investigation. They went back to Judge Biggers with a new request, which would remain secret, seeking authorization to intercept calls made on Patterson's telephone.

In the affidavit submitted by the prosecutors, at least four suspects were singled out. "There is probable cause," the document stated, "to believe that Timothy Balducci, Richard 'Dickie' Scruggs, Steven A. Patterson, Presley L. Blake a/k/a 'P.L.' and others as yet unknown, are in the process of committing and will continue to commit violations" of bribery, wire fraud, and money laundering.

Biggers, who had been following the progress of the investigation, approved the new wiretap of Patterson on October 16.

CHAPTER 17

If Dick Scruggs's name was essential to the success of the superfirm that Tim Balducci and Steve Patterson envisioned, so was the name Biden. From the time that the pair had formed a partnership they invoked the names of Scruggs and Biden, when they could, to impress others.

There were legitimate connections. Patterson had known Scruggs from the time P. L. Blake brought them together. Balducci had also worked alongside the Scruggs defense team while he was associated with Joey Langston's firm. They were not the types to belong to Scruggs's social circle. Certainly they would never have been welcomed by Diane. But Scruggs, ever enchanted by consorting with "the dark side," had respect for what he called their "low cunning."

The Biden connection went back more than twenty years, to the time when Patterson signed on as a southern coordinator for the young Delaware senator in his first, quixotic campaign for the party's presidential nomination. In the intervening years, Patterson stayed in touch with Biden and became acquainted with members of Biden's family, who formed the nucleus for the senator's political operations.

Patterson and Balducci were both supporting Biden's quest for the 2008 nomination, and co-sponsored with Scruggs and three others a fund-raiser when the candidate came to Mississippi in August 2007. On that visit, Biden was accompanied by his brother Jim, who used the trip to cement plans with the Mississippians to open a Washington office that would capitalize on the name Biden.

Langston was conspicuous in his absence at the Biden event in Oxford. Once he had hosted Joe Biden there; now Patterson and Balducci had cut off his access.

The presidential candidate made a rousing appearance on behalf of his autobiography, *Promises to Keep*, before a full house at a book store on the square, then went up the street for a small evening reception at the Oxford University Club. Dick Scruggs was out of town, but his son, Zach, attended. The crowd was small, but the hosts succeeded in producing nearly $70,000 in contributions for the Biden campaign.

While the senator charmed the Mississippi guests at the party, his brother was busy talking with the hosts. It was determined that Jim's wife, Sara, an attorney, could credibly bring the family name to the firm they planned.

Though purportedly a "law group" with a base in Washington, the firm would specialize in lobbying. No law degree was necessary for any of the firm's associates in the District of Columbia, freeing Patterson and others to operate under the banner of an office engaged in legal work. But they would be dealing with power and political connections instead of legal briefs, and they would be drawing on relationships the Bidens and Patterson had developed over the years.

A month later, the idea had become a reality. On September 27, the same day Balducci handed over the first $20,000 payment to Judge Lackey, Balducci also visited Scruggs's office to tell him of a more savory initiative. Enthusiastically, he described plans for the firm of Patterson, Balducci and Biden.

"We've formalized our relationship with the Bidens," he told Scruggs. "It's not going to be some bullshit thing, with a bullshit shingle hung somewhere in a window. This is the real deal. Sara's coming on as a named partner with an equity share in the venture, and we're changing the name of the firm to include her." Speaking of the senator's son, Balducci said, "Hunter's going to be involved, and Jim Biden, too."

He told Scruggs it was critical for them to be able to have some kind of association with the Scruggs Law Firm. "We need you," Balducci said, stressing the word *need*.

Balducci's animosity toward Langston spilled over during the conversation. He warned Scruggs that Langston was "overselling his relationship" with the powerful Oxford lawyer while attempting to subvert their New Albany firm. "He's out there trying to put a little piss on the fire that we're building."

Scruggs laughed. He had long ago recognized that all three men—Langston, Patterson, and Balducci—were using their proximity to him to promote their own interests. Sometimes it was annoying. But he considered all three men his friends, and he had no intention of siding with one or the other in the current feud.

Scruggs told Balducci he would be willing to join them on any reasonable project they might put together, but he was careful not to denigrate Langston. At Balducci's request, he made two calls, leaving phone messages with both Gabor Ondo overseas and Jim Biden in Washington, assuring them that the nascent firm had his blessing.

As soon as he left Scruggs's office, Balducci reported a more glowing version of the meeting to his new partner. He told Jim Biden that Scruggs had said, "Tim, I know what a fireball you are. I know you're out there beating the bushes. I know how hard you're gonna work, and with the political connections you guys are putting together now, I know you're going to do really, really well. The fact is that Joey doesn't have that anymore. Anything y'all want me to be involved in, I want to be."

Balducci sounded ecstatic. "Joey may be out there pissing and moaning and scratching, but at the end of the day, if we bring a deal together on a project that's gonna make money, Scruggs is in. Scruggs is in! Shit, that's his real interest, making money. So at the end of the day, whatever we want him to do, if it's the real deal, then he's gonna be in."

Over the next twenty-four hours, Balducci and Jim Biden had several other conversations as the Mississippians prepared to fly to Washington to join Senator Biden and other members of his family at a black-tie dinner sponsored by the Congressional Black Caucus, where they hoped to recruit Charles Stith to give them clout in Africa.

They also discussed the race for the Democratic presidential nomination. Joe Biden had just appeared in a televised debate with the field of Democratic presidential hopefuls, and Balducci and Jim Biden were scornful of his rivals as they discussed the event.

"I thought it went well with what he had to work with," the senator's brother said.

"He was stuck over in the fucking corner," Balducci complained. "He didn't get much time, and the questions were stupid fucking questions. That sucked."

"We got to do something to break out here," Jim Biden said. "That

Edwards is such a screaming fucking asshole," he added, referring to former North Carolina senator John Edwards.

"I'll tell you what: he is!" Balducci agreed. "And I tell you I thought Obama looked like a fucking retard last night. And Clinton—boy, she looked like a damn raving bitch, I thought."

"Yeah, so did I," Biden said. He carped about "all the time that fucking moron from New Mexico got. I mean, shit . . ." He was talking about New Mexico governor Bill Richardson.

"Yeah, what the hell was that?" Balducci said. "What a blithering idiot that guy is. But, hell, you're right. Looked like this was the 'Prop Up Bill Richardson Show' last night."

"Yeah, I know," Biden said, offering withering words for yet another candidate, Senator Chris Dodd of Connecticut. "That fucking Dodd. Joe has to be frustrated beyond belief."

One of the earliest trophy names in Mississippi to be identified with the new firm was that of Ed Peters, a former district attorney in Jackson and a durable figure in the sprawling political network that Eastland had built. Peters had held the office for seven terms, between 1972 and 2000, and over the years he developed his own personal power base in the state capital. For more than a quarter century, he had given thumbs up or thumbs down on criminal prosecutions, collecting countless IOUs from those who sought his favor. Peters was well known in the state for his ability to control the courts in Jackson, to clear the docket of names of friends, and to threaten enemies with prosecution.

He was a longtime associate of Steve Patterson's. It was Peters who had been prepared to have Dick Scruggs indicted in 1992 and who, just as quickly, was willing to drop the case when others in the organization were told to lay off in the directive delivered by P. L. Blake. He was not only a member in good standing of what Scruggs called "the dark side of the Force," Peters was a ringleader.

When Peters signed on with Patterson and Balducci in the spring of 2007, he was billed as the head of the firm's "civil rights defense and victim protection practice." In the first public manifestation of the firm, Peters and Balducci were hired to represent the family of a young black man killed by police in Jackson, Tennessee. The pair held a press conference to denounce the shooting.

. . . .

Patterson also persuaded another prominent Mississippian to lend his name to the firm's letterhead. Though he was nearly eighty and enfeebled, former governor Bill Allain became associated as a "public policy advocate and constitutional scholar."

Allain was another product of the political organization that had once permeated the state. Elected attorney general in 1979, he ran for governor four years later as the Democratic nominee. In the last days of that race, a wealthy Jackson oilman and right-wing Republican, Billy Mounger, financed one of the most vicious campaign attacks in the state's history to try to defeat Allain. Mounger was not so much interested in reform; rather, he wanted to break the old Democratic monopoly in the state. Relying on the work of private detectives and a spokesman who had credibility with the press, the Republican interests sponsored a lurid news conference in which Allain was accused of having sex with several black transvestites who trolled the streets of Jackson. Allain's alleged consorts—who went by such pseudonyms as "Nicole Toy"—were paid a fifty-dollar per diem and sequestered in a Louisiana hotel across the Mississippi River from Vicksburg to be available for interviews.

Patterson was deeply involved in the defense of Allain and helped devise the Democratic counterattack, which denounced the GOP maneuver as an outrage so unbelievable that no self-respecting Mississippian would fall for the story. Allain won the election, and the transvestites later recanted their story. But Allain never really recovered from the ordeal. His counterpart in Arkansas, Bill Clinton, said that Allain seemed so shell-shocked by the experience that he played little role at southern governors' meetings. Still, he served for four years and continued to practice law for another two decades, holding the portfolio of a former attorney general and governor. On paper it looked impressive.

Patterson also arranged to use the name of the former attorney general from Louisiana, Richard Ieyoub, as their firm's "public policy advocate, governmental affairs liaison and legislative consultant." In fact, Ieyoub practiced law with a prominent Baton Rouge firm. But he had been involved, on behalf of the state of Louisiana, in Scruggs's offensive against the tobacco industry, and he and Patterson were friends.

Ieyoub's background was not without controversy. When he had been a candidate for a U.S. Senate seat in 1996, the Public Integrity Section of the U.S. Justice Department investigated charges that he had used earlier campaign contributions improperly. When the inquiry was dropped two years later, Ieyoub claimed to have been vindicated.

But Jack Wardlaw, a columnist for *The Times-Picayune* of New Orleans, wrote, "Now wait a minute. Federal grand jury or no federal grand jury, there seems to be no dispute that Ieyoub used campaign contributions to do his laundry, buy groceries, move from Lake Charles to Baton Rouge, join something called the Churchill Society, carpet his home and other things that would seem to bear little relation to running for office. All that has been decided is that this behavior did not warrant a federal indictment."

Yet Patterson assured Balducci, "You're gonna love this guy." Patterson reported that Ieyoub told him he wanted to do more than simply let the Mississippi firm "use my name because I'm attorney general. I want us to go make some money."

Balducci approved. "Man, that's incredible," he told Patterson. "Two former attorney generals on our letterhead!"

There were no boundaries to the pair's zeal to extend their operations outside the United States. Besides Stith, who would presumably handle business in Africa, the firm claimed to have a Venezuelan associate with ties to the oil industry. Their brochure also boasted of a native of Argentina who "serves our firm as a litigation consultant and interpreter."

But the biggest international associate they hoped to land was the Swiss lawyer Gabor Ondo, who had represented a subsidiary of the Swiss-based Sulzer Orthopedics in a massive settlement earlier in the decade growing out of hip replacement joints made by Sulzer.

It was a highly complicated case involving thousands of claims and millions of dollars. In a departure from his customary role as a plaintiff's lawyer in product liability cases, Scruggs had been brought into the litigation on Sulzer's side as a "resolution counsel." Using his powers of diplomacy, Scruggs helped convince the various plaintiffs that the firm would go broke, rendering the lawsuits worthless, unless a settlement could be reached.

Scruggs was given $50 million from Sulzer to broker the settlement. He brought in Joey Langston to help complete the deal, giving Langston 25 percent of the fee. In gratitude for his cut, which amounted to roughly $12 million, Langston gave Scruggs a black Thunderbird. (Scruggs noted to his friends that it was a "cheap model.") He also showered Scruggs with a Rolex watch and a framed letter signed by Clarence Darrow, one of the more famous lawyers in American history. The letter hung in Scruggs's office.

During the Sulzer negotiations, Langston developed a friendship with Ondo and believed that he might be the entrée to more big licks on the European continent. Balducci had been working for Langston at the time; he didn't get to share the Sulzer wealth, but he established contact with Ondo and also saw the possibility of a partnership. So he set out to wrest Ondo away from Langson and into a relationship with the Patterson-Balducci-Biden firm.

In mid-October, Balducci flew to Zurich to meet with Ondo. He returned to report to Patterson that he had not succeeded in signing up the Swiss attorney, but he felt they were close to an agreement. Following the debacle over the hip replacements, Sulzer had spun off the subsidiary responsible for the problem and renamed it Centerpulse. According to a financial statement, Ondo held a position in Centerpulse USA Holding Co. in Houston, Texas, that appeared, on paper, to be worth millions.

Balducci could barely control his enthusiasm. "He's rich as hell. He's got a twelve-million-dollar house. He's loaded with stock redeemed out of Sulzer. He's a lot bigger fish than I thought of."

Patterson was doubtful about their ability to form an alliance with Ondo. "Joey has submarined us pretty good with him," he said.

"That's true," Balducci said. "Gabor can't get his mind around the fact that we busted up" with Langston. "He can't get it in mind that Dickie's with us and supporting us."

Patterson grunted.

"Gabor's very impressed with the Bidens," Balducci insisted. "He's very impressed with that dogshit brochure I got printed up."

Balducci had gone to Switzerland with a slick twenty-four-page brochure featuring photographs and biographies of all of the associates of the Patterson, Balducci and Biden Law Group. Patterson was billed as the president. Though his home was in New Albany, Mississippi, he was described as a world traveler and "a familiar face on Capitol Hill."

Balducci used two pages to tell of his attributes as "part of a dynamic legal team" that had recovered $125 million from WorldCom/MCI and as "lead counsel" in other litigation.

Sara Biden's page said that she "worked closely with both Houses of Congress." The brochure pointed out that she was married to the brother of Senator Joe Biden.

Former governor Allain, former district attorney Peters, and former attorney general Ieyoub were listed, too.

The brochure gave the firm's main office address as 818 Connecticut

Avenue in Washington, with branches in Maracaibo, Venezuela; Merion, Pennsylvania; and Oxford and New Albany, Mississippi.

Balducci said Ondo wanted to come to Miami and meet with Patterson and Jim and Sara Biden. "He wants to meet the Big Fish," he said. "He wants to talk to Dickie. It would be great to have Dickie go to Miami to see him."

Patterson said it would be equally important to undercut Langston. "You're going to have to start your dumping on Joey, as bad as I don't want to do that."

There was nothing that Balducci would have liked more than to undercut Langston. But he had another concern. "We got to rope Dickie in on this Gabor thing. Gabor asked if Dickie would go on the letterhead as a joint venture partner, and I said, 'Sure.' "

"Which he actually hasn't," Patterson said.

Patterson and Balducci wanted respect for their firm. Judge Lackey fit the profile of the "of counsel" associates they wanted: older, experienced figures with no blemish on their background. Another older attorney, Norman Gillespie, matched that description, and he came to their attention as coincidentally as Lackey had.

One day in the spring of 2007, Gillespie, a retired seventy-two-year-old former state chancery judge and federal magistrate, called on Patterson. Gillespie was on the board of trustees for Blue Mountain College and out to raise money for the small Southern Baptist school. A native of New Albany himself, Gillespie had heard that Patterson, the son of a truck driver, had moved back to town, acquired a fancy home, and had access to lots of money. Patterson agreed to make a contribution to the school. Encouraged, Gillespie asked if he might help get a donation from Scruggs and Langston, too.

Although Balducci had left Langston's firm on bitter terms, Patterson still had a somewhat amicable relationship with his old associate. So he accompanied Gillespie and a Baptist minister on the thirty-mile drive to Booneville to solicit a contribution. When they reached Langston's office, they discovered he was not there. Gillespie left his card and thought that was the end of it. A few days later he was called by Patterson, who told him he was forming a partnership with Balducci and aligning with the likes of Allain and Peters. He asked Gillespie if he would be interested in joining their group "of counsel."

Gillespie thought about the proposal overnight, then called the next day to accept. He would be paid $1,000 a month and have no real duties. He would be able to use the Oxford office Patterson and Balducci were renting, second-floor space over a clothing store on the square. But the telephone there was wired to ring in New Albany, and all Gillespie wound up doing in the office was reading his own books and papers. The Oxford office was as hollow as the firm's letterhead.

As they plotted to build their firm, Patterson and Balducci sometimes sounded like Abbott and Costello impostors, at other times like characters from Mel Brooks's madcap comedy *The Producers*.

At least they thought big. At one point, Patterson told Jim and Sara Biden that he was "ninety-nine percent sure" he could convince Martin Luther King III to join the group in some capacity. "He's a good friend of mine, been involved in my politics in the past," Patterson said. "He could be of great benefit to us if we get into mass tort stuff, direct mailing. We'd use him where we need him. This is one of the biggest names in the world . . . This is Gandhi, you know."

They even tried to enlist John Hailman, the man who initiated the undercover operation targeting the pair.

After thirty years' service as a federal prosecutor, Hailman had dealt directly with hundreds of lawyers in the state and was highly regarded in legal circles. He would be a logical choice to add cachet to a law firm, and he was already getting feelers about new jobs as his retirement approached.

But when called by Patterson to see if he might be interested in going to work for their firm, Hailman was struck by the monstrous irony of the situation. He had been the prosecutor to whom Judge Lackey took his concerns over Balducci's request for a favorable ruling for Scruggs. He had urged Lackey to stick to his role of undercover agent at a time when the judge was wavering. In recent weeks, he had listened to the FBI wiretaps that implicated Balducci and Patterson. And now the unwitting pair thought he might like to join their firm.

Hailman was in a clumsy position, but he agreed to meet for lunch with Patterson and Norman Gillespie, whom he had known for years. They were given seats in a corner by a French door, the most favored spot at Oxford's leading restaurant, City Grocery. Hailman, a connoisseur, took advantage of the wine list, but Patterson, coming off his stomach surgery, was reduced to picking at a salad. Hailman had to draw upon his acting ability, in the same way Judge Lackey had carried out his deception with Balducci. He listened as Patterson described plans for the superfirm. Hailman told his host that it was likely he would accept a fellowship at Ole Miss, where he taught law part time. Throughout their conversation, the prosecutor was anxious not to give away any hint of the investigation.

The lunch proceeded uneventfully, until Dick Scruggs and other members of his firm walked into the restaurant. Hailman thought Scruggs looked startled when he saw Patterson's party. The two groups waved at each other. Hailman worried that his meeting had somehow blown the cover of the investigation. But the moment passed.

For all of their grandiose schemes, Patterson and Balducci were hemorrhaging money, even while they laid plans with Jim Biden to open a costly operation in Washington.

In their efforts to impress potential clients and associates, the pair had adopted a lavish lifestyle. They borrowed private jets for travel and checked into expensive hotels. Balducci had made a hurried trip to Switzerland to try to bring Gabor Ondo into their fold, and Patterson and his wife planned a trip to Israel.

But by October, only months after they had established their firm with high hopes, Patterson and Balducci were desperate for funds. The $500,000 they'd anticipated from their Texas connection had never materialized. Balducci cursed him repeatedly for his perfidy and called him "a little spic."

In a bid to recover money they had given a Jackson consultant to obtain an introduction to the new chief of the Mississippi band of Choctaws, Balducci exerted muscle. He was indignant that the payment had not resulted in any contact with the Choctaws, who controlled a prosperous gambling resort in Neshoba County and wanted to build a casino in Jackson County. The prospective casino was the subject of a referendum scheduled the next month in the Gulf Coast county, and Balducci wanted in on the action.

When it was helpful, Balducci could project the manners of a religious man; other times, he sounded as though he watched too much of *The Sopranos*. He resorted to the cheap gangster approach when he telephoned the Jackson consultant, eschewing pleasantries for a direct opening line: "I want to take you back to a meeting we had in the conference room at the Smoke Shop in Jackson."

"I remember it well," the consultant replied.

"Okay. So do I. Where I gave you guys a check and said, 'This isn't one of those deals where I give you the money and I hear three or four months down the road that you guys can't deliver.' . . . You didn't deliver. That's okay. But I want my money back, and I'm gonna get my money back, that's all there is to it . . . We're all big boys here. You guys have fucked it up, and now you better fix it."

"I haven't fucked up anything."

"You have fucked up tremendously, son. That's what I'm trying to tell you. You guys fix this, or it's going to be a problem."

The consultant said an associate was to blame.

Balducci interrupted. "I don't give a shit, because you're just as liable."

"You can keep cussing at me, and it ain't gonna help our conversation at all."

"You're right," Balducci admitted, while making his point again, without cursing. "What matters to me is I hired a consulting firm to give me access to the chief so I could make a pitch to the chief about being retained as counsel. That didn't happen. That consulting firm didn't do their job. That consulting firm, frankly, took our money under false pretenses, and I want my money back."

Shortly after the conversation, Balducci called Ed Peters, the former district attorney in Jackson.

"Ed, I have gotten screwed over by some guys in Jackson on a deal," he said. "Do you think we can get two boys indicted down there that have screwed us over on some false pretenses and stole some money from us?"

"Uh-huh," Peters replied. "In fact, there's a lawyer—the D.A., or the D.A.-to-be. He's got a couple of them he's fixing to do the same thing to—that tried to screw him out of a percentage of fees and things."

Federal authorities listening to the telephone conversation figured Peters was referring to Robert Shuler Smith, the local candidate for district attorney. With Peters's backing, Smith had already won a Democratic primary and seemed certain of victory in the general election in November.

Balducci said he wanted to come to Jackson to discuss the case with Peters.

"Perfect," Peters said. "I'll have Robert with us when we do. You need to meet Robert anyway. It'll be good for you."

The Mississippi band of Choctaws represented a big target for investment. After struggling for more than a century following the Treaty of Dancing Rabbit Creek in 1830, an agreement with the U.S. government that ceded eleven million acres in Mississippi to the Choctaws in exchange for fifteen million acres in Indian territory in Oklahoma, the Mississippi band began to flourish late in the twentieth century. Two giant casino-hotels were built on Choctaw land in Neshoba County, complemented by the Dancing Rabbit Golf Club, carved out of rolling woods. The unlikely location began to attract tourists and conventions—and outsiders who wanted a piece of the action.

Jim Biden and Balducci had one long conversation about finding well-connected operators who could link them to the Choctaws. "They could vouch for us as 'not scumbags,'" Balducci quipped cheerily.

Biden agreed. "We're coming in as problem solvers."

Problem solvers were needed, Balducci said. "The new chief doesn't know shit and needs help."

In late October, Judge Lackey attended a judicial conference at the Silver Star Hotel and Casino on Choctaw land, where he met privately in his room with U.S. attorney Jim Greenlee and his chief deputy, Tom Dawson. They were joined briefly by Jim Smith, the chief justice of the state supreme court, who was given some details of the investigation.

After Smith left, the prosecutors tried to buck up Lackey's spirits. Lackey described the meeting in his journal:

> Tom and Jim talked for a little while. They were trying to give me some assurance that they would stand behind me. I told them I knew the suspects were going to come after me tooth and nail, but I can take it since I was certain I was doing the right thing. I related to them my affection for Tim Balducci and what a bright future he had because of his ability, intelligence, and how I was so disheartened because it was apparent Tim had sold his soul to Scruggs and the other blood-sucking scum he was associated with.

While Judge Lackey was feeling some apprehension, Balducci and Patterson were confronted with severe money problems. They got $40,000 from Scruggs on October 18, the payment he had told P. L. Blake he would make. In a letter he left with the check Balducci picked up, Scruggs wrote, "Thanks, once again, for undertaking the analyzing of the voir dire" in a recent Katrina case and "constructing one for me to adapt" in a forthcoming trial. Scruggs attached a transcript for study. The voir dire work involved jury preparation.

When Balducci picked up the package, he left an invoice for $40,000 for a "retainer fee for preparation of voir dire for trial."

(The prosecutors would later describe the documents as a cover for reimbursing Balducci the cash he'd paid Judge Lackey; they also suggested that $40,000 was a preposterous figure to pay for voir dire work.)

It did not take Patterson and Balducci long to spend the money. By the end of October, Patterson calculated their dwindling resources and reported that they needed to write bad checks in order to maintain the appearance of solvency. He looked to an officer at his bank in New Albany to cover the overdrafts until their accounts could be replenished.

Meanwhile, their credit cards were on the verge of maxing out.

One afternoon, Patterson's wife, Debbie, interrupted her husband's meeting with Scruggs in Oxford with a cell phone call warning her husband that a check was due in New Albany. "We got to have that check today," she hissed with an anxious note of urgency. Patterson told her to put off the creditor. His meeting with Scruggs, he explained, "is more important than that."

As November approached, the New Albany partners saw they couldn't make their payroll. Not only had Norm Gillespie and others "of counsel" failed to get their $1,000 payments, but the principal members of the firm had stopped returning their phone calls.

Balducci was asked by one of their employees if a contingency plan existed to keep the firm afloat.

"I have Band-Aids to get us through if Zeke sends the money," Balducci said. "But if Zeke doesn't send the money, there is no contingency for that. It's just a gauze pad. We need fucking surgery, open heart surgery. We don't need a fucking Bayer aspirin."

As Halloween approached, the Mississippi partners of Patterson, Balducci and Biden papered over their financial woes by considering the upcoming evening. Patterson playfully announced that he intended to be the Incredible Hulk and asked Balducci about his disguise. "I'm going to be a squirrel," Balducci replied, chirping squirrel-like clicks of his tongue.

In Oxford, Halloween had grown into an extravaganza in recent years. On the witching night, hundreds of children—infants in red wagons pulled by parents and schoolkids in elaborate costumes representing all sorts of characters from Batman and Princess Leia to angels and skeletons—clogged the residential sidewalks in an informal parade, seeking treats at every home near the square.

Few found their way to the Scruggs's new mansion, tucked away on a wooded hill several blocks from the revelry, where the owner had other concerns on his mind. State elections would be held the next week, and though the Democrats had no chance of unseating Governor Haley Barbour, Scruggs continued to pour money into the campaign of Gary Anderson, the party's candidate for insurance commissioner.

Scruggs had already spent hundreds of thousands of dollars to drive George Dale out of office in the primary, and now he was dumping thousands more into a one-man effort to ensure that a sympathetic figure would govern state policy for insurance over the next four years.

He called Patterson to inquire about ways of routing another

$100,000 to buy more advertising. Scruggs said he was willing to make the expenditure because he had been told that Anderson was "within the margin of error" in polls that showed him still trailing the Republican. "I need you to contact Howard Dean," he said, referring to the chairman of the Democratic National Committee.

Patterson said he did not know Dean and preferred to deal with Congressman Bennie Thompson, who represented the predominantly black Mississippi Delta and presumably had an interest in seeing Anderson, another African American, elected.

But there was confusion. Thompson agreed that the DNC could handle Scruggs's contribution, while Anderson maintained it was illegal to channel the money through the party apparatus. The candidate suggested that it be sent to a friend, who would then pass it on to the campaign. When Patterson mentioned this approach to Jere Nash, a Democratic operative working with Scruggs, Nash emphatically discouraged the idea. "I don't think Dick wants to be within five hundred miles of any kind of fucking conduit going to Gary Anderson."

Nash was able to speak from his own experience. Ten years earlier, after serving as a consultant in a Teamsters election, he had pleaded guilty to a federal charge of illegal fund-raising and was put on two years' probation. It had been an embarrassing experience for a man ordinarily identified with liberal causes.

Patterson reported the problem to Scruggs, who said he was willing to send the money "as long as it's kosher." He said he would not pass it through Anderson's friend. "I'm not going to do anything like that, that blows back on him or me."

Patterson was relieved until Scruggs told him he had already sent Anderson "two hundred grand last week as a loan to him along with a promissory note. He's loaned that to his campaign." The transfer of money was of questionable legality.

Patterson called Nash again. "The plot thickens," he said. "Guess where the loan came from?"

"Oh, no," Nash said, moaning. "That is not pretty."

"Jere, what kind of idiot is it that does that when he's just been through this crap with Minor and all that crowd?"

"And got his hands full in Alabama," Nash added. "You're right. And Minor's going to jail."

The next day dawned with barely a hint of autumn chill, the sky clear of clouds and the early sun winking on the land.

As he drove toward Calhoun City, Tim Balducci was able to forget some of his financial worries because he had an important task ahead: delivering the remaining $20,000 in cash due to Judge Lackey.

Though some of his associates teased him for "trying to be Joey" in his choice of clothing, Balducci was hardly dressed for a court appearance. He wore a light button-down-collar shirt, jeans, and boots. Nor did he have the air of a supplicant before the bench when he sat down in Lackey's office to talk with the judge. Making himself comfortable, Balducci twirled a cord attached to the telephone on Lackey's desk while he discussed one of his clients, whom he described as "just a habitual fuck-up."

The young man, Balducci explained, was the nephew of a state official, and he faced a drunk driving manslaughter charge. His father had already paid Joey Langston a $30,000 fee in cash—"which Joey pockets"—to deal with the case.

"He's eaten up with money," the judge observed.

Balducci, who despised Langston, his former boss, agreed. "I'm not going to just screw people over like that," he said.

The drunk driving case was still pending, and Balducci was ready to take it.

With confidence that he and the judge had formed a partnership to fix cases, Balducci boldly mentioned a new deal. If Judge Lackey could intervene by postponing the trial and quashing his client's indictment, it could prove profitable.

Balducci said he would be able to tell the father of the defendant, "I think I've got a good theory. I can get the legs cut out of this beforehand. Gimme twenty grand to do it." Then he looked to the judge. "If he does, then I thought me and you could split it and we could get it taken care of."

"We can do that," Lackey said, still playing the role of a corrupt judge willing to sell decisions to get over a personal hump.

They also talked about the attorney general's race, which would be decided the next week. Balducci said he believed Jim Hood would "pull it out."

"Maybe he'll get that tit out of Joey's mouth," the judge said, referring to Langston's agreement with Hood to represent the state in recovering back taxes from the bankrupt company MCI/WorldCom. In the current campaign, Hood was under fire from Republicans for the pact with Langston, who had earned $7 million in the case.

As Balducci prepared to go, he left an envelope containing cash on

Lackey's desk. The two men shook hands, then shared a hearty embrace.

When Balducci was gone, the judge thumbed through the bills for a moment, paused, then held his hands to his head. "Oh Lord," he said, sighing, as if in recognition of the lives, including that of his younger friend, that would soon be devastated by the sequence of events nearing their climax. "Oh Lord."

While Lackey sat at his desk with his head bowed, the torso of an FBI agent became visible on the video, walking toward the hidden camera to shut it down. It was as if the curtain fell on the last act of the short life of Patterson, Balducci and Biden.

Shortly after Balducci drove away from Lackey's office, he was pulled over by Bill Delaney and another FBI agent, Gil Surles. The two men had a disk recording of his encounter with the judge minutes before, and they did not have to play much of it for Balducci to realize he was trapped. The agents gave him options. He could be taken to the Lafayette County Detention Center in Oxford, which doubled as a federal jail, or he could talk with the chief U.S. prosecutor, Tom Dawson. If he refused, he would be free to go, but he could not escape the consequences. He agreed to go see Dawson, and was driven to Oxford in a car with tinted glass.

Along the way, they passed pastoral scenes in the North Mississippi landscape. Hills where cattle grazed. Fields where the remnants of the year's cotton crop still clung to stalks like scattered popcorn. It was the first day of November, and though the oaks had lost much of their summer luster, the leaves had not yet fallen. Balducci was unable to appreciate the scenery. In a few minutes, his dreams of a rich life had been destroyed, and all he could now consider were ways in which he might salvage something out of his dilemma.

To ensure that no one saw him, the FBI team drove Balducci into a parking garage in the basement of a building housing the U.S. Attorney's Office, a couple of blocks from the Oxford square. Dawson, who had been notified by Delaney, sent for another prosecutor, Bob Norman, to join them.

Balducci was led into an interrogation room upstairs. Dawson told Balducci that he was not under arrest, but needed to understand that "your life, as you know it, is over." Oddly, Balducci did not ask for a lawyer to represent him. He said he would do it himself.

Dawson informed him that he could plead guilty to one felony charge of conspiracy that carried a maximum sentence of five years. If Balducci cooperated, he would be able to see his twin sons graduate from high school.

Balducci said he understood the situation and wanted to cooperate. Then he began to pour out some of the history of the last seven months. His cooperation would also involve a role as the newest undercover agent for the federal government. He attempted to make a telephone call to Scruggs's office that would be recorded, but Murphy's Law—the theory that had hampered the investigation all fall—intervened. The recording device did not work. So Balducci, who appeared remarkably composed, said he would deal with the contact personally. He knew his future depended on it.

Less than four hours after he had been intercepted in Calhoun City, Balducci was back on the street in Oxford and off to meet his friends at the Scruggs Law Firm. This time Balducci wore, under his clothing, a device given to him by the FBI. Before he dealt with anyone, he cleared his throat and announced:

"My name is Tim Balducci. Today's date is November the first, 2007. The time is approximately one twenty p.m., Central time. I'm attempting to make a consensual recording of a conversation between myself and Sid Backstrom at the Scruggs Law Firm—and possibly with Richard Scruggs."

He was standing on the west side of the square when he spotted Dick and Zach Scruggs walking back to their office after lunch. Without betraying any trace of his traumatic morning, Balducci greeted them: "Hey, man. What's happening?" He said he had come to see Backstrom, but needed to talk with Scruggs as well. As they climbed the stairs leading to the firm's second-floor office. Scruggs seemed preoccupied. He said he had to deal with something "time critical"—the new transfusion to the Gary Anderson campaign—so Balducci wound up talking with Zach for a few minutes.

"I just hate how bad our Kentucky thing turned out," Zach said. "Joey came over on Sunday."

(A few days before, the Scruggs firm had pulled out of plans to work with the other Mississippi lawyers on the Kentucky coal miners' mask litigation. The arrangement had collapsed after bickering broke out between the pair from New Albany and Langston, who was attempting to get in on the deal. To undermine his rivals, Langston had routed to Kentucky some uncomplimentary documents concerning Patterson and Balducci. Patterson and Balducci, in a snit, withdrew from the project, too, sending a colorful letter declaring they had no interest in "filthy lucre."

(The quarrel among the three men had become increasingly unpleasant to Scruggs. He had been visited the previous weekend by Langston, while Scruggs tried to relax beside his swimming pool. Langston warned Scruggs about his association with Patterson and Balducci. "Look," he said, "I'm telling you this as a friend. You don't need to be doing business with these guys." Langston made the same argument with Scruggs's son while he was in Oxford that day.)

The dispute still burned four days later when Balducci, wearing the FBI wire, encountered Zach. "I know Joey's been dumping on me a lot," Balducci said. "That issue is squarely just a pissing match between Joey and us, and I feel like y'all have gotten caught in the crossfire. I hate it."

"Joey didn't intend that consequence, either," Zach said. Like his father, Zach was reluctant to choose a side in the feud. Langston, after all, had been like a solicitous older brother, introducing Zach to criminal defense strategy in the two trials they worked together.

Balducci, whose mission was to record incriminating remarks by Backstrom, strolled toward his office in the rear of the suite.

"When did you get here?" Backstrom asked. "I thought you were coming before lunch."

"Well, I got tied up," Balducci said. "You know how it is."

During his painful session with the federal authorities, Balducci agreed to try to strengthen their case against Scruggs. He had no choice other than to betray some of his closest friends and associates to spare himself a harsh prison sentence. To develop more explicit evidence, he said he could go talk to Scruggs and Backstrom to ask for another $10,000 to fix the Jones case. If he could implicate Zach Scruggs, all the better.

Balducci had a good relationship with the firm. He had been professionally associated with them when, working for Langston, he helped represent Scruggs in the bitter litigation with Luckey and Wilson. Backstrom, in particular, had become a close friend. Balducci seemed to be able to draw out a playful side of Backstrom's personality. While Backstrom usually appeared serious and rarely seasoned his conversations with profanity, he grew robust in Balducci's company. They greeted each other with salutations such as "dude" and "my man" and exchanged wisecracks. Mutual friends, curious about the unlikely fellowship that had developed between the two men, wondered if Backstrom seized upon Balducci as a source for high spirits, as a means to lift him out of the boredom of the straight and narrow. Whatever the reason, Backstrom represented Balducci's strongest link to the Scruggs Law Firm.

In the privacy of Backstrom's office, Balducci told him he had "a couple of things I wanted to run through with you. First things first, let me tell you about the deal with Judge Lackey."

Concocting a false story, Balducci said that Grady Tollison, Jones's lawyer, had "filed a bunch of shit" before Lackey could enter his order sending the case to arbitration. The new motions by Tollison, he explained, were forcing the judge to draft different language in his order.

As they inspected the proposed order, Balducci hovered close to Backstrom to ensure that the recording device caught their conversation.

Zach Scruggs, who had left to take a call, returned. It was an opportunity for Balducci to implicate him, too, so he said, "Zach, let me bring you up to speed," and he repeated his tale of complications.

Trying to understand, Zach asked, "So he's drafted a new order . . ."

Balducci completed Zach's sentence: ". . . addressing that recent filing. He wanted me to approve it. The problem is I didn't have the institutional knowledge of the case to know if it was okay or not. So I wanted y'all to look at it and tell me if it's okay, and if not, make whatever edits need to be made."

Backstrom said he was confused by the wording of the document, purportedly sent by Lackey. Zach agreed. "I don't know how to clean it up because I don't know what he's trying to say."

"I'm not sure, either," Balducci volunteered. His claims of new Tollison motions set off a brief tirade against the Oxford lawyer, who was rapidly becoming as implacable an enemy to Scruggs's interests as Charlie Merkel.

Zach complained that Tollison had been using the Jones case as a device to obtain information from the Scruggs firm in connection with the State Farm action. Tollison was known to be close to the pair of lawyers in Jackson, Danny Cupit and Crymes Pittman, who were advising Attorney General Jim Hood on a separate track in the State Farm negotiations.

Zach speculated that Tollison had obtained some of Backstrom's emails regarding State Farm through the discovery process—in which rival sides can demand material that might otherwise be unavailable—in the

Jones case. "They're citing Sid's email, just one little part of it—just chickenshit shit," Zach said. "I mean, State Farm is using Johnny Jones's action and all the shit they're getting from it. They're getting all these internal emails." He said the latest filings in the Jones case might reflect "all kinds of crooked shit" invented by Tollison. "There's no telling. He might have pulled all kinds of crazy-ass emails."

"I think he's probably doing that because he knows that it's causing us pain elsewhere," Backstrom added.

"What do we do about him releasing privileged stuff?" Zach asked. "Do we file a bar complaint that he's filing a bunch of stuff that has nothing to do with his dispute against us to try to get it in the public domain?"

Backstrom said Lackey's order should be entered, followed by a request to seal the Jones case "because there's a bunch of shit in here that is just inflammatory and not helpful to us in connection with the other litigation."

Balducci offered a suggestion. "Let's get this order entered, and then if you want to go back to the well later and get an order sealing the file, we can do that later."

"What if Judge Lackey retires on the bench and some other asshole gets a hold of it?" Zach asked.

"Well, if he compels it to arbitration, then they gotta wait until arbitration is over," Backstrom said.

Balducci offered a solution. "Do you wanna put in there that the action's dismissed? Put that it's compelled to arbitration, and the proceedings before this court are dismissed? He could dismiss it without prejudice instead of staying it."

That sounded reasonable to Zach. "I might be overlooking a drawback to doing that. I don't know what it would be. I mean, Lackey's fine. But you know, who the fuck else is gonna get this thing?"

If another judge were appointed to hear the case, Balducci said, "I don't know that I'll have the stroke with the next one."

"This is the proper thing to do," Zach said. "It's just so unprofessional what these guys have been up to. Attaching all these things that they're ciphering through, and God knows what Grady's talking to State Farm lawyers about."

Backstrom said arbitration would be the best and simplest course to take. Zach approved of this approach, too. Just as Zach was called out of the room to take another telephone call, Balducci tried to insert a damning line into the conversation. "The other piece of this puzzle

I hadn't told you yet is: get it how you want it, because I've got to go back for another delivery of another bushel of sweet potatoes down there. Get it how you want it, because we're paying for it to get it done right."

But by this time, Zach was leaving the room and was no longer listening.

Balducci and Backstrom continued their conversation on other topics. Backstrom said he was surrounded by constant discussion of the State Farm–Jim Hood situation. Both Dick and Zach Scruggs seemed obsessed with the matter, he said, while the Jackson lawyers, Cupit and Pittman, were "trying to gum up the deal so they could get paid." It had been difficult "to keep my sanity" in the Scruggs office, he said.

Balducci said he had not seen Hood in months. "I think he's firmly attached at Joey's hip," he said, implying that Langston enjoyed closer proximity to the attorney general.

The visitor changed the subject abruptly. "When I talked with you last night, you said Dick was walking the floor or something over this Lackey deal. Is he okay? Or is he pissed at me over this?"

Backstrom was elliptical in his response, using interchanging singular and plural references.

"I told him, guys, part of the reason why it hadn't been on the front burner is because we told him it didn't have to be. And I oversold that a little bit. I said, we're defendants. We can wait till the cows come home. They bought that for a while, but then, you know—When you gonna get that order? We need that order. Well, we really don't. Our lawyers aren't billing us anything because they ain't doing anything. But, you know, they just got it in their heads that they wanted it."

Federal agents, listening to the dialogue later, interpreted Backstrom's remarks as an indication that Zach was part of the plan to obtain the order from Lackey.

"So, they were like," Backstrom continued, "Can you call Tim? And I was like, yeah, I can call Tim. No problem. Then later that day, Dick was like, no we can go about this another way. Don't call Tim. I'll go about it another way, a more indirect way. And I was like, What are you planning on doing? And he was like, I'm a gonna handle it. And kinda giving me the: you don't wanna know kinda thing. So I don't know what he did."

Backstrom said Scruggs had a habit. "Whenever he talks to somebody, he automatically thinks of something that they could do on something else." He said he could only speculate on what Scruggs might do in the Jones case.

"I can put his concerns to rest," Balducci said. "It's all done. He had paid the money, and he was probably upset, you know, or concerned that it wasn't getting delivered like it was supposed to be. That may have been part of the problem."

Backstrom shrugged, then he and Balducci turned to talk of what their children had done on Halloween night.

Before he left the law firm, Balducci finally made his way into Scruggs's office.

Scruggs, who was completing a telephone call, looked up. "Hey, man, I don't practice law. I talk on the phone."

Balducci asked for a minute of his time.

To Scruggs, the Jones case was a minor distraction compared to the war with State Farm, so he welcomed his visitor and began talking about the legal argument over wind and water damage. He showed Balducci satellite photos that he believed would demonstrate that homes had been destroyed by wind rather than a surge from the gulf. And he mentioned a trial scheduled soon on the coast where he would need the same sort of advance jury work that he had sought from Balducci earlier.

Scruggs was in his afternoon mode. He had taken another dose of Fioricet after lunch and felt washed over with optimism and a sense of well-being. Sometimes the drug made him manic in conversation.

Scruggs continued to elaborate on the satellite photos. "This is a hell of a lot better shit than you can get on Google Earth."

"That's great stuff," Balducci said. But he knew he had other matters the FBI wanted him to discuss. "Just very quickly," he said, "I need to talk to you about the Johnny Jones order."

Balducci explained that Tollison had filed new material before Lackey had time to enter his order, so the judge "pulled back that other order and has drafted this new one that I want to show you."

Scruggs felt the change was inconsequential. "I'm sorry you came over here for this," he apologized.

Balducci pressed forward. What the judge had done, he said, was to add one paragraph. "So I needed to get it cleared before I told him to go ahead with it. So read it and tell me if that's okay, that language."

Scruggs quickly edited the document, observing "that last sentence is not really a sentence." He added that another sentence "needs a colon." He returned the order to Balducci.

"So you want me to go ahead? No problems with having this entered?"

"No problems at all," Scruggs said.

Balducci knew he had to follow through on his plan with the FBI to raise the payment another $10,000.

"I know I keep going back and forth about this, Dick, and I'm sorry," Balducci said. The judge had become "a little bit nervous with that last filing by Grady because he thinks they've made a decent argument. He's gonna do this, but he says he thinks he's a little more exposed on the facts and the law than he was before, and did I think you would do a little something else, you know, to about ten or so more?"

Scruggs paused and thought about the request for a moment. He knew Balducci and Patterson were in troubled financial straits. He had given their fledgling firm $500,000 to use their influence with Jim Hood and his advisors earlier in the year. Encouraged by P. L. Blake, Scruggs had given the pair another $40,000 a month ago. That payment was ostensibly for help in preparing for jury selections. But Balducci's new suggestion seemed blatant in its criminality.

Suddenly, Scruggs became peeved with Balducci—and Patterson as well. He thought: What in the fuck are these guys doing? Is this another excuse to ask for money?

His concentration was broken by his secretary announcing a telephone call from Governor Minner of Delaware.

"I'll call him back."

"Sounds like fund-raising," Balducci said.

"Shit," Scruggs said. "Don't know who that is." That was obvious. The caller was not a "him," but Governor Ruth Ann Minner, a political ally of Joe Biden's.

Balducci brought Scruggs back to the $10,000 question. "Do you want me to cover that or not?"

Scruggs paused again, noncommittal.

"Because I've already taken care of everything," Balducci said.

Scruggs grunted. "I'll take care of it." To ensure that he had a reason for writing another check, Scruggs added, "I need some suggested voir dire from you."

In a letter dictated later that day, Scruggs wrote Balducci, "Great seeing you this p.m. and more than appreciate your suggestion to draft proposed instructions . . ."

. . .

Balducci felt he had completed his assignment. He made contact with Delaney at a prearranged site.

"Howdy. How you doing? I hope this fucking thing's working," Balducci said, referring to the recording device. It was. His voice could be distinguished clearly over the background noise of traffic and barking dogs.

"Go ahead and get this thing shut off," the FBI agent told Balducci.
"Go ahead and say the time."

Balducci glanced at his watch and spoke again into the device: "It's
almost three, about two fifty-eight Central time. October first. Excuse
me, November first."

By the time Balducci reached the outskirts of New Albany later
that afternoonn, his voice had lost its confident timbre. He sounded
weary and defeated as he talked on his cell phone with a friend at his
firm. He explained that he had been incommunicado all day because
"I been monkeying around doing some personal shit."

He was told that the firm's American Express credit card had been
cut off. "I figured that out when I tried to get gas," Balducci replied.

Since the firm needed money, Balducci was informed of a potential
case that might grow out of a disaster that morning: "A gas line explo-
sion in Clark County—two people were killed."

"I'm sure Joey's on it," Balducci replied sarcastically. Nevertheless,
he discussed how the names of the victims and their families might
be obtained. Patterson, Balducci and Biden was sinking to ambulance
chasing in the lowest form.

There seemed to be no end to discouraging news. Balducci sighed
and closed the conversation with a crude announcement. "I'm fixing to
go into my house and take a monster shit."

Although Balducci had been debriefed by the FBI before he left
Oxford, the authorities were still not sure what had actually been recorded. The listening device, now in Delaney's hands, had to be downloaded and taken to FBI headquarters in Jackson for scrutiny.

The next day, Delaney called. "We got the five words we needed," he
told Tom Dawson.

They were Scruggs's words: "I'll take care of it."

On the same day, Tim Cantrell, the financial officer for the
Scruggs Law Firm, emailed two secretaries:

"Ladies, we need to prepare an additional check to Tim Balducci, the same payee as the last check, for $10,000. This is for assistance with the Lisanby case. We need first thing Monday."

The following day was a Saturday, and in homes across the state there was an autumn ritual to be followed. Like thousands of others, Dawson prepared to attend the Ole Miss football game, along with homecoming festivities in the Grove. His plans were interrupted by a telephone call from his colleague Bob Norman.

Tim Balducci was rushing to Oxford. In the secret agent atmosphere, Balducci had alerted his control, Bill Delaney, and said he needed to talk with the prosecutors.

Norman, who did not know what to expect, arranged to meet Balducci in the rear of the U.S. attorney's building. Once Balducci was safely inside, he and Norman were joined by Dawson.

Balducci said he had reflected on their interrogation two days earlier. At the time, he had replied negatively when asked about any other cases involving Scruggs. Now the witness said he'd remembered something. He began to talk, and what he told the prosecutors was startling and significant.

Dawson never made it to the football game.

Three weeks later, on the day after Thanksgiving, many Mississippi-ans concentrated on a more important contest than the one Dawson missed: the annual football game between Ole Miss and Mississippi State. Though neither team had enjoyed a stellar season, fifty thousand fans traveled to Starkville and several million others watched the game on national television. For Ole Miss partisans, it morphed into a horror show. Winless in the Southeastern Conference for the first time in the school's history, Ole Miss appeared to be certain of victory in their last match of the season. With the Rebels in control of every aspect of the game and leading 14–0 in the fourth quarter, the Ole Miss coach, Ed Orgeron, unaccountably decided to run rather than punt on a fourth-down play in Rebel territory. The running back was stopped short of a first down, momentum vanished, and a collapse ensued. Ole Miss lost in the final minute. "Thinking is not what Orgeron does best," wrote sports columnist Geoff Calkins the next day in the Memphis newspa-per *The Commercial Appeal.* "There may be dumber calls in the history of the world, but none immediately leaps to mind. OK, maybe Napo-leon, when he decided to invade Russia."

With his brusque manners, Cajun dialect, and dubious intellect, Orgeron had never been a happy fit in Oxford. Now his critics were baying like bloodhounds.

Some Ole Miss supporters believed Orgeron had been installed in the head coaching job by Dick Scruggs. Some felt the lawyer had used his money to act as de facto athletic director at the school. So amid the post-game cursing and gnashing of teeth, a bit of the anger was directed toward Scruggs.

In fact, Scruggs had played a role in Orgeron's hiring three years earlier, but it was largely through his agreement to help pay off the contract of the previous coach, David Cutcliffe. Like other wealthy, enthusiastic alumni at football powers across the country, Scruggs was quick to get involved in the Ole Miss athletic program. Sometimes without being asked.

During an early-season game in 2003, Scruggs and his friend Richmond Flowers, once an outstanding receiver at the University of Tennessee and now father of one of Eli Manning's favorite targets at Ole Miss, had watched in dismay from Scruggs's luxury box as Texas Tech outscored the Rebels 49–44. Scruggs and Flowers agreed that a coaching change was needed. Flowers recommended Rick Neuheisel, a well-traveled coach looking for a job. So Neuheisel was invited to come to Ole Miss as Scruggs's guest for the climactic game with LSU in two months. When the Rebels proceeded to win six straight games, Scruggs felt compelled to withdraw the invitation. But fortunes turned badly the next year, Cutcliffe was fired, and Scruggs helped complete the financial arrangements for his ouster.

(Orgeron was hired, but before he came to Ole Miss he was allowed to discharge his duties as Southern California's defensive coach one last time in a contest with Oklahoma for the national title. Scruggs deployed his Gulfstream to fly Ole Miss chancellor Robert Khayat, athletic director Pete Boone, and several others from Oxford to Florida for the game.

(En route, Khayat, under criticism by some alumni for a procession of liberal speakers on campus, asked for suggestions of a respected Republican who might come to Ole Miss. Scruggs volunteered the name of his friend from the tobacco wars, Senator John McCain. Once on the ground, as if on cue, the Ole Miss group encountered McCain at a pre-game party. Introductions were made, and McCain spoke the next year before a full house at the school's biggest auditorium. Scruggs had a front-row seat for the occasion.)

Three years later, following the debacle at Mississippi State, Orgeron was sacked. As usual, Ole Miss turned to Scruggs. As much as $3 million remained on Orgeron's contract, and the Athletic Department counted on Scruggs to come up with some of it. But there was a more immediate concern. A replacement for Orgeron had to be found quickly, because recruiting season loomed. The university asked Scruggs to provide his private jet to fly school officials to interview prospects for the job.

He had loaned planes during the coaching quest three years earlier and learned that enterprising sportswriters could track the aircraft's movements by obtaining flight plans to determine which candidates were being visited by Ole Miss delegations. This time, Scruggs spent part of the weekend gleefully submitting bogus flight plans to outwit the pesky reporters. His tactic led to one erroneous report that Ole Miss was in consultation with Neuheisel, by then the offensive coordinator for the Baltimore Ravens, and to another false bulletin that Ole Miss had a prospect in Cincinnati.

On Monday night, November 26, Scruggs's Falcon 20 was actually in Fayetteville, Arkansas, where it carried athletic director Pete Boone to sign up Houston Nutt, who had just quit as coach at the University of Arkansas.

But by this time, other events had claimed Scruggs's attention.

On the Sunday after Thanksgiving, Scruggs got a telephone call from his brother-in-law, who told of his plans to resign from the Senate. Though the Scruggs and Lott families had celebrated the holiday together at Lott's new home—an estate near Jackson called "Sub Rosa," bought with the help of a low-interest loan from Scruggs—there had been no whisper of the shocking announcement that would change the face of Mississippi politics and have national implications.

Lott had served less than a year of his new six-year term and had regained some of his old power in the Senate. Though still a loyal Republican, he had seemed to mellow in the years following his disgrace over the Strom Thurmond encomium. At times, he appeared downright ecumenical in his dealings with Democrats, and he took on their rhetoric when inveighing against State Farm's failure to cover losses from Katrina. He seemed in good health and unbeatable in Mississippi. Now, with no warning, he was giving it all up.

When Lott made a public announcement the next morning, he cited a verse from Ecclesiastes: "To every thing there is a season, and a time to every purpose under heaven." Skeptics speculated that Lott had lined up a lucrative lobbying job and wanted to beat a December deadline, imposed by recent legislation, that would prevent him from engaging in the practice for two years after leaving office. Even after

Lott joined John Breaux, a former Democratic senator from Louisiana, to found a bipartisan lobbying firm, there were others who suspected a more sinister explanation, especially after the events that followed.

Both Lott and Scruggs would say there was no connection, that the timing was an extraordinary coincidence.

When Scruggs was asked on Monday about Lott's decision by Humphreys McGee, a young lawyer working for his firm, he said he had heard of it only the night before. "I was just as surprised as the rest of the state," he said.

There was a greater shock coming. Federal authorities were poised to strike the next morning, swooping in on some of the suspects and raiding Scruggs's office.

The move created new dissension between the Oxford FBI office and the prosecutors. Although the agents had been cut out of the plans, they learned of the investigation a few weeks earlier when a visiting colleague, assuming they knew of the operation, talked about surveillance of Scruggs's office.

Indignant over being excluded by the U.S. Attorney's Office, the Oxford agents questioned the wisdom of a daylight raid that would be highly publicized. They, too, had little doubt of Scruggs's guilt, based on the intercepted telephone calls, but they advocated a different approach. Knowing of a loose network of public officials and private fixers who had been swaying the outcome of court cases in North Mississippi for years, the Oxford FBI agents felt that Scruggs should be privately confronted with the incriminating information and squeezed into testifying against these powerful political figures. Even if the trail led to his brother-in-law.

And after hearing of Lott's announcement, several of the agents were convinced that someone in the U.S. Attorney's Office, while retaining deniability of doing it directly, had managed to get word of the investigation to the senator.

The prosecutors dismissed these contentions as petty carping by disgruntled agents who had no role in the investigation. For the U.S. attorneys, Scruggs served as the ultimate Big Fish.

Early on the morning of November 27, Scruggs's junior partner Sid Backstrom was dressing for work when his three-year-old son informed him that someone was knocking loudly on their front door. Backstrom found that the noise came from two FBI agents, who displayed their badges and said they wanted to talk with him. He invited them inside his home. They said they preferred to talk outside or in their car.

"Can you tell me what this is about?" he asked.

"The bribery of a judge," one of them answered.

At their car, a laptop was produced and a recording of one of Balducci's conversations with Backstrom began. The audio lasted two minutes. In it, Backstrom heard a replay of a call he had received while working on the Gulf Coast five weeks earlier.

Balducci: "I swung by your office a little while ago and saw Zach and dropped off a copy of those papers that we've been waiting on."

Backstrom: "Oh, great!"

Balducci: "Everything looked just right. Just like we wanted . . . That'll probably get distributed in the mail here in the next few days so you'll probably get an official call with the good news directly."

Backstrom: "Good."

Balducci: "But we got us a little advance copy this afternoon."

Backstrom: "Good deal, good deal."

Balducci: "Just so you'll know, Dick hired me to prepare the voir dire for the upcoming Katrina trial y'all got in Jackson County, and to review the other voir dire, et cetera, from some of those other trials, and do a little analysis and summary of that. And he gave me a retainer check today for forty grand for that."

Backstrom: "Oh, great! Well, that's a good deal for everyone."

To the FBI, the call illustrated a cover story Scruggs conceived to justify the $40,000 payment: that the money had gone to Balducci for his work on jury consultation for the Scruggs Katrina Group.

The agents asked Backstrom if he recognized the voice other than his own.

"Sounds like Tim Balducci," Backstrom said. He struggled to think clearly. He was not sure what the FBI visit meant, but he knew it could not be good.

The agents—one of them was Bill Delaney—asked Backstrom to come with them to the U.S. Attorney's Office. Backstrom said he preferred to drive himself, explaining that he had a flight to catch later that day to go to the Gulf Coast for a Katrina settlement hearing. The agents insisted that he come with them. Backstrom, just as adamantly, refused.

In his own car, he followed the pair to the back entrance of the downtown building, where several men were waiting sternly at the gate. In their dark suits they looked ready for a funeral. Among them, Backstrom recognized only Tom Dawson, the chief prosecutor, who worked out regularly at the same health club where Backstrom was a member.

"You're dressed differently," Backstrom quipped. Dawson neither answered nor smiled.

Upstairs, Backstrom was led to a windowless room where he was given a chair across the table from six glowering men. Thinking about the encounter later, Backstrom was certain the authorities failed to give him the standard Miranda warning: that he had the right to remain silent and to seek legal counsel.

Instead, Dawson opened the interrogation on a chilling note. "There's only one question you need to answer this morning," he said. "Do you want to be able to see your children graduate?"

Backstrom asked for an explanation.

Another of the prosecutors, Bob Norman, said they would "show a little leg," and began to recite some of the recent dates and conversations that Backstrom had had with Balducci.

The prosecutors said he could cooperate with them and probably escape with a five-year prison sentence. Backstrom was stunned. To him, this constituted a threat, not an offer. He fumbled for a response and said he could not give an answer right away. He reminded the group he had a flight to catch and a court appointment.

Backstrom asked if he was under arrest. No, but he was urged not to leave Oxford. The prosecutors warned him not to reveal a word of their meeting to anyone.

He reiterated that he had to fly to the coast.

They suggested that he call in sick. "I can't do that," Backstrom said. "I haven't missed a day of work in years. They'd know something was wrong."

His interrogators suggested that he call the judge hearing his case and ask for a postponement. Backstrom said he was unwilling to give a bogus reason. He was struck by the fact that after their initial questions, the first request the federal authorities made of him was to ask him to lie to a judge.

Backstrom was free to go, but before he left, he wanted to ensure that he was not wiping out a window of opportunity for further talks. He said he wanted to consult with a lawyer. If he chose to talk later, he asked, "will I still be in the realm of cooperation?"

Only if he acted quickly.

Norman warned Backstrom, "There may be contact with your office today." If he revealed anything about their meeting to his associates at the law firm, he would jeopardize any possible agreement with the prosecutors.

As soon as he left the building, Backstrom called Rhea Tannehill, a good friend whom he had planned to meet at a Bible study group at eight o'clock. Tannehill was a lawyer with experience in criminal defense.

"Rhea," he said, "I need your help."

Across town, an unsuspecting Dick Scruggs prepared to leave his own home, an architectural masterpiece built in the style of a Louisiana plantation house, with twelve white Ionic columns accentuating a front gallery with a view of the long landscaped lawn sloping toward Old Taylor Road. Complete with a pool, a guesthouse, and another building housing elaborate exercise equipment in the back, the complex had cost more than $6 million. It had taken nearly two years to complete, and even after Dick and Diane moved in during the summer, workers had continued to troop through the house like so many nettlesome insects at a picnic. "I think they are living in our attic," Diane complained.

Diane was not well. She still suffered from Crohn's disease, a persistent illness that frequently left her debilitated. On one occasion, her weight had fallen to a mere eighty-four pounds, and she sometimes required hospitalization. She had undergone surgery earlier in the year and was weak. But she and Dick were getting ready for a large party on Saturday that would christen their home and further establish them as permanent members of the Oxford community. On top of that, in two weeks they would be hosting former president Bill Clinton at a fundraising reception for his wife, Hillary, a candidate for the Democratic presidential nomination.

Scruggs was proud of his place in American politics. For years a dominant player in his home state, he had begun to reward his allies on the national scene after the tobacco settlement made him wealthy. Though Trent Lott had warned him not to squander his money on the woebegone presidential campaign of Senator Joe Biden, Scruggs made a significant contribution. He also funneled thousands of dollars to Republican senator John McCain, his compatriot in the tobacco wars. But these contributions were merely gestures to old friends. Scruggs was really counting on Hillary Clinton to win back the White House for the Democrats.

At the Ole Miss–LSU football game earlier in the month, Scruggs had clambered over a low railing separating Chancellor Robert Khayat's suite from Joey Langston's box, which Scruggs had been visiting. He wanted to greet Tom Brokaw, whom he had met on the NBC anchorman's previous visit to Oxford, and to invite Brokaw's local hosts to the Clinton reception. Scruggs seemed almost childlike in his enthusiasm. His pride in the event had been boosted by Steve Patterson, who praised him for attracting "the most popular man in the world" to Oxford.

As he left for work that Tuesday, Scruggs had less happy concerns—restoring his wife's health, fighting Judge Acker's contempt citation in Alabama, getting ready for approaching trial dates in Katrina litigation, remembering to fine-tune his home before the upcoming parties—but no overwhelming worries.

Driving his black Porsche SUV out of his winding driveway, he passed William Faulkner's home, Rowan Oak, around a bend in Old Taylor Road, and turned onto South Lamar Boulevard, flanked by stately old mansions, on the way to the square. It was a brisk, invigorating autumn morning.

Zach Scruggs had just dropped off his two children at a Montesorri school en route to the office when his cell phone rang. Don Barrett was calling from his home in Lexington. "Have you heard anything about that damned Jones case?" he asked. Zach said he thought it was going to arbitration; he was more concerned with a pending Katrina case he had argued in Jackson the day before, a case that the judge had continued, to Zach's chagrin, until January.

Arriving at the office, he encountered Backstrom, who was about to fly to the coast to deal with another of the Katrina cases. Backstrom looked a bit wan. Zach said he was sorry he could not accompany him, then thought to mention: "Don just called and asked about the Jones case. Have you heard anything?"

Backstrom's expression changed to one of surprise. He had spent much of the early morning fending off FBI questions on the case and was laboring under his promise of silence.

"Uh-uh," Backstrom said. "I'm just tired of dealing with those guys." The "guys" were Balducci and Patterson.

Outside the Scruggs Law Firm, a team of FBI agents waited in their cars, frustrated by yet another hitch in their plans. Two members of the U.S. Attorney's Office in Memphis, assigned to serve as a "taint team" for the raid on Scruggs's office, had not arrived in Oxford on time. The government attorneys were needed to ensure that documents irrelevant to their search were separated from pertinent papers. Otherwise their collection of evidence might be legally compromised.

It was not the first delay. A search warrant issued earlier in the month by Judge Biggers had expired before it could be used. Plans for a coordinated move against members of the Scruggs firm and Steve Patterson had been thwarted when Patterson left the country. A second search warrant had been signed the day before by Biggers. An eleven-page affidavit accompanying the request for the authorization had been prepared by Delaney. In it, the FBI agent spelled out the government's pursuit of evidence in the bribery case over the months and asked for permission to seize computer hardware and software and digital storage devices at the law firm.

Delaney was accompanied by agents who specialized in high technology. The FBI had also moved a van bearing heavy-duty equipment into a parking place on the square near Scruggs's office.

Finally, at mid-morning, the taint team arrived, and the federal authorities went bounding up the twenty-four steps leading from the sidewalk to the lobby of the law firm.

Scruggs was standing at the threshold of his son's office, discussing the stalled case in Jackson, when receptionist Vicki Evans came running down the hall. "The FBI is here," she announced, "and they want everybody out front."

There was a confused scene in the lobby. A son-in-law of Trent Lott's, stopping in for a casual visit, found himself herded with a small group of office workers. One of the agents informed Scruggs, "We're here to execute a search warrant."

Scruggs thought at first that the raid had been triggered by Judge Acker's contempt citiation. But inspecting the warrant—attached to a streamlined version of the FBI affidavit (with some of the names redacted)—Scruggs saw that it apparently involved the Jones case. The warrant indicated that the FBI was looking for at least one document, a September order signed by Judge Lackey.

Zach's first impression: This is some more of Grady Tollison's bullshit.

But it was obviously serious stuff. The Scruggses needed someone with experience in criminal defense. So they called Joey Langston in Booneville, and he literally flew, eight minutes in his jet, to Oxford.

Around the corner from the square, inside a cloistered room in the red brick federal courthouse, Tim Balducci had begun testifying before a grand jury. Under rules governing grand juries, there is no defense. Potential defendants—targets of investigations—have no representation, and prosecutors lead the examination of witnesses. Grand jurors are offered the opportunity to ask questions, but the process is a distinctly one-sided affair.

Under the direction of assistant U.S. attorney Bob Norman, Balducci spilled out his story. He said that members of the Scruggs Law Firm had come up with the scheme for Balducci to approach Judge Lackey. "The issue of the litigation that had been filed against them by the Jones law firm came up" in a discussion, Balducci testified. "Zach Scruggs or Sid Backstrom—I'm not sure which one—initially brought up the fact that the case had been assigned to Judge Henry Lackey."

Balducci continued: "Both Zach Scruggs and Sid Backstrom knew that I had a long history of a close professional and personal relationship with Judge Lackey . . . He and I have been friends for going on the better part of fifteen to twenty years. We were very close. And during the course of that meeting, members of the Scruggs firm approached me and asked me if I thought it would be possible for me to use my personal relationship with Judge Lackey to influence him to assist them in something that they wanted done in the case."

Asked which member of the Scruggs firm had made the overture, Balducci answered, "It was a group discussion from them. It was presented to me in sort of a free-form discussion during the meeting, with all three of them interacting with me on that issue."

Balducci added: "What they were asking me to do was to influence Judge Lackey and get him to send that case to arbitration and take it out of his court. So when they asked me if I thought, based on my relationship with him, if I could do that, I told them that I was willing to try."

Balducci said he was motivated by the belief that he would be invited into the Scruggs Katrina Group to replace Johnny Jones. "I had just left the Langston firm and got out on my own in New Albany. And I did not have any resources. I was trying to start this business and, you, know, I needed the money, and I didn't have it. And it was the lure of that, in large part, that convinced me to do it."

He said he had been willing to approach Judge Lackey in order to stay in the good graces of Dick Scruggs. He claimed that Backstrom had held out the possibility that Balducci's firm could be given a seat in the Scruggs Katrina Group, a move that could lead to "potentially millions of dollars in fees." Balducci added that he had wanted to ensure that Scruggs would pay the full $500,000 promised to Balducci and Patterson to convince Attorney General Jim Hood to drop his criminal case against State Farm.

Of P. L. Blake's role in the payment to Lackey, Balducci said, "It's hard to explain and it's hard to understand." Yet he tried. "Mr. Blake has served for many years as a conduit and a layer of separation, if you will, between Mr. Scruggs and other people on sensitive issues."

Balducci said that he and Patterson "sort of play by the rules that we knew Mr. Scruggs normally played by." As a result, he said, Patterson talked with Blake about a $40,000 "problem."

A subsequent conversation took place between the two men, he said, "where P.L. told Steve that P.L. had relayed that information to Dick Scruggs and that Dick Scruggs had said for us to go ahead. Finish the job and that he would cover the $40,000."

Though the grand jurors who would soon vote indictments had no way of knowing it, there were discrepancies between Balducci's presentation and the recollections of others.

Those who were involved in the meeting when Balducci volunteered to meet with Judge Lackey recalled that it was Patterson, not members of Scruggs's firm, who had first suggested the approach.

Speaking of Balducci's initial encounter with Judge Lackey, the prosecutor, Bob Norman, said, "Of course, at that time, you didn't know that he picked up the phone and called the U.S. Attorney's Office as soon as you walked out."

"No, sir," Balducci said.

In fact, it took Judge Lackey two weeks to decide to call the U.S. Attorney's Office.

Balducci's belief that he would be welcomed into the Scruggs Katrina Group was, at best, a pipe dream. The partners would never have accepted him.

Balducci also testified that Backstrom emailed him a proposed order for the judge on May 4. After receiving it, he said, "then I generated an original document on my own computer system so that I would have the original order."

No copy of the purported order, which had been sought during the raid on Scruggs's firm, had ever been found. Members of Scruggs's firm insisted that it had never existed.

More important, Balducci testified that after he had been wired by federal authorities on November 1, he told Backstrom and Zach Scruggs about a new $10,000 demand by Judge Lackey.

"How did Zach Scruggs and Sid Backstrom react?' Balducci was asked by the prosecutor.

"It was not a problem," he said.

In the actual conversation, recorded by federal authorities, Balducci made no specific mention to either Zach Scruggs or Backstrom of the $10,000.

While Balducci was testifying, Zach tried to call him at his New Albany office. A secretary said Balducci was in Oxford, but she did not know where to reach him. A runner from the Scruggs firm was sent to the meager Patterson-Balducci office across the square, but no one was there.

Calls were made to Patterson, who was also unavailable.

In a coordinated strike, two agents had confronted Patterson at his New Albany office at the same time the raid began in Oxford. Norman Comeaux and Christopher Michaelsen identified themselves, told Patterson of a judicial bribery investigation, and said they had some audio recordings he might want to hear.

Patterson escorted them to another office a few blocks away, where he listened, with growing dismay, to a telephone conversation between himself and Balducci in which they discussed payments to Judge Lackey.

Patterson's hands began to shake perceptibly. The agents said there were other incriminating calls on the disk if he would like to hear them. "Not now," he said. Instead, he asked about the investigation and the charges he faced.

Their discussion was interrupted by the voice of a secretary on the intercom: "Steve, Dickie Scruggs calling on line one."

"Tell him I'm tied up," Patterson said.

His conversation with the agents resumed. He was told he was "a subject of the investigation," along with Scruggs and others. And he was informed that his partner, Tim Balducci, was cooperating with authorities.

"Sounds like I need a lawyer," Patterson said. Nevertheless, he agreed to go to Oxford to talk with the prosecutors first. Riding in the front seat of the agents' car, Patterson gave an account of his recent trip to Israel. As they approached Oxford, he reminisced about his Ole Miss years, when he had obtained a master's degree in political science in 1974. He offered directions into town and joked that it represented "my first act of cooperation" with authorities.

Once hurried, out of sight, inside the U.S. Attorney's Office, Patterson learned more details of the case against him. David Sanders, one of the prosecutors, told him of the raid going on simultaneously at Scruggs's office. Sanders also spoke of impending indictments.

The group quizzing Patterson expressed interest in Attorney General Jim Hood and his predecessor, Mike Moore. Balducci had already told the prosecutors of the $500,000 Scruggs had given to him and Patterson. The payment raised natural questions, and the federal prosecutors already had suspicions about both Hood and Moore because of their connections to Scruggs.

Although the prosecutors told Patterson he could expect a twenty-year prison term unless he cooperated, he was unwilling to concede guilt. He argued that the case was not nearly as "clear-cut" as the government was portraying it.

According to an FBI report, Patterson acknowledged that the $40,000 transaction with Judge Lackey constituted a "quid pro quo," but Patterson said irregular measures had been necessary because he'd heard that someone from Grady Tollison's law firm had already "ear-wigged" the judge on behalf of Johnny Jones. He added that another circuit judge in the district, Andy Howorth, was known to be a close friend of Jones and would "trump" Judge Lackey in the case.

Patterson insisted that "the law" was on Scruggs's side in the dispute with Jones. To ensure a favorable ruling, a decision had been made to pay Lackey after the judge appealed for money to bail himself out of a personal debt.

Patterson, who claimed he knew less about the deal than anyone else, was vague when asked about P. L. Blake. He described Blake as a "friend and protector" of Scruggs. Patterson suggested that Blake enjoyed deniability in the case because he had never been given details. Describing his September 27 conversation with Blake, when Patterson sought Blake's assistance in getting Scruggs to reimburse the $40,000 payment, Patterson said he told Blake the money involved "a problem and it needed fixing." According to Patterson, Blake reported the next day that the issue with Scruggs had been "handled."

After listening to Patterson, the prosecutors emphasized the strength of their case. They played more recorded conversations between Patterson and Balducci. Patterson squirmed in discomfort.

Dawson, the chief prosecutor, instilled even more dread. He said Balducci feared for his safety and was fleeing New Albany with his family. Patterson's life could also be in danger, Dawson said.

Patterson was told it would be futile to ask Joey Langston for help. Langston, they said, represented "every thug in North Mississippi," and the prosecutors hinted that Langston would wind up tainted in the case himself.

Patterson asked about the possibility of speaking with Balducci. He was further demoralized after the prosecutors put Balducci on the phone. Patterson could hear his partner weeping. "I'm so sorry," Balducci moaned. "I fucked up. I fucked everybody. I fucked up everybody's life."

When the conversation ended, Patterson blurted, "Let's trade." He asked to talk with John Hailman.

Patterson and Hailman had both worked for Senator John Stennis in the early 1970s. Patterson held a patronage job as an elevator operator on Capitol Hill; Hailman wrote speeches. Despite their different backgrounds, Patterson never forgot a connection. Only two months before, he had tried to hire Hailman, not knowing he'd helped initiate the investigation.

Hailman had just retired from the U.S. Attorney's Office, but he continued to follow the Lackey case. He knew the raid was taking place, yet the call to his home, asking him to come to his old office, surprised him.

Hailman found Patterson in a penitent mood. The suspect described himself as a bit actor in the bribery case and asked for advice. He told Hailman he was inclined to cooperate with the authorities, but unsure about pleading guilty.

Patterson was told that if he dealt information to the prosecutors in the hope of winning leniency, he would have to pass a polygraph test during plea bargaining.

Patterson appeared conflicted. Hailman said he could not represent him, but recommended a couple of lawyers with experience in dealing with the U.S. Attorney's Office.

"Which one is the closest?" Patterson asked.

"Ken Coghlan," Hailman said.

Coghlan's office was on the square, and within a few minutes he arrived to offer counsel to Patterson.

At Scruggs's office, Zach placed a call to Backstrom and left a terse message on his voice mail. "The FBI is here. It has something to do with the Jones case. Call when you get a chance."

He also called his wife, Amy, to tell her of the raid. He professed bewilderment and told her not to worry. It would not amount to anything.

His father, genial by nature, attempted to engage the agents in conversation. Delaney said little. Scruggs noticed a bulge under Delaney's green jacket and thought: These guys are armed to the teeth. Finding Delaney unresponsive, Scruggs turned to others who were more talkative. He discussed old navy days with one of them.

Zach was not as hospitable. He expressed indignation over the raid and demanded to know on whose authority it was being conducted.

He grew angrier when he looked out the French doors leading to the firm's balcony and saw, across the square, members of the Tollison law firm standing on their own balcony watching the commotion.

Zach's father was concerned about his son's arguments with the FBI. It was not helping anything, and it would become obvious later that Zach was sowing seeds of resentment with the federal authorities. He was branded that day as a spoiled, intemperate rich kid, and over the next months federal officials would whisper accounts of Zach's impertinent behavior to reporters.

At the same hour, a mile away on the Ole Miss campus, hundreds of students and alumni were flocking to the Ford Center for the Performing Arts, the school's largest auditorium, to greet the new football coach, Houston Nutt.

Television news crews and reporters crowded near the orchestra pit, straining for a chance to question Nutt. Every seat in the hall was taken. Dozens of spectators crouched in the aisles or stood in the back of the balcony. The building resounded with Rebel yells and rollicking chants of the school's cheer, "Hotty Toddy."

The chancellor, Robert Khayat, came to the stage with a smiling Nutt and several other university officials. Trying to quiet the din, he began to thank those who had helped make the event possible. He singled out Dick Scruggs for praise.

On the coast, Sid Backstrom tried to carry out his arguments in the Katrina case without betraying his inner turmoil. Before leaving Oxford, Rhea Tannehill had suggested that Backstrom retain a seasoned criminal defense lawyer in Jackson, Frank Trapp. During a lull in the legal proceedings on the coast, Backstrom confided to Mike Moore, who was working with Scruggs on the Katrina litigation, that he had been questioned earlier. Not only that, Backstrom said, but the Scruggs firm was under suspicion of bribery.

To escape the unpleasant presence of the FBI, Scruggs, his son, and Joey Langston strolled around the corner for lunch at a popular Italian restaurant called L&M's. Though the name was resonant of a cigarette brand or a truck stop, the place resembled a trattoria, with curing meat on display behind glass and a chef who had learned the trade with Mario Batali at his famed New York location, Babbo.

L&M's was another example of Oxford's cosmopolitan lifestyle in the hills of North Mississippi. But for the trio that day, it was an unsettled meal.

On the sidewalk afterward, Zach tried, without success, to talk with Delaney.

"Can you tell us what this is about?" he asked.

"You got any information for us?" Delaney countered.

"I'm asking," Zach shot back.

He spotted Jim Greenlee, the chief U.S. attorney, heading back to his office from a shopping errand for his wife. Greenlee had paused to watch the activity outside Scruggs's office. To Zach, Greenlee seemed embarrassed. They shook hands, but the prosecutor imparted nothing about the case.

By this time, news of the raid had spread. A merchant on the square, noticing the swarm of FBI agents, called *The Oxford Eagle*, and the local newspaper responded by sending a reporter and a photographer to the scene. Calls were also coming in to the Scruggs office from the Associated Press, *The Clarion-Ledger* in Jackson, and the *Sun-Herald* in Biloxi.

Langston decided to hold an impromptu press conference on the sidewalk. He misled the reporters, suggesting that the raid might be linked to Judge Acker's contempt citation. The agents were seeking some unknown document related to the Katrina litigation, he said. Langston also claimed that Dick and Zach Scruggs were "cooperating one hundred percent."

The attorney adopted a philosophical air. "Sometimes, when you are a successful, high-profile attorney, you have to deal with unpleasantries. This is one of those times."

FBI agents continued to carry material out of the office. Gesturing toward them, Langston remarked, "I don't think they will leave here with anything. I don't think whatever exists is in this building. A search warrant doesn't mean anyone's being arrested or that they've done anything illegal."

Later in the afternoon, once the FBI departed, Langston and his partner, Billy Quin, huddled with the Scruggses in their office suite. Langston had been fishing for information with the authorities. Shut out, he asked his close friend Tony Farese, an attorney with strong connections with the U.S. Attorney's Office, to see if he could break their reticence.

Finally, Langston got a call from Tom Dawson, the prosecutor.

"Can you tell us what's going on?" he asked Dawson.

"Your client knows damn well what this is about," Dawson said.

Langston insisted that Scruggs knew nothing.

"Your client knows damned well."

"Is he a target? A subject?" Langston asked.

"I don't talk in those terms."

"Can we talk? Me? Or Dick? Or both?"

"I guess I could send a couple of FBI agents who would talk with you," Dawson said.

Following the conversation from across the room, Zach Scruggs felt, for the first time, a sinking sensation.

Langston continued to probe. "We're willing to cooperate," he said, "but we're in the dark."

Dawson scoffed at the suggestion that Scruggs knew nothing. "The train's leaving the station," he said before closing the conversation.

After hanging up, Langston tried to reassure Scruggs and his son. "I've been in several cases with Dawson, and he always says that," Langston said, explaining that Dawson used a hoary threat—that the prosecutor's train was leaving the station and that those who wanted to cooperate were already on board and those who refused would be left behind, damned to face trial and prison.

As late November darkness closed in on Oxford, the group moved to Scruggs's home, where they gathered in a small parlor with a fireplace, just off the gleaming new kitchen. They were joined by Diane and the Scruggses' college-age daughter, Claire. Langston, working his phone feverishly, talked with his brother, Shane Langston, a Jackson attorney with his own knowledgeable sources. He passed on a bit of troubling intelligence: not only was Balducci cooperating with the authorities, but the FBI was said to have "everybody on tape."

Langston and Quin were still trying to locate Balducci or Patterson by phone when a call came from Ken Coghlan, who had just met with Patterson at the U.S. Attorney's Office. He reported that Patterson had been given until 6:00 a.m. the next day to make a deal and possibly escape with probation. Patterson had been told, Coghlan said, that there was enough evidence for multiple indictments in connection with an effort to bribe Judge Lackey.

Langston turned to others in the room and repeated what he had just heard from Coghlan. "They've got film of Tim giving cash in a bag. They have Patterson on tape, Balducci on tape. Sid on tape."

Backstrom dropped by the Scruggses' house briefly after flying home on the firm's jet from his assignment on the coast. It was an awkward appearance. He said nothing about his interrogation by the FBI that morning. Instead, he told Dick and Zach Scruggs that reports of the raid "are all over the news." He agreed that Balducci was behind the FBI's action. "I remember Tim saying some crazy stuff," Backstrom said. He left to go home. Zach could only think of a cliché to describe Backstrom's appearance: He looks like he's seen a ghost. And at that point, Zach began to put together some of the pieces of the puzzle.

Later that night, he called Backstrom and learned of his morning visit by the FBI. Backstrom explained that he had been squeezed by the prosecutors and feared for his future. He and Zach agreed to meet early the next day.

As more news of Balducci's betrayal began to trickle in, an ominous realization settled on the assembly of lawyers: the members of the Scruggs Law Firm were going to be indicted.

They needed nothing more to discourage them. But then Langston shared a telephone call he had just completed with Patterson's wife, Debbie.

"Tim is a Judas," she had screamed. "Tim is a Judas!"

CHAPTER 20

Facing the threat of an indictment, Zach Scruggs woke early the next morning. He dressed in a suit and tie, kissed his sleeping children, and set out to find Sid Backstrom, whose behavior had seemed suspicious the day before. Zach wondered if he, too, was cooperating with the federal authorities.

He drove across town to Backstrom's residence, located in an upper-middle-class neighborhood known as The Cove, where most of the homes were occupied by young families. He talked briefly with Backstrom's wife, Kelli, who was tearful and upset. She said her husband had already left for the office. "I'm so sorry about all of this," Zach told her before driving away.

He found no sign of Backstrom at their office, either, concluding that he might be meeting with his friend Rhea Tannehill. As he figured, Zach found Backstrom's car outside Tannehill's office, yet when he went inside, no one was there.

Troubled by Backstrom's absence, he went to his parents' home, where they were soon joined by Langston and Quin. The lawyers had been trolling for information and had learned from Ken Coghlan that his new client, Steve Patterson, had not yielded to the prosecutors.

Langston was also getting reports from Tony Farese, who was trying to milk the U.S. Attorney's Office for any piece of intelligence.

There was another dynamic at work that morning that the Scruggs family knew nothing about. From the moment he realized Balducci had become an informant, Langston suspected that he might be pulled into the investigation. After he left the Scruggses' home late the night before, his associate, Quin, had spoken of the potential for trouble. "You know you've got to be prepared against Balducci," Quin warned him. "You know he's going to try to save himself. He's going to turn in big fish, and you're the biggest fish. You know he's gonna lie. You gotta assume he's gonna lie. And you know Balducci's number one motivation will be to sink you."

While the lawyers worked their cell phones, Dick Scruggs and his son sought refuge in the guesthouse beside the swimming pool. For diversion, they watched television. Each local news break contained references to the raid at the Scruggs firm.

Don Barrett called again. As a principal partner of the Scruggs Katrina Group, he raised questions about the future of the initiative. "What are we going to do?" he asked Scruggs. "We've got all these clients." Scruggs wanted to be rational about the situation, to show no indication of panic. He hoped they could soldier on, but Barrett was not so sure. If Scruggs were indicted, it would be necessary for him, Barrett said, to step back. In his mind, Barrett was already thinking of the letter that would be sent to their clients in a few days:

"The Scruggs Law Firm has informed us that in the interest of its clients, it has withdrawn from the group of attorneys who represent your claims until legal matters have been resolved, . . . The Scruggs Law Firm has assured us that they engaged in no wrongdoing, and we are confident that they will be cleared of the charges."

Scruggs faced the reality that his law firm would suffer. A few minutes later, his personal prestige took another blow. A representative from Hillary Clinton's campaign called to say that "it might be better" for Scruggs to cancel the fund-raiser set for December 15. The former president would not be coming.

At intervals during the morning, Langston strolled out to the guesthouse to give the latest news. None of it sounded encouraging.

Zach persisted in his efforts to locate Backstrom. He left a message on Tannehill's voice mail, but his calls were not returned.

Backstrom and Tannehill, along with Frank Trapp, who had driven up from Jackson, were meeting with the prosecutors at that hour. Backstrom told the authorities their offer of five years in prison was unacceptable. He was not prepared to negotiate. To convince Backstrom that his position was untenable, the prosecutors played a number of recordings of conversations between him and Balducci. Two of them, recorded by Balducci earlier in the month while he wore a wire, seemed incriminating. The prosecutors again pressed Backstrom to plead guilty and become a cooperating witness, but he was not persuaded. He thought: They believe I'm the weak link and they think they can break me. With his slight frame and colorless pallor, he knew he might look vulnerable. He knew his indictment was imminent. Still, he refused to make a deal.

Eventually, an unfamiliar voice, using Tannehill's cell phone, returned Zach's message. The caller identified himself as Frank Trapp.

"Are you representing Sid?" Zach asked. "Are you talking to the prosecutors?"

Trapp seemed to be intentionally vague. "I'm just getting into this," he said. "I may need to talk to your lawyer."

Actually, Zach had no lawyer. Even as events unfolded, he considered the crisis unthinkable, the prospect that he might be indicted unbelievable.

Langston, however, had prepared for that eventuality. He summoned Farese to Scruggs's house. "Tony's going to be your lawyer," he told Zach. "It's a good idea."

Farese had been on the defense team, with Langston, for the first criminal trial in which Zach had been engaged, so Zach agreed to the choice. But he was adamant about his innocence when he talked with Farese. "I don't know what's going on. But I'm not pleading to anything," Zach said. "Even if it means one day in jail or ten years, I'm not pleading to anything."

Zach seemed overcome with nervous energy and worry. He appealed to his father. "If anything happens to me, I want you and Mom to take care of my family."

Recognizing that his son was becoming frantic, Scruggs assured Zach that his family would never be neglected.

Zach's mood lifted a bit when Tannehill finally called to say that Backstrom was not cooperating with the prosecutors.

Around noon, Farese got a call from the prosecutors. Everyone had been indicted. Dick Scruggs. Zach Scruggs. Sid Backstrom. Steve Patterson. Tim Balducci. Federal marshals were being sent to Scruggs's home to make the arrests.

"That won't be necessary," Farese said. "They'll voluntarily surrender."

. . .

The Scruggses and their lawyers rode to the federal courthouse in Zach's Suburban, with Zach wedged in the back between car seats for his two children. Photographers and television crews, alerted by authorities, were waiting.

The defendants were processed through the probation office, where they briefly encountered Patterson. He looked at them and shrugged, as if he were helpless to explain their quandary.

Urine samples were taken, and questions were asked about the men's net worth. Then they were taken to a cell upstairs where they were stripped of ties and belts and put in shackles. One of the marshals on guard offered a copy of the indictment, enabling them to see, for the first time, the official charges. It appeared clear that Balducci was responsible. He was listed as their co-defendant, but was not in a cell in Oxford with them.

After fingerprints and mug shots were taken, Dick Scruggs and his son, still handcuffed but relieved of their leg shackles, were led into the courtroom of federal magistrate Allan Alexander. Dick had gone to law school with her; Zach had worked for Alexander when he was in law school.

In the audience, Zach spotted a woman he recognized as the daughter of his father's nemesis Roberts Wilson. In a halcyon time, nearly thirty years before, Zach and Elizabeth Wilson had played together on the Gulf Coast when their fathers were partners in asbestos litigation. Now she sat, like an avenging angel, watching the Scruggses' humiliation.

Both Scruggs men pleaded not guilty. The prosecutors asked for Dick to post a $5 million bond before he could be released; he was reputed to be a billionaire, wealthy beyond reason from his tobacco windfall. But the magistrate said she had already seen a preliminary report from the probation officers that indicated that Scruggs's assets fell considerably short of a billion dollars. Instead, she set bond at $100,000. After the prosecutors argued that Scruggs represented a flight risk, Alexander ordered his plane grounded and collected his passport.

Dispirited by the experience, Dick and Zach and their lawyers regrouped afterward at the Scruggs home with Diane, daughter Claire, and Zach's wife. Langston and Quin attempted to boost morale by expressing doubts about the strength of the government's case. Dick vowed to summon every weapon available to fight back, telling the group he would bring in John Keker, the high-powered lawyer from

San Francisco who was already defending him in the contempt case in Alabama.

There were other issues to consider. One of those was the Christmas party the Scruggs planned to co-host in three days with Marla and Lowry Lomax, their old friends from Pascagoula who had moved to Oxford earlier in the decade. Invitations had been mailed and catering arrangements made. After talking with the Lomaxes, they decided to go ahead with the party. It would be a demonstration of resolve.

But Zach felt beaten down. After he and Amy drove to their own home, he put their children to bed. As they fell asleep, he kissed them, wondering: How many times will I get to do that again?

The prosecutors, who had concealed the investigation carefully, felt it would be important to go public with a post-indictment press conference to maintain an advantage in the running narrative. As long as the newspaper and television reporters fed on information from the government side, the prosecutors would control the flow of the story. They were assisted by bloggers—virtually all of them critical of Scruggs—who would follow the case, posting pertinent documents on the Internet, developing a wide readership, and, in some instances, guiding the news coverage.

At the press conference, U.S. Attorney Jim Greenlee elaborated on a few details of the case and denied that Trent Lott had been given any advance warning. "To my knowledge, there is absolutely no connection" between Lott's resignation and the charges against his brother-in-law, Greenlee said.

One of those who attended the press conference was not a reporter at all, but Scruggs's adversary Grady Tollison, who listened with satisfaction as the prosecutors tightened their grip on Scruggs. At one point, Dawson, the lead prosecutor, leaned toward Tollison and whispered, "Merry Christmas."

Scruggs's voice was shut down on the advice of his lawyers. Instead of using his own charms, which he had relied upon in the past to engage reporters, the key defendant was kept on the defensive. Friends who were inclined to side with him wondered why he did not hold his own press conference to pronounce his innocence.

Despite the crisis, the Scruggses' Christmas party was carried off with aplomb. Promptly at five o'clock, as light began to fade from the late autumn sky, guests began to arrive. Because the winding driveway was narrow and space outside the house limited, they were asked to park at the foot of the hill, in a university lot usually reserved for campers on football weekends, and to ride the rest of the way in jitneys.

Inside the high-ceilinged home, tables were spread with an assortment of miniature lamb chops and rich seafood dishes. Bartenders handled drinks at several stations, while attendants passed through the rooms offering hors d'oeuvres.

There was a temptation for journalists covering the case to compare the evening to one of Gatsby's parties, but the analogy didn't really work. Though Scruggs now carried a scent of impropriety, he was neither a stranger to Oxford nor gauche about his wealth. His Ole Miss background and his generosity since arriving there four years ago had made him welcome to the community.

Among the first to arrive were Scruggs's friends from his boyhood in Pascagoula: Khayat, the chancellor, and Sam Davis, the dean of the law school. They were followed by dozens who, if gathered for a still photograph, would have represented a portrait of men and women of influence in Oxford: physicians and ministers; faculty members and businessmen; attorneys and entrepreneurs. Andy Kennedy, the Ole Miss basketball coach fresh from his team's 85–77 victory over the University of New Mexico a few hours earlier, was there, along with the school's popular baseball coach, Mike Bianco. Despite their personal agonies, Zach and Amy Scruggs and Sid and Kelli Backstrom made appearances. The only absentees from the guest list were local judges and prosecutors who felt their presence would be inappropriate. The previous December, many of those same officials had attended the joint Lomax-Scruggs Christmas party held at Lomax's new mansion, never imagining the future events that would disrupt their relationships.

Dick and Diane circulated among their guests. Occasionally friends gathered Scruggs in an affectionate embrace. His wife, recovering from an attack of Crohn's disease and the shock of her husband's and son's indictments, maintained a smile, but it looked forced and weak.

As the party gathered momentum, voices grew merrier. When the subject of the government's accusations came up in conversation, Scruggs expressed bewilderment and innocence. More comfortable topics involved his brother-in-law's sudden departure from the Senate and the new football coach at Ole Miss. In a nod to the sport's importance in the region, a television in the exercise room by the pool was tuned to the Southeastern Conference championship game, and some of the guests abandoned the main house to watch it. Since the evening had been planned as an opportunity for friends to see the new house, others wandered through the downstairs rooms marveling at a clothes closet containing what seemed like a hundred suits. Or they penetrated the wine cellar in the basement, where Scruggs was just beginning to accumulate stocks of the best vintages.

Earlier in the year, he had enlisted the advice of John Hailman, the federal prosecutor–cum–wine critic. He told Hailman he wanted to assemble a selection to rival Lowry Lomax's wine cellar. At the last Christmas gathering, Lomax's collection, climate-controlled and bristling with bottles of impressive California vintage and wooden crates bearing labels from France, had generated the buzz of the party. Scruggs had offered to put Hailman "on the clock" to act as his advisor. Hailman dismissed any suggestion of a fee. "We'll just have fun drinking good wine," he had said to Scruggs. Hailman envisioned trips to France in Scruggs's jet; visits to vineyards in Burgundy and the Rhone Valley to choose wines worthy of Scruggs's cellar.

That was before Judge Lackey came to Hailman with his troubling story.

Amid the strained gaiety of the evening, at least one other reminder of the adversaries facing Scruggs lay outside. Behind his house and through the woods, the nearest structure was a brick batting clinic beside the Ole Miss baseball park. It was named for its donor, Charlie Merkel.

The party was off limits to reporters, but Paulo Prada and Peter Lattman of *The Wall Street Journal* were on assignment in Oxford, and began pulling together a story with accounts of the evening and comments from several who attended the Scruggs affair.

"People appreciate him for his support of the community, and we're all willing to stand by and support him," said Oxford's mayor, Richard Howorth. (For his statement, Howorth was criticized in a letter to the editor in *The Oxford Eagle* later in the month.)

As a shot in the dark, the reporters called Steve Patterson's home the night of the Scruggs party. Patterson did not want to talk, but his wife, Debbie, was quite loquacious. "We didn't know any of this," she said. "We were in the Holy Land seeking edification and returned home to this mess." She laid all of their problems at the feet of Tim Balducci, whom she characterized as "a short, midget Italian." That quote worked its way up the ladder of editors at *The Wall Street Journal* before the story was published. A top editor, exercising political correctness, took out the Italian reference.

On Monday following the party, the two reporters decided to make a call on Scruggs at his office. To their surprise, Scruggs greeted them cordially. He said he could not discuss the case, but invited them into his private office for an informal chat. For fifteen minutes, they talked. Seeing his old aviator's helmet on his desk, one of his visitors asked about his experiences as a pilot. He said he rarely flew anymore. When Scruggs learned that Prada lived in Atlanta, he told of how the military school there had "whipped me into shape." A photograph of Diane led to questions about how Scruggs had met his wife. She had not been his high school sweetheart, Scruggs said. "She had much better sense than to hook up with me back then."

Leaving the law firm, the reporters were struck by Scruggs's polite reception. But he seemed to them somewhat disoriented and not quite on top of his game.

Another curious turn occurred the next day, after their article appeared. While they were in Oxford, the reporters had talked with many people who seemed supportive of Scruggs. They began to receive emails from Oxford, some from the same people whom they had seen the week before. These messages now expressed doubts about Scruggs's innocence—and even resentment of him.

During the first two weeks after the indictment, Joey Langston served as Scruggs's primary lifeline to the press. John Keker, the lead attorney on Scruggs's defense team, preferred not to talk with reporters. So it was left to Langston, a Mississippian, to deal with local journalists and with those who had begun descending on Oxford from across the country. He seemed to speak with confidence and authority. But behind his façade of self-assurance lay growing concerns. Langston knew, as early as the night of the raid on Scruggs's office, that if Balducci was cooperating with the authorities, he himself would be exposed to criminal charges on a different case.

Keker had picked up on Langston's uneasiness from the time he arrived in Oxford. There was something a bit squirrelly and defensive in Langston's manner, as though he were hiding something.

The source of Langston's discomfort became clear to others on December 7, the day the defendants and their lawyers met at Scruggs's office to review the first piece of evidence handed over by prosecutors in accordance with rules requiring them to do so. The group had been given a recording of the most damaging material: Balducci's visit to the law firm on November 1 when he was wearing a wire, only hours after his arrest. "Balducci should get an Academy Award for his performance," Langston said of Balducci's ability to carry off his undercover assignment.

The recording represented obvious trouble, but the mood became grimmer later in the day when Farese reported that investigators were digging into a second case. Scruggs was standing on the balcony outside his office, looking out at the old courthouse, swaddled in scaffolding during a renovation project, when Farese said cryptically that the new investigation involved "a case down south." Since much of the Scruggs litigation dealt with Katrina cases to the south, Farese was asked to be more specific. "They're looking at the Wilson case," he said, referring to the *Wilson v. Scruggs* lawsuit in Jackson.

Scruggs thought the litigation had been resolved satisfactorily. Following his $17 million setback to Al Luckey and Charlie Merkel, he had taken the Wilson case out of Jack Dunbar's hands and entrusted it to Langston, who had said he could draw upon his connections in Jackson to ensure that Scruggs would not suffer another embarrassing defeat. Sure enough, a series of rulings in 2006 by state circuit judge Bobby DeLaughter effectively limited Scruggs's losses.

DeLaughter had a sterling reputation among members of the bar association in Jackson, a high regard that originated with his performance as a local prosecutor in the office of District Attorney Ed Peters years before. The judge was thought to be irreproachable.

That evening, Dick Scruggs and his son talked over the events of the day on the driveway in front of Scruggs's new home. After the intrusion of the wiretaps, they had developed a sense of paranoia, suspecting that even conversations with their wives might be overheard. While outside, Scruggs talked with Langston by cell phone about the "case down south."

Though the prosecutors were crowing about sensational evidence that would implicate Scruggs in a new case, Langston said there was nothing to fear. Judge DeLaughter had never been promised any money, he said, and had relied on the law to make his decision.

But Langston and Scruggs both knew that Senator Lott had called DeLaughter to ask about his interest in a federal judgeship while he was considering the Wilson case.

.   .   .   .

Another alarm was sounded that Friday. Farese mentioned that the government might try to seize the assets of the defendants. He startled Zach by asking for full payment of his $300,000 retainer—as if the Scruggses' treasury would soon be looted by federal agents. To satisfy his attorney, Zach instructed the firm's bookkeepers to issue a check. Farese still seemed upset. He fretted that it could not be deposited until after the weekend.

The next afternoon Zach drove to Holly Springs, halfway between Oxford and Farese's home in Ashland, to meet his attorney at a gas station, where he was given another disk of the FBI's recording of Balducci's visit to the Scruggs Law Firm.

Farese provided some new intelligence. Steve Patterson might be forced to plead guilty because he had run out of money and could not pay his attorney's fees. There was one possibility for help, Farese said. Patterson was going to Alabama to meet with someone who might be able to finance his defense.

P. L. Blake now lived in Birmingham.

Farese said he had looked closely at the evidence. He told Zach there was nothing to incriminate him. He offered further assurance: "Your dad's fine."

Two days later, Dick Scruggs got an astonishing call from Farese, telling him that the FBI was in the midst of a raid on Langston's law office.

"Oh, my God," Scruggs said.

The agents were collecting papers dealing with Langston's representation of Scruggs in the Wilson lawsuit, he said. It was an attempt to find evidence that would link Scruggs to another case of judicial bribery. The value of a second charge was contained in a provision in the Federal Rules of Evidence known as 404(b). The rule could be used to introduce evidence that a defendant had a record of engaging in criminal activity.

Tom Dawson liked the tactic so much that he had a vanity license plate on his car bearing the number 404.

Scruggs had been talking with his son, outside in the cold, when the message came. A few minutes later, Langston called. He told Zach, "I just want to let you know, they're searching my office, looking for 404 stuff on Wilson. I hope they find what they're looking for, because it will show that nothing happened." He added, "None of this makes me diminish my faith in Dick and you."

"Nor should it," Zach said, a bit annoyed at Langston's comment.

Farese, who was at the scene in Booneville—"holding Joey's hand," as he described it—reported back to the Scruggses. "I just talked with the prosecutors," he said. "They told me Joey's not a target, that they're just looking for 404 on Dick. And they told me they're not going after anybody's assets."

Despite the bravado, the latest turn in the case brought new threats. Just as Billy Quin had predicted and Langston had feared, Tim Balducci had implicated the Booneville attorney in a widening conspiracy. It involved the move to hire Ed Peters, the former district attorney in Jackson, to use his influence with Judge DeLaughter in the Wilson case.

A few days after the raid on Langston's office, Scruggs and his son drove to New Albany—midway between Oxford and Booneville—to meet with Langston and Farese. By this time, no one trusted telephones. They were wary of public places, too. Finding the café where they planned to meet filled with customers and offering no intimacy, the four men conducted their talks while driving around town.

Langston told Scruggs the FBI was "looking at the Wilson case real hard." He said it represented no significant threat, describing the investigation as a "fishing expedition." The only person vulnerable, he said, might be Peters, who could face an income tax evasion charge if he failed to report a $50,000 payment he had gotten in cash after agreeing to get involved in the case.

Scruggs grew apprehensive. He had authorized Langston to make payments to Peters for his assistance in the case, but he did not recall all of the details. Nor did he remember the $50,000 in cash.

Langston sought to ease Scruggs's mind. He speculated that the FBI action had actually been intended to disqualify Langston as Scruggs's attorney. "It's all a bunch of bullshit," he said. In fact, Langston was very worried.

The government's principal witness was frightened, too. During his confessions, Balducci reminded federal prosecutors that Langston had defended some of the most notorious figures in North Mississippi; he claimed Langston had enough acquaintances among these criminal elements, who lived in gritty little communities in the hills, to hire someone to kill him. One of these characters was a man Langston had defended successfully in a couple of murder cases. Around the office, Langston jokingly referred to that client as "the devil from Jumpertown."

The prosecutors were well acquainted with some of the defendants Langston had represented over the years. They were known at the U.S. Attorney's Office as "stone killers," men willing to perform murders for hire to settle domestic turmoil or personal disputes in the area. In fact, rural Prentiss County, where Langston lived, was so notorious that prosecutors claimed, only half-facetiously, that a car stolen in Chicago would wind up in a Prentiss County chop shop within hours.

In a meeting with Langston shortly after it became obvious that Balducci was cooperating with federal authorities, Dawson gave the Booneville lawyer a stern warning. "I want you to know that if anything at all happens to Tim Balducci—or anybody else in this case—I'm not going to look at anyone but you first, and I'm going into Prentiss County."

Langston's face flushed. He knew there were men in Prentiss County who would be willing to exterminate Balducci, free of charge, merely as a favor to him. The prospect frightened him, too. "I swear on the heads of my children," he told Dawson, "I'll have nothing to do with that."

Balducci remained terrified. On the weekend after his grand jury appearance, Balducci took his wife and children to a motel near Jackson, Tennessee, for refuge, then panicked when he feared that one of his accomplices had booked a nearby room.

He returned to his home in New Albany and asked for protection. For weeks, until he could be settled elsewhere, Balducci was guarded around the clock by teams of Mississippi Highway Patrol troopers and FBI agents trained in surveillance. Members of Balducci's protective units wore camouflage and hid in the woods. Bob Norman, one of the prosecutors, planned to visit with his witness and deliver a couple of board games for entertainment to Balducci's twin boys, who were confined with him. Before going, Norman was given specific instructions regarding two blinks of his headlights at a specific location near Balducci's home. Norman had served in the Marines and considered himself adept at security practices, but even he was impressed by the armed guards' speed and stealth as they surrounded his car. Members of the protective unit became known around the U.S. Attorney's Office as "the snake-eaters."

Balducci and his family were eventually relocated in a Mississippi hamlet a hundred miles south of New Albany, where Balducci took a temporary job with a construction company while awaiting the forthcoming trials and the disposition of his own case.

At his hideaway, Balducci pondered his bleak future, which would surely include time in prison. He grew morose. Two weeks before Christmas he sent a sheet of parchment he once cherished to Norman Gillespie, one of the former judges who had joined his firm "of counsel." It was Balducci's certification to practice before the U.S. District Court, and it had been signed in 1991 by Gillespie when he was clerk of the court.

On the back, Balducci printed a message: "Dear Judge Gillespie," he began,

I am sorry for not contacting you sooner, but it has taken me a while to come to terms with my present situation and be able to even discuss it with friends like you. I sincerely apologize for the pain and embarrassment I have caused you . . . Judge, my heart is broken over the loss of my ability to continue to be associated with you; you are the book-ends of my career—swearing me in back in 1991 and present for my fall from grace now. I send you this certificate as my olive branch peace offering that it might remind us both of happier and simpler days. Judge, I failed you and everyone else I cared about. Although my sins are many and great, I am committed to walk on a path of redemption and reconciliation, I hope that one day I can see you again and rejoice in a brighter day . . . May God bless you richly, Tim.

It was a troubled Christmas for the members of the Scruggs family, and their concerns increased when Diane was hospitalized at the beginning of the new year after a flare-up of her illness. On Monday, January 7, she seemed stable enough to be discharged, but after the hospital staff disconnected some of the medical tubes, she suffered an embolism. The stroke-like seizure left her temporarily paralyzed on the right side of her body.

The relapse occurred around lunchtime. Early that afternoon, both Dick and Zach were at her bedside. She was conscious but able to say little.

Scruggs's cell phone rang. John Keker, his San Francisco attorney, was calling with urgent news. Scruggs left the room and walked to the end of the hospital hall to carry on the conversation without disturbing his wife. Already burdened by criminal charges and his wife's grave illness, Scruggs was stunned by Keker's report. According to a friend with connections in the Justice Department, Joey Langston was, that afternoon, in a closed federal courtroom in Oxford pleading guilty to conspiring with Scruggs and Steve Patterson to ensure "favorable consideration" for an appointment to a prestigious federal judgeship to the state judge who heard the Wilson case.

Incredulous, Scruggs walked back to his wife's room, turned to his son, and asked, "Zach, what in the hell is Joey doing?"

CHAPTER 21

Like Dick Scruggs, Paul Minor, and other Mississippi attorneys who became rich during the 1980s, Joey Langston had acquired all the trappings of success: the private jet, the vacation home in Telluride, the taste for a luxurious life that eluded most citizens of the hardscrabble hills of northeast Mississippi at the tail end of Appalachia.

No place in Booneville came close to matching Langston's estate on Old Highway 45 south of town. Set behind iron gates and a long brick wall, it occupied 250 acres of groomed land. His mansion was flanked by a swimming pool and marble statuary that had once graced Gianni Versace's palace in Miami. Langston purchased the pieces after the fashion designer's murder in 1997. He built a guesthouse with a game room bigger and finer than that of most full-time residences in the region. Paved footpaths meandered into a forest, past a tennis court. Langston had been a standout player at Millsaps College before he went on to graduate from Ole Miss law school in 1983.

He came home to a firm established by his father, Joe Ray Langston, known in the area for representing the common man, serving as a lawyerly equivalent of a country doctor building a popular practice while making house calls. But Joe Ray died a few years after his son joined him, and it was left to Joey to keep up the tradition. His siblings, Shane and Cindy, were lawyers, too. But they chose to start their careers under the more radiant lights of Jackson.

Everyone knew the lawyer as Joey; the name had a nice, homey ring. His middle name was Cashe, and that fit, too, for money seemed to flow to his office like rainwater seeking low ground. Some of his colleagues, described as "trial lawyers," were not actually trial lawyers at all. They preferred to bring their adversaries to their knees before court convened, to secure a big lick settlement. Scruggs took that approach. But Joey Langston liked to engage in trials, both civil and criminal.

He defended a number of thieves and killers and developed a reputation around the state's FBI shops as a mouthpiece for villains. Long before Langston became involved in the Scruggs case, federal prosecutors looked into allegations about him. He was never charged with misconduct until the Scruggs case, but the prosecutors were wary of him because Langston's father and law partner had been under investigation at the time of his death.

Because Langston had won so many acquittals for his clients, his supporters dismissed the allegations by the prosecutors as the juice of sour grapes. No question that he was effective in the courtroom. He had argued close to one hundred cases in trials, and had scored some stunning victories in criminal cases and civil litigation.

By 1990, when he bought the property he turned into his estate, Langston was a millionaire. He got richer. After a young boy was electrocuted when he touched a poorly wired hand-drying device in the men's room of a Pizza Hut, Langston won an eight-figure settlement from the parent company, Pepsico. He followed that up by convincing a federal court jury to deliver a $20.8 million judgment against another fast food franchise, Captain D's, after a customer was left paralyzed from a beating by employees of the seafood chain.

These cases resulted in news stories that spread Langston's name far beyond Booneville. But he was also successful in matters that were never publicly known.

One of his unpublicized achievements aided a Florida lawyer trying to unlock money won in a $187 million judgment against the government of Cuba.

The families of four men belonging to a Cuban American group called Brothers to the Rescue had received the award in federal court in Miami in 1997, nearly two years after the men were killed when Cuban jets shot down their planes on a Brothers mission in the Caribbean. However, there seemed to be no way to collect the money from a hostile government.

Langston learned of the situation in an offhand conversation with a Miami lawyer named Aaron Podhurst whom he knew from work with Scruggs in an unrelated case. Podhurst told Langston of his Cuban American clients who were sitting on a potential fortune and looking for a method to extract it from Cuba. Did Langston have any influential friends in Washington? Langston knew of one: Joe Biden, a senior member of the Senate Foreign Relations Committee. Langston was acquainted with Biden through Steve Patterson, whom he had hired because of his political associations.

Langston initiated discussions with Biden's office about the case. Talking with key members of the Delaware senator's staff, Langston helped line up Biden's support for complicated legislation that would enable the Cuban American plaintiffs to reach the foreign money. It turned out that there were other claimants against other countries. Americans who had been held hostage by Iranian-backed terrorists in Lebanon were also intent on getting payments from the government of Iran. As a result, many lawyers and sympathetic senators were involved. For all of the people and money involved, the effort required quiet, behind-the-scenes work.

One legislative victory had been a tiny provision that took up less than a page in a 3,825-page budget bill in 1998. But more work needed to be done. This was accomplished two years later during consideration of a pet bill of Biden's called the Victims of Trafficking and Violence Protection Act of 2000. The measure drew overlapping interest from the Foreign Relations and Judiciary committees; as a member of both, Biden occupied an important position. But at the time, the House and Senate were in a virtual meltdown, triggered by partisan bickering in the wake of President Clinton's impeachment. During conference meetings between members of the two congressional houses to reconcile their differences in the bill, little was being accomplished. Some thought certain elements of the bill, such as the Brothers to the Rescue claim, represented a bad precedent, and they opposed these sections. Other obstructionists wanted to block the legislation altogether. Yet Biden remained a forceful advocate for the bill, especially on behalf of language dealing with violence against women.

At the eleventh hour, congressional staff members got a mysterious call from President Clinton's National Security Council insisting that the Brothers to the Rescue provision be kept in the bill. One key staff member involved in crafting the legislation was puzzled by the intrigue. He later described the final product as a "strange animal" cob-

bled together "in a midnight sort of way." But the claims against Cuba
and Iran survived as Section 2002 of Public Law 106-386, and the
Cuban Americans got access to nearly $100 million.

For his troubles, Langston told his colleagues, he was paid several
million dollars.

When Langston boasted of his triumph in Washington back
home in Booneville, he provoked envy rather than admiration among
one of his associates. Tim Balducci yearned to make a big lick for himself. Though he was well paid as a young lawyer in Langston's office,
he wanted more.

Balducci had first worked for Langston shortly after law school, left
for several years, and then returned to the firm in 2000. He seemed
smart and clever, and for that Langston gave him a base salary of
roughly $300,000 a year. At the end of each year, Langston calculated
bonuses for his associates, and Balducci usually took home twice his
annual salary. That put his income in the top percentile of the population in Mississippi, but it was not enough for Balducci.

When Balducci visited his boss at his home, Langston could sense
that the younger man coveted his possessions. Balducci dreamed of a
private jet, a getaway place at a popular resort area; he desired to join
the ranks of the elite trial lawyers.

Balducci wanted to be made an equity partner in the firm, and
that had not happened. He also felt he had been deprived of his fair
share of Langston's spoils, especially the bonanza that came after the
multimillion-dollar settlement with MCI/WorldCom. When Langston
informed him in 2006 that he had no plans to yield any of his ownership
in the Langston Law Firm, Balducci made plans to leave. And he left in
the company of Patterson, another of Langston's longtime associates.

Langston was more troubled by Patterson's departure. The two men
had been friends since Langston, while a student at Millsaps, served as a
volunteer in a 1975 gubernatorial campaign directed by Patterson. Two
decades later, Patterson called upon Langston to defend him against
criminal charges brought by Attorney General Mike Moore. An investigation into the embezzlement of thousands of dollars from a police
chiefs' organization had led Moore to the state auditor's office, which
was headed by Patterson. Since Moore and Scruggs had been targeted
by Patterson a few years earlier, the attorney general had no reluctance
about pursuing the auditor. Moore's investigators developed a list of al-

legations, including falsified expense accounts and favors offered in exchange for money. Moore was prepared to seek Patterson's indictment.

After assessing the situation, Langston saw that his client faced serious charges being pressed by a personal and political enemy. He knew
of Patterson's earlier attempt to undercut Moore via the action against
Scruggs in 1992. "When you take a swing at the king, you better knock
him down," Langston told Patterson, reminding him of his failure to
take out Moore.

In an effort to resolve the case out of court, Langston met with
Moore. He argued that Patterson was an elected official and a Democrat. Moore countered that Patterson was a dishonest man dealing with
state money. The attorney general insisted that Patterson give up his
office, and he delivered Langston a deadline to make a decision. He
warned that Patterson would be indicted the next day.

The talks ended in an agreement. Patterson would plead guilty to a
misdemeanor—failing to pay taxes on a car—and would resign as state
auditor. By doing so, he avoided a messier set of charges.

Patterson lost his portfolio as state auditor, but he retained his
Rolodex. Though he had no law degree, he was hired to join the Langston Law Firm to lure clients and to lobby, unofficially, for special projects. Patterson not only served as Langston's introduction to Joe Biden,
he also wired Langston into P. L. Blake's circle of cronies.

"I introduced Mr. Langston to an awful lot of people that he made an
awful lot of money out of," Patterson once boasted.

As his renown grew, Langston became a campaign issue during
state elections in 2007.

Jim Hood, the incumbent attorney general, came under attack by his
Republican opponent for the arrangement with Langston to represent
the state in an effort to recover funds from MCI/WorldCom, the bankrupt telecommunications giant that had headquarters in Mississippi. In
a way, it was a throwback to the dispute over Mike Moore's decision to
appoint Scruggs as a special assistant attorney general to handle litigation involving asbestos and tobacco.

After a period of spectacular growth from a little company do-
miciled in Clinton, Mississippi, to a $37 billion merger with MCI
Communications—the largest in U.S. history at the time—MCI/World-
Com crashed in 2002. Its CEO, Bernard Ebbers, and other officers were
sent to prison for fraudulent accounting practices that hid losses and

inflated revenue to stabilize its stock price. The state of Mississippi, among others, was left holding the bag.

But Billy Quin, a young lawyer in the Jackson office of a Louisiana law firm, Lundy and Davis, was intrigued by the idea that the state could prove that the company evaded taxes through deceptive reporting practices. After reviewing records for several days, he was convinced the state could make a substantial claim. Using a friend in the legislature as an intermediary, he presented his case to the attorney general. Hood liked Quin's theory, but wanted to pair the Louisiana firm with Mississippi lawyers. He shopped the case among friendly trial lawyers, such as Scruggs. After Langston showed more enthusiasm for the case than others, he was given the job.

It resulted in 2005 in a payment of more than $100 million by MCI to the state to cover back taxes owed by its predecessor company, WorldCom. The company also turned over to the state a building it owned in downtown Jackson. Langston and the Louisiana law firm negotiated a separate fee for themselves of $14 million, which they split. (Quin, who had worked closely with Langston on the case, was dissatisfied with the share his firm gave him and wound up going to work for Langston, replacing Tim Balducci.)

With Hood facing a reelection campaign, Langston made a $100,000 contribution to the attorney general and channeled another $100,000 to him through an attorneys general organization. Hood was accused by the Republican candidate, Al Hopkins, of awarding state contracts to lawyers, who reciprocated with big political contributions.

Hood won reelection easily, the only Democrat to survive in statewide office. (Scruggs's candidate for insurance commissioner, Gary Anderson, was among the losers.) Langston weathered criticism on the grounds that he had succeeded in winning the state far more than expected and negotiated his own payment from the company rather than taking a contingency fee from the state.

All seemed calm. Then, three weeks after the election, the Scruggs case exploded on the scene.

Ever since the raid on Scruggs's office, and then his own, Joey Langston recognized that he had a problem. Balducci, the government's chief witness, was consumed with ill will and envy and would do anything in his power to bring him down. Langston could trace his vulnerability to the handling of the lawsuit against Scruggs by his former partner Roberts Wilson. First filed in 1993, the case had wandered through different courts and jurisdictions until it settled on the docket of state circuit judge Bobby DeLaughter. After suffering from the companion action by Al Luckey, Scruggs was determined not to lose to Wilson. Circumstances seemed to call for different tactics.

Langston and Balducci had helped represent Scruggs in the Luckey trial. With the Wilson case looming, Langston had some new ideas. He warned Scruggs that he might be "home-cooked" in Jackson. "They'll be out to strike against you," he told Scruggs, referring to a cadre of lawyers in the state capital who resented Scruggs. On the plaintiff's side, Wilson had hired a Jackson lawyer, William Kirksey, to help represent him. Kirksey had once been in the same law firm as Judge DeLaughter. Langston warned Scruggs that Kirksey's presence might sway the judge's decision. To counter Kirksey, Langston suggested that Scruggs retain the services of Ed Peters, a longtime player in the old political network. The former district attorney had once been DeLaughter's boss.

Peters was familiar with Wilson's lingering dispute with Scruggs. Years before, after Scruggs made his peace with the "dark side of the Force," Peters had obligingly threatened Wilson with prosecution over a tax issue.

Peters had a history of using his office as district attorney in the state's largest county as a weapon, to run interference for his allies and to punish their enemies.

He was reelected repeatedly, although newspapers reported on some of the seamy episodes that tarnished his record. He escaped conviction after being acquitted of extortion charges in 1975, four years after he was first elected. He was also reprimanded by the Mississippi Bar Association after a federal judge found that an insurance company he represented had been involved in deceptive sales of securities. Later in the decade, he came under investigation by the FBI over allegations that prisoners at the state penitentiary were paying $1,000 a year to have their sentences reduced in Hinds County courts. In 1977, he was investigated as a result of reports that he accepted payoffs rather than prosecute prostitution rings. No charges were ever filed, and the muckraking Jack Anderson, a nationally syndicated columnist, attributed the lack of action to intervention by Senator Eastland, the original king of the dark side of the Force.

With his connections to the Eastland apparatus, Peters built a reputation over the years. One of his close associates was Steve Patterson, who said of him, "Ed Peters ran the Hinds County courthouse for twenty years. Period." Patterson elaborated on his own political antennae in a 2009 deposition. "You tell me a county, and I'll tell you who you need to hire." In Hinds County, where the state capital of Jackson was located, Patterson said Peters "could find out virtually anything on any subject."

Although Peters no longer held public office, he still wielded influence—especially, Patterson and Langston thought, with his former deputy who had become a judge, Bobby DeLaughter. "Anyone who understands Hinds County politics and Hinds County's judicial system knows that's a very close relationship," Patterson said.

Peters and DeLaughter had been heroes in national news stories in 1994 when they carried out the successful prosecution of Byron De La Beckwith, an aging white supremacist accused of the civil rights–era assassination of Medgar Evers, an NAACP leader in Mississippi. Although Beckwith had been arrested shortly after the 1963 murder, two trials in that decade ended in hung juries, and the state made no further efforts to convict him.

Beckwith maintained his notoriety. He ran for lieutenant governor of Mississippi in 1967 as a "straight shooter"—Evers had been shot in the back by a high-powered rifle. He finished fifth in the race while winning thirty-four thousand votes. In 1973 he was arrested in New Orleans, with a time bomb ticking in his car, on a mission to dynamite the home of a prominent Jewish activist. After serving three years in a Louisiana prison, Beckwith retreated to a mountaintop near Chattanooga where he flew the Confederate battle flag from his porch and periodically issued racist proclamations.

By refusing to fade away, Beckwith ensured that people would not forget him. When news stories uncovered evidence of jury tampering in his long-ago trials, a clamor arose in Mississippi to bring the old man back for another courtroom drama.

DeLaughter, an energetic prosecutor in Peters's office, advocated a new trial, and the district attorney—knowing that black voters represented a significant percentage of his constituency—agreed. In the first of a series of redemptive southern trials that obtained convictions in racial murders, DeLaughter and Peters built a formidable case that resulted in a guilty verdict. Beckwith died in prison.

DeLaughter wrote about his experiences in a prize-winning book, *Never Too Late*, and was gilded by a 1996 movie, *Ghosts of Mississippi*, in which his character was portrayed by Alec Baldwin. Three years later he was appointed to a vacant county judgeship, elected to a full term, and then appointed in 2002 by Governor Musgrove to serve an unexpired term as circuit judge.

The movie reduced Peters's character to a bit role, played by an actor named Craig T. Nelson. The script even gave DeLaughter credit for Peters's tough cross-examination of a defense witness. Afterward, Peters complained to a reporter, "At first, it didn't bother me. I always thought of movies as fiction anyway, and Bobby told me he had protested. Then I talked with Rob Reiner [the director], who told me the purpose of the movie was to record history. So you are recording history, but the moment everybody considers to be the turning point of the trial, you're giving it to someone else?"

If Peters was irked that DeLaughter won most of the praise, he did not show it publicly. Instead, the two men remained close friends. Though DeLaughter occupied a place on the bench, Peters was still considered his mentor.

The idea to use Peters in the *Wilson v. Scruggs* case had actually come from Steve Patterson, who had been dealing for years with Peters, his confederate in the network. At the time, Patterson was still working for Langston's law firm. The plan made sense to Langston, who sold it to Scruggs. It was agreed that Peters would not serve as Scruggs's attorney of record, but would represent his interests quietly outside the formal constraints of the court.

Scruggs asked his financial advisors to determine an amount that represented a "best-case scenario" of his prospective cost in the case. They arrived at a figure of $2.5 million. Negotiating through Langston, Scruggs proposed a "reverse contingency fee." If the final judgment came in under $2.5 million, the Langston-Peters team could keep the difference. If the judgment exceeded $2.5 million, the former district attorney would get nothing.

Peters asked for $50,000 up front. Patterson suggested that he be paid in cash as a favor. "Nothing sinister about it," he later explained. Peters was remodeling a fishing camp in Louisiana. "You know, you can pay contractors with cash pretty easily in Louisiana."

Langston did not keep that much cash on hand, and was pleasantly surprised when his associate, Balducci, volunteered to provide the money. It came from a cache Balducci called his "slush fund." With $50,000 in U.S. currency tucked into a thick envelope, Langston, Patterson, and

Balducci flew to Jackson to deliver the payment to Peters. They met at a private hanger at the Jackson airport. When Balducci, who had, after all, supplied the money—was asked to stay behind in a reception area to watch television while Langston and Patterson met privately with Peters, it became another grievance Balducci accumulated against Langston. He wanted to be an inside player, too. At least he was repaid. The $50,000 was reimbursed under the guise of payments for a swimming pool being built at Balducci's home.

Scruggs said nothing about giving Langston primacy in handling the Wilson case. Johnny Jones, a member of the legal team, learned about Langston's new role indirectly. He called Jack Dunbar in Oxford to tell him that "Joey Langston's down in Jackson saying he's now in charge of the Wilson case." It was the first that Dunbar, who had been Scruggs's lead attorney, knew he was being replaced.

Jones and his partner Steve Funderburg stayed on the case. They did not know of Peters's involvement, but felt comfortable that Scruggs would win in DeLaughter's court on the merits of his argument. DeLaughter seemed to have taken an interest in the nuances of the case that other judges had ignored.

Zach Scruggs was confident, too. He sent Jones an email hailing his firm's work and DeLaughter's grasp of the facts.

"I know Steve has been working hard on the Wilson case and has done a great job on briefing and getting Joey and Tim up to speed," Zach wrote. "But I can tell you that you could file briefs on a napkin right now and get it granted given the Judge's view of the case . . . Joey and Tim have this situation well in hand . . . I think they have turned this thing around before a judge who is fair, doesn't hate Dick or want to punish him for making money like the other 2 [judges], and actually understands the case."

Jones replied by email the next day. He told Zach: "You have some misconceptions about Joey and Tim that I hope do not ultimately need to be explored." Jones considered the two Booneville lawyers high-caliber bullshit artists and was resentful that Langston had been given the lead in the case. "If we win, it will be because the law says we win. Letting J.D. [Judge DeLaughter] have 2 days to read the file and all the briefing back in February helped our cause tremendously. He finally did the hard work that no other judge (including Davis) would do to figure out where the merits lay in these cases."

By this time, however, Scruggs had received a thirdhand message from Peters. The former D.A. was more concerned in gaining an advantage for Scruggs than in studying the merits of his case. It would help, Peters reported, if DeLaughter were considered for an open federal judgeship in Mississippi. Peters had passed the word to Patterson, who relayed it to Langston, who told his client.

Scruggs reminded Langston of his poor track record in recommending judicial nominations to his Republican brother-in-law. But he had known DeLaughter in law school and felt his moderate background might prove acceptable to Lott. At least, Scruggs thought, DeLaughter's name could be put on a list of candidates that Lott and his fellow senator from Mississippi, Thad Cochran, would consider.

So he called Lott to suggest DeLaughter's name. Lott, who constantly fended off supplicants for patronage jobs and federal appointments, asked if DeLaughter was seriously interested. Assured by Scruggs of DeLaughter's qualifications and desire, Lott agreed to call the judge. They had a pleasant conversation, which Lott concluded by suggesting that DeLaughter send him a résumé.

For all of the activity, it was unlikely that Lott would recommend DeLaughter to the White House. The judge was perceived as too liberal. Besides, he had a beard, and the senator did not care for beards.

Even as he implicated his former associates during his confessions to the FBI, Balducci told the agents that Scruggs never promised a federal judgeship for DeLaughter. Balducci said he overheard Scruggs, "on more than one occasion," tell Patterson and Langston that he could only "make sure that DeLaughter would be considered" for the post.

Lott's call to DeLaughter came on March 29, 2006, a month after DeLaughter had already delivered an important ruling rejecting a finding by a special master in the case that recommended a $12 million judgment against Scruggs. By the time DeLaughter issued his final declaration in July, determining that Scruggs owed Wilson no more money, the vacant judgeship was on its way to another man.

Still, there were doubts about DeLaughter's decision. When Wilson's attorney, Charlie Merkel, got word of DeLaughter's ruling, he cried out to one of his partners, "Somebody got to him."

Balducci, who had been overheard on FBI recordings bragging of "slush funds" and "bodies buried," turned over the names of Joey

Langston and Ed Peters to the U.S. attorneys two days after he was first confronted by the FBI. That was the Saturday that Tom Dawson had to skip the Ole Miss homecoming game.

Balducci's information not only imperiled Langston and Peters, it exposed Scruggs to a second charge of bribing a judge. This opened the door for the government to use the 404(b) provision to show that Scruggs had a predilection for criminal behavior.

Langston knew that he, too, would be targeted as soon as he heard the prosecutors play their 404(b) card against his client Dick Scruggs. Sifting through what he knew, Langston realized that Ed Peters would be a critical figure to the investigation.

On a dreary Saturday in early December—after Patterson had been indicted but before Langston's office was raided—Langston and Patterson decided that they needed to make a pilgrimage to Jackson. Despite Patterson's break with Langston's firm, the two men had maintained an odd friendship throughout Patterson's ill-fated alliance with Balducci. Langston continued to pay Patterson $80,000 a month for his role in helping to resolve the tangled tobacco lawsuit involving the Butler family, and they still had things in common. It would be in their interest, Langston said, to go see the former district attorney.

(The government would eventually allege that the trio—Langston, Patterson, and Peters—divided equally a $3 million payment from Scruggs. Like so much in the case, it was never as simple as the government indicated.

(Peters had gotten $50,000 in cash, up front. After DeLaughter ruled favorably for Scruggs, Peters demanded all of Scruggs's $2.5 million. Because Scruggs had been forced to pay Wilson several million dollars over the long duration of the suit, he refused to hand over the full amount. Instead, he sent Langston a check for $1.9 million, earmarked primarily for Peters. Later, he sent a second check for $600,000 to settle Peters's demand.

(Rather than turn the money directly over to Peters, Langston kept some for himself and wired Peters monthly increments that finally totaled $950,000. Added to the $50,000 in cash, Peters wound up with $1 million.

(To compensate Langston for his representation in the Wilson case, Scruggs also forgave a $2 million debt Langston owed. Scruggs had loaned him the money to help finance a Fen-Phen case.

(Patterson never received the $1 million the government alleged he got for his one-third cut of the deal. When he bolted from Langston's firm to join Balducci, Patterson left his share of Scruggs's money behind. He claimed that Langston used him as a "pawn" by telling Peters the money would be split three ways. As a result, Peters got only one third. Langston kept the rest,

(Although Patterson felt shortchanged in the deal, he continued to get piecemeal payments from Langston for other services rendered over the years.)

Against this backdrop of tangled transactions and a federal investigation, Langston and Patterson went to Peters's house. They gave him five minutes' notice, calling him just before arriving. Though surprised, Peters was cordial yet guarded in his comments as they discussed the ramifications of the case.

Peters was seventy. His hair, which had grown gray years before, had now gone white and wispy. He was growing deaf and suffering from a cold; his sneezes interrupted their conversation. Though known as the chief fixer of Hinds County, he did not appear very menacing. He merely looked old and harmless.

Langston told him that the prosecutors kept bringing up 404(b) in connection with the DeLaughter case.

"We didn't give Bobby any money," Peters rationalized. "Besides, I think he followed the law" in deciding the Wilson case.

"I do, too," Langston agreed. Still, he was apprehensive.

Patterson appealed to his old friend to help him in the case involving the bribe to Judge Lackey. Peters said he would like to help. After forty-five minutes of rambling conversation, Langston and Patterson rose to leave.

Peters looked at his guests. "Boys," he said, "I'd cut my own throat for you." Then he made a slashing gesture across his neck with his hand.

Instead of protecting his old friends, Peters and his attorney, Cynthia Stewart, began meeting with federal authorities in Oxford just before Christmas. A veteran prosecutor himself, Peters realized that his position was tenuous. But he also knew that his cooperation would be invaluable to the U.S. attorneys trying to build a case against Scruggs and Langston. He was prepared to make a "Rule 11 proffer," in which he would tell all that he knew of the maneuvering with Judge DeLaughter in exchange for an agreement not to bring charges against him.

Because the case involved a public official—an elected judge—representatives of the Public Integrity Section of the U.S. Justice Department sat in on the discussions. Peters did not know the federal prosecutors well, and appeared to be floundering. At one point, his own attorney burst into tears, charging that one of the FBI agents was being unduly harsh toward her client. Peters seemed relieved and visibly brightened when Tom Dawson came into the room during the negotiations. They had known each other for more than thirty years, from the time Dawson was a young attorney in Meridian and had been hired by Peters's district attorney's office to help select a jury in a trial moved from Jackson to Meridian.

Peters rose to shake Dawson's hand, then awkwardly embraced him.

"It's good to see you, Ed," Dawson told him. "But I'm sorry it's under these circumstances."

During a series of meetings with the prosecutors, Peters laid out the details of his discussions with DeLaughter and the money that had been sent to Peters. It essentially corroborated what Balducci had said earlier. Peters's account implicated Scruggs as the beneficiary of the scheme and the ultimate source of the money. The information also put Langston in what the prosecutors called their "trick bag," enabling them to squeeze him further.

The U.S. attorneys were confronted with a hard decision: to offer protection to a venal man who had held an important public office for decades in exchange for his testimony. In the end, they agreed to do so.

Under the terms of their secret agreement with Peters, the prosecutors gave him transactional immunity from prosecution in the case they would begin to call Scruggs II. Not everyone was satisfied with the arrangement; especially the Public Integrity officials from Washington, who were dismayed over the deal Dawson had struck with his old friend and fellow prosecutor. But Peters's cooperation would make it possible for the government to move against Langston, Scruggs, and DeLaughter. Peters would give up his license to practice law, turn over to the government $450,000 left from his share of the deal, and continue to be exposed to criminal charges if other cases developed. Nevertheless, the veteran dealmaker in the state capital would once again escape prosecution.

Patterson, who described himself as "somewhat of a switchboard" between Peters, Langston, and Balducci, had a different account of Scruggs's role. Scruggs had not been a party to discussions with Peters, he said later in confidential testimony never publicly released. "No one had a conversation with Mr. Scruggs. Mr. Balducci, I don't think, had much conversation with Mr. Scruggs about this case . . . Mr.

Scruggs was the guy with the money. Mr. Langston, above all others, recognized that fact, and therefore he kept me or Mr. Balducci—or anyone else who might get credit with Mr. Scruggs for having done anything—far away as he possibly could from Mr. Scruggs."

Patterson testified that P. L. Blake knew about the arrangement with Peters. "My guess is, I told him . . . We talked all the time. Mr. Blake was the kind of guy who, shall we say, dealt in information."

Throughout December, Langston worried over reports that the government was preparing a case against him. Despite the presence of three sons—two in college and one in high school—at home for the holidays, Christmas held little gaiety for Langston and his wife, who agonized over the situation. The most successful member of the Booneville bar felt that events were closing in on him.

On the first Thursday of the new year, Langston and his associate Billy Quin flew to Washington on Langston's jet to consult with a prominent criminal defense lawyer. Reid Weingarten had defended Bernard Ebbers, the former WorldCom executive whose case had been the state's greatest white-collar crime story until the Scruggs affair.

Langston thought the federal case being constructed against him might be handled out of Washington, rather than North Mississippi, so he wanted to play all of the angles available to him. He thought a Washington lawyer familiar with the criminal division of the Justice Department might be able to waylay an indictment. But Weingarten offered little help.

On the flight home, Langston began speaking of himself in the past tense. It troubled Quin, who had worked for him for a year. The last time Quin had heard someone use the past tense in referring to himself, it had been his father, deflated after the death of Quin's mother. He decided Langston needed a pep talk.

"Joey," Quin said as the small jet made its way back to Mississippi, "let's talk about this. There are five people involved. There's Dickie and Trent, DeLaughter and Peters and you. What are they going to say? Dickie's going to say: 'I didn't do anything.' Lott's going to say the same thing. That leaves DeLaughter, Peters, and you. DeLaughter's going to say: 'I didn't do anything.' So what does Peters have to say?"

Back home, Langston concluded that Peters had a lot to say. Peters and his attorney had been incommunicado for several weeks, not responding to Langston's call for a joint defense agreement between the prospective defendants. Langston also worried over what Scruggs might tell the prosecutors. That Friday he called Scruggs's office, but failed to reach him. He left a mysterious message with the receptionist: "Tell Dick that I'm no Tim Balducci."

While Langston was in Washington, his friend Tony Farese had begun plea bargaining with prosecutors in Oxford. Farese asked for immunity for Langston in exchange for his cooperation in the case the prosecutors were calling Scruggs II. No deal. As a fallback, Farese indicated that Langston would be willing to plead guilty to a reduced charge, a misdemeanor that would enable him to continue to practice law. No deal.

The federal government held over Langston the specter of the Racketeer Influenced and Corrupt Organizations (RICO) statute, which empowered them to seize any assets he might have gained illegally.

Langston realized that aside from harming his professional reputation, the government might confiscate his personal possessions. The thought that he might lose his Booneville estate, his Colorado vacation home, his jet, became as great a concern to him as an indictment.

Over the weekend, as he drove aimlessly around Booneville, he called Scruggs at home. They had a convoluted conversation that Scruggs thought quite pointless. It consisted largely of Langston making ad hominem observations that had little to do with the case.

All that Langston had built seemed to be crumbling. Only a few weeks before, the Langston Law Firm had been represented in a back-cover advertisement of *MidSouth Super Lawyers 2007*, a slick supplement inserted in every copy of the *The New York Times* Sunday edition distributed in the region. The text of the announcement sang of Langston's recent accomplishments—winner of the 2007 Mississippi Trial Lawyer of the Year, winner of an annual award given by the state Democratic Party.

Langston had great pride in appearances, so much so that some detractors referred to him as Joey the Blade. He paid a local stylist to groom his hair. He wore tailored dress suits, silk ties, and shoes made of costly leather. Ordinarily his face had a cherubic glow, a picture of innocence. But now, it had taken on a washed-out, unhealthy pallor.

Langston drove to his office, which was shuttered and unoccupied. He sat on a couch, in the darkness, and contemplated his situation. He tried to determine, in his mind, how the case might play out. He knew Balducci was already aligned against him and that Peters had probably become a cooperating witness. He wondered about Scruggs. He knew from his experience as a criminal defense attorney how the U.S.

Attorney's Office in Oxford operated. He realized they would make threats and offer deals. If he chose to fight the charges, he believed the government would go to Scruggs and say: Here's our deal on the indictments in Judge Lackey's case. If you testify against Langston in the DeLaughter case, we won't prosecute your son, Zach. Langston had three sons himself. He felt certain that Scruggs would turn on him to save his own son.

Early Monday morning, he made one last attempt to contact Scruggs. Getting no answer, he left another message on voice mail. "Dick," it said simply, "I need to talk to you."

The prosecutors had given Langston until that afternoon to make his decision. Expecting a breakthrough, Tom Dawson arrived at his office by 6:00 a.m. It was cold and rainy outside. An hour later, Joey Langston showed up, trembling and distraught.

CHAPTER 22

Joey Langston's illustrious career, his life as a pillar in the northeast Mississippi community, were coming to an end, and he asked for a few days to wind up his affairs. U.S. District Judge Michael Mills, who had been given the case, was willing to grant him that much. It would be unpleasant duty for everyone involved. Mills knew Langston well. They came from the same part of the state, and Mills had presided over the Captain D's trial, one of Langston's great triumphs. So the judge allowed Langston to come quietly into his private chambers to finish the business. Mills agreed to seal the results of the hearing for a week, but he also showed that his lenience had limits. When he saw Shane Langston in the room and learned he was not formally representing his brother, the judge had three words for him: "Hit the door."

The hearing took only twenty-five minutes and followed a script the two sides had agreed upon. Although he had not been indicted, Langston would plead guilty to charges of conspiring with Dick Scruggs, Steve Patterson, Tim Balducci, Ed Peters, and others to corruptly influence Judge DeLaughter. Langston faced a maximum sentence of five years in prison, but the prosecutors, who were counting on Langston to cooperate, agreed to seek no more than three years' imprisonment. The critical element in the plea bargain was contained in one line of Tom Dawson's brief remarks: "The United States agrees not to seek forfeiture of the defendant's assets."

The arrangement between Langston and the prosecutors had been completed quickly that morning. He pleaded guilty and told Judge Mills he intended to surrender his license to practice law. Then his voice gave way to crying.

Langston's lawyers, Tony and Steve Farese, asked if he could sit down. The defendant was able to regain his composure, but there was little left to say.

As Judge Mills prepared to recess the hearing, he told a marshal, "Let's not get into all that handcuff stuff if we can avoid it," and then asked the fallen lawyer, "Can you behave, Mr. Langston?"

"Yes sir," Langston replied, weeping again. "I'm embarrassed and ashamed. And I should be."

"You've earned it," Mills said.

"Yes, sir, I have."

And with that, a few minutes before two o'clock on the afternoon of January 7, 2008, the public stature of Joey Langston and the law practice his father had established was extinguished.

Langston's associate Billy Quin was in Jackson when Brook Dooley, an associate of Scruggs's chief defense lawyer, John Keker, called him later that day. "We know what your partner's up to, and we know what's going on," Dooley told him.

Quin was baffled by the accusatorial manner. "What's going on?" he asked.

Dooley said Langston had spent the afternoon in the federal courthouse in Oxford, probably turning on Scruggs.

"That's news to me," Quin said. As soon as their short conversation was over, he tried to reach Langston.

He was interrupted by an incoming call, this one from Rhea Tannehill, the Oxford lawyer representing Sid Backstrom in the Lackey case. Quin and Tannehill, fraternity brothers at Ole Miss, were old friends, but Quin was suspicious. He thought that Tannehill, like Dooley, was fishing for information.

Quin professed that he knew little. He told Tannehill of the trip to Washington with Langston a few days before to meet with Reid Weingarten, but he was stunned by news of Langston's court appearance. "Listen, Rhea," he told his friend, "if y'all think I know about this, you'd be wrong." He was concerned that the other defense lawyers with whom he had been working would think that he, like Langston, had been double-dealing.

He finally reached Langston on his cell phone. Their conversation lasted less than a minute. "I've taken care of my problem," Langston said simply. He promised to tell Quin more later.

When Quin got back to Booneville, Langston explained that he had had no choice other than to plead guilty. It was his only way out of a terrible bind.

In a tearful session, Langston met with members of his staff at the Langston Law Firm. He begged their forgiveness and expressed hope that the firm could continue. He asked Quin about the possibility of his staying; he even talked of changing the name of the firm. But Quin was uncomfortable with the proposition. Booneville was Joey Langston's town; it would never be Quin's. He had come there to work with Langston, had even handled an awkward commute to Booneville each day from Tupelo, where he had settled his family. It would be best for Quin to move back to Jackson and open his own firm.

Langston's plea threw the Scruggs defense team into disarray as soon as they learned of it. Dick Scruggs suddenly faced a situation in which his own lawyer was prepared to implicate him in another bribery. His son had also been put in a difficult position. Zach's defense attorney, Tony Farese, now represented someone planning to testify against his father.

Dick Scruggs felt betrayed; Zach, enraged. For several weeks, Zach had been troubled by Farese's behavior, and as he absorbed the news of Langston's guilty plea, he began to retrace his recent dealings with the two men.

Zach believed that both Farese and Langston had lied during their conversation with him and his father as they drove around New Albany before Christmas. At the time, they dismissed the likelihood that Langston would be charged. Zach also wondered about Farese's connections with the U.S. Attorney's Office. A couple of weeks before, Farese had complained that a motion by Keker had "pissed off the prosecutors." Who cared if they annoyed the prosecutors if it helped Scruggs's defense? Zach remembered that Farese had made an unauthorized overture to the prosecutors about a possible plea arrangement for his father the day after Christmas. When Zach questioned the wisdom of making this signal to the government lawyers, Farese said, "Things could get worse for Dick."

A few hours before Langston appeared before Judge Mills, Zach had a phone conversation with Farese, who had failed to return several calls over the weekend. Where had he been? "I'm in Oxford, killing some snakes on a Monday," Farese said. A few minutes later, the lawyer came to Zach's office but appeared in a rush. He said he had papers that Langston's "D.C. lawyers" wanted Zach to sign, a "waiver of conflict of interest" form, which would enable Farese to represent Langston and Zach at the same time. He told Zach it was "no big deal . . . a pretty standard form."

Zach was puzzled by the request. Farese had reassured him that Langston was not a target, explaining that the waiver would merely authorize Farese to assist Langston's Washington lawyers in dealing with documents before a grand jury as a result of the FBI raid on Langston's office.

Before leaving, Farese made copies of the waiver and said hello to Sid Backstrom.

Later, Zach concluded that Farese was on his way to the U.S. Attorney's Office, a few blocks away, to complete the plea bargain for Langston.

Farese would insist that the contract signed that day formalized an agreement he and Zach had reached orally on December 11, the day after Langston's office was searched by the FBI. At that time, Farese said, he and Langston became part of a joint defense agreement with other defendants and their attorneys.

Zach maintained that he never agreed to have Farese represent Langston at the same time. It was the beginning of yet another ugly dispute between lawyers.

Farese, Farese and Farese had amassed a powerful reputation in the years since "Big John" Farese founded the firm in 1939 in the remote North Mississippi village of Ashland. The son of an Italian immigrant, Farese had come south from Boston on a football scholarship at a Mississippi junior college. He stayed to work his way through Ole Miss law school and open an office in Ashland, where his new wife, Orene, had a job as a schoolteacher. As more members of the Farese family arrived in Benton County, they gave up Catholicism for the fundamentalist Protestant faiths popular in the region. They also became political players in a rural area along the Tennessee state line that has no major highway. "Big John" and his wife served together in the state legislature. After a nephew, Anthony Farese, joined the law firm, he went on to be elected chancery judge for the district. By the latter part of the twentieth century, a new generation of Fareses, including Steve and Tony, took over the firm and specialized in criminal defense work.

When students at Ole Miss, fifty miles away, ran afoul of the law, their parents often turned to the Farese firm for help. But when the Fareses opened an Oxford office, they had another reason. They were increasingly involved in cases in federal court there. The firm appeared proficient in hammering out plea bargains with federal prosecutors for their clients. Robert Whitwell, U.S. attorney for the Northern District of Mississippi during President George H. W. Bush's administration, joined the Farese firm after he left office in 1993. And it did not go without notice that Whitwell's brother-in-law Jim Greenlee was appointed U.S. attorney after the election of the second George Bush.

The Farese firm boasted of acquittals won in state courts in Mississippi and Tennessee, which sprang a variety of clients from murder charges. Just months before the Scruggs case broke, Steve Farese was instrumental in reducing the jail sentence of Mary Winkler to a matter of days to end a sensational case. Winkler had originally been charged with murdering her husband, a Church of Christ minister, in Selmer, Tennessee, by shooting him in the back with a shotgun while he slept. She was convicted of a lesser crime, voluntary manslaughter, during a trial that drew breathless television coverage in the Mid-South and further publicity for the Farese firm.

The Fareses won favorable verdicts in federal court, too. Steve and Tony, working with Joey Langston and Zach Scruggs, had earned acquittals for the two Lee County deputies in Zach's introduction to criminal trials. But the Fareses were better known in federal court circles for their ability to cut deals with prosecutors, who trusted their word and completed their agreements with simple handshakes rather than court papers.

Zach Scruggs's problem was that he wanted no plea bargain. He insisted upon his innocence, and he felt his position had been jeopardized by the latest turn in the case.

After learning of Langston's plea, Zach returned to his office late that afternoon and called Farese for details. Farese said he did not want to talk about the case on the phone, implying that Scruggs's phone might be tapped by the FBI. Within an hour, he appeared at the office. They were the only people left in the darkened upstairs suite on the square, and they sat in the same conference room where Balducci had volunteered to approach Judge Lackey more than eight months earlier.

Farese explained that Langston had pleaded guilty because prosecutors were threatening to indict him for money laundering, mail fraud, wire fraud, and racketeering. In addition, Farese said, the government attorneys had been ready to initiate RICO action to seize all of Langston's assets.

While Zach listened in disbelief, Farese said Langston was now cooperating with the federal government and would be willing to testify against his own client, Dick Scruggs. In an attempt to mollify Zach, Farese said Langston would say that Zach knew nothing of the plot to influence Judge DeLaughter. Langston also sent word that he "would not lie on Dick."

Zach retorted that his father had done nothing illegal and should not have to worry about lies.

"Well, there are some things you do not know about your dad," Farese replied.

The conversation grew heated. Zach demanded to know why Farese had failed to share with him the knowledge that Langston would soon plead guilty. Farese told Zach, "You were not entitled to that information."

Despondent, Zach drove home. On the way, his cell phone rang. He could see the call came from Langston. He refused to answer.

Instead, he called the man who had been close to him for most of his life, Mike Moore, and poured out his problem to the former attorney general. After hanging up and reflecting on their conversation, Moore told his wife, "You know, I think Zach wants me to represent him."

Tisha Moore had a quick reaction, invoking the name of their own son. "What if Kyle were in trouble and he called Dick? Don't you think Dick would help?" Her husband immediately called Zach and agreed to take his case.

During the ordeal in early January, Dick Scruggs maintained a certain calm—with the aid of Fioricet. His son did not take developments as quietly. Zach lashed out at those who he felt had betrayed the Scruggs family. After learning that Langston had wept as he pleaded guilty before Judge Mills, Zach was scornful. He remembered that Langston had bragged privately about his uncanny ability to cry when delivering passionate closing arguments. He told Zach how he would concentrate on an unhappy experience—the death of his father, for example—in order to establish a mood that would help him shed tears. He said the tactic often led jurors to weep themselves. Langston suggested that he should be awarded a "tear bonus"—a symbolic tear for each juror who cried—much in the same way that ace pilots in World War II earned an insignia of the enemy on the fuselage of their planes for each rival aircraft shot down.

Zach remembered this as he pondered the situation in the privacy of his small office, down the hall from his father's room overlooking the square. Zach had an inelegant view of the backsides of buildings from his window, but his wall was brightened with framed school degrees and other mementos, including the front page from the Tupelo newspaper with Langston's congratulatory inscription. Zach was confused by the move of a man who had been a friend and a mentor. But for Tony Farese, Zach had only contempt.

Though Zach was a novice in the field of criminal defense work, he felt he had enough innate intelligence and confidence to make some moves of his own. Without consulting his father, who no longer seemed to be thinking clearly under the pressure of prosecution, Zach decided to break with members of the defense team.

His cell phone rang, and he saw he was getting another call from Langston. Instead of answering, Zach called Farese and told him, in dismissive tones, "Your client called me again. If he's got a message, tell him to give it to you."

Farese said Zach should understand that Langston had no choice. "They were going to take his assets."

Twenty-four hours later, Zach placed another call to Farese.

"Tony," he said. "First of all, you're fired. And I think you know why." Farese said nothing.

"I paid you three hundred thousand dollars," Zach continued, "and I want it back, along with all of the evidence you gathered." For the past month, the Scruggs defense team had been getting copies of wiretaps and other FBI material to which they were entitled under the federal rules that require prosecutors to share material evidence with defendants.

Farese protested that Zach owed him $100,000 for the work he had done since his indictment six weeks earlier. He followed up with a three-page letter to Zach the same day. In it, Farese said he had been representing Langston since the day the FBI raided his office a month earlier, and he detailed the work he had done. "I checked with you to see if you had any conflict of interest with Joey," Farese wrote. "I was assured by you that you had no conflict of interest with Joey, and that you had no objection to me representing him."

Noting that "Joey's situation changed," Farese said, "I certainly understand that you may wish to obtain new counsel" because the new case affected Zach's father. "I was assured by Joey that you had no involvement in that case," Farese added. "I was also assured by the government that you were not a suspect nor a target in that investigation."

He closed with personal regards. "I only want what is best for you and your family," Farese wrote. "I would never do anything to compromise your case nor your well being. I certainly wish you the best of luck on these charges."

They settled their financial dispute by splitting the difference. Farese returned $250,000. He said later that he was not obligated to return any of the "non-refundable" retainer. "I did not take that position because I did not feel that was fair."

Zach remained indignant, and even as he prepared for his own defense, he compiled a ten-page treatise against Farese with the thought of seeking sanctions against his former lawyer from the state bar association.

The morning after Joey Langston pleaded guilty in the closed chambers of Judge Mills, three federal officers took a commercial flight from Memphis to Washington to begin a sensitive mission. U.S. attorney Jim Greenlee, chief prosecutor Tom Dawson, and an FBI agent from Tupelo named John Quaka were on their way to interview Trent Lott.

The former senator had already figured in speculation about the Scruggs case. Lott's resignation from the Senate came only two days before his brother-in-law's indictment, triggering suspicions that his decision was related to the events about to unfold in Mississippi. The investigators had tried to hold knowledge of Operation Benchmark to a handful of people, and Greenlee insisted there had been no leak. Lott's spokesman also claimed the timing was "totally coincidental." Nevertheless, there were skeptics wary of Lott's Sigma Nu network.

Just as activities by the CIA during the period that George H. W. Bush served as vice-president and president were traced to his college connections with Skull and Bones, a secret society at Yale that produced its share of Bonesmen who became spies, political favors distributed by Lott were often linked to the Ole Miss chapter of Sigma Nu, where Lott had been the group's "commander." The fraternity kept a preternatural hold on its alumni. Aging Sigma Nus sent daily postings via the Internet to their old frat brothers, with personal news of births and weddings, illnesses and deaths. Lott seemed to rule as Commander for Life, and members of the brotherhood were loyal to him.

In the hothouse climate of the Scruggs case, some of those involved in the investigation wondered about the objectivity of Greenlee, a Sigma Nu. Their qualms doubled when Quaka, another Sigma Nu, was chosen to accompany him to see Lott.

At the meeting with Lott, who was accompanied by a lawyer, Dawson felt he had to take charge. He had doubts about Lott's innocence. Yet Greenlee seemed deferential, and Quaka had no hard questions. Dawson pressed the former senator about the impact of a call to a judge who might hope to be elevated to the federal bench. Lott insisted that his discussion with Judge DeLaughter had been nothing more than a routine follow-up to Scruggs's recommendation about an open federal judgeship. Lott told the prosecutors that he did not know Scruggs had a case pending before DeLaughter.

He reminded his visitors that DeLaughter never got the nomination. Lott was also in a position to say that his call on March 29, 2006, came after DeLaughter had already made one decision favorable to Scruggs in February, and the process to fill the judgeship with another candidate was well under way before DeLaughter's final decree.

Dawson remained dubious about Lott's explanation. A few months later, the prosecutors stopped short of a subpoena, but asked Lott to make available his records concerning his reviews of candidates for federal judicial positions.

After the group finished with Lott, Greenlee and Quaka went back to their hotel. Dawson headed to the suburbs of northern Virginia, where his daughter lived. As he was riding across the Fourteenth Street bridge over the Potomac he got a call from his associate in Oxford, Bob Norman. Scruggs's lawyer John Keker had just telephoned and said he wanted to talk.

Keker's overture set in a motion a series of meetings between the prosecutors and defense attorneys in which the two sides privately probed each other for strengths and weaknesses. Because the prosecutors were required by law to turn over evidence, including the wiretaps and the videotapes of Balducci's conversations with Judge Lackey, the defense attorneys saw some of the hard facts that confronted them.

It became something of a grim poker game, in which the prosecutors had aces and royal face cards showing. There were bluffs and bravado in the talks. If the defendants wished to avoid a trial, the prosecutors suggested prison sentences—as much as ten years for Scruggs—they might be willing to offer in exchange for guilty pleas. Both sides realized that a trial conviction could result in much harsher prison terms.

The prosecutors figured that Dick Scruggs would take the gamble. He had the reputation of a risk-taker, a fighter pilot, a man always skating on the edge. But Langston, who was now cooperating with the prosecutors, confided to them his belief that Scruggs, his former client, would plead guilty in the end.

After the defense attorneys reported to their clients the gist of their talks with the U.S. Attorney's Office, all early proposals by the prosecutors were rejected.

In the councils of the Scruggs defense team, it was time to regroup and rebuild after Langston's abrupt departure. Keker took complete control of Dick Scruggs's case.

Sid Backstrom would be represented by Rhea Tannehill, a friend he trusted, but they would rely on the more experienced criminal defense lawyer from Jackson, Frank Trapp.

Zach felt comfortable with the man close to his family, Mike Moore, but developments in the case prompted him to retain others. During the exploratory talks, prosecutors hinted they might drop charges against Zach if persuasive evidence could be produced that he had not been in Backstrom's office during a critical point in Backstrom's conversation with Balducci on November 1—the day Balducci first wore a body wire.

Zach hired Todd Graves, a former U.S. attorney from Missouri, to handle negotiations with the federal prosecutors. Graves had been recently forced out of office during a purge of U.S. attorneys by the Bush administration, one of ten officials believed to have been targeted by the White House and Attorney General Alberto Gonzales for failing to carry out prosecutions sought by Republican interests. Charges of political prosecutions were dominating headlines, and a congressional investigation led by Democrats was under way. With U.S. attorneys' offices across the nation, including the one in Oxford, on the defensive, Graves was considered an ideal choice to assist Zach. Graves was joined by his partner Nathan Garrett. In addition, Zach retained another Missouri lawyer, Edward "Chip" Robertson, a former state supreme court justice who had been involved in some of Scruggs's litigation against State Farm.

Steve Patterson pleaded guilty a week after Langston. His capitulation came as no surprise. He had been implicated in telephone conversations recorded by the FBI and had been floundering in the days since his indictment. Unwilling to pay the retainer sought by his first attorney, Patterson turned to Ron Michael, a friend who had once worked with him at Langston's firm. For good measure, he also called on another lawyer with a familiar name, Hiram Eastland, a cousin of the late senator. But the name Eastland no longer carried much weight outside the organization the old senator once directed.

Appearing before U.S. District Judge Neal Biggers the week after Langston had been reduced to tears in the same building, Patterson could not resist a bit of theatrics. As he stood before Biggers, the judge said, "Mr. Patterson, I thought I was having a Kafkaesque moment this morning when I read the paper: you'd already entered a plea of guilty. You know, that's like that novel by Franz Kafka where this guy was charged, he was convicted, and he was executed, and he never went before the court. It was like a surreal thing. But you haven't been before the court on a guilty plea, have you?"

"No, sir," Patterson deadpanned. "The press stays ahead of me all the time."

He admitted guilt to one count of conspiring to bribe Judge Lackey. Patterson said he had never set out to corrupt a judge, implying that he had been drawn into the crime by others. "I stand here a blessed man," he said. "My family, church and community have stood by me." To complete the deal in which all other criminal charges against him were swept away, Patterson promised to cooperate with the prosecutors and to submit to a polygraph to verify that he was telling the truth.

Patterson offered no defense in the Lackey bribery. Though he had been involved in hiring Peters in the second case, Patterson subsequently ridiculed the decision to ask Senator Lott to contact DeLaughter. In testimony Patterson gave more than a year later in a deposition, he said he learned of Lott's action in a telephone call from Langston. "I shall never forget that call because I thought that was the most insane thing I had ever heard in my entire life," Patterson said. "That a United States senator whose brother-in-law was in a case of this magnitude would actually call the judge and ask him—I thought that was just going way over the line. I thought it was politically stupid, thought it made no sense."

With Patterson's plea, Scruggs recognized that the prosecutors now had four witnesses—Patterson, Langston, Balducci, and Peters—prepared to testify that he had been involved in an attempt to sway Judge DeLaughter in the Wilson case. It not only opened Scruggs to a second charge in Scruggs II, but it also gave the prosecutors a powerful weapon: Rule 404(b).

Keker, who commanded a fee of $900 an hour, found himself facing a difficult task, but it was hardly the first time he had been in that position. In the thirty years since he and a partner founded the law firm of Keker and Van Nest in San Francisco, the office had swelled to a force of fifty attorneys, and Keker had won a reputation as one of the leading criminal defense lawyers on the West Coast.

He came from a city with a long history of colorful advocates. Melvin Belli, the first to claim the title of King of Torts, had represented an impressive cast of characters in his heyday; his clients ranged from Jack Ruby and Errol Flynn to the Rolling Stones. During the cold war, Vincent Hallinan, another San Francisco lawyer, was known as a passionate defender of leftist causes, an unpopular job in that period. Keker helped win an acquittal for Hallinan's son Patrick—a criminal defense lawyer himself—in a celebrated case in 1996 involving a questionable drug charge brought by the federal government. Defending Hallinan, Keker lashed out at a U.S. attorney as "a chicken-shit" and complained about "fanatic prosecutors who believe that people who represent people accused of crime are the same as the people who are accused of crime."

Keker stood as erect as a sentry in the courtroom, and he was naturally combative. Rather than covering his walls with plaudits, he displayed busts of Napoleon to garnish his office. After graduating cum laude from Princeton in 1965, he served as a Marine lieutenant in Vietnam. Seriously wounded there, he returned stateside and obtained a law degree from Yale. He clerked for the chief justice of the U.S. Supreme Court, Earl Warren. His Marine background, coupled with his own liberal views, became special credentials when he took a leave from private practice to become associate independent counsel during the investigation of the Iran-Contra affair in the 1980s. His tough cross-examination of Marine Lt. Col. Oliver North, who claimed he was a patriot following orders from the Reagan White House, broke down North's wall of self-righteousness and won a conviction.

Yet Keker became best known for his defense work. When his friend, the commentator Ben Stein, was arrested for passing through an airport metal detector with an unloaded gun, he contacted Keker. "He got them to drop the charges," Stein told reporters afterward. "He even got my gun back."

Keker's clients included Black Panther Eldridge Cleaver. Even as he prepared to take up Scruggs's defense, there were reports that Barry Bonds, the embattled home run king, wanted to hire Keker to represent him against perjury charges growing out of an investigation of steroid use in baseball.

Instead, Keker devoted most of his time that winter to the Scruggs case as it played out in Oxford, nearly two thousand miles from San Francisco. His room at a bed-and-breakfast a few blocks from the federal courthouse was no match for the Four Seasons Hotel off Union Square, and local cuisine, while acceptable, offered no real substitute for the feasts of dim sum he found in Chinatown near his home office.

For the cosmopolitan Keker, Oxford represented an out-of-the-way location. But he had another high-profile client whose case attracted coverage in newspapers across the country. And he had a familiar foe: a U.S. attorney's office run by a Republican appointee and staffed with many Republican partisans.

Although the government's pursuit of Scruggs smacked of entrapment to his supporters, that defense could not be used because he had not dealt directly with a federal agent or an informant when he covered Balducci's original payments with a $40,000 check. Instead, the defendants from the Scruggs Law Firm settled on a defense built around the argument that the government had created the crime for which they were being falsely accused.

In a lengthy motion filed with the court on February 11, Keker asked for dismissal of the indictments on the grounds of "outrageous government conduct." The document not only accused the federal government of turning Judge Lackey into an agent involved in "manufacturing a crime," it charged that the government had "engaged in a pattern of concealing from this court" exculpatory evidence helpful to the defendants.

The motion was carefully crafted and consisted of several key points:

- Balducci's suggestion concerning an "of counsel" position for Judge Lackey at their March 2007 meeting was not intended as a quid pro quo for a favorable ruling in the *Jones v. Scruggs* case. Nothing of value was ever mentioned until the judge became aggressive.

- During the six-month interval between Balducci's original meeting with the judge and the September day when Lackey asked for

money, it was the judge, rather than Balducci, who repeatedly initiated contact.

- While the case lay dormant, with Balducci failing to follow through
  with any further improper requests, "the government and its agent
  Judge Lackey decided to instigate the crime . . ."

- It was the judge who called Balducci "out of the blue, using hushed,
  conspiratorial tones" to ask if the defendants in the Jones case would
  help him if he helped them.

- The government instructed Judge Lackey to ask for money.

- On the day Balducci delivered the first installment of cash, he told
  Judge Lackey "this is just between me and you . . . there ain't another soul in the world that knows about this." When Lackey interjected Scruggs's name Balducci responded, "He's not even involved
  at that level, Judge . . . Doesn't wanna be. Doesn't need to be."

- Despite Balducci's assertion that Scruggs had no part in the conspiracy, the government continued to pursue him.

- In its applications for wiretaps on Balducci's phone, the FBI omit-
  ted information that cast doubt on the case the government was
  building.

- The FBI also submitted misleading summaries of recorded telephone conversations, never mentioning in documents filed with the
  court during the covert investigation that Judge Lackey had recused
  himself.

- Once Balducci was arrested, the government used him the same
  way it used Lackey: "as an agent sent on a mission to create evidence
  of a criminal scheme that did not exist other than through the government's own machinations."

As a result of all of the overzealous investigation, Keker submitted,
"the seed that the government planted in the spring and cultivated
over the course of the summer and fall finally bore its bitter fruit": the
indictments of Dick and Zach Scruggs and Sid Backstrom.

Drawing upon similar arguments, the defense also offered a motion
to suppress evidence obtained from wiretaps on the grounds that the
FBI had filed "false or misleading statements" to the court.

The motions led to a critical hearing before Judge Biggers only nine days later.

The case had been on a fast track ever since it was assigned to Biggers. Cases are routinely given by the federal court clerk to judges on a rotating basis, but the selection of Biggers raised some questions in legal circles because he had been the judge who earlier considered the FBI requests for wiretaps and issued the authorizations. Ideally, the judge who hears a case is not the same one involved in preliminary rulings during an ongoing investigation. With jurisdiction over the Scruggs case, Biggers was effectively sitting in judgment over some of his own decisions and presiding over a case he had been secretly following for weeks before arrests were made.

Judge Biggers originally scheduled the trial for January, less than two months after the indictments. After the defense asked for more time, he pushed the trial date back to February. Following another request for a delay, Biggers yielded one more month. He set the trial for March and indicated that the date was firm.

As a former prosecutor, Biggers had a reputation as a stern jurist with little sympathy for defendants. Even some bloggers who were demanding Scruggs's head referred to the judge as "Maximum Neal." In a recent case involving a local contractor for the failed state-owned beef processing plant, Biggers had rejected a plea bargain submitted by prosecutors that would have enabled the defendant to avoid prison. The judge wound up sentencing the contractor to twenty-two months.

While Judge Biggers's rulings in criminal cases seemed fearsome, he was generally respected for his judicious handling of a torturous civil case that had spanned decades in a race-related argument over state funding for higher education. He had been a state judge in 1982 when Senator Thad Cochran sent his name to the White House, and President Reagan followed through with the nomination. Biggers had never been considered an activist Republican or unduly political, and he drew little criticism. The only obstacle to Senate approval had been a scathing attack by his former wife, and that was resolved quietly, outside of any public hearing.

After a quarter century on the federal bench, Biggers had become the senior judge in the Northern District of Mississippi. Whether the cases before him were criminal or civil, he was a grave presence in the courtroom. Peering over his glasses, he brooked no inappropriate humor nor any flippant remark. He epitomized the power of federal judges. Appointed for life, he could command marshals with the wave of his hand, reduce errant attorneys to mumbled apologies, and consign miscreants to prison without remorse.

In hearing pretrial motions, Biggers approved two requests by the prosecution that were ordinarily reserved for cases involving the Mafia or mob-connected defendants. He ordered that the jury be sequestered for the duration of the trial and that their names be kept secret. The rulings carried an implication that the defendants might try to rig the jury.

But he granted Scruggs and the other two defendants a hearing on their "outrageous conduct" motion and their attempt to suppress evidence gathered from wiretaps. The defense team was eager to get a chance to cross-examine Tim Balducci and others, but members of the group were not sanguine about appearing before Judge Biggers.

As they anticipated, the hearing became an uphill battle from the outset. Biggers said he had no intention of allowing the arguments to turn into a trial, and he limited Keker's questioning of Balducci to three areas: the meeting at Scruggs Law Firm when the idea to approach Judge Lackey was first broached; Balducci's meeting with Lackey later that same day; and the judge's recusal.

When Balducci was sworn in, it offered the defendants their first chance to see him since he had fed their names to the prosecutors and gone into hiding. He now seemed to them a bit weaselly. But he spoke with confidence as assistant U.S. attorney Bob Norman guided him.

Balducci said that he and Patterson had gone to Scruggs's office to discuss another matter—the Kentucky coal miners' mask litigation—"when the real reason for the meeting was revealed." Johnny Jones had just filed his suit against Scruggs, and the case was in the hands of Judge Lackey.

"It was generally known about my relationship with Judge Lackey," Balducci testified, "and Zach was the first one to bring that up and asked if I thought it would be possible for me to go and have an off-the-record conversation with Judge Lackey and see if I could persuade him to rule in their favor."

Watching from the defense table, Zach had to restrain himself from shouting, "Liar!"

Balducci recounted details of his meeting that same afternoon with the state judge. He admitted that his request of Lackey was unethical, but said he never intended for his suggestion about an "of counsel" position with the Patterson-Balducci firm to be considered a quid pro quo for the ruling he sought.

Judge Lackey, he testified, "never gave me any indication that he was offended by it or that he felt that what I was doing was improper."

Weeks later, Balducci said, he learned from Sid Backstrom that Lackey had recused himself from the case. He described Backstrom as "frantic and angry" as he directed him to "get ahold of the situation and find out what's going on and let us know."

It was Backstrom's turn to be dismayed as he listened to Balducci's testimony implicating him. Balducci said he called Backstrom immediately after Judge Lackey asked for a payoff six months after the first meeting.

"I advised him that I'd just left a meeting with the judge; that the judge wanted forty thousand dollars to enter the order compelling the Jones case to arbitration," Balducci said. "And I asked him [Backstrom], is that what they wanted done? Did they want to pay the money? And, if so, how did they physically want to do it? Did they want me to pay it? And, if so, were they going to cover me?" He said Backstrom promised, "Let me find out, and I'll call you back."

Asked about his use of a plural pronoun, Balducci said that "they" referred to "the three defendants."

He also directly implicated Dick Scruggs. Balducci said that he and Patterson went to see Scruggs in late September to ask about a reimbursement for the $40,000 they were giving to Judge Lackey.

"He said that he knew that we had talked to P. L. Blake, and that he had talked to P. L. Blake. And he knew that we needed the forty, and that we would be covered and not to worry about it."

In his cross-examination of Balducci, Keker pounced on several inconsistencies.

One involved a classified FBI report, known as a 302 document, describing an interview with Balducci on November 2, the day after he had been stopped by the FBI leaving Judge Lackey's office. In the report, Balducci is referred to as CHS, FBI lingo for "confidential human source." Describing Balducci's account of his first meeting with Scruggs concerning Judge Lackey, the agents paraphrased Balducci's words and wrote, "DS [Scruggs] said he was not asking the CHS for anything illegal, but could the CHS see if the judge would move the matter to arbitration."

In a later 302 filed by Bill Delaney, the FBI agent who controlled

Balducci's movements in the case, it is clear that Balducci wanted to change the FBI report. On December 14, Delaney wrote, "The CHS advised he did not recall making" the statement that Scruggs "did not ask the CHS to do anything illegal." Delaney reported that he had reviewed his own notes of the interview and concluded that "the original draft was an accurate reflection of that debriefing." After telling Balducci of his conclusion, "the CHS believed if both interviewing agents recalled the interview as originally documented, then the CHS would concur."

Keker approached the witness and asked, "Did Dick Scruggs say he was not asking you for anything illegal, but would you see if the judge would move the matter to arbitration?"

"Yeah," Balducci said. Then he quickly corrected himself. "No—that's not accurate." He explained, "I understand that that's written in that 302 . . . And I think that was incorrectly written down by the agent in that first debriefing, and I brought it to their attention later."

"So, later they let you see the 302 that they wrote, and you corrected it?" Keker asked.

"No. We had a discussion about that . . . I explained to them, 'If that's what I said, that's not what I meant. If that's what they heard, that's not what I said.'"

Later in his cross-examination, Keker bore in on the P. L. Blake connection.

Balducci said Patterson had not been satisfied with Sid Backstrom's assurance that their $40,000 would be repaid by Scruggs. "Steve said that he was going to contact P. L. Blake and make certain that he—Steve—got a direct word from Dick that Dick wanted us to go forward."

Keker: "And when Mr. Patterson contacted P. L. Blake, he never told P. L. Blake what you and he needed the forty thousand dollars for, did he?"

Balducci: "I wasn't privy to their conversation, sir."

"Did he tell you that he had not told P. L. Blake what you needed the forty thousand dollars for?"

"Patterson told me that he told P. L. Blake that we were working on a problem to solve for Dick that he wanted us to solve, and that it was going to cost forty thousand dollars, and that we needed to know if he wanted us to solve the problem."

"Did Patterson tell you that he had never told P. L. Blake what the problem was?"

"Yes."

. . .

After Keker completed his questioning—which had been limited by Judge Biggers—prosecutor Bob Norman opened a new line of inquiry to tie the government's case to accusations of a second bribery involving Judge DeLaughter.

He led Balducci to testify that he had felt comfortable in telling Judge Lackey there would be no problem in getting him $40,000 because "I had been privy previously to another matter in which Mr. Scuggs bribed another judge for a favorable outcome in a case, and I was aware of that."

"Your Honor," Norman said to the judge, "that is the subject of our 404(b) motion . . . and I will leave that at this point."

Keker was not ready to abandon the subject and asked for permission to reexamine Balducci. Judge Biggers gave him five minutes to do so. The following colloquy took place:

Keker: "You said you were privy to another matter where Dick Scruggs bribed a judge. What matter are you referring to?"

Balducci: "A case involving an attorney named Bob Wilson who had sued Mr. Scruggs for asbestos and possibly tobacco fees."

"Was that case pending in Hinds County before Judge Bobby DeLaughter?"

"It was."

"Was Judge Bobby DeLaughter bribed in that case?"

"He was."

"By whom?"

"By Dick Scruggs."

"And was the bribe a money bribe?"

"No, sir."

"What was the bribe that you're referring to?"

"He was offered a federal judgeship or he was offered the influence of Mr. Scruggs's brother-in-law, who was Senator Trent Lott, to put him on the list for consideration of an open federal district judgeship."

"So we can get it, what do you understand—Mr. Scruggs called Mr. DeLaughter and said something?"

"No, sir. Mr. Lott called Mr. DeLaughter."

"What are you saying?"

"I'm saying that Mr. Lott called Judge DeLaughter, at Mr. Scruggs's request, and told him that he was being considered to be put under— or put on the list for consideration for an open judgeship in that district, and that that was during the pendency of the case involving Mr. Wilson that was before Judge DeLaughter."

"And how do you know that that happened? You talked to Senator Lott about that?"

"No, sir."

"How do you know that that happened?"

"Because I was directly involved in the conversation between Mr. Scruggs and Mr. Langston where they were discussing it, where they discussed that the call would be made. And then I was privy to conversations after the call was made."

"When was that discussion, the one before?"

"It was during the pendency of the Wilson case."

"Do you remember more specifically than that?"

"It would have been around the summer of '06."

"2006. So, June, July, or August 2006."

"I think the Wilson case—my best recollection is the Wilson case was tried in August of '06. So it was shortly before that."

"Like within a month or two?"

"Yes."

"Okay. You're sure about that?"

"It's my best recollection, yes, sir."

"Because you were there. So if these conversations didn't happen in June or July, then you're just completely wrong about this, right?"

"No, no. The conversation—I think that the call was made—maybe I misunderstood what you were asking. I think that Senator Lott made the call to Judge DeLaughter sometime in the first quarter or so of '06."

"And what was Judge DeLaughter supposed to do? What was he going to do? You said it was a bribe. What was he going to do?"

"Rule favorably for Mr. Scruggs."

"On what? Some particular motion or just anything that came along?"

"There were several, yes, sir, and it was for a favorable outcome."

"And you know that because you heard Mr. Langston and Mr. Scruggs talking about it?"

"I know it for a lot more reasons than just that, but, yes."

"What are the rest of the reasons?"

"I was privy to several meetings with Ed Peters where we discussed strategies about the case. Where we previewed filings in the case. Where we were provided with draft copies of orders that Judge DeLaughter was going to enter in the case. There was a lot of stuff."

"What did that have to do with this call from Senator Lott?"

"I'm not sure I understand your question."

"I'm not sure I understand your answer. What did it have to do with what you just said? These meetings. What did that have to do—"

"That was part of implementing the favorable outcome in the Wilson case."

"Are you aware, sir, that the judgeship Judge DeLaughter was interested in was given to somebody else by, say, April of 2006. It was gone?"

"My understanding is that there were about three different judgeships that were pending during the Wilson case before it was tried, and that the last federal judgeship was filled within just a couple of weeks after the trial, that there was—during the pendency of the Wilson trial, in other words, there was always an open judgeship on the federal bench."

"Did the Wilson trial end in a settlement whereby Mr. Scruggs paid Mr. Wilson some money?"

"He did."

"How much money did he pay him?"

"My best recollection is that he paid him $3.9 million."

Judge Biggers instructed Keker that his time had expired but gave him two or three minutes more "to wrap it up."

Keker asked Balducci if he "were going to do any work for Mr. Scruggs for the forty thousand dollars."

"At that time, Mr. Scruggs had not created this cover story for me doing this voir dire for him, if that's what you're asking," Balducci replied.

Keker asked Judge Biggers for permission to call Judge Lackey as a witness. He said Lackey "can fill in how this crime was created." In remarks earlier that morning, Keker talked of how Lackey had been "pushing, pushing, pushing" for six months to insert Scruggs's name into his dialogues with Balducci.

"I don't mean to be harsh about this," Keker said, "but at that point, it's almost extortion."

Keker felt that Lackey's credibility would not hold up under strong questioning. He believed that Lackey, acting out of his hatred of Scruggs, had prodded and goaded his younger friend, Balducci, into the crime. Keker wanted to force Lackey to explain fully his role in the case. It might be possible to transform Lackey's image from that of a heroic judge defending the principles of justice to that of a contemporary Iago.

Judge Biggers was unwilling to call Lackey to the stand. He had already heard enough of the defense's claim that Lackey, acting as a government agent, had created a crime by asking for money. The defense had failed, Biggers ruled, to demonstrate "outrageous conduct" by the government.

"The law required that in order for such a motion to be successful, the defendants must not have participated in any active way in the carrying out of the crime," Biggers said. "All the evidence to this point is that they did. So it would seem to the court it would be futile to bring in these other witnesses to testify about what they did and what the defendants did because the defendants are unable, will be unable, to show that they were merely passive participants in this crime."

Scruggs and the others at the defense table could not believe what they were hearing. In their interpretation of Judge Biggers's remarks, he had found them guilty before their trial.

Keker made a final attempt to argue that the defendants were drawn into the crime by government action and "extortion circumstances."

But Judge Biggers cited precedent: "A defendant claiming outrageous conduct bears an extremely high burden of proof."

Additional witnesses, he said, "would not wipe out the clear evidence that's before the court now that there was an active participation of the other defendants in the carrying out of this crime."

Three hours after the hearing opened, the "outrageous conduct" motion was denied, and the defense was left with only its effort to suppress evidence obtained through wiretaps and search warrants authorized by Judge Biggers.

That, too, failed.

Disheartened by the setbacks, the Scruggs defense team explored another avenue. They would stage a mini–mock trial in early March before a group of independent "jurors," to weigh their chances in the real trial set to begin in less than a month.

It was an elaborate production, arranged by a consultant specializing in pretrial focus groups, and carried out in deepest secrecy. The setting bore no resemblance to a federal courtroom. Sam's Town Hotel and Casino, overlooking the Red River in Shreveport, Louisiana, was chosen as the site, and dozens of residents of the area who knew nothing of the case were hired to serve on four separate jury panels. Scruggs agreed to underwrite the costs—which were considerable.

On the night before the formal arguments would take place, eight members of the team, along with one defendant, Sid Backstrom, flew into Shreveport to begin planning for the war game. Neither Dick nor Zach Scruggs attended.

The format required a reversal of roles for some of the group. Mike Moore, calling on his courtroom experience as a prosecutor, would present the government's case. The defendants would be represented by other attorneys on the team. Chip Robertson, one of Zach's lawyers, was given the task of delivering the government's rebuttal to the defense.

To begin the long day of deliberations, the "jurors" and the attorneys gathered in a large ballroom of the hotel. In lieu of witnesses, the "trial" consisted of five presentations—one by Moore, three on behalf of each of the defendants, and a closing argument by Robertson. At the end of each performance, the "jurors" adjourned to four smaller rooms to consider the merits of what they had just heard. Each time, they were asked to fill out questionnaires and to indicate whether they were leaning for conviction or acquittal.

In spite of his close friendship with the Scruggs family, Moore gave a fervent argument for conviction. He cited the evidence that would be introduced in the actual trial and did his best to damn the defendants. "This is not the first time they've done this," Moore thundered, referring to the second case involving Judge DeLaughter.

The defense lawyers followed, using a line of attack just rejected by Judge Biggers: that the government had created a crime. They also accused one of the witnesses, Balducci, of perjury in his grand jury testimony and implied that another principal witness, Judge Lackey, had had ulterior motives in initiating the investigation.

The concept of the exercise was to evaluate the strength of the prosecution's case and to give the defendants a realistic view of the risk they were taking if they actually went to trial. Robertson, acting as a prosecutor, was given the final word, and he hit hard with the 404(b) evidence that Scruggs had been involved in a second bribery.

At the end of the day, the panel members were asked to sit in judgment. While the "jurors" debated, video cameras in each room fed their discussion to four different monitors in an adjacent room. The lawyers, wearing headsets, were able to follow the various deliberations. In some talks, participants felt the defendants should be held to a higher standard because they were lawyers. On the other hand, there were "jurors" who expressed doubts concerning the government's case and speculated about the extent of entrapment. But ultimately, the same conclusion was being reached in every room: the defense had been overwhelmed by the introduction of the second case and the suggestion that Scruggs had a history of bribing judges.

All four of the panels voted to convict both Dick Scruggs and Sid Backstrom. Zach escaped with a couple of hung juries. There were no acquittals.

Faced with the unhappy results from Shreveport and a federal judge they believed hostile, the Scruggs group grew pessimistic as their options ran out.

If convicted in the fast-approaching trial, the defendants would more than likely spend many years in prison. Scruggs, approaching his sixty-second birthday, would be an elderly man if he survived to see freedom again. Backstrom's small children would be grown before he was released, and no one was quite sure what might happen to the fine new home under construction for his family. For thirty-three-year-old Zach, the idea of any time in prison was unthinkable.

Alone among the three members of the Scruggs firm under indictment, Zach had begun to feel isolated by events. With his knowledge of the evidence in the government's possession, he realized that his father and Backstrom were vulnerable. But he felt strongly that he would be exonerated by the lack of any explicit demonstration of his guilt. He began to wonder if his father might use him as a bargaining chip, offering a guilty plea in exchange for dropping charges against his son.

If the defendants chose to plead guilty in order to be ensured lighter sentences, the deadline set by Judge Biggers to enter pleas in the case was even more imminent: only a week away.

Publicly, the defendants gave every indication that the case would be fought to trial. But inside the strategy sessions at the Scruggs Law Firm, emotions ran from anxiety and anger to resignation that guilty pleas might become necessary.

With access to much of the government's evidence, the defendants were able to anticipate the testimony against them. Scruggs listened to disks containing nearly one hundred recordings of conversations involving Balducci, Patterson, Lackey, and sometimes himself. Much of it was irrelevant to the case or too elliptical to be used against him. But one recording was damaging: his November 1 conversation with Tim Balducci regarding an additional payment to Judge Lackey. Scruggs could hear himself say, "I'll take care of it." He thought to himself: That's what put the noose around my neck.

As they reviewed the potential witnesses with their lawyers, the defendants felt contempt for their onetime associates who had turned on them: Tim Balducci, Joey Langston, and, to a lesser extent, Steve Patterson. But they reserved their greatest resentment for a man they did not know, Judge Lackey. They felt him duplicitous, conniving, and a philosophical partner of Grady Tollison in the effort to bring them down. To lighten the atmosphere, some members of the defense team would break into a riff from the old Johnny Rivers song "Secret Agent Man," to refer sarcastically to the judge.

Scruggs had hired a private detective to look into the backgrounds of various characters involved in the case. After the investigator began making inquiries into some of Lackey's private business dealings in Calhoun City, the judge was said to be incensed when he learned of it. The defendants knew Lackey's position would only harden.

In moments when they resorted to mordant humor, members of the defense team joked that they might better address their remarks to Biggers's life-size portrait, which hung in the courtroom, rather than to the judge himself, in order to get a more sympathetic hearing. The oil painting, a fine likeness by the Oxford portraitist Jason Bouldin, became a subject of their derision, for special temperature controls had been mounted on the courtroom wall to prevent the canvas from rotting.

Scruggs felt that Biggers had turned his courtroom into a modern-day Star Chamber, where a defendant had no rights. At a trial, he said facetiously, he expected to have a black hood placed over his head, and if he lost, he might be sentenced to twenty-five years in prison. Paul Minor's conviction in a trial where another federal judge had made a number of adverse rulings played into Scruggs's thinking. So did Minor's prison term of eleven years.

Scruggs was tormented by his son's predicament and tearfully talked about it with Chip Robertson, who had worked with the elder Scruggs in earlier litigation and now helped represent Zach. "I don't care what happens to me," he told Robertson. "I want to help my boy. He's only involved in this because of me—and it's killing me."

Scruggs's sleep deteriorated, and he fell back increasingly on the barbituates for relief. His life had gone into a sickening spiral, from the high of his tobacco triumph, when he had been hailed as a champion of the little man, to the lowly feeling that prison lay in his future. At home, he tried to maintain a stout appearance of innocence. Diane remained convinced that Dick would take the fight to trial. But in his deepest and most private thoughts—and in his counsel with John Keker—he knew that events had closed in on him.

Less than four months after the nightmare day in which he was arrested, was arraigned in a magistrate's courtroom, and announced himself "not guilty," Scruggs decided, as he later told a friend, "I had to stand there before Biggers and take an ass-whipping."

Scruggs's decision set off a scramble on both sides.

Keker asked for a meeting with the prosecutors on Wednesday after returning from Shreveport. Acting alone, he initiated the first round of serious plea bargaining. The discussion was general and conducted in utter secrecy in a first-floor conference room at the U.S. Attorney's Building, which is guarded and closed to unauthorized visitors. After talking with Keker, the three prosecutors—Dawson, Norman, and David Sanders—were left with the impression that Scruggs was willing to plead guilty to one count of conspiracy in the bribery case involving Judge Lackey and accept a five-year sentence. On the second case dealing with Judge DeLaughter, the prosecutors understood, Scruggs would not plead guilty unless a sentence for that offense ran concurrent with the first case; that is, Scruggs would face a total of no more than five years in prison.

The prosecutors were unwilling to agree to the proposal and renewed a demand for at least a seven-year sentence for Scruggs. They also expressed interest in a "global settlement" in which all of the defendants pleaded guilty in the Lackey case. Although Scruggs faced potential charges in the DeLaughter affair, neither Zach nor Sid Backstrom was implicated in the second case.

Keker came back with what became known as the "5-3-1" suggestion: five years for Scruggs, three for Backstrom, and one for Zach, in exchange for their guilty pleas in the Lackey case.

"What about Scruggs Two?" Dawson asked of the second case.

"We'll take our chances on that," Keker said.

Dawson said he had no authority to seal such an arrangement and asked for time to talk with his boss, Jim Greenlee, who was in Washington. Dawson thought to himself: This is a case a prosecutor lives to bring to trial, an arena with spotlights and headlines. He would never again have the opportunity to challenge a defendant so famous and high powered, to move from the shadows of an assistant prosecutor to the forefront of one of the biggest cases in memory. But a guilty plea would ensure a victory, and if Dick Scruggs was willing to stand up and admit his guilt, Dawson could say that justice had been served. When he reached Greenlee by telephone, he explained that the proposal was not entirely satisfactory. "But it doesn't give me heartburn, either," he added. "These things never please everybody. The big thing is that everybody will be convicted of a felony, and they'll be disbarred forever."

Greenlee approved of the 5-3-1 deal. "But what about the second case?" he asked.

"We'll go ahead with that one," said Dawson, who told Greenlee he was surprised Scruggs had left himself open to further charges in the DeLaughter case.

Dawson called Keker to tell him he had a deal. He asked Keker, who represented only Scruggs, if he could be assured that the other two defendants would accept the agreement. Backstrom was believed ready to surrender, but Zach had shown no indication that he would plead guilty. Keker said it might be a hard sell with Zach, but he felt he would do it.

After the Shreveport experience, Backstrom was leaning toward a guilty plea. He sensed that he had been doomed by a recorded November 13 telephone call with Balducci in which his friend talked explicitly about the bribe to Judge Lackey.

"He's in a posture where he'll play ball with us on whatever we want to do," Balducci had said. "You know, it'll take some more money . . . I mean, we've given him fifty to get us to where we are now, but you know, for a little bit more, he's willing to play ball, I think, and get this thing like we want it . . ."

And Backstrom had jokingly replied over the phone, "We just cut out for about three minutes there, and I didn't hear any of that." Then he laughed and said, "I know what you're saying."

If Dick Scruggs felt trapped by his own "five words," Backstrom wished that his phone had actually malfunctioned.

Scruggs broke the news to his family on Thursday morning. He called Diane, who had been planning to go to lunch with friends. Throughout the ordeal, she had tried to maintain a normal appearance. She went out to public places, and instead of avoiding her friends, she relied on their company to help her face the crisis. Her husband's words stunned her. "Don't go to lunch," he told her. "I need to talk with you. I'm going to have to plead." He explained that two men who had once represented him, Balducci and Langston, were prepared to testify against him. The judge, he said, could put him away for twenty-five years if he went to trial and were convicted.

Diane was shocked, for she thought he would contest the charges to the end.

After informing his wife of his plans, Scruggs had to tell his son.

Zach was meeting with his own attorneys in a conference room at the law firm when Mike Moore took him aside. "We need to talk," Moore said. They were joined by Scruggs in Zach's small office.

Scruggs took a seat in an armchair by a window, looked at his son, and said, "This is the latest government offering: They're willing to give me five years, Sid three, and one for you." He paused. "I'm going to take it. I wish you would, too."

Zach was stunned. He had never expected the case to come to this. "Hell, no," he said. "I'm not going to do it." He rose from behind his own desk, repeated his vow, and walked out.

Moore followed Zach from the room and led him to Scruggs's office, where Keker was waiting. The San Francisco lawyer explained some of the details of the prosecutors' offer and the reasons why he felt it would be best for the defendants to accept the plea bargain.

"Look," Keker said, "we've been overruled on every motion. I can destroy Tim Balducci and I can destroy Henry Lackey on cross-examinaton, but at the end of the day we're still looking at this November the first tape." He reminded Zach of the negative results of the mock trial in Shreveport where the "jurors" had had little sympathy for the lawyer-defendants. A real jury in Oxford would likely come down hard, too, Keker said. "Zach, they'll look at you like a rich white boy."

"I'm not doing it," Zach said.

"You don't want to blow up the deal, put your dad in trouble."

Zach scoffed at the suggestion. "There's no way in the world they'll refuse a deal on Dick Scruggs and hold out for me. I'm not going to do it."

"All right," Keker said. He did not press Zach further.

Zach walked back to his own office. His father was still there, sitting quietly, staring out the window. His son was overwhelmed by the poignancy of the moment. He thought the scene would stay with him the rest of his life: the sight of his father, as if he were a monarch, looking out at his kingdom and watching it disintegrate—Zeus, the king of the gods, falling.

Father and son sat together saying nothing.

Elsewhere, there was frantic activity. Frank Trapp was not pleased to learn that Keker had suggested a three-year sentence for his client. After thirty-five years in the trenches, with countless criminal defendants, Trapp could be stubborn and unyielding. He often exasperated prosecutors with counter-demands on behalf of his clients, and now it seemed as if Keker had spoken for Backstrom before Trapp could negotiate in earnest.

Keker had a national reputation, but Trapp was regarded as one of the most formidable criminal defense lawyers in the state. Scruggs had wanted to hire him in 1992 when Steve Patterson and Ed Peters threatened him with indictment, but Trapp had a conflict and couldn't accept the assignment. Fifteen years later, after Backstrom had been advised to retain Trapp, Backstrom had asked Mike Moore about the lawyer's reputation. "You can't do any better," Moore had told him. For the past four months, Trapp had traveled back and forth between Jackson and Oxford to defend Backstrom.

In the courtroom, Trapp presented an unlikely sight. While others dressed formally, he preferred a sports jacket and slacks to distinguish his client from "the suits." His graying hair curled over his collar like shoots of dry grass that had not been mowed. His manner seemed deceptively informal. Trapp grew up in Neshoba County, the place made notorious by the 1964 murders of civil rights workers Chaney, Schwerner, and Goodman; local residents preferred that their home be known for the Neshoba County Fair, an annual event billed as "Mississippi's giant house party." Though he had played football at Ole Miss, Trapp became identified around the state through his profession, which he practiced at the Jackson office of Phelps Dunbar, one of the most respected law firms in the South.

After hearing of the 5-3-1 proposal, Trapp met with Backstrom, then went to see the prosecutors himself.

He knew his client had been implicated in the recordings, but he told the prosecutors he was prepared, in a trial, to impeach Balducci's grand jury testimony, concentrating on the passage where the witness claimed that he had talked with Backstrom about a $10,000 payoff to Judge Lackey when a recording of that conversation showed that he had done no such thing.

The prosecutors offered to knock six months off Backstrom's prison time, to reduce their recommendation to two and a half years.

To Zach, the case against him seemed to be built on a conversation he emphatically denied he had not heard—Balducci's mention of "sweet potatoes" in Backstrom's office on November 1—and by the fact that he had been the only one left in the Scruggs office on the night of October 18 to accept an envelope from Balducci containing Lackey's order. Zach handed over another envelope containing a check for $40,000 from Scruggs in exchange for an invoice from Balducci for work on a voir dire project.

Zach had been enthusiastically planning his own defense. He would charge the government with using the recorded conversations out of context, and he was prepared to question the FBI's failure to produce a record of a critical exchange on November 19, while Balducci was still acting as an undercover agent. Balducci had come to the Scruggs Law Firm that day—eighteen days after he had last visited, wearing a body wire—and briefly interrupted a meeting between Zach and several others. Zach had reminded Balducci of the voir dire assignment that needed to be completed quickly. There had been no mention of Judge Lackey. When Zach's attorneys asked the FBI for a tape of that conversation, they were told none existed. The FBI explained that Balducci had not been equipped with a body wire that day; his assignment had been to lure Backstrom across the square to the little Patterson-Balducci office, rigged with listening devices designed to plunge Backstrom deeper into a conspiracy. (The plot failed—Murphy's Law, again—because Backstrom had been out of town.)

Zach complained, repeatedly and bitterly, that the government's case against him had been constructed on a foundation of lies and deceit. He considered himself an unwitting victim of circumstances.

Mike Moore buttressed the argument that Zach had not been present for the critical part of Balducci's conversation with Backstrom. Zach had been quite vocal earlier in the FBI recording, but his voice was missing when "sweet potatoes" were mentioned. Since Zach was known to be very loquacious—a characteristic he demonstrated in his running commentary while in Backstrom's office—Moore said it was inconceivable that Zach would have let Balducci's cryptic message pass without making some remark himself.

Keker reported to the prosecutors that Zach would not be a part of any agreement. To them, Keker sounded exasperated and concerned that Zach's reluctance might upset the plea bargain. His comments pleased the prosecutors. It reflected disarray in the defense camp. In truth, the prosecutors had little patience or sympathy for Zach. They had developed a dislike for him from the day of the raid at Scruggs's office, when the FBI reported that Scruggs's son acted intemperately.

The three-man prosecution team decided that Zach would not be a deal-breaker. They agreed on five years for Scruggs and two and a half years for Backstrom—with the stipulation that Backstrom cooperate with the investigation. Dawson declared of Zach, "We won't let this jerk hold things up. We'll try his ass by himself. We've got significant evidence against him, and if he's convicted, he'll be looking at about fifteen years."

By Thursday night, the cases of Dick Scruggs and Backstrom were settled, but Mike Moore was just beginning intense negotiations to try to save Zach. He felt that Norman and Sanders showed some leniency, though Dawson was holding out for a felony plea and some prison time.

In a hushed conversation on the balcony of the law firm, Moore told Zach of his talks with the U.S. attorneys. He saw encouraging signs. "Go home, get some sleep, and pray," Moore told his client. They would talk about it again the next day, after Scruggs and Backstrom formally entered their guilty pleas.

On Friday morning, March 14, Zach and Backstrom gathered for the last time, as law partners and co-defendants, at their firm on the square. The office was steeped with sorrow and melancholy. Members of the staff were weeping; Backstrom was crying, too. He embraced Zach, telling him, "I'm so sorry, but I'm going to get you out of this."

Zach could not bear to go with the others as they made the short walk to the federal courthouse where his father and Backstrom would commit themselves to prison sentences and give up their law licenses.

Judge Biggers had already scheduled a hearing on another motion in their case that morning, so there were a few people on hand for what was expected to be a routine session. Bruce Newman, a photographer for *The Oxford Eagle*, was surprised to see Dick Scruggs walking toward the federal courthouse hand in hand with his wife.

Diane had always been in court with Dick when he wanted her there. She had once spent weeks in a California courtroom, under happier circumstances, when he had been involved in a long civil case. So she would be with him now. But she was in a daze, moving in tandem with Dick as if by rote. She recognized some of the reporters and photographers whom she had once considered friendly. Now they seemed part of an enemy army.

Though the late winter day was clear, it felt as though there had been an instant, stormy change in atmospherics.

There had been no public indication of a breakthrough. The night before, Jere Hoar, a retired journalism professor, had been talking with Biggers about protocol at a Delta hunting camp when the judge said, "You're a crime writer, aren't you?" Hoar had written one well-received crime novel, *The Hit*. Without revealing the case, Biggers suggested, "There's a hearing at ten tomorrow that you might find very interesting."

Hoar was waiting when Scruggs walked into the courtroom a few minutes before the appointed hour. He heard a stir. Some spectators bolted from the room to alert others. Scruggs moved inside the rail separating the general public from the counsels' tables. He shook hands with all of the prosecutors and court officers, then went, with Backstrom, into the judge's chambers for a few minutes. Scruggs was still smiling when he emerged, but Backstrom looked miserable.

While they waited on the judge, Scruggs worked the crowd like a politician. He leaned toward Hoar, extended his hand, and said, "I'm Dick Scruggs." Hoar thought: As if the whole world didn't know.

Scruggs somehow maintained a dapper appearance throughout his ordeal. Backstrom did not fare as well. He trembled and wept. His friend Rhea Tannehill helped prop him up as he pleaded guilty.

Backstrom's day was not done. As required by the plea agreement, he would be interrogated that afternoon and would submit to a lie detector test. The prosecutors anticipated that he would implicate Zach and close the circle on the last defendant.

But through three hours of questioning, Backstrom gave them little more evidence than they already had. He said that Zach had not been in the room to hear Balducci's remark; nor did Zach know of any conspiracy to bribe Judge Lackey. Backstrom had flight records and credit card receipts to prove that he and Zach had been in New Orleans on the day Balducci claimed to have talked with Backstrom in Oxford about the Lackey bribe. There were other instances where Backstrom was prepared to demonstrate that Balducci had lied.

Backstrom's attorneys, who were with him, told Moore shortly afterward that Backstrom had "exonerated Zach."

With new resolve, Moore and Todd Graves approached the prosecutors about dropping the case against Zach. But they were told by Dawson that Keker's 5-3-1 proposal implied that Zach was guilty.

When Zach heard of this kink in efforts to extricate him from the indictment he marched to the bed-and-breakfast establishment where Keker was staying. Keker told him he was appalled that the government had interpreted the 5-3-1 proposal that way, and he called Dawson to say he believed Zach was innocent. He recommended a deferred prosecution for Zach and a short suspension of his law license. A deferred prosecution effectively meant a dismissal of the charges, though the government would reserve a future right to revive the case against him. In exchange, Zach would be willing to acknowledge that he knew of unethical plans to earwig Judge Lackey.

Dawson, already weary of the events of the past two days, said any decision was too important to be made right away. He suggested that everyone wait until the weekend passed.

To the astonishment of the Sunday brunch crowd at the Oxford University Club, Scruggs appeared, en famille. He greeted friends as though little had happened. At one table he said that the weekend had not been devoid of good news. "At least Mississippi State lost," he said of the upset Saturday of his alma mater's top-ranked rival in the Southeastern Conference basketball tournament.

Zach was there with his wife, Amy, and their two small children. To those who wished him luck, he assured them he intended to fight until vindicated.

Despite his father's guilty plea, Zach felt confident. When he met with Rhea Tannehill later in the day, he was further encouraged. "Everything is cool," Tannehill told him. "Sid blew the air out of their case" when he met with the prosecutors. "Your biggest challenge is not to be cocky."

Zach's mood changed Monday morning when he saw Moore talking on his cell phone with Dawson as he walked up the interior steps to Scruggs's office. Zach was troubled by Moore's expression, and he overheard him say, "That's not what you told me on Friday."

The compromise Moore felt he had in hand Friday night had fallen apart over the weekend. "What about the deferred prosecution?" Moore asked.

"Greenlee wouldn't do it," Dawson said. He encouraged Moore to persuade Zach to plead guilty. "You should be scared at how many years Judge Biggers would lay on him. He could get fifteen to twenty years."

The prosecutors were prepared to accept a plea on one count of misprision of a felony, an obscure charge that would accuse Zach of knowing about a crime and failing to report it. In exchange, they would recommend that he serve no time in prison.

Zach told Moore he was not sure what "misprision of a felony" meant, and he was still unwilling to give in, especially if it meant the loss of his law license. But for the first time, he seemed less adamant.

To ensure that Zach would not go to prison, Moore suggested to the prosecutors that they meet collectively with Judge Biggers to finalize the deal. Dawson told Moore that contact of this sort with the judge was out of the question. "You might do this in state courts, but you can't do that with a federal judge," he said.

The federal prosecutors had a poor relationship with Moore. Despite his years as attorney general and district attorney, they'd never considered him one of their own. They thought him glib and naïve, and because of his friendship with Scruggs, they had suspicions about his honesty. They had pumped some of the defendants—notably Steve Patterson—with questions about the two Democratic attorneys general, Moore and Jim Hood.

It sounded as though the prosecutors would be delighted to be able to indict Moore, too, and accounts of their interest in him were relayed to him. At one point, during a recess in a hearing in the case, Moore approached the prosecutors' table and made a caustic remark. "Do you guys have any questions you want to ask me?"

No one responded to Moore's dare. Still, the prosecutors regarded him with disdain. Like his client, they thought Moore far too slick, and they considered him tarnished by an association with Dick Scruggs.

Moore worried that Zach, left alone, would wind up with the wrath of the federal government upon him. Following another meeting with prosecutors Tuesday morning, he told his client of his concerns at a meeting that afternoon at the law office while they nibbled at orders of take-out pizza. Dick was also there, as Moore presented the argument for a guilty plea.

Moore cited Judge Biggers's hostility. "This judge will send you to the moon if you're convicted," he said. "And if it comes to that, I don't know that I could ever practice law again."

Zach's father offered his own warning about the judge. "Don't fool around with this guy."

Zach felt he had been put in a hotbox by his best friends. For days he had the sensation, as he described it, of "being left wounded on the beach." His father had capitulated to the government without ensuring that his son would escape. Zach believed that his father, under stress, had lost judgment, and he blamed Keker for failing to press for Zach's freedom. At the same time, Zach recognized that Keker was, after all, representing Dick's interest, and not his. The situation seemed hopelessly confusing.

Still, he resisted the advice to accept the results of the plea bargaining.

"Dick got five," Zach said, calling his father by his first name, as had become his practice. "Sid got two and a half. There's no way the judge will give me more than that. I'll take my chances with five years."

"If you're convicted, it will be more than that," Moore countered. He pointed out that a guilty plea would allow Zach to maintain his freedom.

"Are you sure about that?" Zach asked.

"Well, no," Moore admitted. But he added, "Dawson says he will make a strong recommendation for probation, and the judge usually accepts his recommendations."

"I need to think about this," Zach said.

That afternoon, Zach met his wife, his parents, and Moore at Dick and Diane's home. Up until then, the women had been supportive of Zach's position, but now they urged him to make a deal with the prosecutors in order to escape a prison sentence.

"Do you want your children to grow up and for ten years not know you?" his mother asked. Diane was already struggling with the realization that her husband would soon be leaving for years in prison. It was unthinkable that her son, too, would be missing from the life of their family.

Zach said he would rather be in prison and have his children believe he had been convicted unjustly than to plead guilty.

Amy, who was pregnant with a child to be born that fall, said it was unacceptable to think that their family could survive without him for a decade.

The women were desperately trying to save him from the possibility of a terrible sentence.

Diane and Amy belittled the stigma of a misprision of felony conviction. "What's that? It's nothing," Diane said. Amy said she could accept the prospect of a relatively short prison sentence, but not the specter of a long one. If the plea bargain ensured that Zach would not be jailed, Diane and Amy argued, he should accept the offer.

Outside, a harsh rain pelted the grounds of Scruggs's property, where the first manifestations of spring were beginning to show in the scores of flowering shrubs planted the year before.

Zach thought to himself: I can fight the government, but I can't fight my family and my lawyer, too.

Three days later, Zach stood before Biggers, laboring to appear as humble as possible. He attached the honorific "Your Honor" to each of his answers as the judge led him through a sequence of pro forma questions. At the end, Judge Biggers asked, "Do you plead guilty or not guilty to count one of this information?"

"I plead guilty, Your Honor."

David Sanders, one of the prosecutors, told the judge that the government would recommend probation. Throughout the negotiations, Zach's attorneys felt comfortable with Sanders. He was younger and seemed to understand the intricacies of Zach's case. They believed Sanders had been consistent in his dealings with them and had pushed for a deferred prosecution in his discussions with his own colleagues. But Sanders was the junior member of the prosecution team, and within days he would be leaving the U.S. Attorney's Office to become a federal magistrate.

Biggers informed Zach that the court would not be bound by the prosecutors' recommendation, and he mentioned that a three-year prison sentence was still possible under the law.

Before the session ended, Zach sought permission to speak. "I'd like to start out by telling the court, and the public, that I had no knowledge that Tim Balducci bribed Judge Lackey," he said.

Zach's comments were a reflection of his attitude. He continued to assert innocence, even though he had just pleaded guilty.

"I didn't conspire to bribe Judge Lackey in connection with an arbitration order," he continued, "and I would have stopped it had I known."

Zach did not realize that his remarks were triggering an adverse reaction among the federal authorities in the courtroom. As he spoke, he ratified their belief that he was prideful and arrogant, a young man who deserved to be cut down a notch.

"As a member of the Mississippi bar," Zach went on, "I had a duty to prevent such contacts from occurring and to report them, and I failed to do so. I am truly and humbly sorry for that, and I apologize to the court, to the legal profession I love so deeply, and to the people of Mississippi." He closed by saying that he hoped his case might serve as a lesson to lawyers in the state.

Zach's speech failed to move Biggers. "All right, Mr. Scruggs," the judge said, dismissing him. "Of course, the legal profession that you say you love so much, you will not be a part of it for the rest of your life."

In the welter of betrayals and personal hatreds that characterized the Scruggs case, one man seemed to emerge with his reputation enhanced: circuit judge Henry L. Lackey. Publicly promoted as a hero by Grady Tollison, whose lawsuit had led to Balducci's bribe, and hailed by federal prosecutors for his willingness to report Balducci's first inappropriate approach, Lackey enjoyed an afterglow of admiration. In commentary headlined "Consider Judge Lackey" displayed on the front page of *The Clarion-Ledger*'s Sunday Perspective section, one Mississippi attorney wrote, "Thank God for men like Judge Henry Lackey!"

After serving in relative anonymity in rural North Mississippi, the old judge seemed to be reaching apotheosis. The Mississippi Supreme Court would give him their highest honor, the Chief Justice Award, while the state bar association added its Judicial Excellence Award.

In interviews, he liked to describe himself as simply a "country bumpkin" who loved the law. But a month after the guilty pleas by the members of the Scruggs Law Firm, Judge Lackey's genial side gave way to a more disagreeable nature when he made a dramatic appearance in the reopening of Johnny Jones's suit against the remnants of the Scruggs Katrina Group.

The case had been moved out of Lackey's hands—for obvious reasons—and assigned to circuit judge William Coleman from Jackson, who presided at a hearing in Oxford to determine the extent of involvement in the bribery by the defendants in the civil action. Lackey's role would shift from that of judge to that of witness.

Before Lackey took the stand, Dick Scruggs was called as a witness, and he repeatedly invoked his Fifth Amendment rights in refusing to answer questions posed by Tollison, who still smoldered. As a regional president of the American Board of Trial Advocates, Tollison sent a fiery email to its members. Though he did not believe in capital punishment, Tollison wrote, he would be willing to make an exception for judge-bribing lawyers.

With Tollison guiding him during his opening testimony, Lackey was loquacious. But the judge's animosity toward Scruggs came tumbling out during a cross-examination by Oxford attorney J. Cal Mayo, who now represented Scruggs in the civil case.

Mayo found himself in a delicate position: the witness was a judge in whose court he would continue to practice. At the same time, he had a responsibility to his client to question Lackey's motives. An additional source of tension existed in the courtroom. A decade earlier, Mayo had been offered a job by Tollison when Mayo worked as counsel for the University of Mississippi. Mayo sought advice from a friend who had experience with Tollison's firm. He was warned of Tollison's volatile personality. "Don't go to work for him," the friend urged Mayo, adding, "And if you don't go to work for him, he'll never speak to you again." The prediction proved accurate. Although they practiced law in the same town for the next ten years, Tollison refused to acknowledge Mayo's existence. During the run-up to the hearing, Tollison would not return Mayo's phone calls or agree to an informal discussion of the case. Mayo decided that Tollison, riding a crest of favorable publicity for his part in bringing down Scruggs, now considered Mayo an acolyte of Satan.

Mayo employed a deferential manner in questioning Judge Lackey, but at the beginning of his cross-examination he touched on a sensitive subject: a suggestion that Tollison had engaged in improper ex parte contact with the judge a year before when he presented Lackey with an order to seal Jones's lawsuit, a move that gave Tollison a tactical advantage.

Mayo: "Was anyone there at this time representing any of the other parties to this lawsuit besides the parties that Mr. Tollison represented?"

Lackey: "Oh, no."

"And did Mr. Tollison tell you who any of the parties were?"

"I don't believe he did."

. . .

"Did he tell you that there was an arbitration agreement that the parties had signed?"

"No."

"Did he tell you that there had been settlement discussions ongoing?"

"Been what?"

"Settlement discussions between the parties."

"No."

"Did he mention that the entry of this order sealing the complaint might impact those settlement discussions?"

"No. He said it might help to keep from hanging their dirty wash out before the public."

Mayo's line of questioning drew Tollison out of his chair. He objected to "all this about my conversations," and said it was irrelevant to the purpose of the hearing.

The objection was sustained, but Mayo managed to pursue Lackey with a few more questions.

"Did Mr. Tollison prepare the order that you signed?"

"He's the one that gave it to me. I assume he did . . ."

"You didn't prepare it?"

"No."

"Had you ever signed an order sealing a case like this before?"

"No. Never been asked."

The exchange set the tone for increasingly acrimonious responses from Lackey. He acknowledged that he'd fabricated several statements during his attempts to incriminate Tim Balducci, including a false claim of being under pressure from Tollison, and another tale of inadvertently having an out-of-court conversation with a member of Tollison's firm. Lackey rationalized his "fabrications" with Balducci.

"I was not being truthful with him, and I didn't think he was being truthful with me, but that doesn't make any difference, his truthfulness to me."

Lackey was asked about Balducci's original request that Judge Lackey perform a "favor" for him by sending the case to arbitration. "Did there come a time, Judge Lackey, when you told him to stop, wait a minute, this is a case I'm involved in?"

"No," Lackey said. "I was shocked that he would make that overture to me. I was incensed. I actually became physically ill because of it."

The judge said he felt an obligation to report the overture by Balducci. "I didn't know who to turn to in this circumstance. I didn't know what kind of monster we were dealing with at this point."

Lackey's use of the term *monster* surprised Mayo, and he would return to that description later.

Scruggs's attorney observed that two months after the first meeting between Balducci and Lackey, "Mr. Balducci has made no quid pro quo offer and he has offered no money" in exchange for a favorable ruling.

"He was lying to me, and I was lying to him," Lackey testified. "That's what happened."

Confused over the lack of progress in establishing evidence of an actual bribe, Lackey had withdrawn from the case. Mayo asked Lackey about his decision. The judge said Bill Delaney, the FBI agent, came to see him immediately to encourage him to remain in the investigation.

"After talking with him and after realizing what a monster that we were probably dealing with, and the lives that he had probably destroyed, and the young lawyers whose lives and their families that he had destroyed, I agreed to get back in it," Lackey said.

"And who is the 'he' that you're referring to, Judge Lackey?"

"Talking about Dickie Scruggs."

"And who was it that told you Mr. Scruggs had destroyed all those lives?"

"It's evident what he's done," Lackey snapped. "It's evident. Don't you think he's destroyed them?"

Mayo asked if this was part of the discussion he had with Delaney and John Hailman, the prosecutor.

"I didn't know for sure at that point, didn't know what type of monster we were dealing with. But I realize now. I think he's done more to destroy this profession than anything that's happened in my lifetime."

During his testimony, Lackey created a new controversy. He said he informed an assistant district attorney, Lon Stallings, about Balducci's visit shortly after it happened but felt reluctant to take the information to a higher level, to Attorney General Jim Hood, after Stallings told him that Scruggs had threatened Hood's political future.

Lackey's statement was somewhat rambling: "I knew from my information—if it was true—that Jim Hood had told Lon Stallings that Mr.

Scruggs, through Mike Moore, had promised him if he didn't go along with the settlement of these State Farm cases and allow them to collect this $26.5 million in attorney's fees, that they would find a candidate that would run against him."

Lackey had not forgotten that Scruggs had driven his friend George Dale out of the insurance commissioner's office the year before. "They would fund" an opponent to challenge Hood "just like they were going to do the commissioner of insurance," the judge declared. "Now, that's what I knew."

Moore, sitting in the courtroom, was outraged by Lackey's statement. At a break in the hearing, the former attorney general told reporters, "Judge Lackey either is very confused or he made up the story out of whole cloth. Jim Hood is a very, very close friend. He worked for me, supported me in my first campaign. I encouraged him to take my place."

Reached later by reporters, Hood said, "Mike Moore never approached me with such a message."

Stallings said of Lackey's testimony, "A few details got confused, but the thrust of his testimony was correct." Stallings said Lackey didn't trust the attorney general's office because Hood, Moore, and Scruggs were all friends.

Before he left the stand, Lackey asked the presiding judge if he could "retrieve my personal notes rather than them being disseminated to the public."

During his testimony he had carried with him, for reference, the journal that prosecutors had asked Lackey to keep concerning his dealings with Balducci. Copies of the document were turned over to attorneys on both sides, but Lackey said they should not be made public.

"I don't mind the lawyers having access to them," he said, "but there are other matters in here of my personal expression about certain things and certain people."

The journal would reflect his ill prediposition toward the Scruggs group, which he had called "scum." In an early entry, Judge Lackey had also referred to Balducci as "the little wop."

Lackey's request to restrict his journal was granted.

Throughout the spring, Scruggs prepared for prison. His sentencing would take place on June 27, and shortly afterward he would lose control of his future. A physical fitness buff, he began trying to work out regularly again at home. Seized by depression in the period after his indictment, his exercises had lapsed and the inactivity had contributed to his malaise. Now he felt a need to build back his strength.

More important, he took steps to deal with a demon that only his family and a few close friends knew about: his dependency on the prescription drug that gave him a sense of well-being, even in times of stress. Fioricet had been readily available on the Internet, ninety tablets for sixty-five dollars. Once, when Sid Backstrom came to work hungover from celebrating a big lick by the firm the night before, Scruggs offered his junior partner a couple of "happy pills." The medicine jolted Backstrom so strongly that he had to be driven home. Employees of the firm were accustomed to the task. Quite often they had to get the boss safely home.

In April, Scruggs quietly checked into a drug treatment center in Hattiesburg, a South Mississippi city 250 miles away from Oxford. He spent a week, cold turkey, in a recovery program, trying to rid himself of the craving.

He came home pronouncing himself cured. But within a few weeks, one of his secretaries, Beth Jones, discovered that he had accessed the office computer to order a new shipment of the drug via FedEx. She alerted Rex Deloach, the financial advisor who had effectively taken charge of affairs at Scruggs's office. Jones and Deloach planned to intercept the shipment. On the day of the delivery, they spotted the FedEx truck parked on the square and waited for the order to be brought upstairs. After an unproductive interval, they peered from the balcony and spied Scruggs below, seated in his Porsche SUV. He had beaten them to the delivery man. Deloach called Diane. "He's outsmarted us," he said, suggesting that she intervene. Scruggs's wife drove quickly downtown.

A few minutes later, Scruggs appeared in Deloach's office. "I want you to be my witness," Scruggs announced. He led his friend to the men's room, where he opened the package and poured the tablets into the toilet.

Despite his action, the close-knit group at Scruggs's office suspected he continued to sneak the medication for himself.

Disgraced by his guilty plea and remorseful over his son's dilemma, it seemed natural for Scruggs to turn to any source of comfort he could find. He not only faced prison and the loss of his law practice, but had become a subject of debate at his alma mater, where there were calls to remove his name from a campus music hall. To spare Chancellor Khayat a wrenching decision, Scruggs wrote to ask that the name be taken down. The job was done overnight. The next day, no traces of the lettering remained on the building's façade. (Scruggs also arranged a discreet disappearance of the words *Scruggs Law Firm* from the front of his second-floor office overlooking the square.)

But his commitment to donate $5 million toward the construction of a new law school complex continued to cause division. The day after his guilty plea, Scruggs called Sam Davis, his childhood friend from Pascagoula who had become dean of the law school.

"Sometime we need to sit down and talk about how I'm going to fulfill my pledge," he told Davis.

The dean, who had tried to reach him earlier to commiserate, said, "Dick, that's the farthest thing from my mind right now."

Scruggs had been the co-chairman of a drive to raise $10 million for the project and helped host a fund-raising gala in Oxford the year before, an event that took place three days after the fateful March 2007 meeting with Balducci and Steve Patterson.

Davis might have wanted to put off his worries about Scruggs's money, but the subject remained very much on the minds of some law school professors who considered the gift tainted. At one faculty meeting, John Robin Bradley, a liberal voice at the school, observed, "We've not had the experience before of having wealthy people donate to us who were crooks. Other universities have had that experience. We should check on this, because I think there's an ethical problem."

Appealing for leniency from Judge Biggers, the Scruggs Law Firm defendants mobilized a letter-writing campaign among their friends.

Backstrom sent an email to his neighbors, thanking them for their "prayers and thoughts" and explaining that he had chosen to plead guilty rather than gambling with a trial that might have resulted in a lengthy sentence. "I think most of you know that I am not a risk taker, either professionally or otherwise," he wrote. The two-and-a-half-year sentence he expected "will allow me to still see most of the years of my children (Jayne is 9, Drew is 7 and Seth is 3) growing up as compared to the terrible risk of not seeing any of those or later years . . ."

In these letters, Backstrom suggested, "you can request favorable consideration or leniency at the sentencing." He added, "I don't want to be presumptuous. If you are not comfortable writing such a letter, you need not."

The request produced 127 letters in support of Backstrom.

Zach's Sigma Nu brothers rallied behind him on the fraternity's email network. But when critical bloggers obtained a copy of the message and gave it wider circulation, with sarcastic comment, the impact of the Sigma Nu effort was diminished. Seventy-one letters were written on Zach's behalf.

Dick Scruggs's case attracted 248 letters to Judge Biggers. Though a couple called for a severe sentence, virtually all of the correspondence noted Scruggs's long record of generosity and asked the judge to take that into consideration.

There were handwritten notes by aging residents of Pascagoula who remembered Scruggs for his kindnesses and letters from influential Mississippians such as former governor William Winter, who wrote:

"I know of the generous financial support which he gave to many worthwhile causes which benefited his community and our state. I always found him to be a highly compassionate and engaged citizen leader who had a genuine interest in the well-being of his fellow citizens."

The childhood friend in Brookhaven whom Scruggs had bailed out of a $90,000 debt sent a letter describing how Scruggs had hired a law firm to negotiate a settlement on the credit card demands and then paid off the settlement himself.

Another wrote of how Scruggs had been a major donor for the Piney Woods School, one of the few institutions for troubled African American youngsters in the country.

Michael Mann, the director of *The Insider*, wrote from Hollywood that he knew Scruggs as "a man of rare character, humanity, and I believe a positivism."

But the letter that generated the most interest came from Scruggs's old friend Robert Khayat. Writing on the university's letterhead stationery, Khayat cited Scruggs's "compassion and generosity" and ended with a proposal:

"It is my belief that any time he spends being incarcerated is an absolute waste of a great deal of talent and ability. He has much to offer society and is a public-spirited person. Furthermore, it would appear to be a waste of taxpayers' money. Punishment is relative to the individual. A man such as Dick has been amply punished by the loss of his profession and public stature."

Scruggs, who received copies of the letters, was able to call upon them for consolation while awaiting sentencing. But Khayat's comments ignited a different reaction elsewhere.

Biggers allowed reporters to read the letters, and excerpts from the messages were published. Learning of Khayat's strong support, Grady Tollison became indignant. Though he had once worked in the same firm with the chancellor, Tollison told friends he hoped the new law school would never be named for Khayat.

The letter also proved counterproductive with a more significant figure. Instead of being persuaded by Khayat's argument, Judge Biggers himself was said to be infuriated.

The evening before Dick Scruggs's sentencing, his California lawyers sampled a taste of rustic Mississippi nightlife. John Keker and his associate Brook Dooley rode with Rex Deloach and others to Taylor, an artsy community eight miles from Oxford, to have dinner at a legendary catfish place called Taylor Grocery. They found themselves in a nest of strange sounds: the hubbub of demin-clad diners and the twangs of a jug band playing for tips in the back. The village occupies a "dry" corner of Lafayette County, where alcohol is illegal, so customers are forced to bring their own. With no notice, the group's table was supplied with the sizable remains of a magnum of wine.

John Hailman, the recently retired federal prosecutor and wine maven, was leaving after dinner, and on the way out he thought to give the visitors what was left in his bottle. "Welcome to Oxford," he said to the group. "Looks like you need some wine." His gesture was a token of the informality at Taylor Grocery. Hailman had recognized Keker, but Scruggs's attorney did not know the identity of the donor.

The next day, a crowd began to gather outside Judge Biggers's courtroom nearly an hour before doors opened. Many of them had come to give moral support to Scruggs: members of his family, including all of Diane's siblings, and close friends such as Mike Moore, Sam Davis, and Robert Khayat. Others, though, had different reasons for being there. Roberts Wilson, the former partner who had fought with Scruggs for fifteen years, had made the trip from his home in Alabama to witness the latest installment in the downfall of Dick Scruggs. Wilson's lawyer, Charlie Merkel, had driven over from Clarksdale to see his old enemy in the dock. And Grady Tollison, whose case had resulted in the bribery, sat inside the rails of the courtroom, uncomfortably close to the defendant's table.

When Scruggs entered, he carried none of the ebullience that had characterized his appearance in the same room three months earlier when he pleaded guilty. He seemed as somber as his dark suit and tie, and he held his hands in a prayerful position.

The terms of Scruggs's five-year sentence were assured, and so was his $250,000 fine. But there were official rulings that needed to be made. Biggers said he was satisfied that Scruggs was "a leader and a planner" of the conspiracy to bribe Judge Lackey, and he said he considered Zach a "particpant" in the conspiracy regardless of the reduced charge Scruggs's son had accepted. The March 2007 meeting between the two Scruggs men, Backstrom, Balducci, and Patterson "was the starting of the scheme to corrupt the integrity of the Lafayette County Circuit Court," Biggers said.

Before undertaking the "very unpleasant duty" of passing sentence, the judge asked Scruggs if he had anything he wished to say.

Standing before Biggers and flanked by Keker, Scruggs said:

"I could not be more ashamed than to be where I am today, mixed up in a judicial bribery scheme that I participated in. I realized that I was getting mixed up in it. And I will go to my grave wondering why."

Sniffles could be heard among his supporters.

"I have disappointed everyone in my life: my wife, my family, my son, particularly. My friends—many of whom were kind enough to come up today and to write to the court. I deeply regret my conduct. I'm sorrowful for it. It is a scar and a stain on my soul that will be there forever."

Keker followed with his own brief remarks. He said it would take mystical southern novelists—William Faulkner or Walker Percy—"to understand how these kinds of things happen." Keker said he was perplexed by Scruggs's "passivity," and added, "In this instance, I think I'm beginning to understand, but I just don't understand about how it all happened."

His client, he said, "has fallen about as far as a man can fall."

Keker asked that Scruggs be allowed to report to prison at a later

date rather than be immediately taken into custody. He requested
that Scruggs be assigned to a federal correctional camp in Pensacola,
Florida, where his family would be able to visit him. And he sought an
additional thirty days for Scruggs to pay the fine.

Biggers accepted the first two requests as "reasonable." Of the third,
he said, "I question why you need thirty days to get up the $250,000
when it's in your checking account."

After Keker referred to "cash flow problems that I can explain to you
if you wanted me to," Biggers approved the delay. But the judge had
sharp words for Scruggs.

Biggers spoke of previous cases in which lawyers, doctors, ministers,
business executives, and bankers had appeared before him. "They were
willing to risk their freedom and their profession to get some money,"
Biggers said. "And yet you neither thought you needed money or did need
money. Yet you committed a reprehensible crime which, in my opinion,
is one of the most reprehensible crimes that a lawyer can commit . . .

"I do not have to know why you've done it," he continued. "I just
have to know that you did it. And there's no doubt that you did it. I've
heard the tapes. I've heard you say you did it."

As the judge who had authorized the wiretaps and search warrant,
Biggers had been in a position to follow the accumulation of evidence
long before any charges were actually filed against Scruggs. "I was personally shocked when I first learned about this situation with you and
your partners," Judge Biggers said. "I was shocked as I learned the evidence as it developed. And when I saw how, when you were approached
with this scheme, I saw how easily and quickly you entered into it. And
it made me think that this, perhaps, is not the first time you've done it
because you did it so easily. You didn't really take time to think about
it. And there is evidence before the court that you have done it before."

Biggers, of course, was speaking of the case involving Judge De-
Laughter in which Scruggs had been implicated. Though Scruggs had
not yet been charged in the second case, the government was using it
to justify their 404(b) tactic. The judge seemed to be throwing his own
weight behind the prosecutors.

Biggers was not finished. He told Scruggs: "You attempted to bribe
Judge Lackey. You found out that Judge Lackey is not a man to
bribe . . . And another thing that doesn't make any sense—it makes
your crime more reprehensible . . . The court system has made you a
rich man, and yet you have attempted to corrupt it."

Scruggs began to quiver. His arms twitched and his knees buckled.

Some of the spectators gasped. While Keker held on to his client's arm, a court officer produced a chair for Scruggs to sit in.

Noting Scruggs's condition, the judge paused briefly, then said that a transcript of his remarks would be available for the shaken defendant. "You may not remember what I'm saying, but there's some people who you're involved with—who I have become intrigued in this situation," Biggers said. It was obvious he was referring to P. L. Blake, long the most mysterious figure in the case.

"When I see, from this case and others, that people who are not lawyers are getting considerable amounts of money from a legal settlement, and, you know, it intrigues me as to what they're doing to earn it, if anything . . . Balducci said that you know where a lot of bodies are buried. If you want to uncover some of those bodies, it might help you in the future in this case and this sentencing."

Judge Biggers had another stern observation about a man sitting in the courtroom, Chancellor Robert Khayat. "One person who wrote a letter said he thought sending you to prison would be a waste of the taxpayer's money. To alleviate any concerns for that person, the taxpayers won't have to pay for your incarceration." Staring at Scruggs, the judge said, "You'll pay for it yourself" with the $250,000 fine.

Scruggs was able to rise and listen as the judge handed down his formal sentence. Though Biggers included a provision for drug treatment in prison, his remark seemed lost, like so much boilerplate language, on others in the courtroom. When the session ended, less than forty-five minutes after it began, Scruggs walked to the spectator's section, embraced Diane, and thanked friends for "being here with me this morning."

John Hailman, whom Scruggs had wanted to commission to help stock his wine cellar before Hailman launched the Lackey investigation, came forward. He offered a curious expression of support, shaking Scruggs's hand and telling him, "I was glad to see you get up just then. That means you're going to make it."

At that moment, in a state courtroom across the Oxford square, Khayat was the subject of more judicial criticism. Judge Lackey was presiding over a case in which the university was the defendant in a small-bore civil action. During the morning session, Judge Lackey had called for pauses in the proceedings while he used a cell phone.

Suddenly, he said he had an announcement to make. "As you know probably, I've been involved in a matter involving Dick Scruggs and others," he explained to attorneys who had been wondering about his behavior. "Mr. Scruggs was just sentenced in federal court about four blocks from where we're sitting today. Receiving sixty months to serve and, I believe, a $250,000 fine. And it's one of these phone calls—or a couple of them—was what that was about."

Judge Lackey had just overruled a motion by the university attorneys for a summary judgment in their favor. Now he was recusing himself. The lawyers were flabbergasted that he was doing both in the same breath.

The judge had more to say.

"It's come to my attention that Chancellor Khayat proceeded with some of the Scruggs family there at the sentencing, and it's come to my attention that the university, speaking through Chancellor Khayat and other faculty and staff members, have spoken out praising Dick Scruggs, requesting leniency from the court and describing him as a model citizen and apparently condoning judicial bribery.

"Ladies and gentlemen," the judge intoned, "I'm embarrassed for our state. I'm ashamed for the public disgrace and the disrepute that has been caused to this great university. I'm mortified that some of our so-called educational leaders and literary icons cannot find the moral courage to publicly condemn and denounce the reprehensible, vile, and evil acts that have besmirched the professional reputation of the many, many honest and trustworthy lawyers of this state."

As a result, Judge Lackey said, he could no longer give the university a fair trial and he pulled out of the case. In closing, he said, "Thank you for allowing me to vent my frustration."

Following his father's sentencing, Zach went to his parents' home for a gathering of close friends. Afterward, he took Amy for a late lunch on the square. Before they entered City Grocery, Zach reconnoitered the crowd. If there were news correspondents present, he wanted to go elsewhere. A couple of weeks earlier, a reporter had spied Zack with a friend in the bar upstairs. The next day, an article in the Jackson paper noted that Zach had been drinking Grey Goose, an expensive vodka.

Instead of journalists, Zach spotted a table he wanted to avoid. Roberts Wilson and several members of his family were celebrating Scruggs's humiliation. The festive group had started with shots of Grey Goose, then moved on to champagne. Buoyed by the spirits, the Wilson family began singing the chorus of an old ballad by a Mississippi country troubador, Jimmie Rodgers, "In the Jailhouse Now."

Zach and Amy left before the Wilson table grew boisterous. After learning of the incident, John Currence, City Grocery's owner, called Zach to apologize. The behavior was regrettable, Currence told him, and did not reflect the feelings of anyone connected with the restaurant.

At two o'clock that afternoon, it was Sid Backstrom's turn to stand before Judge Biggers. Backstrom's wife, Kelli, was there with many of their friends, wiping away tears. Backstrom tried to smile from across the courtroom in support, but appeared close to breaking down, too.

With Frank Trapp and Rhea Tannehill at his side, Backstrom pulled notes from his pocket and addressed the judge.

He said he wanted "to express my profound sorrow to my family, to this court, and the bar" for his involvement in the case. "I have been haunted by the events leading to my indictment every day since late November, and will likely be for the rest of my life. I have cried with my wife and my children too many times to count. That punishment, along with always wondering of the damage I've caused to my family and three children, will never leave me."

Backstrom's voice broke. Tannehill held the back of his suit jacket to keep him from falling, then put his arm around his shoulders, rubbing gently.

First Trapp, then Tannehill, told the judge of their client's remorse and contrition. But when Tannehill described Backstrom as a "caretaker" for his elderly grandmother, his widowed stepmother, and his brother, who was imprisoned himself, Biggers asked, "What does being a caretaker have to do with the reason he's standing before the court?"

"Your Honor, I think that in some ways he was just trying to help the situation," Tannehill said, "and I think he takes responsibility for that."

"Well, thank goodness all caretakers are not before the court having been convicted of a serious crime," the judge said.

Despite the tone of Biggers's comment about caretakers, he appeared pleased by Backstrom's picture of abject remorse.

"Frankly, I've been kind of surprised at the lightness with which this judicial bribery case has been taken by some people who are supposed to be role models to law students and to other students, generally, young people, as to how they should conduct themselves," Biggers said, adding that he was impressed by Backstrom's "state of mind."

"I remember when you pled guilty, Mr. Backstrom, you were very remorseful at that time," he said, referring to Backstrom's tearful appearance three months earlier. "I cannot say that I have seen that type of remorse with some of your co-defendants."

Zach was sitting in the courtroom with his mother, but he failed to appreciate the portent of Biggers's remarks.

Even as Biggers complimented Backstrom for his penitence, he complained about his failure to implicate Zach. "There's one thing that I have not seen from you that I thought I would see," Judge Biggers said, "and that is some kind of cooperation on your part with the government. They gave you a plea agreement that provided your sentence would be capped at half of Mr. Scruggs's sentence, and that was based on assumed cooperation from you. I understand there was a proffer of some kind of cooperation before the plea agreement was made, but there has been no cooperation."

"I think we've done what we've been asked to do," Trapp replied.

"You think so?"

"Yes, sir."

"Well, I haven't heard any testimony or any proffer from the government about his knowledge of the others' activities—especially one co-defendant I was interested in."

"There has not been any knowledge of that, that he has, Your Honor," Trapp said.

"Well, all right," the judge said. "I question about what he knew about the other things. But based on that, I will accept the plea agreement."

Backstrom's day in court was done, but Zach's lay ahead, a week later. Zach continued to believe that he would not be saddled with a prison sentence, but his friends and family were no longer sure.

By the morning that Zach faced Judge Biggers, he finally understood the precarious state of his position. Before leaving his office the night before, he told his father's longtime secretary, Charlene Bosarge, "I may have to serve some time." But Zach was resolute about his courtroom appearance. He would not be craven. And he asked Mike Moore to defend him if the judge said anything objectionable.

Zach's formal remarks were very brief. "I am deeply sorry and regretful for my involvement in this case. I wish that I could go back and change what happened a year ago. And I should have stopped what happened," he said, "I didn't do that . . . For that, I'm deeply sorry and remorseful. And I ask this court's forgiveness. And my challenge now is to try to rebuild my life, Your Honor."

Before Biggers issued his sentence, Tom Dawson rose to say that the prosecutors recommended probation when Zach pleaded guilty. "We meant that then, and we mean that now."

Biggers pointed out that he was not bound by any agreement.

"Your case is a sad case, Mr. Scruggs," the judge said. "The primary actor in this case was your father. It would not have happened without him. And it makes it even sadder that you, his son, was [sic] brought into it. The evidence in this case shows that you were fully aware of this corruption—attempted corruption of Judge Lackey. You took that order that Balducci brought up to your law office, the corrupt order that was attempted to be bought from Judge Lackey. And you made comments on it. You said where commas should be and what things should be said about it, what the order would say."

Listening to the judge, Moore began to shake his head. Biggers seemed to be confusing Zach with his father's comment to Balducci about a colon in the punctuation of the order during the damning November 1 conversation recorded by the FBI.

Biggers said he had listened to the recordings. "It was just clear that you not only knew what was going on," he said, "you were participating in what was going on. You helped write that order."

He stopped and glared at Moore. "You shake your head, Mr. Moore, but I heard the tapes. He suggested what should be in that order, that corrupted order. Have you heard that?"

"Judge, I've listened to every tape . . ."

"Well, then, you've heard that if you've listened to every tape."

"I hope I get a chance to respond," Moore said.

"You've had your chance to respond," Biggers snapped, then reconsidered. "Well, you can respond to that. Go ahead."

It seemed as if arcs of electricity were shooting between the two men.

"Zach Scruggs never had any knowledge whatsoever that there was any conspiracy to bribe a judge in this case," Moore began.

Biggers interrupted. "He's not being sentenced for conspiring to bribe a judge."

"I understand, Judge."

"He's being sentenced for misprision of a felony. But the underlying offense is the corruption of a judge. He knew that Judge Lackey was being corrupted—"

"Your Honor, I—"

"And whether it was for money or whatever else is really immaterial. It was a corrupt order."

"The only difference—and I don't want to offend the court," Moore responded, "but the only difference is that the only thing Zach knew was that Tim Balducci went to have a conversation with Judge Lackey. He never knew that anybody conspired to bribe a judge or to do something untoward. The tape you're talking about is a tape that occurred after Tim Balducci came to the Scruggs Law Firm on November the first, wired up, saying he was there to meet with two individuals, Sid Backstrom and Dick Scruggs. Zach Scruggs, all the evidence would show, happened to walk in the room that day. He was never a part of that. And that's the only evidence the government ever had in this case. And that may be a distinction without a difference in Your Honor's mind, but it's a distinction in Zach's mind."

"Well, that's something you can argue. Whether or not that's true remains open," Biggers said. "You know, when Mr. Backstrom—who's admitted he was part of the bribe—and your client are as close as they were; they're up there in that office every day talking about legal projects for the firm. It's kind of a stretch of credulity to believe that Backstrom never mentioned that money was being sent down to Judge Lackey. You can claim that. You can argue that. And as far as the law is concerned, I'm going to base the sentence on that. But whether or not I believe that is something else."

Moore said that in all of the hundreds of conversations recorded by the government, "there's no mention of Zach Scruggs in this case anywhere."

"What do you say, Mr. Dawson?" Biggers asked the prosecutor.

"I'd have to disagree with that statement. Zach Scruggs is mentioned on some of the tapes."

Zach's name had not only been mentioned in some of the captured conversations, but his voice could actually be heard in the November 1 conversation with Balducci in Backstrom's office. The judge seized on that.

"When you—Mr. Scruggs—and Mr. Backstrom were talking with Mr. Balducci over this order that he had brought to you before it had been entered by Judge Lackey, it was an order that you were commenting on how it should read and what it should say."

The judge recalled Zach's earlier comments when he pleaded guilty concerning his respect for the legal profession. "You certainly had no great respect for the Circuit Court of Lafayette County or Judge Lackey, because the tapes show that you told Mr. Balducci and Mr. Backstrom that we need to hurry up and get this order signed before some other 'asshole' gets the case. Now that's a total thumb in your nose at the Lafayatte County Circuit Court. And it contradicts your statement to the court that you have a great love and respect for the legal profession."

Judge Biggers reminded Zach that his plea bargain did not bind the court.

"Your Honor, we were informed by the government on that matter," Moore said. "We asked for a binding plea—"

"You didn't get it," Biggers said. "You were here when he entered a plea of guilty. I told you it was not binding."

"Judge, we know that," Moore said, "I just—"

"If I want you to say any more, Mr. Moore, I'll ask for it."

"Judge, I appreciate that. I thought a lawyer could always respond to the court respectfully."

"No, you do not. I didn't ask you to respond. I wasn't saying anything to you. I was saying it to your client."

Moore apologized "if I've offended the court in some way representing my client."

"I'm not going to argue with you about it," Biggers said, repeating that there was never a binding plea agreement.

"The only response I have," Moore said, "if it's okay for me to respond . . . is that we attempted to do a binding plea, and the government informed us that this court would not accept a binding plea on probation. And that's why we did not do it that way."

Biggers put an end to the colloquy and moved to his decision. He said that presentencing guidelines called for a twenty-one- to twenty-seven-month sentence. "I am giving some weight to the government's recommendation for leniency," he said.

Nevertheless, he sentenced Zach to fourteen months in prison.

Biggers declared a recess. As Zach turned toward his supporters in the courtroom, he could see that many of them were sobbing in shock over his prison sentence. Zach's expression was grim, but he did not cry.

He was approached by a man who wanted to offer a formal introduction. "Zach, I'm Tom Dawson. I don't believe we've met."

Zach stopped him with a baleful eye. "You broke your deal, and we're not going to meet now."

Surprised by Zach's brusque response, Dawson had a curt rejoinder. "Well, enjoy your time."

The courtroom was emptying. Several of Zach's fraternity brothers gave him condolences. He was hugged by others, and he exchanged a long *abrazo* with Ollie Rencher, a priest at St. Peter's Episcopal Church, where he and Amy were communicants.

Jim Greenlee, the U.S. attorney, was moving toward the door when confronted by Diane Scruggs. By this time, she was beyond tears. Clear-eyed, she looked at Greenlee and stretched her arms wide.

"I thought we had an agreement," she said.

Greenlee did not reply. He was not sure what Diane had said, and even if he had understood her, he had no answer.

CHAPTER 27

More than a year passed.

Alone among those who pleaded guilty, Zach Scruggs continued to protest that he was innocent, the victim of a crime created by his own government. His defiant attitude fit the image the federal authorities had cast for him—that of a spoiled, hot-tempered brat—and it did him no favors. His six months in a low-security prison camp in Forrest City, Arkansas, were spent uneventfully, broken only by the birth of a daughter, Ellie, in October. He was not allowed to be with his family for the occasion.

From Arkansas, Zach followed, with some annoyance, that fall's election in Mississippi, where Roger Wicker campaigned to hold on to the Senate seat vacated by Zach's uncle Trent. No matter that Zach, a fellow Sigma Nu, had once worked in Wicker's congressional office or that Wicker had been the recipient of campaign contributions from him and his father. Wicker, a Republican, was being challenged by former governor Ronnie Musgrove. In spite of his own background with the Scruggs family, Wicker tarred his opponent for his association with the new felons. The text of one Wicker flyer, distributed statewide by the Republican Senatorial Campaign Commmittee, read:

"Convicted trial lawyer Dickie Scruggs guaranteed a loan for Musgrove's campaign. Dickie Scruggs guaranteed a loan for $75K for Musgrove's campaign for lt. governor and has given over $110K in campaign contributions to his campaigns. Scruggs met privately with Musgrove in the governor's office to discuss a judicial appointment. Scruggs is now in prison for bribing a judge."

Wicker won the election, ensuring the continuity that Trent Lott had preserved between Washington and the old conservative network in Mississippi.

On February 24, 2009, the day Zach transferred from Forrest City to a halfway house in Tupelo, Mississippi, he stopped in Oxford to pick up non-prison clothes and to have lunch downtown with members of his family. Though he felt that no rule specifically forbade the activity, the Bureau of Prisons cracked down on him following newspaper reports of a Zach "sighting" on the square. He was thrust back into the hands of U.S. marshals and put in the county jail in Oxford, which doubled as a federal facility, for ten days.

While there, he caught the first glimpse of his father since they were imprisoned. Dick had been brought back to Oxford to appear before a grand jury.

Zach's temporary job with family friend Lowry Lomax was nixed by authorities, but he was eventually allowed to return to the halfway house and begin working weekdays for a catfish farming operation with offices in Oxford. Soon he was able to spend weekends, with strict curfews, at home with Amy and their three children.

He was the first to go free, in August 2009, but he retained an abiding bitterness. His friends and family worried about his unforgiving mood. They counseled him to try to put the experience behind him, to meet the years ahead with as positive an outlook as possible. But Zach continued to seethe.

Sid Backstrom had also been assigned to prison in Forrest City, and he handled his sentence with more equanimity. Since the facility was only a two-hour drive from Oxford, he regularly saw his wife and friends. By serving his time without attracting attention, he expected to be free before the end of 2010.

The Backstroms had moved into their new home in a secluded cul-de-sac on the outskirts of Oxford shortly before he was incarcerated. Settling down in the house, which had been designed for them in detail, offered a diversion for the family. But there was one drawback: it was quite close to the home of Judge Biggers.

.   .   .

Joey Langston had hoped for a reduced sentence. The U.S. Attorney's Office filed a motion—which became public after the document was posted on the court's Internet connection by mistake—asking Judge Michael Mills to look sympathetically on the case. After pleading guilty, the prosecutors said, Langston had "cooperated to an extent that clearly exceeds the government's expectation." He had informed authorities about his knowledge of Scruggs's role in the bribery case involving Judge DeLaughter, described how he had arranged to pay Ed Peters, and answered questions about P. L. Blake.

Moreover, the prosecutors pointed out, Langston had recently suffered a heart attack, and the grounds of his home in Booneville had been visited by a "possible intruder" driving a van "packed with electronic equipment."

Langston's friends filled the courtroom on the day he faced formal sentencing. When Judge Mills refused to pare any time from the three-year prison sentence agreed upon in the plea bargain, Langston wept, and so did many of his supporters. He was sent to a facility in Montgomery, Alabama.

Steve Patterson joined his former partner in the Montgomery prison camp. He was sentenced on the same morning, Friday, February 13, 2009, as his more recent partner, Tim Balducci, but the courtroom styles of the two men were strikingly different.

Patterson walked boldly past a gauntlet of photographers and television cameramen outside the courthouse and later told Judge Biggers that he was "an embarrassed man with much to be embarrassed about." He quoted his grandmother and Winston Churchill.

Before sentencing Patterson, the judge revealed some startling information from a presentencing report compiled by federal probation officers. Patterson had been receiving $80,000 a month from the tobacco spoils, a payment that had been reduced to $20,000 a month. Biggers did not explain the source of the income.

(It came from Langston for Patterson's help in smoothing some of the rough edges of the byzantine settlement in the Butler secondhand smoke case. Langston paid Balducci a $100,000 bonus for his role in the affair and agreed to pay Patterson a "consulting fee" of $80,000 a month as long as the "three points" money came in from Scruggs.)

Described by federal prosecutors as a "minor" player in the scheme to bribe Judge Lackey, Patterson drew a two-year sentence.

· · ·

Minutes later, Tim Balducci appeared in the same courtroom. He had asked federal marshals to allow him to enter the building through a back door, out of sight of the cameras. Once inside, he stood by himself, with no lawyer to represent him. He had little to say. All of Balducci's brashness seemed washed away, and he actually looked diminished in size.

Prosecutors praised Balducci for his cooperation in breaking the case he had actually conceived. He was also given a two-year prison sentence, which he began serving in a federal facility in Estill, South Carolina.

After fourteen years as chancellor of the University of Mississippi, Robert Khayat retired in the summer of 2009. He was seventy years old. Though he had aggravated a few critics because of his support of Dick Scruggs, Khayat was almost universally praised for his leadership at the end of his career. Not only had the school's enrollment increased 44 percent during his stewardship, but the number of "minority" students had grown by nearly 80 percent. Over the same period, the Ole Miss endowment had tripled.

No less than six new academic centers had been built, and a long-sought chapter of Phi Beta Kappa had been established at Ole Miss. It was a different campus from the one Khayat had inherited.

Scruggs could no longer be counted on for gifts to the school, but the new law school center he had helped develop was nearing completion. It would be named for Robert Khayat.

Wilson v. Scruggs, thought finished with Judge DeLaughter's declaration in 2006, was reopened in 2009 and lurched into its fifteenth year under a new heading: joining Scruggs on the list of defendants were Ed Peters, Steve Patterson, Tim Balducci, Zach Scruggs, and various "John Does."

Wilson finally settled with Scruggs for an undisclosed amount in the fall of that year. A few months later, Wilson purchased the office suite that had housed the Scruggs firm on Oxford's square. The Scruggs family would never have sold him the property—which had been on the market for a year—so Wilson used a third-party straw to complete the deal.

Meanwhile, Johnny Jones obtained out-of-court settlements from some of the partners in the Scruggs Katrina Group in connection with his lawsuit, including Dick Scruggs. He continued to pursue the case against his personal bête noire in the group, Don Barrett, but Barrett refused to consider any measure of compromise.

In 2009, Grady Tollison presided over a spring convention of the southeastern region of the American Board of Trial Advocates at the grand old Peabody Hotel in Memphis. The program he arranged was dominated by two sessions dealing with professional ethics. Both panels were composed of only Tollison, Johnny Jones, and Charlie Merkel.

The title of their discussion: "Icarus, the Rise and Fall of Dickie Scruggs; Or, a Lesson in Hubris."

A smaller number of lawyers than usual chose to attend.

In his most extensive comment about the case, U.S. attorney Jim Greenlee also called upon the words of ancient Greeks in a private speech about the Scruggs case at a litigation conference in Phoenix, Arizona.

He quoted from Plato's *Republic:* "What shall he profit, if his injustice be undetected and unpunished? He who is undetected only gets worse, whereas he who is detected and punished has the brutal part of his nature silenced and humanized; the gentler element in him is liberated, and his whole soul is perfected and ennobled by the acquirement of justice and temperance and wisdom . . ."

Before he reached that lofty passage, Greenlee spoke of the painful aspects of the Scruggs case. Personal relationships are interwoven in a state like Mississippi, and he noted several associations he had with those he had investigated. He and Zach had served together on Sigma Nu committees; his nephews had been fraternity brothers with young Scruggs. He and the Backstroms had attended the same church; Balducci, too, before he moved from Oxford. Trent Lott had helped him to become U.S. attorney. He and Langston had attended law school at the same time. Greenlee's children were friends of Patterson's children. The relationships, he said, are "indicative of a very small bar in a small district and in a small state that is known for its hospitality, and in a bar where collegiality is practiced."

The healthy balance in the legal community had been threatened, Greenlee said. "Because of the wealth and power and connections of Dickie Scruggs and the other defendants, they demonstrated tremendous influence over others in the state."

Their interests were thwarted, Greenlee said, by an undercover operation so tightly held that virtually no one knew about it. The timing of Lott's resignation from the Senate was coincidental, he said, for there was no way for the senator to have known about the investigation of his brother-in-law.

Turning to the case of Scruggs's son. Greenlee said, "There has been hushed criticism of our office for prosecuting such a young attorney. Zach, to this day, will probably tell you that he is not guilty, that he did not know of a planned payment to Judge Lackey. Of course, we had evidence otherwise."

In closing, the U.S. attorney described a country judge as the real hero of the Scruggs story. "The tide was turned because of the courageous Henry Lackey, a frail man liked by all, an elected public official who said 'enough is enough,' who risked his life and his position. He has done more than any other I know to halt the tidal wave of attempts to corruptly influence our judges."

Back home, Judge Lackey continued to be honored. When a former federal prosecutor was sworn in as a state appellate judge in ceremonies in Oxford, Lackey was asked to deliver welcoming remarks on a program that included Senator Thad Cochran and several federal judges.

At the reception afterward, Lackey could be seen chatting with his friend, former insurance commissioner George Dale.

Though Greenlee, a Republican appointee, was not quickly replaced by the Democratic administration of President Obama, there was turnover in his office. Tom Dawson retired. David Sanders departed to become a U.S. magistrate. John Hailman, who left shortly after setting the Scruggs investigation in motion, devoted much of his time to completing a book about wine and a memoir of his experiences as a prosecutor.

The remains of the Scruggs case—embodied in the prosecution of Judge Bobby DeLaughter—was entrusted to the last member of the team that conducted the investigation, Bob Norman.

In court elsewhere, a federal district judge from Florida, Roger Vinson, dismissed the criminal contempt case against Scruggs initiated by the judge in Alabama, William Acker.

Undeterred, Judge Acker ordered Scruggs and the Rigsby sisters, who had turned over State Farm documents to Scruggs, to pay $65,000 in attorney fees to the Rigsbys' former employer. The elderly Acker was still angry. In a sharp attack, he described Scruggs as "too cute by half," referred to Mississippi attorney general Jim Hood as a "so-called law enforcement officer," and said that Scruggs and the Rigsbys were as "joined at the hip as any set of Siamese twins."

In July 2009, the Eleventh Circuit Court of Appeals vacated Acker's order on the grounds that the judge had no jurisdiction in the case. The appellate panel wrote, "Finally, in the interests of fairness to both the district court [Acker] and Scruggs we shall exercise our supervisory powers to direct that all remaining issues pertaining to Scruggs in the Renfroe case should be assigned to a different district court judge."

As he began his third year in prison, Paul Minor continued to come into the news. His case had been highlighted in a congressional report in 2008 concerning "selective prosecutions" by U.S. attorneys appointed by President George W. Bush. Noting that Minor had been a "major contributor" to the Democratic Party, the report suggested that "politics may have influenced" his prosecution.

The report was issued by the House Judiciary Committee, whose chairman, Representative John Conyers, Jr., of Michigan, is a Democrat. It also touched on Scruggs.

"While Mr. Minor was indicted by U.S. Attorney Lampton for making or guaranteeing loans to Mississippi judges, including Justice Diaz, another prominent Mississippi trial lawyer alleged to have engaged in virtually the same conduct, Richard Scruggs, was not. Mr. Scruggs, however, has been reported to have supported Republican candidates in other elections and is the brother-in-law of Senator Trent Lott. Indeed, Senator Lott himself acknowledged speaking to prosecutors about the case, stating that Mr. Scruggs had nothing to worry about regarding an investigation of connections between Mississippi judges and lawyers . . ."

Minor filed another lengthy appeal of his conviction, and part of his sentence was vacated by the Fifth Circuit Court of Appeals, a ruling that brought some joy to Minor shortly before Christmas 2009.

But earlier in the year, Sylvia Minor, his wife of forty-one years, died after a long struggle with cancer. Minor was not allowed to visit her in her last days or to attend her funeral.

Karl Rove, the chief political advisor to former president Bush, was interviewed by the staff of the House Judiciary Committee in the summer, six months after Bush left office. Asked about the appointment of Dunn Lampton as U.S. attorney in Mississippi's Southern District, Rove said he was the product of a routine process involving the state's two Republican senators. "One of them, in particular, has strong feelings about anything that is connected with southern Mississippi," he said. "I speak of former Senator Lott."

Rove said he had no knowledge of the prosecution of Paul Minor. The case took place in "a distant part of the country," he said. "It was not the policy of the White House to directly or indirectly attempt to influence any specific case."

But Rove volunteered that the Scruggs case "makes for entertaining reading."

Scruggs asked to serve his time at a federal prison in Pensacola, Florida, where Minor was being held. Not far from his and Diane's former home in Pascagoula, the location would be convenient for visits. His request was denied on the grounds that he represented a "flight risk." The prison facility was adjacent to a naval air station where he had once flown, and it was theorized that he could somehow commandeer a plane and fly away.

He was sent, instead, to a correctional facility in Ashland, Kentucky, a hard day's drive for his friends and family members in Oxford. In the first week of his imprisonment, Scruggs suffered a seizure believed to be related to his withdrawal from the drugs on which he had grown dependent. He was hospitalized for several days. After recovering, he was given a job as a janitor; his first cellmate was a young man serving twenty years for operating a meth lab.

Although the Kentucky prison was far away, Diane made the trip to visit her husband almost every weekend.

Zeus Scruggs had fallen to unimaginable depths, but he kept the "stiff upper lip" so prized in the military. And a sense of humor. Two months into his sentence, he wrote a friend, "I am now teaching a phase of the GED course work. I just knew that someone would spot my genius by how I pushed that mop."

Later, he told of how he had been subjected to "tobacco's curse" years after his assault on the industry. "I got promoted," he wrote. "I no longer mop the hall every day. Now I only have to clean the guards' lounge and bathrooms on weekends. You cannot imagine how much spit tobacco can fit into one trash can. These good old boys use empty pop bottles for cuspidors. After I carry this trash to a bin, it is culled by a group of inmates who reprocess this slimy stuff in a microwave and smoke it! I kid you not. These guys even get mad at me when there's not enough. Tobacco's curse is getting even with me."

Early in 2009, the federal prosecutors made another run at him. Threatened with indictment in connection with Senator Lott's call to Judge DeLaughter and the judge's favorable ruling in the Wilson case, Scruggs faced the possibility of spending the rest of his life in prison if convicted of another bribery. His first instinct—to fight the charge—gave way to a decision to plead guilty in the case prosecutors called Scruggs II.

He did so in the little North Mississippi town of Aberdeen before U.S. District Judge Glen Davidson. Although Roberts Wilson and Charlie Merkel were again present in the courtroom, the ambience seemed less ominous than his dates in the federal building in Oxford. Scruggs was allowed to wear a suit, but he moved toward the bench in a halting pace, still shackled by leg irons.

He told Judge Davidson that he had promised Judge Biggers "to be a better man" when he accepted his sentence for Scruggs I. "I hope what I am doing today is a major step toward redeeming that pledge."

By this time, Bob Norman was in charge of the prosecution, and he told the judge that Scruggs had already begun talking. "His cooperation has opened several doors we need to investigate."

The judge accepted Scruggs's plea and added another two and a half years to his sentence. He also delivered a mild lecture about Scruggs's "sad" thirst for money. Instead of citing the wisdom of ancient Greeks, Davidson invoked Scottish philosopher William Barclay: "The Romans had a proverb that money is like sea water. The more you drink, the thirstier you become."

When the session was finished, Scruggs was taken to another room, where he was stripped of his business suit. Photographers were waiting when the prisoner, manacled and wearing a vivid orange jump suit, was led from the building.

While he was being shuttled from one location to another by the Bureau of Prisons, Scruggs once found himself briefly in the company of two other prisoners, Steve Patterson and Joey Langston. He had a conversation with Patterson, but refused to speak to Langston.

The prosecutors felt confident that Scruggs's testimony would finally lead them to P. L. Blake. At last, they believed, they had in their crosshairs the most intriguing figure in the case, the veteran of the old Mississippi organization.

In the spring of 2009, Scruggs was brought to the Lafayette County Jail in Oxford—where he came within sight of his son but was unable to speak with him—to appear before a federal grand jury. But his testimony failed to win an immediate indictment of his old associate. In fact, the prosecutors were disturbed over the paucity of Scruggs's remarks. His session with the grand jury was so unproductive that it lasted only fifteen minutes.

He was kept in a windowless cell in Oxford for two months as talks continued between prosecutors and his attorneys.

One of the most remarkable statements in their dialogue came from Bob Norman. It occurred in a conference room at the U.S. Attorney's Office in late March, almost exactly two years after Tim Balducci had approached Judge Lackey. Representing the government were Norman, his associate Chad Lamar, and Bill Delaney. Scruggs was accompanied by two lawyers from John Keker's office, Jan Little and Brook Dooley.

At the beginning of the conversation, Norman tried to establish a convivial mood by remarking that the federal government had come to realize that none of the members of the Scruggs Law Firm had originally set out to bribe Judge Lackey.

Scruggs was astonished by the statement. Across the conference table, it seemed to him that Delaney had grown uncomfortable, for Norman's remark carried an implication that the government investigation had turned an unethical overture to Judge Lackey into a crime that reached monstrous proportions.

"We tried to tell you that," Scruggs said.

That had been at the heart of Scruggs's explanation of the crime: That Balducci had been instructed to do nothing that would break the law in his ear-wigging conversation with Judge Lackey. That Scruggs had not known of the payments to the judge until they had already been made in his name by Balducci. Even as he had pleaded guilty, Scruggs insisted in his remarks before the court "there was no intent to bribe the judge; it was an intent to earwig the judge."

But Scruggs had acknowledged, "I joined the conspiracy later in the game."

More than a month later, Scruggs was returned to prison in Ashland. He spent his sixty-third birthday in a solitary cell known by inmates as "the hole." Prison authorities said he had been put there because it was feared he might have been exposed to swine flu while away.

In the fall of 2009, after more than a year in confinement, Scruggs was moved to a prison camp at Ashland where inmates had more freedom. Reflecting on the variety of cellmates he had during his journeys he wrote a friend, "So far, I've learned how to run a Ponzi scheme, an Internet porno network, a still, a meth lab, proper bank robbery, espionage, and now pimping. Surely there is a degree for this."

Diane was capable of her own displays of black humor. When their daughter, Claire, was married in September 2009 at the family home in Oxford, Diane had a life-size pasteboard cutout of Dick, grinning and wearing a tuxedo, on hand for the ceremony. Guests posed for photographs with the facsimile of the missing father of the bride.

Anticipating the need for a defense team, P. L. Blake began hiring lawyers shortly after Scruggs's second guilty plea. Blake's attorneys dispatched two private detectives to Pascagoula, where they went to see Diane Scruggs's twin brother, David Thompson. He was not quite sure what to make of their visit. One of the detectives was quite intimidating in size, though nothing that was said seemed overtly threatening. They told Thompson that Blake "thought the world of Dick Scruggs."

When Thompson told his sister of the visit, she found it unsettling. Diane felt that Blake was trying to send some sort of message, but she was not sure what.

At the end of July 2009, Bobby DeLaughter pleaded guilty to one of five counts in an indictment against him. His decision came after intense plea bargaining in the days before his trial, which had been set for August.

DeLaughter admitted guilt in lying to an FBI agent when asked about his contacts with Ed Peters. The charge constituted obstruction of justice and carried a maximum sentence of twenty years' imprisonment. The government chose to recommend an eighteen-month sentence, and the remaining four counts of the indictment were dropped.

The sentence was formally imposed in November 2009.

Before agreeing to the reduced charges, the prosecutors realized they would have problems in a trial. There was no hard evidence of a quid pro quo that DeLaughter received in exchange for his ruling in the *Wilson v. Scruggs* case, and the key witnesses—Tim Balducci, Joey Langston, Ed Peters, and Steve Patterson—might display shaky credibility on a vigorous cross-examination. If Trent Lott appeared as a witness, he would be expected to testify that his call to DeLaughter had been merely a courtesy, and that no federal judgeship was ever offered. But if the former senator were not called, he would represent a hole in the government's case.

The federal courtroom in Aberdeen was crowded for DeLaughter's appearance. Earlier in the day, he had resigned as circuit judge, and his guilty plea would end his legal career. Charlie Merkel drove across the state, as he had done several times previously, to see justice done. But there was a new face among the spectators who wanted to witness DeLaughter's final disgrace: Byron De La Beckwith, Jr., the son of the assassin whom DeLaughter had sent to prison for the remainder of his life.

At the first of the new year, DeLaughter went to prison himself, assigned to a federal facility in distant Kentucky.

In January 2010, a federal grand jury in Oxford indicted FBI agent Hal Neilson on charges of attempting to cover up his financial interest in a building housing the local FBI offices. He was also accused of lying to his own bureau. The formal charges came nearly two years after the U.S. Attorney's Office recused itself from the investigation and the case had been turned over to federal prosecutors in Baton Rouge, Louisiana.

Neilson's fellow agents in Oxford were angered over the action. A member of an old Mississippi family—Neilson's is the name of a venerable department store in Oxford that survived the Civil War—Neilson had many other friends in the area who rallied to his side. Considered part of the fabric of the community, he held undergraduate and law degrees from Ole Miss, and he and his wife and four children had settled in Oxford years earlier.

He had been reassigned to Washington in 2009 during the turmoil, but after his indictment he was suspended by the FBI—eleven months from retirement.

Neilson vowed to fight the charges, even though he underwent major heart surgery days after the indictment.

· · ·

A week after Neilson's indictment, Jim Greenlee announced that he would retire as U.S. attorney. The Obama administration had still not found a replacement for him, but Greenlee considered his work done.

Though the wreckage of the house Zeus Scruggs built had been strewn about the landscape, the Force he dealt with endured.

The Washington branch remained intact. Trent Lott had yielded his power on Capitol Hill, yet he flourished in his new lobbying job, building a strong list of clients who would both enrich him and enable him to maintain influence. His Senate seat was retained by another member of the brotherhood, Roger Wicker. And Lott's alter ego, Tom Anderson, a man who left few footprints, continued to get $1.5 million a year from Scruggs. The money is wired to the Burke and Herbert Bank and Trust in Alexandria, Virginia, to be credited to the account of Bainberry LLC in Middleburg, Virginia, where Anderson lives. Bainberry is not registered as a corporation with the secretary of the Commonwealth of Virginia.

Down south, more than two years after the investigation began, two of the darkest figures in the Force, P. L. Blake and Ed Peters, remained free.

EPILOGUE

June 2011

By the beginning of the summer of 2011, only Dick Scruggs remained in prison in Kentucky. Though his surroundings offered him greater liberty, he still faced as many as three more years of confinement. He seemed to have adapted to his situation philosophically, teaching in-house history classes and acting as a "jailhouse lawyer," crafting legal appeals for fellow inmates. He awaited transfer, approved by authorities, to a more desirable facility in Montgomery, Alabama, and looked even further ahead to his return to Oxford. Once free, he hoped to work for a nonprofit organization such as the Southern Poverty Law Center, which champions civil rights and monitors extremist groups.

Scruggs was still besieged by lawsuits filed by rival attorneys and former associates. He settled some cases for undisclosed amounts, including an old action brought by Charlie Merkel that was resolved just before a trial in 2011. Yet other litigants waited in the wings to nibble at his fortune. Even while in prison, Scruggs continued to earn several million dollars a year in deferred income. His financial interests were managed by Rex Deloach from a small unmarked office off of Oxford Square.

Diane Scruggs remained at home. Over the past three years she made trips to see her husband most weekends, using a private plane made available by David Nutt, Scruggs's partner in the tobacco initiative. Diane's health had improved dramatically after her crisis in early 2008. Rather than retreating socially, she played an active role in the community, serving on one high-profile committee appointed by the mayor, and she could frequently be seen dining on the square with friends.

Their son, Zach, rejoined his wife and their three children at their own home in a high-end Oxford development flanked by a golf course. Zach explored an investment in a restaurant but found that his criminal record would block a liquor license and keep him from other business opportunities. He chafed at the restrictions and initiated a legal challenge that provided new drama and brought many of the players in the Scruggs case back under the roof of the Federal Building in Oxford for several days in May 2011.

While Zach petitioned the court to vacate his conviction and restore his good name, the other defendants moved more quietly back into life outside the walls.

Sid Backstrom found a promising job in Texas. He and his family moved there shortly after spending their last Christmas in Oxford in 2010. Though he reappeared the next spring to testify on Zach's behalf, Backstrom appeared anxious to put his costly experience behind him.

Steve Patterson came home to New Albany after being away nearly two years. In December 2010, he sent a five-page Christmas letter to friends, thanking them for standing with him during "the furious storm that turned my life upside down." Though he acknowledged that his "judgment and actions were horribly flawed," Patterson lashed out at the government's handling of the case. "I fervently believe these prosecutions were in part politically motivated and largely media driven" and abetted by "two persons whose mercenary and deceitful acts brought about the devastating deluge that needlessly engulfed so many."

He did not name the "two persons," but he was clearly thinking of Judge Henry Lackey and his former partner, Tim Balducci.

"One, a senior state court judge, was a self-described close friend and mentor to the other, an ambitious younger attorney who was a business associate of mine at that time. At the urging of the government, the judge exploited his special relationship by artfully feigning personal financial distress, and then begging for money, all in order to callously ensnare and eventually corrupt his admiring protégé. You see, at its inception, the sole intent of the government's scheme was to use the judge's young friend to bring down its true target, a nationally known and politically active trial attorney who was already swamped by controversy."

Balducci, who was freed a day after Patterson in December 2010, resumed life in the same, small north Mississippi town where he had sought refuge during the months between his apprehension in November 2007, when he began his role as a cooperating witness for the FBI, and his imprisonment. The former lawyer went to work for a construction company.

The two prominent figures who were jailed as a result of the "Scruggs II" case, former judge Bobby DeLaughter and one-time "Mississippi Trial Lawyer of the Year" Joey Langston, were also released from federal custody in the spring of 2011. DeLaughter, who sold his antebellum home near Jackson, slipped into a new life elsewhere without leaving public traces. Langston returned to his comfortable estate in Booneville, where he continued to enjoy the support of many friends. Though he would be unable to practice law again, Langston retained most of his wealth and continued to get substantial quarterly payments from Scruggs's tobacco account.

In the climax to a subplot in the Scruggs story, Oxford FBI agent Hal Neilson won his fight against the same federal prosecutors who brought down Scruggs. Earlier in the decade, Neilson and other agents in his office disagreed sharply with the U.S. Attorney's office in Oxford over an investigation of shop owners with Middle Eastern backgrounds. The dispute escalated over the handling of the Scruggs case. Neilson blamed the prosecutors' anger at his opposition to their policies for his own indictment in 2010 on charges of having an improper interest in a building housing the FBI office. Because of the conflict between federal authorities in Oxford, the prosecution was turned over to representatives of the U.S. Attorney's office in Baton Rouge.

After a two-week trial in Aberdeen, Mississippi, in November 2010, a federal jury acquitted Neilson on two of the five counts and failed to reach a verdict on the remaining charges. Neilson's joyful family and friends wept and gave thanks in an impromptu "circle of prayer" in a witness room moments after the jury announced its findings. Word of the decision soon made its way to Oxford on a Saturday afternoon while many townspeople were watching an out-of-town Ole Miss football game on television.

The chagrined prosecutors dropped the remaining charges before the end of the year, enabling Neilson to go back to work with the FBI. He was reassigned to an office in nearby Tupelo.

A greater rebuke to the team that prosecuted the Scruggs case came the following spring when U.S. District Judge Neal Biggers disqualified assistant U.S. attorney Bob Norman from participating further in Zach Scruggs's case. The unusual action came after a hearing in which Norman admitted that he failed to correct misstatements submitted to the court during the prosecution of Scruggs's son three years earlier.

Biggers faulted Norman as well as Tom Dawson, who had retired as lead prosecutor, for submitting to him a document Biggers described as "puzzling, to say the least" and "inconsistent with the government's position . . . and inconsistent with information which had been provided" to young Scruggs.

(A year and a half earlier, Norman and Dawson had been among the recipients of a U.S. Department of Justice award for superior service in connection with their work in the Scruggs case. "Their accomplishments have advanced the interests of justice on behalf of the American people," Attorney General Eric Holder said at the time.)

The judge based his ruling on the prosecution's claim in 2008—while Zach was contesting charges of bribing Judge Lackey—that Zach would be implicated in a second case involving Judge DeLaughter. Norman had announced during a preliminary hearing that Joey Langston would say "Zach Scruggs was fully aware of what was going on" in the second case. The prosecution used the threat of an additional set of charges to pressure the younger Scruggs.

In the hearing three years later, Langston testified that Norman misinterpreted a remark he had made. Langston's lawyer, Tony Farese—who at one time had represented Zach Scruggs—was more precise, recalling that after Norman had made his assertion, he approached Norman and told him "that was incorrect."

In an exchange during the new hearing, Norman admitted to Farese: "In all candor, I believe I basically blew you off that afternoon and said, 'I'm tired. I'm going home. We'll talk about it later.' "

Although the misunderstanding was eventually clarified, the court was not notified. In fact, the prosecutors submitted a motion to Biggers saying that "there have been no substantial changes" in the case—when, in fact, there had been a critical one. In his new ruling, Biggers said he was "baffled" and "nonplussed by the government's failure to correct this mistake."

The hearing carried a bit of irony. As Zach Scruggs watched from the same spot where he pleaded guilty in 2008, he saw Langston and Farese—whom he felt had betrayed him—actually testifying on his behalf. (Zach's complaint charging Farese with conflict of interest in representing Langston at the same time he had Zach as a client failed to generate any action from the state bar association.)

The hearing also produced evidence that the prosecutors realized that their chief witness, Tim Balducci, was giving inaccurate information to the grand jury in November 2007, when he testified that he told Zach Scruggs and Backstrom that Judge Lackey was demanding an additional $10,000, and that the two young lawyers in the Scruggs firm had assured him "It was not a problem."

An FBI recording of the conversation had no record of these purported remarks. The discrepancy was never corrected explicitly, though Dawson, who appeared uncomfortable in his new role as a witness, explained that he believed the misstatement had been clarified later when prosecutors elicited testimony from Balducci that he used "sweet potatoes" as code for "money."

With Norman missing, Judge Biggers reconvened an extraordinary session on Zach's thirty-seventh birthday to hear testimony on his petition to erase his conviction. Zach based his motion on a 2010 U.S. Supreme Court decision narrowing the definition of "honest services" fraud, a charge used against him by federal prosecutors. Zach argued that the "crime"—to which he originally pleaded guilty of knowing about—no longer constituted criminality. He acknowledged that he was aware of a scheme to influence Judge Lackey but renewed his protest that he had never known about a bribe.

(The Supreme Court decision also encouraged Dick Scruggs and another prominent trial lawyer, Paul Minor, imprisoned in a different case, to seek a reduction of their sentences.)

Zach's hearing took on elements of the trial he had denied himself three years earlier when he pleaded guilty. This time, however, Zach found himself in a legal position where the burden of proof was on him to establish his innocence.

Although Judge Biggers again presided, the courtroom atmosphere was drained of much of the tension and hostility that characterized the 2008 hearings. There were odd—and sometimes awkward—reunions.

When Balducci encountered Judge Lackey before the hearing began, the pair embraced and had a quiet conversation.

Balducci spent all day on the stand. At one point, Zach's attorney, Edward "Chip" Robertson, asked the witness why he had not said, "I've been entrapped here," when he left Lackey's office for the last time in 2007 and was stopped by FBI agents. Balducci did not reply. "That was a question," Robertson prompted. Balducci continued to stare wordlessly. Finally, he said, "I chose to listen."

Robertson attacked Balducci's credibility repeatedly. The witness admitted that he "misspoke" before the grand jury about mentioning a new $10,000 demand to Zach and Backstrom. He said he assumed Zach knew of the bribe, but testified that he had not talked directly about money in any of the three conversations he had with Zach during the six months between Balducci's first visit to Lackey and his interception by the FBI on November 1, 2007.

Although Balducci wore an FBI body wire to the Scruggs Law Firm later that same November day, the question of whether Zach was still in the room when Balducci talked of "sweet potatoes" drew conflicting testimony. There were several seconds of silence in the recorded conversation as Zach left the room.

Other witnesses refuted Balducci's contention that Zach conceived of the idea to approach Judge Lackey for a favor in March 2007.

Patterson, who had been in the room at Scruggs Law Firm that day, testified that he had no recollection of Zach playing a primary role in the decision to send Balducci to seek a favor from Lackey. Patterson seemed to enjoy his return to the courtroom. Asked about his reputation as a rainmaker, Patterson quipped, "I helped make a pretty damn good storm here, didn't I? A hurricane." When questioned if Zach had been "in any way aware or involved with the plan of the actual payment of money to Judge Lackey," Patterson replied, "Well, there never was a plan. We were asked for the money . . . We were extorted . . . "

On cross-examination, federal prosecutor Scott Leary returned to the subject. In an incredulous tone, Leary asked, "You say that Judge Lackey extorted money from Tim Balducci?"

"That's how I felt about it," Patterson responded. "I think he was operating at the instruction of the government."

"You think the government coerced Judge Lackey?"

"I do."

In the end, Zach's attorneys chose not to call all of the witnesses they had summoned. Judge Lackey, who had proved to be a volatile witness three years earlier, was not brought to the stand. Nor was Zach, who was already on record denying knowledge of the bribery in his appearance before Judge Biggers when he pleaded guilty.

The decision not to use the witnesses was tactical—based on concerns that harsh questioning of a fellow jurist might anger Judge Biggers, and that Zach's testimony might rekindle the hostility his lawyers felt Biggers displayed toward Scruggs's son in 2008.

Biggers promised a decision in the weeks ahead.

After the hearing, Zach's family felt that he had won a measure of public vindication, regardless of how Biggers ultimately ruled.

Notes

Virtually all interviews for this book were conducted in 2008 or 2009. Exceptions will be noted, such as cases where the author drew upon informal conversations that took place earlier.

page   Preface

2   *Two months* . . . Letter from Curtis Wilkie to Dick Scruggs, Jan. 31, 2008.

3   *Afterward, I got* . . . Letter from Scruggs to Wilkie, Feb. 12, 2008.

Chapter 1

5   *In the summer of 1992* . . . Interviews with Dick Scruggs, Mike Moore, confidential sources.

7   *In Pascagoula* . . . "The Asbestos Industry on Trial," Paul Brodeur, *The New Yorker*, June 24, 1985.

7   *Scruggs missed out* . . . *Assuming the Risk*, Michael Orey (Little, Brown and Co., 1999); interviews with confidential sources.

8   *After winning election* . . . Interviews with confidential sources.

9   *The network teemed* . . . Interviews with confidential sources.

9   *It was Eastland* . . . Interview with Robert Khayat.

9   *Judge Cox* . . . *Robert Kennedy and His Times*, Arthur M. Schlesinger, Jr. (Houghton Mifflin Harcourt, 1980).

10   *Khayat fought the charges* . . . "Settlement Ends Saga," *Sun Herald*, March 22, 1985.

10   *Emboldened by success* . . . "Background of Asbestos Cost Recovery Litigation by the State of Mississippi," attachment to letter from Attorney General Mike Moore to State Auditor Steve Patterson, July 31, 1992.

10   *At first, nothing appeared* . . . Interviews with confidential sources.

10   *As money poured in* . . . "A Bitter Battle for Tobacco Spoils in Mississippi," Curtis Wilkie, *Boston Globe*, Oct. 18, 1998.

11   *One of the principal figures* . . . 2007 brochure for Patterson, Balducci and Biden PLLC Law Group.

11   *After Winter won* . . . Interviews with confidential sources.

12   *One document prepared* . . . Response of Steve Patterson to motion, document filed in Circuit Court of Jackson County, Mississippi, Aug. 13, 1992.

12   *Moore would be cited* . . . Undated memorandum prepared for Patterson by William Liston.

12   *Scruggs would be implicated* . . . Interview with confidential source.

12   *To handle the criminal charges* . . . Interviews with confidential sources.

13   *Peters had a history* . . . Interview with Dan Goodgame.

13   *One evening in 1992, as Scruggs struggled* . . . Interview with Dick Scruggs.

13   *Blake had been charged* . . . Newspaper clip, interviews with confidential sources.

14   *By normal standards* . . . Interviews with Micajah S. Mills, confidential sources.

14   *Blake was a standout* . . . *Southeastern Conference Football Encyclopedia*.

14   *Sometime in the 1960s* . . . Interviews with Pete Johnson, confidential sources.

14   *When David Bowen* . . . Interviews with David Bowen, confidential sources.

15   *When Scruggs told his wife* . . . Interview with Diane Scruggs.

15   *Despite Diane's misgivings* . . . Interview with Dick Scruggs.

15   *The case was effectively settled* . . . Letter from Steve Patterson to District Attorney Edward J. Peters, Aug. 31, 1992.

15   *Patterson would also* . . . Letter from Patterson to Steve Hicks, Dec. 29, 1992.

16   *For his part* . . . Letter from Thomas E. Royals to Patterson, Sept. 14, 1992.

16   *To cement the understanding* . . . Interview with Dick Scruggs.

Chapter 2

17   *For all of the wealth* . . . Interview with Dick Scruggs.

17   *Scruggs worked out compulsively* . . . Interview with Johnny Morgan.

18   *He was a bona fide* . . . Interviews with Bill Furlow, Dick Scruggs.

19   *Forty years* . . . *The Horse Soldiers*, a film directed by John Ford, 1959.

19   *In the seventh grade* . . . *Pascagoula*, Jay Higginbotham (Gill Press, 1967).

21   *Their homeroom teacher* . . . Interview with Robert Khayat.

22   *Otherwise, his was a normal* . . . Interview with Sam Davis.

22   *Just as he had been* . . . Interview with Dick Scruggs.

23   *The Pascagoula newspaper* . . . *The Race Beat: The Press, the Civil Rights Struggle, and the Awakening of a Nation,* Gene Roberts and Hank Klibanoff (Knopf, 2006).

23   *"A pall of contradiction"* . . . Editorial, *The Chronicle,* September 1962.

23   *For challenging orthodoxy* . . . *The Smell of Burning Crosses: A White Integrationist Editor in Mississippi,* Ira B. Harkey (Harris-Wolfe, 1967).

23   *To ensure that her son* . . . Interview with Dick Scruggs.

25   *There were few navy guys* . . . Interview with Johnny Morgan.

26   *In the summer of 1968* . . . Interview with Dick Scruggs.

26   *Diane attended* . . . Interview with Diane Scruggs.

27   *A few years earlier* . . . Interview with Dick Scruggs.

Chapter 3

29   *To his delight* . . . Interviews with William Winter, Dick Scruggs.

30   *After graduation* . . . Interview with Bill Reed.

30   *The firm entrusted* . . . Interview with Dick Scruggs.

31   *When he decided* . . . Interview with confidential source.

32   *Before Scruggs made* . . . Interview with Diane Scruggs.

32   *Most of these local attorneys* . . . Interview with Lowry Lomax.

33   *One of the more* . . . Interviews with confidential sources, confirmed in conversation with Joe Colingo.

34   *At Ole Miss, Lott joined* . . . "Secret History," Curtis Wilkie, *George,* June 1997.

36   *Thad Cochran* . . . *Dixie: A Personal Odyssey Through Events That Shaped the Modern South,* Curtis Wilkie (Scribner, 2001).

38   *After he entered politics* . . . Interviews with confidential sources.

38   *Blake once described himself* . . . P. L. Blake deposition in connection with *P. L. Blake v. Gannett Company, Inc., Gannett News Service, Inc., and Mississippi Publishers Corp.,* April 9, 1985.

38   *Court documents* . . . "The P. L. Blake Empire Has Good Credit in Washington," Mark Rohner and Dennis Camire, Gannett News Service, *Clarion-Ledger,* Dec. 11, 1983; Blake deposition; interviews with confidential sources.

39   *Though he posed* . . . Blake deposition.

39   *The Louisiana Buccaneers* . . . "Year-to-Year Notes" on New Orleans Buccaneers/Memphis Pros, courtesy of Robert Bradley.

39   *In another sporting gesture* . . . Interviews with confidential sources; Blake deposition.

40   *The Reaganites* . . . Interview with Clarke Reed.

40   *In 1982, Jim Lake* . . . Blake deposition.

40   *In 1984, the U.S. Department of Agriculture* . . . "FmHA at Fault in

Blake Loan, Inspectors Say," Mark Rohner and Dennis Camire, Gannett News Service, *Clarion-Ledger*, Sept. 15, 1984.

40   *The news report* . . . "Pleading Poverty, He Makes Millions," an article in Gannett News Service Special Report: "FmHA: The Golden Yoke," December 1983.

40   *According to court papers* . . . Schedule of Dewitt Corp. assets filed in tax returns, from documents in connection with *Blake v. Gannett*.

40   *The grain was stored* . . . Interviews with confidential sources; "The P. L. Blake empire . . .," *Clarion-Ledger;* "The Billie Sol Estes Scandal," *Time*, May 25, 1962.

41   *Blake, in applying* . . . "The P. L. Blake empire . . .," *Clarion-Ledger*.

41   *(Perry was later fired* . . . "Cochran's Record of USDA Jobs Patronage Less Than Stellar," column by Bill Minor, *Clarion-Ledger*, Oct. 17, 2008.

41   *Anderson, for his part* . . . "The P. L. Blake empire . . .," *Clarion-Ledger*.

42   *Outraged by the Gannett series* . . . Blake deposition.

42   *In a decision* . . . Supreme Court of Mississippi ruling in *Blake v. Gannett*, May 25, 1988.

42   *Later in the decade* . . . Interview with Dick Scruggs.

42   *After obtaining records* . . . "Patterson Linked to Farmer in Bank Case," Associated Press, June 30, 1997.

42   *Although Scruggs* . . . Interviews with Mike Moore, Diane Scruggs.

42   *Nevertheless, both Patterson and Blake* . . . Interview with Joey Langston.

43   *Blake also retained* . . . "Blake Still Enigma," William Browning, *Greenwood Commonwealth*, Feb. 26, 2009.

43   *When . . . Tom Anderson . . . Washington Times*, Oct. 3, 1989.

43   *The Democratic Congressional Campaign Committee* . . . Associated Press, Oct. 16, 1989.

43   *According to Blake's testimony* . . . Blake deposition.

43   *In November 1993* . . . Interview with Dick Scruggs.

Chapter 4

44   *The asbestos industry* . . . *Civil Warriors: The Legal Siege on the Tobacco Industry*, Dan Zegart (Delacorte Press, 2000); "Orey, *Assuming the Risk*."

45   *He began to acquire* . . . Interviews with confidential sources.

45   *While lavishing millions* . . . Interviews with confidential sources; letters in support of Dick Scruggs, filed in 2008 in U.S. District Court in connection with *U.S.A. v. Scruggs*.

46   *Scruggs and Wilson* . . . Interviews with Dick Scruggs, Diane Scruggs, confidential sources.

46   *After Wilson threatened* . . . Letter from Dick Scruggs to Roberts Wilson, Feb. 17, 1992.

47   *The contentions . . . Boston Globe*, Oct. 18, 1998.
47   *Though it seemed relatively insignificant* . . . Interview with Charles Merkel.
47   *The lawsuits got uglier* . . . Affidavit of Mitchell Tyner, filed in Hinds
County Circuit Court in connection with *Luckey v. Wilson, Scruggs, and
Asbestos Group*, Dec. 8, 1996.
47   *He followed developments* . . . Interviews with Dick Scruggs, Don
Barrett; Orey, *Assuming the Risk.*
49   *The mother of Lewis's secretary* . . . Interviews with Mike and Pauline
Lewis, Mike Moore, Dick Scruggs; Orey, *Assuming the Risk.*
50   *A few months later* . . . Interviews with Dick Scruggs, Mike Moore,
Danny Cupit, Crymes Pittman.
51   *In casting about* . . . Interviews with Mike Moore, Dick Scruggs, Crymes
Pittman, Don Barrett, confidential sources.
52   *Despite his misgivings* . . . Interview with Mike Moore.
52   *As they plotted* . . . Interviews with Dick Scruggs, Don Barrett, Mike
Moore.
53   *Scruggs reflected* . . . Interview with Dick Scruggs.
53   *While men such as Blake* . . . Interview with Pete Johnson.
55   *Johnson was not a registered lobbyist* . . . Interviews with Johnson,
confidential sources; Mississippi 1994 Session Laws, Senate bill 2503:
Medicaid—General Revision.
55   *Later in the decade* . . . Orey, *Assuming the Risk.*

Chapter 5

56   *For much of his life* . . . Interviews with Dick Scruggs, Don Barrett; Orey,
Assuming the Risk.
57   *The same spring* . . . Interview with Mike Moore.
58   *For Mississippi* . . . Interviews with Scruggs, Barrett, Moore;
confidential sources; details of joint venture agreement for HALT, signed
autumn 1994; deposition given by Scruggs on Aug. 25, 2004, in connection
with *Wilson v. Scruggs.*
59   *As Mississippi's case* . . . Orey, *Assuming the Risk*; interview with
Scruggs; deposition given by Scruggs, Aug. 25, 2004.
60   *(A few years* . . . Interview with Scruggs; *The Insider*, a film directed by
Michael Mann, 1999.
60   *In the fall* . . . Interview with Scruggs.
61   *The tobacco issue* . . . *Herding Cats: A Life in Politics*, Trent Lott
(ReganBooks, 2005).
61   *The process* . . . Interviews with confidential sources.
61   *After Liggett* . . . Interview with Scruggs, confidential sources; Orey,
Assuming the Risk; Lott, *Herding Cats.*

61   *After seventeen years* . . . Wilkie, "Secret History"; interviews with
confidential sources.

62   *Though both Anderson and Sears* . . . Interviews with confidential
sources; letter from John P. Sears to Richard Scruggs, Jan. 12, 2000.

62   *Hoppenstein's curriculum vitae* . . . Joel Hoppenstein biography posted by
Jewish Policy Center.

62   *There was never* . . . Interviews with Scruggs, confidential sources.

63   *Before the struggle* . . . Deposition given by Scruggs, Aug. 25, 2004.

64   *At the same time* . . . Lott, *Herding Cats.*

64   *The deal was set back* . . . "Plan to Settle Tobacco Case Draws Fire," Milo
Geyelin, Suein L. Hwang, and Alix M. Freedman, *Wall Street Journal,* Aug. 27,
1996.

64   *Scruggs felt betrayed* . . . Interview with Scruggs.

65   *On June 20* . . . "The Tobacco Settlement—Elements of the Deal: Pros
and Cons," *New York Times,* June 21, 1997.

65   *For the next twenty-five years* . . . HALT documents.

65   *Looking back* . . . Interview with Scruggs.

66   *Less than two months* . . . "Plaintiff in Tobacco Suit Targets a New
Adversary: Her Lawyer," by Milo Geyelin, *Wall Street Journal,* Aug. 19, 1997;
interview with Scruggs, Joey Langston, confidential sources.

67   *Diane Scruggs* . . . Interview with Diane Scruggs.

68   *While various claimants* . . . Interview with Mike and Pauline Lewis.

69   *There were other* . . . Interviews with Scruggs, Pete Johnson,
confidential sources.

70   *There were others* . . . "Tobacco Wars' Huge Legal Fees Ignite New Fight,"
Myron Levin, *Los Angeles Times,* May 20, 2001; interview with Scruggs; flow
chart of payments by Delmas Capital, LLC.

70   *A particularly nasty* . . . Interview with Scruggs, letter from Scruggs to
John P. Sears, Developing Markets Group LLC, Jan. 13, 2000.

70   *Nevertheless, according to court documents* . . . Deposition given by
Scruggs, Aug. 25, 2004; testimony of Scruggs in trial transcript, *Alwyn H.
Luckey v. Richard Scruggs,* U.S. District Court, Northern District of Mississippi,
June 8, 2005; interviews with Scruggs, confidential sources.

71   *Charles Merkel* . . . Interview with Merkel.

71   *But U.S. District Judge* . . . Injunction ordered by U.S. District
Judge Allen Pepper in Northern District of Mississippi in connection with
*P. L. Blake and Shirley Blake v. State Bank and Trust Co. of Greenwood,
Mississippi,* Jan. 3, 2005.

71   *Back at Ole Miss* . . . Wilkie, "Secret History."

71   *Scruggs attributed* . . . Interview with Scruggs.

71   *When Scruggs was asked* . . . Deposition given by Scruggs, Aug. 25, 2004.

71   *Blake's explanations* . . . Deposition given by P. L. Blake in connection
with *Wilson v. Scruggs*, August 2004; "Blake's Information 'Right-on,' " Anita
Lee, *Sun Herald*, Dec. 17, 2007; interview with Scruggs.

71   *While Blake got* . . . Deposition given by Scruggs, Aug. 25, 2004.
Interviews with confidential sources.

72   *In addition* . . . Deposition given by Scruggs, Aug. 25, 2004. Interviews
with confidential sources.

72   The New Yorker . . . "Fight on the Right," Philip Gourevitch, *The New
Yorker*, April 12, 2004.

72   *Scruggs's contribution* . . . Interview with Scruggs.

72   *After Michael Kranish* . . . "Special Interests Aided Tax-reform
Advocate," Michael Kranish, *Boston Globe*, March 31, 2006.

72   *Later, after Scruggs* . . . Interview with Scruggs.

72   *In 2000 the bickering* . . . Letter from John P. Sears to Scruggs, Jan. 12,
2000.

72   *He told Sears* . . . Letter from Scruggs to Sears, Jan. 13, 2000.

73   *Sears wrote back* . . . Letter from Sears to Scruggs, Jan. 24, 2000.

73   *In a subsequent letter* . . . Letter from Sears to Scruggs, Jan. 25, 2000.

73   *Scruggs finally came* . . . Interviews with confidential sources; flow chart
of Delmas Capital, LLC; deposition given by Scruggs, Aug. 25, 2000.

73   *In addition* . . . Interview with Rex Deloach.

73   *On a schedule* . . . Flow chart of Delmas Capital, LLC; interviews with
Deloach, confidential sources.

74   *At night* . . . Interview with Scruggs, Sept., 1998; *Boston Globe*, Oct. 18,
1998.

Chapter 6

75   *Politics had been embedded* . . . Interview with Dick Scruggs.

76   *To protect their position* . . . Interview with Danny Cupit.

76   *The idea took form* . . . Interview with Jere Nash.

78   *A lengthy 1999 profile* . . . "Who's Afraid of Dickie Scruggs?," Adam
Bryant, *Newsweek*, Dec. 6, 1999.

78   *To extend his influence* . . . Interviews with Scruggs, confidential sources.

78   *The logical choice* . . . "Ferris Displayed Amazing Public Education
Credentials," column by Bill Minor, *Clarion-Ledger*, June 27, 2008.

78   *But Scruggs's "dark side"* . . . Interview with Scruggs; "Tuck's Amended
Report Discloses Loan from Scruggs," Bobby Harrison, Northeast Mississippi
Daily Journal, July 9, 2003.

80   *Abuses also ran rampant* . . . Interviews with confidential sources.

80   *Business interests* . . . "Jackson Action," op-ed piece by Charlie Ross, *Wall*

Street Journal, Sept. 15, 2005; bulletins by American Tort Reform Association; "Mississippi Tort Reform in 2004," memorandum prepared by Wells Marble and Hurst PPL.

81   *After market research* . . . "New Names, New Strategies," Terry Carter, *ABA Journal*, Feb. 21, 2007.

82   *One judge* . . . Interview with confidential source.

82   *Scruggs threw his own money* . . . Interviews with Scruggs, Richard Phillips.

82   *A Jackson attorney* . . . "Court Is Ignoring Juries: Victims Losing 100 Percent of Appeals? Is the Mississippi Supreme Court a 'rubber stamp' for powerful corporate entities?," op-ed piece by Alex A. Alston, Jr., *Clarion-Ledger*, June 29, 2008.

83   *With Big Business* . . . *The Appeal*, John Grisham (Doubleday, 2008).

84   *In 2000* . . . Interview with Scruggs.

Chapter 7

85   *Their choice* . . . Transcript of grand jury testimony by Richard Scruggs, U.S. District Court, Southern District of Mississippi, May 16, 2003.

86   *Minor was often* . . . Interviews with confidential sources.

87   *After their meeting* . . . Scruggs's testimony before grand jury.

88   *As GOP theoretician* . . . *Politics by Other Means*, Benjamin Ginsberg and Martin Shefter (W.W. Norton, 1999).

88   *In a move approved* . . . "A Minor Injustice," "Why Paul Minor?" and "Justice in Mississippi," articles by Scott Horton, *Harper's*, Autumn 2007; "The U.S. Attorney Who Wasn't Fired: How Bush Pick Helped Prosecute Top Democrat-backed Judge," Larisa Alexandrovna and Muriel Kane, *The Raw Story*, April 1, 2008; "The United States Attorneys Scandal Comes to Mississippi," signed editorial by Adam Cohen, *New York Times*, Oct. 11, 2007; "Congress Probes Witch Hunts," Adam Lynch, *Jackson Free Press*, May 28, 2008; appeal filed by Paul Minor in connection with *U.S.A. v. Minor*, U.S. District Court, June 30, 2008.

88   *Scruggs was accustomed* . . . Letter from Minor to Scruggs.

88   *A few years later* . . . Scruggs testimony before grand jury.

89   *During his grand jury* . . . Scruggs's testimony before grand jury.

90   *Minor and Scruggs* . . . Interviews with Scruggs, confidential sources.

91   *A year later* . . . Interviews with confidential sources.

Chapter 8

92   *He had been exceedingly generous* . . . "Mississippi Madness: A Spat Over a Mansion Turns Ugly," Michael Orey, *Wall Street Journal*, May 1999; interviews with Dick Scruggs, Diane Scruggs, confidential sources.
94   *Much of his spending* . . . Interviews with confidential sources; letters in support of Scruggs, filed with U.S. District Court, Northern District of Mississippi.
95   *In a startling act* . . . Interview with Robert Khayat.
96   *Rex Deloach* . . . Interviews with Khayat, Dick Scruggs, Rex Deloach.
97   *But he followed up* . . . Interviews with Deloach, confidential sources.
98   *Among those* . . . Interviews with Sid Backstrom, confidential sources.
99   *Another significant change* . . . Interviews with Dick Scruggs, Diane Scruggs, confidential sources.
99   *Scruggs was approaching* . . . Interviews with confidential sources.
100   *At the beginning* . . . Lott, *Herding Cats*.
100   *South America* . . . Interviews with Dick Scruggs, Lowry Lomax, George Shaddock.
100   *He wanted his son* . . . Interviews with Dick Scruggs, Zach Scruggs.
102   *In many ways* . . . Interview with Zach Scruggs.
104   *Before making the move* . . . Interviews with Zach Scruggs, Joey Langston.
105   *Though the tactic* . . . Interviews with confidential sources.
105   *Scruggs wanted the best* . . . Interview with Deloach.
105   *The visiting novelist* . . . *The Raw and the Cooked: Adventures of a Roving Gourmand*, Jim Harrison (Grove/Atlantic, 2001).
106   *Scruggs wanted nice art* . . . Interview with Deloach.
106   *The Scruggses, père et fils* . . . Interviews with Dick Scruggs, Zach Scruggs, confidential sources.

Chapter 9

107   *Diane Scruggs* . . . Interview with Diane Scruggs.
108   *Time magazine* . . . "Sick of Hospital Bills," Daren Fonda, *Time*, Sept. 19, 2004.
108   *A federal judge* . . . Opinion by U.S. District Judge Loretta A. Preska, U.S. District Court, Southern District of New York, Point of Law Forum, Manhattan Institute, April 12, 2005.
108   *Undaunted by the setbacks* . . . News release by Scruggs, *Patient Financial Services Weekly Advisor*, Feb. 11, 2005.
109   *Still, a big lick* . . . Scruggs interview in *Chief Executive* magazine, June 2002; "The Bribe," Peter Boyer, *The New Yorker*, May 19, 2008.

109   *Although they wound up* . . . Interviews with Charles Merkel, confidential sources.

110   *Merkel was known* . . . Interviews with confidential sources.

110   *Said Sherlock Holmes* . . . "The Final Problem," a short story by Arthur Conan Doyle, *Strand Magazine*, December 1893.

110   *Said Merkel* . . . Interview with Merkel.

111   *Contending* . . . Flow chart of Delmas Capital, LLC.

111   *The psychic battering* . . . Interview with Diane Scruggs.

111   *Scruggs had retained* . . . Interviews with Jack Dunbar, confidential sources.

112   *In June 2005* . . . Interviews with Merkel, Dunbar, U.S. Magistrate Jerry Davis; email from Timothy Balducci to John Jones, others, Oct. 27, 2004.

113   *"What about the stock?"* . . . Interview with Vaughn Grisham.

113   *The trial opened* . . . Trial transcript, *Alwyn H. Luckey v. Richard F. Scruggs, et al.*, U.S. District Court, Northern District of Mississippi, June 6, 2005.

113   *Scruggs was prepped* . . . Interviews with confidential sources.

114   *During nearly two weeks* . . . Trial transcript.

114   *Scruggs took action* . . . Trial transcript; interview with Scruggs.

115   *Merkel, who had been using* . . . Email from John Jones to Dunbar and others, Nov. 30, 2004; interviews with confidential sources.

115   *Dunbar and Rex Deloach* . . . Interview with Rex Deloach.

115   *But as Merkel* . . . Interviews with confidential sources.

115   *As the case wound* . . . Interviews with Scruggs, Deloach, Joey Langston.

115   *In a July 8* . . . Letter from Langston to Deloach, July 8, 2005.

116   *Scruggs responded* . . . Letter from Scruggs to Langston, July 18, 2005.

116   *Deloach was more blunt* . . . Letter from Deloach to Langston, July 20, 2005.

116   *Doubting Langston's claims* . . . Interviews with Scruggs, Deloach, Langston.

116   *Diane Scruggs* . . . Interview with Diane Scruggs.

116   *On July 20* . . . Memorandum opinion by U.S. magistrate judge Jerry Davis, U.S. District Court, Northern District of Mississippi, July 20, 2005.

117   *Scruggs was staggered* . . . Interviews with Dick Scruggs, Zach Scruggs.

118   *Scruggs smoldered* . . . Interview with Merkel.

118   *The setbacks* . . . Interview with Deloach.

119   *A few days later* . . . Interview with Zach Scruggs.

120   *Two days after Katrina* . . . Interviews with Dick Scruggs, Zach Scruggs.

Chapter 10

123   *Jones charmed his way* . . . Email from John Jones to Dick Scruggs, Danny Cupit, and others, Sept. 14, 2005.

123   *Papers formalizing* . . . Joint Venture Agreement, In Re: Katrina Litigation, Scruggs Katrina Group, Nov. 8, 2005.

124   *Scruggs, as usual* . . . Interviews with Scruggs, Don Barrett, confidential sources.

125   *Jones was bookish* . . . Interviews with Jones, confidential sources.

127   *Tim Balducci had also served* . . . *The Delta Italians*, Paul V. Canonici (Calo Creative Designs, 2003); interviews with confidential sources.

127   *Tim Balducci never strayed* . . . Interview with confidential source; Bolivar County statistics for 2000, U.S. Census Bureau.

128   *As he said later* . . . Testimony by Balducci in hearing in connection with *U.S.A. v. Scruggs*, U.S. District Court, Northern District of Mississippi, Feb. 20, 2008.

129   *For Jones, bad news* . . . Interview with Jones; deposition given by Jones in connection with *Jones, Funderburg, Sessums, Peterson & Lee PLLC v. Richard Scruggs, et al.*, Circuit Court of Lafayette County, Mississippi, July 22, 2008.

129   *In a move* . . . Deposition given by Jones.

129   *Like Johnny Jones* . . . Conversation between Balducci and Judge Henry Lackey, recorded by the FBI, Sept. 21, 2007.

130   *Tommy Cadle* . . . Telephone conversation between Balducci and Judge Lackey, recorded by the FBI, Sept. 18, 2007.

130   *Driving in Oxford* . . . Conversation between Balducci and Judge Lackey, recorded by FBI, May 9, 2007; interview with Diane Scruggs.

130   *Though the Georgia* . . . Conversation with Senator Joe Biden, August 2000.

131   *Under the contract* . . . Joint Venture Agreement.

131   *Barrett had doubts* . . . Interview with Barrett.

131   *If Scruggs Katrina Group* . . . Joint Venture Agreement.

132   *In the first blush* . . . Letter from Jones to Dick Scruggs, Dec. 11, 2006; interview with Jones, confidential sources.

132   *Patterson had lived* . . . Interviews with confidential sources.

133   *When a young woman* . . . Letter from Steve Patterson to Thomas D. McDonough, July 2, 2007.

133   *Patterson's letter* . . . Letters from Stephen P. Livingston to the Mississippi Bar, July 11, 2007; July 19, 2007; July 26, 2007, with attachments.

133   *Balducci responded* . . . Letter from Balducci to Livingston, Aug. 1, 2007.

133   *Livingston dismissed* . . . Interview with Livingston.

134   *When Jones walked* . . . Interview with Jones.

134   *Barrett had tried* . . . Deposition given by Jones.

134   *Barrett was annoyed* . . . Interview with Barrett.

134   *At the outset* . . . Deposition given by Jones.

135   *Scruggs, who seemed* . . . Interviews with Jones, Dick Scruggs, Zach
Scruggs.

136   *Driving from the meeting* . . . Interview with Jones.

136   *His partner* . . . Email from Steve Funderburg to Dick Scruggs, March
4, 2007.

136   *He turned* . . . Interview with Jones.

136   *Cupit explained* . . . Interview with Cupit.

Chapter 11

137   *Grady Tollison* . . . Interviews with confidential sources.

137   *In 1994* . . . Interview with Grady Tollison.

137   *During one* . . . "Ex-Head of Baptist College Pleads Not Guilty to
Fraud," *New York Times*, Sept. 23, 1994.

138   *As one* . . . Interview with confidential source.

138   *For such an unusual* . . . Interviews with Tollison, confidential sources.

140   *Tollison had never* . . . Interview with Tollison.

140   *Scruggs sensed* . . . Interview with Dick Scruggs.

140   *There was one particular apostasy* . . . Interview with Tollison.

141   *If the four sides* . . . Interview with Mike Moore.

141   *Tollison's animosity* . . . Interviews with Tollison, Scruggs.

142   *Less than two weeks* . . . *Jones, Funderburg, Sessums, Peterson & Lee LLC
v. Richard Scruggs, Don Barrett, Scruggs Law Firm, Barrett Law Office, Nutt &
McAlister, PLLC, and Lovelace Law Firm,* Circuit Court of Lafayette County,
Mississippi, March 15, 2007.

143   *On March 15* . . . Transcript of testimony of Judge Henry L. Lackey in
connection with *Jones, Funderburg v. Scruggs* hearing in Circuit Court of
Lafayette County, Mississippi, April 15, 2008.

143   *Lackey signed* . . . Order signed by Judge Lackey sealing case, Circuit
Court of Lafayette County, Mississippi, March 15, 2007; testimony of Lackey
in April 15, 2008, hearing.

143   *With the judge's order* . . . Letter from Tollison to Scruggs and others,
March 15, 2007.

143   *Scruggs recognized* . . . Interviews with Dick Scruggs, Zach Scruggs.

144   *On the morning* . . . "Law Firm Sues State Farm Opponent Scruggs,"
Associated Press, *Clarion-Ledger*, March 28, 2007.

Chapter 12

145   *On the same day* . . . Interview with Zach Scruggs.
146   *Everyone at the conference* . . . Interviews with Dick Scruggs, Zach
Scruggs, Sid Backstrom, Joey Langston; Confidential Human Source (CHS)
Reporting Document of the FBI giving Tim Balducci's account to agents of
bribe to Judge Henry L. Lackey, Nov. 2, 2007.
146   *Despite that possibility* . . . Transcript of testimony by Balducci in
hearing in connection with *U.S.A. v. Scruggs*, U.S. District Court, Northern District of Mississippi, Feb. 20, 2008; testimony by Judge Lackey in April 15 hearing; interviews with confidential sources.
146   *Lackey had the appearance* . . . Interviews with confidential sources.
147   *He described himself* . . . Boyer, "The Bribe."
147   *He handled* . . . Interviews with confidential sources.
147   *Lackey seemed jolly* . . . Testimony by Judge Henry L. Lackey in April
15 hearing.
148   *In the Baptist fashion* . . . Conversation between Lackey and Balducci,
recorded by the FBI, May 9, 2007.
148   *Only three days before* . . . "Lipstick on a Pig" advertisement in *The
Clarion-Ledger*, March 25, 2007.
148   *Before he left* . . . Testimony by Balducci in hearing, Feb. 20, 2008.
149   *Baffled and offended* . . . Testimony by Lackey in hearing, April 15.
149   *On the morning* . . . Interview with John Hailman; testimony by
Lackey, April 15.
149   *Hailman was an interesting* . . . Interview with Hailman.
151   *Hailman closed the door* . . . Interview with Tom Dawson.
151   *"Henry"* . . . Interview with Hailman.
151   *The prospect* . . . Interviews with confidential sources.
153   *A serious schism* . . . Interviews with confidential sources.
153   *The bureaucratic clash* . . . "Request for Legal Opinion," a confidential
FBI paper sent to the "Director's Office" by five agents, Sept. 22, 2004;
interviews with confidential sources.
154   *In the meantime* . . . Interviews with confidential sources.
154   *In March* . . . FBI report drafted by Philip H. Neilson alleging "Civil
Rights violations, Intelligence Oversight Board (IOB) violations, and privacy
violations" by the United States Attorneys Office, Northern District of
Mississippi, March 21, 2006.
155   *Determined to keep* . . . Interviews with Hailman, Dawson, confidential
sources.
155   *For several months* . . . Interview with Dawson.
155   *Despite these efforts* . . . Interviews with confidential sources.

Chapter 13

156   *In the beginning* . . . Interview with Tom Dawson.

156   *Using his own* . . . Interviews with John Hailman, confidential sources.

156   *Bill Delaney* . . . Transcript of testimony by William Delaney, hearing in connection with *U.S.A. v. Scruggs*, U.S. District Court, Northern District of Mississippi, Feb. 20, 2008.

157   *On May 4* . . . Telephone conversation between Judge Henry L. Lackey and Tim Balducci, recorded by the FBI, May 4, 2007.

157   *He even had a cheery greeting* . . . Meeting between Lackey and Balducci, recorded by the FBI, May 9, 2007.

160   *When he finally found* . . . Telephone conversation between Lackey and Balducci, recorded by the FBI, May 21, 2007.

160   *That same day* . . . Letter, transmitted by fax, from Lackey to Larry D. Moffett and Grady Tollison, May 21, 2007.

161   *He even concocted* . . . Lackey testimony, April 15, 2008. Balducci testimony, Feb. 20, 2008.

161   *Though no one else* . . . Interviews with Dawson, Hailman.

162   *Over lunch* . . . Balducci testimony, Feb. 20, 2008.

162   *Afterward, Lackey* . . . Personal journal of Henry Lackey, entry dated June 4, 2007.

162   *On June 4* . . . Letter, transmitted by fax, from Lackey to Moffett and Tollison, June 4, 2007.

Chapter 14

163   *While Judge Lackey* . . . Interviews with Dick Scruggs, Zach Scruggs.

163   *The tone* . . . "Biloxi Attorney Paul Minor and Two Former Mississippi State Court Judges Convicted for Role in Bribery Scheme," U.S. Department of Justice news release, April 2, 2007.

163   *Minor was sentenced* . . . "Biloxi Attorney Paul Minor and Two Former Mississippi State Court Judges Sentenced on Conviction in Bribery Scheme," U.S. Department of Justice news release, Sept. 7, 2007.

163   *Even vacations* . . . Interviews with Diane Scruggs, Rex Deloach.

164   *En route* . . . Interview with Parham Williams.

164   *Attracting the famed* . . . Words of Wisdom, Chapman University website.

164   *Continuing west* . . . Interviews with Diane Scruggs, Deloach.

164   *On the last day* . . . Interview with Mike Moore.

165   *The trouble with Dale* . . . Interview with Dick Scruggs.

165   *A hundred days* . . . Deposition given by David Lee Harrell in connection with *Thomas C. and Pamela McIntosh v. State Farm Fire & Casualty*

Co., Forensic Analysis & Engineering Corp., and E.A. Renfroe & Co., U.S. District Court, Southern District of Mississippi, Oct. 31, 2007.

165   *He felt* . . . Interview with Dick Scruggs.

166   *In a cartoon* . . . "Lipstick on a Pig," *Clarion-Ledger*, March 25, 2007.

166   *Diane Scruggs* . . . Interview with Diane Scruggs.

166   *The head* . . . "The Man Who Sold the War," James Bamford, *Rolling Stone*, Nov. 17, 2005.

166   *The Republican governor* . . . Unpublished interview with George Dale, 2008.

166   *Dale sued* . . . "Dale Says He'll Fight Removal from Mississippi Ballot," Emily Wagster Pettus, Associated Press, March 21, 2007.

167   *But Dale blamed* . . . Unpublished interview with Dale.

167   *Hood convened* . . . Interview with Danny Cupit.

168   *In a twist* . . . Interviews with Dick Scruggs, confidential sources.

168   *When Hood* . . . Interviews with Zach Scruggs, Dick Scruggs, confidential sources.

168   *Scruggs and Cupit* . . . Interviews with Scruggs, Cupit, and confidential sources.

170   *In the case* . . . Interview with Dick Scruggs.

171   *Drawing upon his wiles* . . . "Katrina: Where Things Stand," *20/20* report by Brian Ross on ABC, Aug. 25, 2006.

171   *A week later* . . . *E. A. Renfroe & Co., Inc. v. Cori Rigsby Moran, et al.*, U.S. District Court, Northern District of Alabama.

171   *The case was assigned* . . . "Federal Judge Challenges Himself on U.S. Cases," William Schmidt, *New York Times*, July 19, 1988; "Alabama Students Say School Punished Them for not Reciting Pledge," Associated Press, July 21, 2000; "U.S. Judge: No Yale Law Clerks," Dee McAree, *The National Law Journal*, Feb. 25, 2005.

172   *In June 2007* . . . Interview with Zach Scruggs.

172   *The day after* . . . Memorandum opinion by U.S. District Judge William M. Acker, Jr., in *Renfroe v. Rigsby Moran, et al.*, U.S. District Court, Northern District of Alabama, June 15, 2007.

172   *There was further irony* . . . Letter from U.S. Attorney Alice H. Martin to Judge Acker, July 25, 2007.

172   *Refusing to give up* . . . Judge Acker's June 15 opinion; "Criminal Contempt Prosecution of Dickie Scruggs," Point of Law Forum, Manhattan Institute, July 28, 2007

172   *Scruggs countered* . . . Interview with Dick Scruggs.

173   *In one of Senter's* . . . "Judge Rules for Insurers in Katrina," Joseph B. Treaster, *New York Times*, Aug. 16, 2006.

173   *Still, Scruggs* . . . Interview with Zach Scruggs.

Chapter 15

174   *Air-conditioning* . . . "Dry September," short story by William Faulkner, *Collected Stories of William Faulkner* (VintageBooks, 1995).
174   *Down the road* . . . Judge Lackey testimony, April 15, 2008.
174   *The federal agents* . . . Interviews with confidential sources.
174   *Finally, on the afternoon* . . . "Gary Anderson Sends George Dale to the Showers," *Jackson Free Press*, Aug. 8, 2007; telephone conversation between Judge Lackey and Tim Balducci, recorded by the FBI, Aug. 9, 2007.
175   *"I'm looking for the piss ant"* . . . Telephone conversation between Lackey and Balducci, Aug. 9, 2007.
176   *Lackey's subsequent attempts* . . . Two failed attempts by Lackey to reach Balducci by telephone, FBI recordings, Sept. 11, 2007; interviews with confidential sources.
176   *"I could not reach* . . . FBI recording, Sept. 11, 2007.
177   *A week later* . . . Telephone conversation between Lackey and Balducci, recorded by the FBI, Sept. 18, 2007.
178   *If he could get* . . . Balducci's grand jury testimony, Nov. 27, 2007.
178   *Listening to the conversation* . . . Interviews with Tom Dawson, John Hailman.
178   *The development* . . . Interview with Dawson.
179   *The event* . . . Panel discussion hosted by Prudential Financial in 2002; Boyer, "The Bribe."
180   *Despite Lackey's admonition* . . . Telephone conversation between Judge Lackey and Balducci, recorded by the FBI, Sept. 18, 2007.
180   *Their money had* . . . Telephone conversation between Balducci and unidentified man in his firm, recorded by the FBI, Nov. 1, 2007.
180   *Showing no signs* . . . Telephone conversation between Balducci and Steve Patterson, recorded by the FBI, Sept. 28, 2007.
181   *Scruggs was their ultimate* . . . Telephone conversation between Balducci and Jim Biden, recorded by the FBI, Sept. 27, 2007.
181   *The conversation* . . . Conversation between Balducci and Judge Lackey, recorded by the FBI, Sept. 21, 2007.

Chapter 16

184   *Four days after* . . . Application for interception of wire communications, filed in U.S. District Court, Northern District of Mississippi, Sept. 25, 2007.
184   *Biggers was* . . . Interviews with confidential sources.
185   *On September 25* . . . Application for interception of wire communications, signed by U.S. District Judge Neal Biggers.

185   *One of the first* . . . Telephone conversation between Patterson and Balducci, recorded by the FBI, Sept. 26, 2007.

185   *Before nine o'clock* . . . Telephone conversation between Balducci and Patterson, recorded by the FBI, Sept. 27, 2007.

186   *A half hour later* . . . Conversation between Balducci and Judge Henry Lackey, recorded by the FBI, Sept. 27, 2007.

189   *Lackey had another* . . . Journal of Judge Lackey, entry dated Oct. 18, 2007.

189   *Driving back* . . . Telephone conversation between Balducci and Jim Biden, recorded by the FBI, Sept. 27, 2007.

189   *Shortly before noon* . . . Second telephone conversation between Balducci and Patterson, recorded by the FBI, Sept. 27, 2007.

190   *The next afternoon* . . . Interview with Joey Langston; two telephone conversations between Patterson and Balducci, recorded by the FBI, Sept. 28, 2007.

192   *Although Patterson* . . . Telephone conversations between Patterson and Balducci, Sept. 28, 2007.

192   *That same afternoon* . . . Interview with Dick Scruggs.

193   *Blake remained vague* . . . Second telephone conversation between Patterson and Balducci, Sept. 28, 2007.

193   *Listening to the recordings* . . . Application for interception of wire communications, filed in U.S. District Court, Northern District of Mississippi, Oct. 16, 2007.

194   *Biggers* . . . Application for interception of wire communications, signed by Judge Biggers, Oct. 16, 2007.

Chapter 17

195   *There were legitimate* . . . Interviews with Dick Scruggs, Diane Scruggs, confidential sources.

196   *The presidential candidate* . . . Interviews with Zach Scruggs, confidential sources; invitation to "A fund-raising reception honoring Senator Joseph R. Biden, Jr. (D-De.)."

196   *It was determined* . . . Telephone conversation between Tim Balducci and Jim Biden, Sept. 27, 2007.

196   *A month later* . . . Telephone conversation between Balducci, Steve Patterson, and Jim Biden, recorded by the FBI, Sept. 27, 2007; telephone conversation between Balducci and Jim Biden, Sept. 27, 2007.

197   *Scruggs laughed* . . . Interview with Dick Scruggs.

197   *As soon as he left* . . . Telephone conversation between Balducci and Jim Biden, Sept. 27, 2007.

197   *Over the next twenty-four hours* . . . Second telephone conversation between Balducci and Jim Biden, Sept. 27, 2007.

198   *One of the earliest* . . . Interviews with confidential sources; brochure for Patterson, Balducci and Biden, PLLC Law Group.

198   *In the first* . . . "Lawyers: Police Shooting Unjust," Tyrone Tony Reed, Jr., *Jackson Sun*, April 19, 2007.

199   *Patterson also persuaded* . . . Brochure for law group.

199   *Allain was another* . . . Interviews with confidential sources; Wilkie, *Dixie*.

199   *His counterpart* . . . Conversation with Bill Clinton, February 1992.

199   *Patterson also arranged* . . . Brochure for law group.

199   *Ieyoub's background* . . . "Ieyoub Claims He's Vindicated," Jack Wardlaw, *Times-Picayune*, June 17, 1998.

200   *Yet Patterson* . . . Telephone conversation between Patterson and Balducci, recorded by the FBI, Oct. 4, 2007.

200   *There were no boundaries* . . . Telephone conversation between Balducci and Patterson, Sept. 28, 2007; brochure for law group.

200   *But the biggest* . . . Telephone conversation between Balducci and Patterson. Sept. 27, 2007.

200   *It was a highly complicated* . . . Interviews with Dick Scruggs, Joey Langston.

201   *In mid-October* . . . Telephone conversation between Balducci and Patterson, recorded by the FBI, Oct. 15, 2007.

201   *According to a financial* . . . Centerpulse Ltd. filing with Security Exchange Commission, April 25, 2003.

201   *Balducci could barely* . . . Telephone conversation between Balducci and Patterson, Oct. 15, 2007.

201   *Balducci had gone* . . . Brochure for law group.

202   *Balducci said Ondo* . . . Telephone conversation between Balducci and Patterson, Oct. 15, 2007.

202   *Another older attorney* . . . Interview with Norman Gillespie; Patterson, Balducci PLLC Law Group of Counsel Agreement, signed May 9, 2007.

203   *At least they thought* . . . Telephone conversation between Patterson and Jim and Sara Biden, recorded by the FBI, Oct. 31, 2007.

203   *They even* . . . Interview with John Hailman.

204   *For all of their* . . . Telephone conversations between Balducci and Patterson, recorded by the FBI, Oct. 8, 2007.

204   *He resorted* . . . Telephone conversation between Balducci and a man identified only as "Bruce," recorded by the FBI, Oct. 3, 2007.

205   *Shortly after the conversation* . . . Telephone conversation between Balducci and Ed Peters, recorded by the FBI, Oct. 3, 2007.

205   *Federal authorities* . . . Interviews with confidential sources.

205   *"Perfect," Peters said* . . . Telephone conversation between Balducci and Peters, Oct. 3, 2007.

206   *Jim Biden* . . . Telephone conversation between Jim Biden and Balducci, Oct. 15, 2007.

206   *In late October* . . . Interview with Tom Dawson.

206   *Lackey described* . . . Journal of Judge Henry Lackey, entry dated Oct. 25, 2007.

206   *While Judge Lackey* . . . Telephone conversations between Patterson and Balducci, recorded by the FBI, Oct. 9, 2007; Oct. 15, 2007.

206   *In a letter* . . . Letter from Scruggs to Balducci, Oct. 18, 2007.

207   *When Balducci* . . . Undated invoice from Balducci to Scruggs Law Office.

207   *One afternoon* . . . Telephone conversation between Steve and Debbie Patterson, recorded by the FBI, October, 2007.

207   *As November approached* . . . Interview with Gillespie.

207   *"I have Band-Aids* . . . Telephone conversation between Balducci and unidentified man, recorded by the FBI, Nov. 5, 2007.

Chapter 18

208   *As Halloween approached* . . . Telephone conversation between Tim Balducci and Steve Patterson, recorded by the FBI, Oct. 18, 2007.

208   *He called* . . . Telephone conversation between Patterson and Jere Nash, recorded by the FBI, Nov. 1, 2007.

209   *Nash was able* . . . "Former Teamsters President Ron Carey Indicted," CNN, Jan. 25, 2001; interview with Nash.

209   *Patterson reported* . . . Telephone conversation between Patterson and Dick Scruggs, recorded by the FBI, Nov. 1, 2009.

209   *Patterson called Nash again* . . . Second telephone conversation between Patterson and Nash, recorded by the FBI, Nov. 1, 2007.

210   *He wore* . . . Meeting between Balducci and Judge Henry Lackey, videotaped by the FBI, Nov. 1, 2007.

211   *Shortly after* . . . Interview with Tom Dawson.

212   *Less than four* . . . Balducci conversation with Dick Scruggs and Zach Scruggs, recorded by the FBI, Nov. 1, 2007, interview with Zach Scruggs.

212   *(A few days* . . . Interviews with Zach Scruggs, Joey Langston. Letter from Dick Scruggs to D. Eric Lycan and William H. May III, Oct. 19, 2007.

212   *The arrangement* . . . Telephone conversation between Patterson and Balducci, recorded by the FBI, Oct. 20, 2007.

213   *Patterson and Balducci* . . . Letter from Patterson and Balducci to Lycan and May, Oct. 20, 2007.

213   *(The quarrel* . . . Interviews with Dick Scruggs, Zach Scruggs, Langston.

213   *The dispute* . . . Conversation between Balducci and Zach Scruggs, recorded by the FBI, Nov. 1, 2007.

213   *"When did you* . . . Conversation between Balducci and Sid Backstrom, recorded by the FBI, Nov. 1, 2007.

213   *During his painful* . . . Interview with Dawson, confidential sources.

213   *Balducci had* . . . Interviews with Zach Scruggs, Backstrom.

214   *In the privacy* . . . Conversation between Balducci and Backstrom, Nov. 1.

214   *As they* . . . Interview with Zach Scruggs.

214   *Zach Scruggs* . . . Conversation between Balducci, Backstrom, and Zach Scruggs, Nov. 1.

216   *Balducci and Backstrom* . . . Conversation between Balducci and Backstrom, Nov. 1.

217   *Before he left* . . . Conversation between Balducci and Dick Scruggs, recorded by the FBI, Nov. 1, 2007.

218   *Scruggs paused* . . . Interview with Dick Scruggs.

218   *His concentration* . . . Conversation between Balducci and Dick Scruggs, Nov. 1.

218   *In a letter* . . . Letter from Scruggs to Balducci, Nov. 1, 2007.

219   *Balducci felt* . . . Conversation between Balducci and Bill Delaney, recorded by the FBI, Nov. 1, 2007.

219   *By the time* . . . Telephone conversation between Balducci and unidentified man, recorded by the FBI, Nov. 1, 2007.

219   *Although Balducci* . . . Interview with Dawson.

219   *On the same day* . . . Email from Tim Cantrell to Meg Grantham, Holly Mooney, Nov. 2, 2007.

Chapter 19

221   *"Thinking is not* . . . "As Usual, Coach O's Bright Idea Leads to a Dark Day for His Ole Miss Squad," Geoff Calkins, *Commercial Appeal*, Nov. 24, 2007.

222   *In fact* . . . Interviews with confidential sources.

222   *During an early-season* . . . Conversation with Dick Scruggs.

223   *He had loaned* . . . Interviews with Dick Scruggs, confidential sources.

223   *On the Sunday* . . . Interview with Dick Scruggs.

223   *At times* . . . Conversation with Trent Lott, September 2007.

223   *When Lott* . . . "Sen. Trent Lott Announces Resignation," Associated Press, Nov. 26, 2007.

224   *When Scruggs was asked* . . . Interview with Humphreys McGee.

224   *There was a greater shock* . . . Interviews with confidential sources.

224   *Early on the morning* . . . Interview with Sid Backstrom.

227   *"I think* . . . Interview with Diane Scruggs.

228   *Scruggs seemed* . . . Telephone conversation between Steve Patterson and Dick Scruggs, recorded by the FBI, Oct. 18, 2007.

228   *Zach Scruggs* . . . Interview with Zach Scruggs.

228   *Outside the Scruggs* . . . Interviews with confidential sources.

229   *A search warrant* . . . Application and Affidavit for Search Warrant, filed by William P. Delaney and signed by Judge Neal Biggers, U.S. District Court, Northern District of Mississippi, Nov. 16, 2007.

229   *A second search* . . . Application and Affidavit for Search Warrant, filed by Delaney and signed by Judge Biggers, U.S. District Court, Nov. 26, 2007.

229   *Scruggs was standing* . . . Interviews with Dick Scruggs, Zach Scruggs.

230   *Around the corner* . . . Transcript of testimony by Tim Balducci before a grand jury, U.S. District Court, Northern District of Mississippi, Nov. 2007.

232   *While Balducci* . . . Interview with Zach Scruggs.

232   *In a coordinated strike* . . . Interview with Tom Dawson. Confidential Human Source (CHS) Reporting Document of the FBI giving details of Steve Patterson's converation with agents, Nov. 27, 2007.

233   *Once hurried* . . . Interviews with confidential sources.

233   *According to an FBI* . . . CHS Reporting Document of the FBI on Patterson.

233   *After listening* . . . Interviews with Dawson, confidential sources.

234   *Patterson and Hailman* . . . Interview with John Hailman.

235   *At Scruggs's office* . . . Interviews with Dick Scruggs, Zach Scruggs.

235   *On the coast* . . . Interview with Backstrom.

236   *By this time* . . . Interviews with Zach Scruggs, Bruce Newman.

236   *Langston decided* . . . *Oxford Eagle*, Nov. 28, 2007.

237   *Later in the afternoon* . . . Interviews with Zach Scruggs, Langston, Dawson.

237   *As late November* . . . Interviews with Zach Scruggs, Langston.

Chapter 20

239   *Facing the threat* . . . Interview with Zach Scruggs.

239   *There was another* . . . Interview with Billy Quin.

240   *While the lawyers* . . . Interview with Zach Scruggs.

240   *"The Scruggs Law Firm* . . . Letter from Don Barrett, David Nutt, and Dewitt Lovelace to clients of Scruggs Katrina Group, December 4, 2007.

240   *Scruggs faced* . . . Interviews with Dick Scruggs, Zach Scruggs.

240   *Backstrom and Tannehill* . . . Interview with Sid Backstrom.

241   *Eventually* . . . Interview with Zach Scruggs.

243   *The prosecutors* . . . Interview with Tom Dawson.

243   *At the press conference* . . . *Oxford Eagle,* Nov. 29, 2007.

243   *One of those* . . . Interview with Dawson.

245   *Earlier in the year* . . . Interview with John Hailman.

245   *The party* . . . Interview with Paulo Prada.

245   *"People appreciate* . . . "It's a Party Time for Dickie Scruggs in Oxford,
Miss.—Home of Faulkner, Grisham Rallies Round a Lawyer Just Indicted for
Bribery," Paulo Prada and Peter Lattman, *Wall Street Journal,* Dec. 4, 2007.

245   *That quote* . . . Interview with Prada.

246   *Keker had picked up* . . . Interview with John Keker.

246   *The source* . . . Interview with Zach Scruggs.

247   *Scruggs thought* . . . Interview with Dick Scruggs.

247   *DeLaughter* . . . Interviews with confidential sources.

247   *That evening* . . . Interview with Zach Scruggs.

248   *Tom Dawson* . . . Interview with Dawson.

248   *Scruggs had been talking* . . . Interview with Zach Scruggs.

249   *A few days after* . . . Interviews with Dick Scruggs, Zach Scruggs, Joey
Langston.

249   *The government's* . . . Interview with Dawson.

249   *Around the office* . . . Interview with confidential source.

250   *He returned* . . . Interviews with Dawson, confidential sources.

250   *Balducci and his family* . . . Interview with confidential source.

251   *At his hideaway* . . . Interview with Norm Gillespie.

251   *"Dear Judge Gillespie* . . . Written message from Tim Balducci to
Gillespie.

251   *It was a troubled* . . . Interview with Zach Scruggs.

Chapter 21

253   *Like Dick Scruggs* . . . Interview with Joey Langston; "Good & Guilty,"
Patsy Brumfield, *Northeast Mississippi Sunday Journal,* Feb. 3, 2008.

254   *He defended* . . . Interviews with confidential sources.

254   *By 1990,* . . . Interviews with confidential sources; "Jury Awards Paralyzed Man $21M," *The Clarion-Ledger,* Oct. 13, 2005

254   *The families* . . . "U.S. Judge Assesses Cuba $187 Million in Death of
4 Pilots," Mireya Navarro, *New York Times,* Dec. 18, 1997.

254   *Langston learned* . . . Interview with Langston.

255   *One legislative victory* . . . Interviews with Langston, confidential
sources; "Justice Nearer for Brothers Fliers' Kin," *Miami Herald,* Oct. 25, 1998.

255   *At the eleventh hour* . . . Interviews with confidential sources;

"Terrorist Victims Set Precedent," Bill Miller, *Washington Post*, Oct. 22, 2000;
Section 2002 of the Victims of Trafficking and Violence Protection Act of
2000.

256   *For his troubles* . . . Interviews with Langston, confidential sources.

256   *Balducci had first* . . . Interview with Langston.

256   *An investigation* . . . Interview with Mike Moore.

257   *After assessing* . . . Interview with Langston.

257   *"I introduced* . . . Deposition given by Steve Patterson in connection
with *Eaton v. Frisby*, June 18, 2009.

257   *Jim Hood* . . . "Plenty of Fireworks in First-ever Held Local Political
Forum," *Desoto Times Tribune*, Aug. 1, 2007.

257   *But Billy Quin* . . . Interview with Billy Quin.

258   *With Hood* . . . "Hood Defends Allegations He's Influence Peddling,"
Madison County Journal, Sept. 27, 2007.

258   *Ever since* . . . Interview with Langston.

259   *Langston and Balducci* . . . Interview with Dick Scruggs.

259   *Peters was familiar* . . . Interviews with confidential sources.

259   *He was reelected* . . . "Ex-DA Leaves Scandal in Wake," Jerry Mitchell,
Clarion-Ledger, Jan. 11, 2009.

259   *With his connections* . . . Deposition given by Patterson.

260   *Peters and DeLaughter* . . . Wilkie, *Dixie*.

260   *DeLaughter* . . . *Never Too Late*, Bobby DeLaughter (Scribner, 2001);
Ghosts of Mississippi, film directed by Rob Reiner, 1996.

261   *The movie* . . . "Hollywood Gave Peters' Big Scene to DeLaughter,"
column by Sid Salter, *Meridian Star*, Feb. 14, 2009.

261   *The idea* . . . Interviews with Dick Scruggs, Langston.

261   *Peters asked* . . . Deposition given by Patterson.

261   *Langston* . . . Interview with Langston.

262   *Scruggs said* . . . Interview with Johnny Jones.

262   *Zach Scruggs* . . . Email from Zach Scruggs to Jones, May 29, 2006.

262   *Jones replied* . . . Email from Jones to Zach Scruggs, May 30, 2006.

263   *By this time* . . . Interview with Dick Scruggs.

263   *Besides, he* . . . Interview with Diane Scruggs.

263   *Even as he implicated* . . . Affidavit for search warrant for Langston Law
Firm, filed by FBI agent John Quaka before U.S. District Judge Michael P. Mills,
Northern District of Mississippi, December 9, 2007.

263   *Lott's call* . . . Interview with Dick Scruggs.

263   *Still, there* . . . Interview with Charles Merkel.

263   *Balducci* . . . Interview with Tom Dawson.

264   *On a dreary Saturday* . . . Interview with Langston.

264   *(The government* . . . Information charging Langston with one count of

violation of Title 18, U.S. Code, Section 371, filed by U.S. attorney Jim
Greenlee in U.S. District Court, Northern District of Mississippi, Jan. 7, 2008.

265   *Against this backdrop* . . . Interview with Langston.

265   *Instead of protecting* . . . Interview with Dawson.

266   *At one point* . . . Interview with confidential sources.

266   *Peters seemed relieved* . . . Interview with Dawson, confidential sources.

266   *Patterson, who* . . . Deposition given by Patterson.

267   *Throughout December* . . . Interview with Langston.

267   *On the flight* . . . Interview with Quin.

268   *Back home* . . . Interviews with Langston, Zach Scruggs.

268   *While Langston* . . . Interviews with Langston, Dawson.

268   *All that* . . . "Mid-South Super Lawyers 2007," advertising supplement
to *The New York Times*, autumn 2007.

268   *Langston drove* . . . Interview with Langston.

269   *The prosecutors* . . . Interview with Dawson.

Chapter 22

270   *Joey Langston's* . . . Transcript of Waiver of Indictment/Filing of Infor-
mation, Plea of Guilty to Count One of the Information, Hearing before U.S.
District Judge Michael P. Mills, U.S. District Court, Northern District of
Mississippi, Jan. 7, 2008; interviews with confidential sources.

271   *Langston's associate* . . . Interview with Billy Quin.

272   *Langston's plea* . . . Interview with Zach Scruggs.

273   *Farese would insist* . . . Personal and confidential letter from Anthony L.
Farese to Zach Scruggs, Jan. 9, 2008.

273   *Farese, Farese* . . . Website of Farese, Farese and Farese law firm.

274   *When students* . . . Interviews with confidential sources.

274   *Just months* . . . "Mary Winkler Gets a Week in Prison, 60 Days in
Mental Health Facility," Clay Bailey, *Commercial Appeal*, June 8, 2007.

274   *After learning* . . . Interview with Zach Scruggs.

275   *Instead, he called* . . . Interview with Mike Moore.

275   *During the ordeal* . . . Interview with Zach Scruggs.

276   *Farese protested* . . . Letter from Farese to Zach Scruggs; exchange of
communications between Curtis Wilkie and Tony Farese: Memo from Wilkie
to Farese, July 28, 2009; Farese letter to Wilkie, July 30, 2009; email from Cal
Mayo to Farese authorizing Farese "to provide truthful responses to Curtis
Wilkie's questions about the subject matter areas identified in his memo of
July 28," Aug. 12, 2009; letter from Farese to Wilkie, Aug. 17, 2009; email from
Farese to Wilkie, Aug. 20, 2009; interview with Farese.

277   *They settled* . . . Interviews with Zach Scruggs, confidential sources.

277   *Zach remained* . . . Undated ten-page document detailing Zach Scruggs's account of "my dealings with my former attorney Tony Farese . . ."

Chapter 23

278   *The morning* . . . Interview with Tom Dawson.

278   *The investigators* . . . Interviews with confidential sources.

279   *At the meeting* . . . Interview with Dawson.

280   *In the councils* . . . Interviews with Dick Scruggs, Zach Scruggs, Sid Backstrom.

280   *Zach hired* . . . "The Scales of Justice," Murray Waas, *National Journal,* May 31, 2007.

281   *Steve Patterson* . . . Interviews with confidential sources.

281   *Appearing before* . . . Transcript of hearing on Change of Plea to Count One of the Indictment Before U.S. District Judge Neal Biggers, U.S. District Court, Northern District, Jan. 15, 2008.

281   *In testimony* . . . Deposition given by Patterson, June 18, 2009.

281   *With Patterson's plea* . . . Interview with Dick Scruggs.

282   *In the thirty* . . . John W. Keker, Lawyer Profile, Martindale.com; "The Man Who Will Prosecute Oliver North; John W. Keker, Ready for the Courtroom Showdown," *Washington Post,* Jan. 31, 1989; "High Profile Corporate Defendants Turn to Keker," Edward Iwata, *USA Today,* Feb. 3, 2004; "Help, I'm in Legal Trouble. Get Me John Keker," *Northern California Super Lawyers 2005;* "Barry Bonds Begins Assembling Legal Dream Team; Eyes Famed Attorney Keker," Christian Red, Michael O'Keefe, and Teri Thompson, *New York Daily News,* Nov. 29, 2007.

283   *In a lengthy motion* . . . Defendants' Motion to Dismiss the Indictment for Outrageous Government Conduct with Combined Memorandum of Law, filed in U.S. District Court, Northern District of Mississippi, Feb. 11, 2008.

285   *The case had been* . . . Interviews with confidential sources.

286   *Balducci said* . . . Transcipt of hearing on Defendants' Motion Before U.S. District Judge Biggers, U.S. District Court, Northern District of Mississippi, Feb. 20, 2008.

286   *Watching from* . . . Interview with Zach Scruggs.

286   *Balducci recounted* . . . Transcript of hearing, Feb. 20, 2008.

287   *It was Backstrom's* . . . Interview with Backstrom.

287   *"I advised* . . . Transcript of hearing, Feb. 20, 2008.

287   *One involved* . . . Confidential Human Source (CHS) Reporting Document of the FBI giving Tim Balducci's account of bribe to Judge Lackey, Nov. 2, 2007.

287   *In a later 302* . . . Confidential Human Source (CHS) Reporting

Document of the FBI giving Balducci's explanation of previous interview, Nov. 14, 2007.

Chapter 24

305   *It sounded* . . . Interview with Moore.

305   *No one* . . . Interviews with confidential sources.

305   *Moore worried* . . . Interviews with Dick Scruggs, Zach Scruggs, Moore.

306   *"Do you want* . . . Interviews with Zach Scruggs, Diane Scruggs.

306   *Three days later* . . . Transcript of hearing on Change of Plea to Count
One of the Information in Connection with *U.S.A. v. David Zachary Scruggs*,
before U.S. District Judge Neal Biggers, U.S. District Court, Northern District
of Mississippi, March 21, 2008.

307   *Throughout the negotiations* . . . Interview with Zach Scruggs.

307   *Biggers informed* . . . Transcript of hearing in U.S. District Court, March
21, 2008.

Chapter 25

308   *In commentary* . . . "Consider Judge Lackey," Lydia Quarles, *Clarion-
Ledger*, Feb. 3, 2008.

308   *The Mississippi Supreme* . . . "Judge Henry Lackey to receive Chief Jus-
tice Award," press release by Mississippi State Supreme Court, July 11, 2008;
"Judge Lackey Honored by Mississippi Bar," Alyssa Schnugg, *Oxford Eagle*,
July 1, 2008.

308   *In interviews* . . . *Oxford Eagle* article, July 1, 2008.

308   *The case* . . . Transcript of hearing before circuit judge William
Coleman, Circuit Court of Lafayette County, in connection with *Jones, Funderburg v. Scruggs*, April 15, 2008.

309   *As a regional* . . . Interviews with confidential sources.

309   *Mayo found himself* . . . Interview with Cal Mayo.

309   *Mayo* . . . Transcript of hearing, April 15–16, 2008.

312   *Moore, sitting* . . . Interview with Mike Moore.

312   *Reached later* . . . "Hood Denies Scruggs Threatened to Fund Opponent," Alyssa Schnugg, *Oxford Eagle*, April 17, 2008.

312   *Throughout the spring* . . . Interviews with Dick Scruggs, Diane Scruggs,
Rex Deloach, confidential sources.

314   *The day after* . . . Interview with Sam Davis.

314   *At one faculty* . . . Interview with John Robin Bradley.

314   *Backstrom* . . . Undated email from Sid Backstrom to friends and
neighbors.

315   *Zach's Sigma Nu* . . . Interviews with confidential sources.

315   *Dick Scruggs's case* . . . Letters of support on file with U.S. District
Court in Oxford; letter from William F. Winter to Judge Biggers, April 14,
2008; letter from Michael Mann to Judge Biggers, May 13, 2008; letter from
Chancellor Robert Khayat to Judge Biggers, April 30, 2008.

316   *Learning of Khayat's* . . . Conversation with Grady Tollison; interviews with confidential sources.

Chapter 26

317   *John Hailman* . . . Interview with John Hailman.
318   *Biggers said* . . . Transcript of sentencing of Richard Scruggs, U.S. District Court, Northern District of Mississippi, June 27, 2008.
320   *At that moment* . . . Interview with confidential source.
320   *"As you know* . . . Transcript of *Shields v. University of Mississippi* before circuit judge Henry L. Lackey, Circuit Court of Lafayette County, Mississippi, June 27, 2008.
321   *Following his father's* . . . Interview with Zach Scruggs.
321   *The festive group* . . . Interviews with confidential sources.
322   *After learning* . . . Conversation with John Currence.
322   *At two o'clock* . . . Transcript of sentencing of Sidney Backstrom, U.S. District Court, Northern District of Mississippi, June 27, 2008.
323   *By the morning* . . . Interviews with Zach Scruggs, Mike Moore.
323   *Zach's formal* . . . Transcript of sentencing of David Zachary Scruggs, U.S. District Court, Northern District of Mississippi, July 2, 2008.
326   *He was approached* . . . Interviews with Zach Scruggs, Tom Dawson.
327   *He was not* . . . Interview with Jim Greenlee.

Chapter 27

328   *"Convicted trial* . . . Campaign brochure in support of Roger Wicker by Republican Senatorial Campaign Committee, 2008.
329   *Zach's temporary* . . . Interviews with Zach Scruggs, Lowry Lomax.
330   *Joey Langston* . . . Motion for Downward Departure, filed by Robert H. Norman, assistant U.S. attorney, in U.S. District Court, Northern District of Mississippi, Nov. 13, 2008.
330   *Patterson walked* . . . Transcript of sentencing of Steve Patterson, U.S. District Court, Northern District of Mississippi, Feb. 13, 2009.
331   *He had* . . . Interview with confidential source.
331   *Prosecutors praised* . . . Transcript of sentencing of Tim Balducci, U.S. District Court, Northern District of Mississippi, Feb. 13, 2009.
331   *After fourteen years* . . . "Friends Reflect on the Legacy of Robert Khayat," *University of Mississippi Lawyer* (Spring/Summer 2008).
331   Wilson v. Scruggs . . . "Scruggs Hit with Another Lawsuit," Holbrook Mohr, Associated Press, *Commercial Appeal*, Jan. 14, 2009.
331   *Wilson finally settled* . . . Interviews with Zach Scruggs, confidential sources; conversation with Roberts Wilson, 2010.

332   *In 2009, Grady Tollison* . . . Email from Tollison Law Firm to members of the Southeastern Region of the American Board of Trial Advocates (SEABOTA), April 15, 2009.

332   *In his most* . . . Prepared speech at Council on Litigation Management annual conference, Phoenix, Arizona, delivered by U.S. attorney Jim Greenlee, March 12, 2009.

333   *Back home* . . . "Newly Renovated Courthouse Packed for Judge Investiture," Alyssa Schnugg, *Oxford Eagle*, May 18, 2009.

333   *In court* . . . Order dismissing contempt in *U.S.A. v. Richard F. Scruggs and the Scruggs Law Firm*, issued by U.S. District Judge Roger Vinson, U.S. District Court, Northern District of Alabama, Feb. 29, 2008.

333   *Undeterred* . . . "Judge Fines Scruggs, Rigsby Sisters," Anita Lee, *Sun Herald*, June 6, 2008.

334   *In July 2009* . . . Order vacating judgment of contempt against Richard F. Scruggs, U.S. Court of Appeals for the Eleventh Circuit, July 21, 2009.

334   *His case* . . . Report by U.S. House Judiciary Committee, April 2008.

334   *Minor filed* . . . Order reversing three counts of Paul Minor's conviction, issued by the U.S. Court of Appeals for the Fifth Circuit, Dec. 11, 2009.

334   *But earlier* . . . Interview with Bill Minor; "Paul Minor Is Not Allowed to Attend His Wife's Funeral," OpEdNews.com. April 20, 2009.

334   *Karl Rove* . . . Transcript of interview with Karl C. Rove by the staff of the U.S. House Judiciary Committee, July 7, 2009.

335   *Scruggs asked* . . . Interview with Diane Scruggs.

335   *Two months* . . . Letter from Dick Scruggs to Curtis Wilkie, Oct. 30, 2008.

335   *"I got promoted* . . . Letter from Scruggs to Wilkie, June 18, 2009.

336   *His first instinct* . . . Interview with Dick Scruggs; plea agreement in *U.S.A. v. Richard F. Scruggs*, filed in U.S. District Court, Northern District of Mississippi, Feb. 9, 2009.

336   *He told* . . . Transcript of sentencing of Dick Scruggs, U.S. District Court, Northern District of Mississippi, Feb. 10, 2009.

336   *While he* . . . Interview with Dick Scruggs.

336   *The prosecutors* . . . Interviews with confidential sources.

337   *One of the most* . . . Interviews with Dick Scruggs, confidential sources; letter from Scruggs to Wilkie, June 25, 2009.

337   *Even as he* . . . Transcript of sentencing of Scruggs, U.S. District Court, Northern District of Mississippi, June 27, 2008.

337   *He spent* . . . Interview with Diane Scruggs.

338   *In the fall of 2009* . . . Letter from Scruggs to Wilkie.

338   *Diane was capable* . . . Interview with Diane Scruggs.

338   *At the end* . . . "Hinds Judge's Plea Calls for 18 Months," Jerry Mitchell, *Clarion-Ledger*, July 31, 2009.

338   *The sentence* . . . Transcript of sentencing of Bobby DeLaughter, U.S. District Court, Northern District of Mississippi, Nov. 13, 2009.

339   *But there was* . . . "This Is Over," Patsy R. Brumfield, *Northeast Mississippi Daily Journal*, July 31, 2009.

339   *In January* . . . "Indicted Agent's History Shows Feud with U.S. Attorney's Office," Patsy R. Brumfield, *Northeast Mississippi Daily Journal*, Jan. 15, 2010.

339   *Neilson's fellow agents* . . . Interviews with confidential sources.

340   *A week after* . . . "US Attorney Set to Retire," Alyssa Schnugg, *Oxford Eagle*, Jan. 21, 2010.

340   *The money is wired* . . . Interview with Rex Deloach.

340   *Bainberry is not* . . . Email from Kenneth J. Schrad, director, Division of Information Resources, State Corporation Commission, Richmond, Virginia, to Wilkie. Aug. 18, 2009.

Epilogue

341   *By the beginning* . . . Emails from Dick Scruggs to Curtis Wilkie, spring 2011.

342   *Their son, Zach* . . . Conversations with Zach Scruggs, 2010.

342   *Steve Patterson came home* . . . Letter from Patterson to numerous friends, December 2010.

343   *After a two-week trial* . . . "Neilson not guilty twice, federal jury declares" by Patsy R. Brumfield, *Northeast Mississippi Daily Journal*, Nov. 21, 2010.

344   *A greater rebuke* . . . Order to disqualify Assistant U.S. Attorney Robert Norman, issued by U.S. District Judge Neal B. Biggers Jr., U.S. District Court, Northern District of Mississippi, May 11, 2011.

344   (*A year and a half earlier* . . . "Norman, Dawson honored by DOJ for work in Scruggs case," *Oxford Eagle*, Dec. 7, 2009.

344   *The judge based* . . . Hearing on motion before Judge Biggers in *U.S.A. v. David Zachary Scruggs*, U.S. District Court, Northern District of Mississippi, May 9, 2011.

345   *With Norman missing* . . . Hearing on motion before Judge Biggers in *U.S.A. v. David Zachary Scruggs*, U.S. District Court, Northern District of Mississippi, May 23–25, 2011.

346   *In the end* . . . Conversation with Zach Scruggs, May 26, 2011.

Author's Note

Dick Scruggs is my friend.

So are many other characters with roles on all sides of the political, civil, and criminal conflicts in this story.

John Hailman, who triggered the investigation against Scruggs, shared an office suite with me at the Overby Center for Southern Journalism and Politics at Ole Miss following his retirement from the U.S. Attorney's Office.

On the same campus, fifty years earlier, Robert Khayat was my platoon sergeant in Army ROTC. He has been a pal ever since.

I attended Ole Miss with several attorneys and officials who appear in the book, including Charlie Merkel, Crymes Pittman, Trent Lott, Thad Cochran, Joe Colingo, George Shaddock, and Ed Peters. I don't remember Peters from that period, but knew the others when we were students.

Judge Neal Biggers and I graduated, several years apart, from the same small public high school in Corinth, Mississippi.

Jack Dunbar has been a close friend from the time we were young men living in Clarksdale, Mississippi, in the 1960s.

During that long-ago time when I was a reporter for *The Clarksdale Press Register*, I covered a local high school football team coached by Grady Tollison and enjoyed our postmortems following each game.

Danny Cupit and I were both antiwar delegates on a biracial Mississippi delegation seated at the 1968 National Democratic Convention in Chicago.

A few years later, as a reporter for the *News-Journal* papers in Wilmington, Delaware, I got to know a bright young New Castle County councilman named Joe Biden and wrote about his rise to the U.S. Senate in 1972.

Frank Trapp is my wife's first cousin.

After Bobby DeLaughter successfully prosecuted Byron De La Beckwith—a trial I covered for *The Boston Globe* in 1994—I got to know him through our mutual friend, the late Willie Morris. We all wrote books that dealt with the racial transformation of Mississippi. If one finds these volumes today, an inspection of the covers will show that I provided a blurb for Bobby's book and he did the same for mine.

The fabric of Mississippi is woven with interlocking interests. In the Scruggs case, that intimacy is especially acute for those who graduated from Ole Miss or live today in Oxford. These relationships were invaluable to me as I pursued this book. But not all of the people I've mentioned above chose to talk with me in connection with my work—and a couple of them quit speaking to me altogether during the course of the book project.

It's a story, I found, where passions and personal hatreds run high.

Acknowledgments

During the two years that I spent developing this book, I spoke with many old friends and made dozens of new acquaintances. I'm deeply grateful to everyone who was willing to share information and their thoughts with me.

I conducted more than two hundred interviews. In some instances, I had multiple discussions, which lasted hours, with a number of individuals who were especially generous with their time. Some of these talks were confidential. In many cases, I was free to use material given to me, but under the condition that their names not be connected with direct quotes or assertions. As a result, I'm unable to publish a complete list of sources to acknowledge. I thank all of these individuals nonetheless. Without their cooperation, the sweep of this book would not have been possible.

In my research, I acquired literally thousands of pages of documents: Old depositions. Court transcripts. Copies of email traffic. Exchanges of letters. Extensive evidence obtained by the FBI through surveillance. Critical testimony from witnesses, including information that has never been made public. Much of this was shared with me in confidence.

I've cited sources from many books and publications in the endnotes but should single out Michael Orey's *Assuming the Risk* as an especially useful guide through the tobacco wars.

Dialogue in the book comes from different sources. Many of the conversations are taken directly from secretly recorded FBI wiretaps and video disks. Courtroom scenes are based on transcripts and on my notes from court sessions I attended. Some quotes come from private depositions made available to me.

In other instances I reconstructed dialogue based on the recollection of participants in conversations. In gathering material, I was struck by how consistent these accounts were, regardless of whether the words came from defendants or prosecutors. When I had only one source, I served as my own judge in determining whether to use the language given to me.

In the end, I take full responsibility for the accuracy of these quotes and for any assertions contained in the text.

I can, at least, offer thanks to my wife, Nancy, who endured the long project and encouraged me throughout this process, and to other members of my family. My son Carter, a published author himself, offered valuable suggestions for the manuscript, while my son Stuart, daughter, Leighton, and six grandchildren provided moral support.

Many thanks, as always, to my agent, Deborah Grosvenor, who understands the publishing world far better than I.

I am very grateful to John Glusman, my editor at Crown Books, who had faith in this project from the time he looked at my proposal in early 2008 to its completion. And to his assistant, Domenica Alioto, who ensured that every *T* was crossed properly.

Special thanks, too, to my old friend, Charles Overby, who made me a fellow at the Overby Center for Southern Journalism and Politics and provided me with a wonderful place to work; to Dawn Jeter, our invaluable office manager at the center; and to Caleb Ballew, a law student who tracked down some valuable research.

Index

Photograph Insert Credits

About the Author

CURTIS WILKIE graduated from the University of Mississippi in 1963. He was a national and foreign correspondent for the *Boston Globe* for twenty-six years. Wilkie is the author of *Dixie* and coauthor of *Arkansas Mischief*. He and his wife, Nancy, live in Oxford, where he teaches journalism and is a fellow at the Overby Center for Southern Journalism and Politics at Ole Miss.